GRECO-ROMAN PERSPECTIVES
ON FRIENDSHIP

SOCIETY OF BIBLICAL LITERATURE
Resources for Biblical Study

Edited by
David E. Aune

Number 34
GRECO-ROMAN PERSPECTIVES ON FRIENDSHIP
edited by
John T. Fitzgerald

GRECO-ROMAN PERSPECTIVES ON FRIENDSHIP

edited by
John T. Fitzgerald

Scholars Press
Atlanta, Georgia

GRECO-ROMAN PERSPECTIVES ON FRIENDSHIP

edited by
John T. Fitzgerald

© 1997
Society of Biblical Literature

Library of Congress Cataloging-in-Publication Data
Greco-Roman perspectives on friendship / edited by John T. Fitzgerald.
    p. cm. — (Resources for biblical study ; no. 34)
  Includes bibliographical references.
  ISBN 0-7885-0271-9 (alk. paper). — ISBN 0-7885-0272-7 (pbk. : alk. paper)
  1. Friendship—Rome—History. 2. Rome—Social life and customs.
I. Fitzgerald, John T., 1948–   . II. Series.
BJ1533.F8G63 1996
177'.6—dc20   96-21409
                                                            CIP

Printed in the United States of America
on acid-free paper

CONTENTS

Preface vii
List of Contributors ix
Abbreviations xi
Introduction 1

1. John T. Fitzgerald
   Friendship in the Greek World Prior to Aristotle 13

2. Frederic M. Schroeder
   Friendship in Aristotle and Some
   Peripatetic Philosophers 35

3. Benjamin Fiore, S.J.
   The Theory and Practice of Friendship in Cicero 59

4. Johan C. Thom
   "Harmonious Equality": The *Topos* of Friendship in
   Neopythagorean Writings 77

5. Edward N. O'Neil
   Plutarch on Friendship 105

6. David L. Balch
   Political Friendship in the Historian Dionysius of
   Halicarnassus, *Roman Antiquities* 123

7. Ronald F. Hock
   An Extraordinary Friend in Chariton's *Callirhoe*:
   The Importance of Friendship in the Greek Romances ... 145

8. Richard I. Pervo
   With Lucian: Who Needs Friends?
   Friendship in the *Toxaris* 163

9. Katherine G. Evans
   Friendship in the Greek Documentary Papyri
   and Inscriptions: A Survey 181

10. Gregory E. Sterling
   The Bond of Humanity: Friendship in Philo of Alexandria... 203
11. Alan C. Mitchell
   "Greet the Friends by Name": New Testament Evidence
   for the Greco-Roman *Topos* on Friendship 225

Index of Names and Places 263
Index of Subjects 269
Index of Greek and Latin Terms 284
Index of Ancient Authors and Texts 287
Index of Modern Scholars 324

PREFACE

Prefaces are traditionally used by authors and editors to express their gratitude to individuals and institutions which have encouraged and supported their research. In keeping with that tradition, the contributors wish to thank our various institutions for their support of this project. In addition, we are grateful to Professor David E. Aune for accepting this volume for publication in the Society of Biblical Literature's Resources for Biblical Study Series.

As editor of this volume, it is not only my privilege to thank my fellow contributors for their essays but also my obligation to apologize to them and to the Society for the inordinate delay in the publication of this volume. As the contributors already know, the delay was caused principally by Hurricane Andrew, which destroyed my family's house in August of 1992 and forced us to move three times within three years (see my "Life in the Wake of a Storm: On Good Friends and 'Good Neighbors,' Prudent Plans and Patient Endurance," *Religious Studies News* 8:2 [May, 1993] 3–6). I wish to thank the contributors, both collectively and individually, for their patience and support during an extremely difficult period. By exemplifying the ancient maxim that "friends share one another's sorrows," they have demonstrated that they are interested not only in the ancient theory of friendship but also in its contemporary practice.

John T. Fitzgerald

LIST OF CONTRIBUTORS

David L. Balch
Professor of New Testament
Brite Divinity School
Texas Christian University
Fort Worth, Texas

Katherine G. Evans
Ph.D. Student in Religions of
the Ancient Mediterranean
World
University of Pennsylvania
Philadelphia, Pennsylvania

Benjamin Fiore, S.J.
Professor of Religious Studies
Canisius College
Buffalo, New York

John T. Fitzgerald
Associate Professor of New
Testament
University of Miami
Coral Gables, Florida

Ronald F. Hock
Professor of Religion
University of Southern
California
Los Angeles, California

Alan C. Mitchell
Associate Professor of Biblical
Studies
Department of Theology
Georgetown University
Washington, DC

Edward N. O'Neil
Professor Emeritus of Classics
University of Southern
California
Los Angeles, California

Richard I. Pervo
Professor of New Testament &
Patristics
Seabury-Western Theological
Seminary
Evanston, Illinois

Frederic M. Schroeder
Professor of Classics
Queen's University
Kingston, Canada

Gregory E. Sterling
Associate Professor of New
Testament and Christian
Origins
University of Notre Dame
Notre Dame, Indiana

Johan C. Thom
Senior Lecturer of Greek
University of Stellenbosch
Stellenbosch, South Africa

ABBREVIATIONS

The abbreviations used for the titles of modern books, periodicals, translations, and series follow, where possible, the guidelines of the Society of Biblical Literature as published in the *Journal of Biblical Literature* 107 (1988) 579-96. Other abbreviations are either self-evident or are derived from *L'Année philologique* (Paris: Société d'Édition Les Belles Lettres).

AB	Anchor Bible
ABD	D. N. Freedman (ed.), *Anchor Bible Dictionary*
AJAH	*American Journal of Ancient History*
AJP	*American Journal of Philology*
ANRW	*Aufstieg und Niedergang der römischen Welt*
BASP	*Bulletin of the American Society of Papyrologists*
BZNW	Beihefte zur Zeitschrift für die neutestamentliche Wissenschaft
CAG	*Commentaria in Aristotelem Graeca*
CP	*Classical Philology*
CQ	*Classical Quarterly*
CW	*Classical World*
EKKNT	Evangelisch-Katholischer Kommentar zum Neuen Testament
EPh	*Études philosophiques*
ERE	James Hastings (ed.), *Encyclopedia of Religion and Ethics*
ETL	*Ephemerides theologicae lovanienses*
EtClass	*Études classiques*
FB	Forschung zur Bibel
G & R	*Greece & Rome*
GIF	*Giornale Italiano di Filologia*
GRBS	*Greek, Roman, and Byzantine Studies*
HNT	Handbuch zum Neuen Testament
HSM	Harvard Semitic Monographs
HSPh	*Harvard Studies in Classical Philology*

HTKNT	Herders theologischer Kommentar zum Neuen Testament
ICC	International Critical Commentary
ICS	*Illinois Classical Studies*
IF	*Indogermanische Forschungen*
JAC	*Jahrbuch für Antike und Christentum*
JBL	*Journal of Biblical Literature*
JHS	*Journal of Hellenic Studies*
JRS	*Journal of Roman Studies*
JTS	*Journal of Theological Studies*
LCL	Loeb Classical Library
LD	Lectio divina
LEC	Library of Early Christianity
LSJ	Liddell-Scott-Jones, *Greek-English Lexicon*
MeyerK	H. A. W. Meyer, Kritisch-exegetischer Kommentar über das Neue Testament
MTZ	*Münchener theologische Zeitschrift*
NedTTs	*Nederlands theologisch tijdschrift*
Neot	*Neotestamentica*
NovT	*Novum Testamentum*
NovTSup	Supplements to Novum Testamentum
NRSV	New Revised Standard Version
OBT	Overtures to Biblical Theology
OCT	Oxford Classical Texts (= Scriptorum classicorum bibliotheca oxoniensis)
OJRS	*Ohio Journal of Religious Studies*
OTNT	Ökumenischer Taschenbuchkommentar zum Neuen Testament
PCPhS	*Proceedings of the Cambridge Philological Society*
PhilAnt	Philosophia Antiqua
PhilWoch	*Philologische Wochenschrift*
PLG	T. Bergk (ed.), *Poetae Lyrici Graeci*
PW	Pauly-Wissowa, *Real-Encyclopädie der classischen Altertumswissenschaft*
PWSup	Supplements to PW
QUCC	*Quaderni Urbinati di Cultura Classica*
RAC	*Reallexikon für Antike und Christentum*
REG	*Revue des Études Grecques*

RevQ	*Revue de Qumran*
RhM	*Rheinisches Museum*
RivB	*Rivista biblica*
RNT	Regensburger Neues Testament
RSR	*Recherches de science religieuse*
RSV	Revised Standard Version
SBLDS	Society of Biblical Literature Dissertation Series
SBLSBS	Society of Biblical Literature Sources for Biblical Study
SBLSP	*Society of Biblical Literature Seminar Papers*
SBLTT	Society of Biblical Literature Texts and Translations
SJLA	Studies in Judaism in Late Antiquity
SNTU	Studien zum Neuen Testament und seiner Umwelt
SVTP	Studia in Veteris Testamenti pseudepigrapha
TAPA	*Transactions of the American Philological Association*
TDNT	G. Kittel and G. Friedrich (eds.), *Theological Dictionary of the New Testament*
TLNT	C. Spicq, *Theological Lexicon of the New Testament*
TLZ	*Theologische Literaturzeitung*
TRu	*Theologische Rundschau*
TU	Texte und Untersuchungen
TZ	*Theologische Zeitschrift*
WMANT	Wissenschaftliche Monographien zum Alten und Neuen Testament
WUNT	Wissenschaftliche Untersuchungen zum Neuen Testament
YCS	*Yale Classical Studies*
ZAW	*Zeitschrift für die altestamentliche Wissenschaft*
ZKG	*Zeitschrift für Kirchengeschichte*
ZPE	*Zeitschrift für Papyrologie und Epigraphik*
ZRGG	*Zeitschrift für Religions- und Geistesgeschichte*
ZWT	*Zeitschrift für wissenschaftliche Theologie*

INTRODUCTION

The essays contained in this volume are the result of research conducted by members of the Hellenistic Moral Philosophy and Early Christianity Group, a program unit of the Society of Biblical Literature. The impetus for the formation of this working group was provided by Professor Abraham J. Malherbe of Yale Divinity School, who suggested it at the 1988 SBL Annual Meeting in Chicago. He wished to see the Society form a collaborative group that would give close attention to ancient texts, both pagan and Christian, treating them in their own right as well as in relation to each other. He envisioned an interdisciplinary group of scholars, diverse in their training and methodological presuppositions, but united in their devotion to the careful study of ancient documents. Such a group would include not only NT scholars, but also classicists, students of ancient philosophy, ancient historians, cultural and historical anthropologists, and others who were interested in Christian origins.

In response to his suggestion, about two dozen scholars held an organizational and planning session at the 1989 SBL Annual Meeting in Anaheim. A proposal for the formation of a program unit devoted to the study of hellenistic moral philosophy and early Christianity was submitted soon thereafter to the Society, which promptly approved it. The first official session was held at the 1990 SBL Annual Meeting in New Orleans. At that session, Professor Malherbe delivered an address on "Hellenistic Moral Philosophy and the New Testament."[1] In that address he not only provided a retrospective analysis of approximately a century of research into the relationship of early Christianity to its Greco-Roman moral and cultural context but also proposed various subjects that the newly

---

[1] The SBL Program Committee gave prominence to Professor Malherbe's address by making it part of the Society's series on "Biblical Scholarship in the 21st Century."

1

formed group might investigate.² Foremost among the topics that he mentioned was friendship, a subject that in recent years has become immensely important to modern scholars in a variety of fields.³ Professor Malherbe's suggestion was seconded by the three scholars who responded to his address, and it was subsequently adopted by the group as its initial research project.⁴

Both of the group's sessions at the 1991 SBL Annual Meeting in Kansas City were devoted to friendship. Given the emphasis that ancient philosophers placed on friendship, the group decided to

---

[2] Relevant portions of the address were incorporated into Professor Malherbe's "Hellenistic Moralists and the New Testament," *ANRW* 2.26.1 (1992) 267–333.

[3] See, for example, M. E. Marty, *Friendship* (Allen, Texas: Argus Communications, 1980); L. A. Blum, *Friendship, Altruism, and Morality* (International Library of Philosophy; London: Routledge & Kegan Paul, 1980); R. R. Bell, *Worlds of Friendship* (Sociological Observations 12; Beverly Hills: Sage Publications, 1981); Gilbert Meilaender, *Friendship: A Study in Theological Ethics* (Notre Dame: University of Notre Dame Press, 1981); Steve Duck, *Friends for Life: The Psychology of Close Relationships* (New York: St. Martin's Press, 1983; 2d ed.; London: Harvester Wheatsheaf, 1991); Michael Argyle and Monika Henderson, *The Anatomy of Relationships* (London: Heinemann, 1985) 64–94; Laurence Thomas, "Friendship," *Synthese* 72 (1987) 217–36; Michael Stocker, "Duty and Friendship," *Women and Moral Theory* (ed. E. F. Kittay and D. T. Meyers; Totowa: Rowman and Littlefield, 1987) 56–68, and "Friendship and Duty: Some Difficult Relations," *Identity, Character, and Morality: Essays in Moral Psychology* (ed. O. Flanagan and A. O. Rorty; Cambridge: MIT Press, 1990) 219–33; Jacques Derrida, "The Politics of Friendship," *Journal of Philosophy* 85 (1988) 632–44; Marilyn Friedman, "Feminism and Modern Friendship: Dislocating the Community," *Ethics* 99 (1989) 275–90; P. J. Wadell, *Friendship and the Moral Life* (Notre Dame: University of Notre Dame Press, 1989); Roy Porter and Sylvana Tomaselli (eds.), *The Dialectics of Friendship* (London: Routledge, 1989); Joseph Kupfer, "Can Parents and Children Be Friends?" *American Philosophical Quarterly* 27 (1990) 15–26; D. K. O'Connor, "Two Ideals of Friendship," *History of Philosophy Quarterly* 7 (1990) 109–22; D. J. Enright and David Rawlinson (eds.), *The Oxford Book of Friendship* (Oxford: Oxford University Press, 1991); Michael Pakaluk (ed.), *Other Selves: Philosophers on Friendship* (Indianapolis: Hackett, 1991); N. K. Badhwar (ed.), *Friendship: A Philosophical Reader* (Ithaca: Cornell University Press, 1993); Allan Bloom, *Love and Friendship* (New York: Simon & Schuster, 1993); L. S. Rouner (ed.), *The Changing Face of Friendship* (Boston University Studies in Philosophy and Religion 15; Notre Dame: University of Notre Dame Press, 1994); Eberhard Bethge, *Friendship and Resistance: Essays on Dietrich Bonhoeffer* (Geneva: WCC Publications; Grand Rapids: Wm. B. Eerdmans, 1995), esp. 80–104 ("Bonhoeffer's Theology of Friendship"); J. Barry Gurdin, *Amitié/Friendship: An Investigation into Cross-Cultural Styles in Canada and the United States* (San Francisco: Austin & Winfield, 1996).

[4] The respondents to Professor Malherbe's address were Stanley K. Stowers of Brown University, Glenn S. Holland of Allegheny College, and S. Georgia Nugent, now of Princeton University.

devote one session to friendship in the philosophical tradition (Aristotle, Cicero, Plutarch, the Neopythagoreans, and Philo of Alexandria). The other session was devoted to an examination of friendship in a variety of Greek authors and documents (Dionysius of Halicarnassus, Chariton, Lucian, the documentary papyri, and the New Testament). Ten of the eleven essays contained in this volume are revised versions of the papers presented at these two sessions.[5]

As the title of this volume suggests, the temporal focus of these studies is the Greco-Roman period. Aristotle was the first to provide an extensive and systematic analysis of friendship, but he was not the first to reflect on the theory and practice of friendship in the Greek world. For that reason, the editor has provided in Chapter One a brief overview of Greek friendship in the periods prior to Aristotle. Emphasis in that discussion is given to the archaic period, and to the depictions and discussions of friendship by Homer, Hesiod, and Theognis.

In Chapter Two, Frederic M. Schroeder turns to Aristotle's treatment of friendship and focuses his comments on two debated issues—the question of altruism in Aristotle's depiction of character friendship and the issue of integrity in the Stagirite's taxonomy of friendship. In doing so, Professor Schroeder not only compares Aristotle to Plato but also discusses later Peripatetic understandings of friendship as reflected in the writings of Theophrastus, Cicero, Arius Didymus, Alcinous, and Aspasius.

Cicero, who also reflects knowledge of Stoic and Epicurean understandings of friendship, is the subject of Chapter Three. Here Benjamin Fiore, S.J., contrasts the idealistic depiction of friendship in Cicero's *Laelius* (*De amicitia*) with the more pragmatic and utilitarian recommendations found in the *Commentariolum petitionis*, a handbook for political candidates that purports to have been composed for Cicero by his brother Quintus.

Of the pre-Socratic philosophers, the one who attached the greatest importance to friendship was Pythagoras (fl. sixth century

---

[5] Unless otherwise indicated, all of the contributors to the volume have provided their own translations of ancient Greek and Latin texts or used those of the Loeb Classical Library (LCL).

BCE). Later Pythagoreans of the Hellenistic and Roman periods continued their founder's emphasis on friendship, and this emphasis is particularly clear in Neopythagorean texts. In Chapter Four, Johan C. Thom discusses the treatment of friendship in four types of Neopythagorean writings: (1) the treatises of Hippodamus, Callicratidas, and Zaleucus; (2) the letters of Theano and Apollonius of Tyana; (3) the sayings collections (the *Sayings of Sextus*, the *Sayings of Clitarchus*, the *Pythagorean Sayings*, and the *Golden Verses*); and (4) the biographical traditions regarding Pythagoras and the Pythagorean life.

Plutarch, who was active during the late first and early second centuries CE, discussed friendship not only in his famous "How to Tell a Flatterer from a Friend" (*Mor.* 48E–74E) and "On Having Many Friends" (*Mor.* 93A–97B) but also in several other works. In Chapter Five, Edward N. O'Neil discusses numerous aspects of Plutarch's extensive treatment of friendship, giving particular attention to his use of various platitudes and *topoi* about friendship. As Professor O'Neil points out, Plutarch drew on Greek traditions of friendship but did so with an acute consciousness of contemporary Roman conditions and customs.

Friendship in the ancient Mediterranean world was not simply an interpersonal relationship but also a political phenomenon.[6] In Chapter Six, David L. Balch examines the depiction of political friendship by Dionysius of Halicarnassus, a Greek rhetorician, literary critic, and historian who was active in Rome at the end of the first century BCE. Professor Balch focuses on four stories of conflict between "friends" in Dionysius' *Roman Antiquities*, two of which concern the Roman general Gaius Marcius Coriolanus. These stories exalt love of country above love of family, depict the reconciliation of different social groups following civic discord, extol the harmony of the state, and examine conflicting views of friendship and their consequences for foreign affairs.

---

[6] See esp. Horst Hutter, *Politics as Friendship: The Origins of Classical Notions of Politics in the Theory and Practice of Friendship* (Waterloo, Ontario: Wilfrid Laurier University Press, 1978). See also his "Friendship in Theory and Practice: A Study of Greek and Roman Theories of Friendship in Their Social Settings" (Ph.D. Diss., Stanford University, 1972).

Introduction

Friendship was an important subject not only for Greco-Roman philosophy and politics, but also for ancient literature. One important but often neglected literary genre for recovering ancient perspectives on friendship is the Greek novel or romance. In Chapter Seven, Ronald F. Hock examines the importance of friendship in the Greek romances. He focuses his attention on Chariton's *Callirhoe*, a novel that probably was written in the first century CE. It depicts the extraordinary friendship of Chaereas and Polycharmus, whom Chariton compares in closeness to Achilles and Patroclus, as well as other types of friendships, both social and political. Of particular interest is Chariton's depiction of friendships involving women. These include Callirhoe's friendships with aristocratic women and her friendship with her husband Chaereas. Professor Hock argues that Chariton depicts Chaereas and Callirhoe as enjoying the highest form of friendship—an idea that was inconceivable to Aristotle centuries earlier.

Although friendship was often extolled and idealized, it could also be satirized. In the view of Richard I. Pervo, that is what Lucian of Samosata does in his *Toxaris*, a work which is cast in the form of a dialogue between a Greek by the name of Mnesippos and a Scythian named Toxaris. Each man relates five remarkable stories about friendship in an effort to prove that his ethnic group is superior in its practice of friendship. In Chapter Eight, Professor Pervo argues that the *Toxaris* is not intended, as certain scholars have maintained, to convey a serious moral message; on the contrary, it is a parody that mocks and ridicules conventional ideas associated with friendship. One likely target of Lucian's irony, paradox, and excess, in Professor Pervo's opinion, is the romantic novel. His essay thus offers a different perspective on the Greek romance from that offered by Professor Hock in the preceding chapter.

The Greek documentary papyri and inscriptions constitute yet another valuable but virtually untapped source for recovering ancient understandings of friendship. In stark contrast to the numerous studies that researchers have devoted to friendship in the philosophical tradition, modern scholarship has sorely neglected friendship terminology in these materials. In Chapter Nine, therefore, Katherine G. Evans breaks new ground by providing the first study of friendship in Greek and Roman Egypt as reflected in private letters, wills, epitaphs, dedications, and devotions. As she demonstrates, friends frequently appear here as proxies in financial and familial matters, though there is also evidence for other types of friendships. These include friendships between males and females as well as adult-child friendships.

The final two essays in the volume examine the ways in which Jewish and Christian authors make use of the Greco-Roman *topos* on friendship. In Chapter Ten, Gregory E. Sterling examines ways in which Philo of Alexandria draws on Greek philosophical traditions about friendship for his explication of the Hebrew Bible. He argues that Philo is particularly indebted to Stoic conceptions of friendship, indeed so indebted that this Jewish philosopher constitutes one of our most important sources for Stoic views on friendship. Yet Philo does not simply adopt Stoic views but also modifies them by wedding them to his Jewish tenets of faith, especially monotheism. As a consequence, friendship becomes a Philonic vehicle for a universal understanding of humanity.

In Chapter Eleven, Alan C. Mitchell surveys recent scholarship on the presence of friendship language in the New Testament. The use of the friendship *topos* has been identified and examined chiefly in the letters of Paul (1 Thessalonians, Galatians, 1 and 2 Corinthians, Romans, and Philippians), Luke-Acts, and the Johannine literature. Professor Mitchell not only provides an extensive *Forschungsbericht* but also contributes to the discussion, especially in regard to Luke-Acts. He argues that friendship language in Luke-Acts has the social function of encouraging Christians to extend friendship to one another across status divisions, thereby creating greater unity within the church. At the same time, Luke also challenges certain conventional aspects of friendship, especially reciprocity, and in the process offers a new understanding of friendship.

The essays in this volume by no means exhaust all of the relevant sources for recovering classical and Greco-Roman perspectives on friendship. Many important authors and texts are mentioned only in passing or not at all, including such authors as

Euripides,[7] Thucydides,[8] Plato,[9] Xenophon,[10] the writers of New

---

[7] See James Tyler, "Philia and Echthra in Euripides" (Ph.D. Diss., Cornell University, 1969); Ute Schmidt-Berger, "Philia: Typologie der Freundschaft und Verwandschaft bei Euripides" (Ph.D. Diss. Universität Tübingen, 1973); David Konstan, "*Philia* in Euripides' Electra," *Philologus* 129 (1985) 176–85; G. R. Stanton, "ΦΙΛΙΑ and ΞΕΝΙΑ in Euripides' 'Alkestis,'" *Hermes* 118 (1990) 42–54.

[8] See, for example, Thuc. 2.40.4–5 and the comments of J. S. Rusten (ed.), *Thucydides, The Peloponnesian War: Book II* (Cambridge Greek and Latin Classics; Cambridge: Cambridge University Press, 1989) 156–57.

[9] See esp. Plato's *Lysis, Phaedrus*, and *Symposium*. For studies of Platonic love and friendship, see Willibald Ziebis, *Der Begriff der* Φιλία *bei Plato* (Inaugural Diss., Friedrich-Wilhelms-Universität zu Breslau; Breslau: Druck der Buch- und Offsetdruckerei Schlesische Volkszeitung, 1927); A. E. Taylor, *Plato: The Man and His Work* (repr. of 6th ed. of 1952; New York: Meridian, 1956) 64–74; Maria Lualdi, *Il problema della philia e il Liside platonico* (Scienze umane 31; Milan: Celuc, 1974); L. Versenyi, "Plato's *Lysis*," *Phronesis* 20 (1975) 185–98; A. Kosman, "Platonic Love," *Facets of Plato's Philosophy* (ed. W. H. Werkmeister; *Phronesis* Suppl. 2; Assen: van Gorcum, 1976) 53–69; Julia Annas, "Plato and Aristotle on Friendship and Altruism," *Mind* 86 (1977) 532–54; David Bolotin, *Plato's Dialogue on Friendship: An Interpretation of the Lysis, with a New Translation* (Ithaca: Cornell University Press, 1979), which contains an interesting appendix on "The Pohlenz-von Arnim Controversy about the *Lysis*" (pp. 201–25); Hans-Georg Gadamer, "*Logos* and *Ergon* in Plato's *Lysis*," *Dialogue and Dialectic: Eight Hermeneutical Studies on Plato* (New Haven: Yale University Press, 1980) 1–20; O. Kaiser, "Lysis oder von der Freundschaft," *ZRGG* 32 (1980) 193–218; Gregory Vlastos, "The Individual as Object of Love in Plato," *Platonic Studies* (2d ed.; Princeton: Princeton University Press, 1981) 3–42; David Glidden, "The *Lysis* on Loving One's Own," *CQ* 31 (1981) 39–59; D. B. Robinson, "Plato's *Lysis*: The Structural Problem," *ICS* 11 (1986) 63–83; M. C. Nussbaum, *The Fragility of Goodness: Luck and Ethics in Greek Tragedy and Philosophy* (Cambridge: Cambridge University Press, 1986); Hutter, *Politics as Friendship*, 93–102; A. W. Price, *Love and Friendship in Plato and Aristotle* (Oxford: Clarendon, 1989); and Catherine Osborne, *Eros Unveiled: Plato and the God of Love* (Oxford: Clarendon, 1994) 58–61.

[10] See esp. Xenophon, *Mem.* 1.2.8,52–55; 2.4.1–2.6.39; *Cyr.* 8.7.13. The theme of friendship is also important in Xenophon's depiction of the trial of Theramenes, where the dissolution of the friendship between Critias and Theramenes (*Hell.* 2.3.15) involves charges of betrayal (2.3.43). For an analysis and comparison of Xenophon's treatment with Plato's depiction of Socrates in the *Lysis*, see Olof Gigon, *Kommentar zum zweiten Buch von Xenophons Memorabilien* (Schweizerische Beiträge zur Altertumswissenschaft 7; Basel: Friedrich Reinhardt, 1956) 118–72.

Comedy,[11] Epicurus[12] and Lucretius,[13] Panaetius,[14] Seneca,[15]

---

[11] See esp. Friedrich Zucker, *Freundschaftsbewährung in der neuen attischen Komödie: Ein Kapitel hellenischer Ethik und Humanität* (Berlin: Akademie-Verlag, 1950). See also P. G. McC. Brown, "Menander, Fragments 745 and 746 K-T, Menander's *Kolax,* and Parasites and Flatterers in Greek Comedy," *ZPE* 92 (1992) 91–107. On Greek and Roman comedy in general, see the two volumes by David Konstan, *Roman Comedy* (Ithaca: Cornell University Press, 1983) and *Greek Comedy and Ideology* (Oxford: Oxford University Press, 1995).

[12] See, for instance, C. Brescia, "La φιλία in Epicuro," *GIF* 8 (1955) 314–32; Jean Bollack, "Les Maximes de l'Amitié," *Actes du VIIIe Congrès, Association Guillaume Budé* (Paris: Société d'Édition "Les Belles Lettres," 1969) 221–36; C. Diano, "Épicure: La philosophie du plaisir et la société des amis," *EPh* 22 (1967) 173–86; J. M. Rist, *Epicurus: An Introduction* (Cambridge: Cambridge University Press, 1972) esp. 127–39, and "Epicurus on Friendship," *CP* 75 (1980) 121–29; Phillip Mitsis, "Friendship and Altruism," *Epicurus' Ethical Theory: The Pleasures of Invulnerability* (Cornell Studies in Classical Philology 48; Ithaca: Cornell University Press, 1988) 98–128; D. K. O'Connor, "The Invulnerable Pleasures of Epicurean Friendship," *GRBS* 30 (1989) 165–86; and Suzanne Stern-Gillet, "Epicurus and Friendship," *Dialogue* 28 (1989) 275–88. On Epicurean friendship, see also Benjamin Farrington, "La amistad epicúrea," *Notas e Estudios de Filosofía* 3 (1952) 105–15, and *The Faith of Epicurus* (New York: Basic Books, 1967) 20–32, 77, 103–04; N. W. De Witt, *Epicurus and His Philosophy* (Minneapolis: University of Minnesota Press, 1954) 101–02, 190–91, 307–10, and *St. Paul and Epicurus* (Toronto: Ryerson Press, 1954) 50, 142, 148–51; A.-J. Festugière, *Epicurus and His Gods* (1955; repr. New York: Russell & Russell, 1969) 27–50; André Tuilier, "La notion de φιλία dans ses rapports avec certains fondements sociaux de l'épicurisme, *Actes du VIIIe Congrès, Association Guillaume Budé* (Paris: Société d'Édition "Les Belles Lettres," 1969) 318–29; Hutter, *Politics as Friendship,* 116–20; Bernard Frischer, *The Sculpted Word: Epicureanism and Philosophical Recruitment in Ancient Greece* (Berkeley: University of California Press, 1982) 75–76, 79; and David Konstan, "Friendship from Epicurus to Philodemus," *L'epicureismo greco e romano* (ed. M. Giannantoni and M. Gigante; Naples: Bibliopolis, forthcoming) 387–96.

[13] W. Allen, Jr., "On the Friendship of Lucretius with Memmius," *CP* 33 (1938) 167–81, and B. Farrington, "Lucretius and Manilius on Friendship, " *Hermathena* 83 (1954) 10–16.

[14] See esp. F.-A. Steinmetz, *Die Freundschaftslehre des Panaitios nach einer Analyse von Ciceros 'Laelius de amicitia'* (Palingenesia 3; Wiesbaden: Franz Steiner, 1967).

[15] See, for instance, Sen. *Ep.* 3; 9; 35; 48; 63; 94; 103; 109; and the references given in A. L. Motto, *Guide to the Thought of Lucius Annaeus Seneca* (Amsterdam: Hakkert, 1970) 88–90, 191–92. For studies, see Ulrich Knoche, "Der Gedanke der Freundschaft in Senecas Briefen an Lucilius," *Arctos* 1 (1954) 83–96, reprinted in *Seneca als Philosoph* (ed. Gregor Maurach; Wege der Forschung 414; Darmstadt: Wissenschaftliche Buchgesellschaft, 1975) 149–66 (cf. also Knoche's comments on the same subject in *Acta philologica aenipontana* 1 [1962] 55–57); R. Schottlaender, "Epikureisches bei Seneca: Ein Ringen um den Sinn von Freude und Freundschaft," *Philologus* 99 (1955) 133–48; and Wolfgang Brinckmann, "Der Begriff der Freundschaft in Senecas Briefen" (Inaugural Diss., Universität Köln, 1963). See also M. F. Manzanedo, "La amistad humana vista por Seneca," *Estudios sobre Seneca:*

Introduction 9

Epictetus[16] and other Stoics,[17] Secundus the Silent Philosopher,[18] Catullus,[19] Horace,[20] Juvenal,[21] the Roman poets,[22] and various

---

Ponencias y communicaciones (Madrid: Consejo Superior de Investigaciones Cientificas, Instituto Luis Vives de Filosophia, 1966) 209–19.

[16] See esp. Epict. *Diss.* 2.22; 3.22.62–66. On the latter passage, see the comments of Margarethe Billerbeck, *Epiktet, Von Kynismus* (Philosophia Antiqua 34; Leiden: E. J. Brill, 1978) 127–30. For the role of friendship in Epictetus' ethics, see A. Bonhöffer, *Die Ethik des Stoikers Epictet* (Stuttgart: F. Enke, 1894) 106–9.

[17] See Hutter, *Politics as Friendship*, 120–32, and Glenn Lesses, "Austere Friends: The Stoics and Friendship," *Apeiron* 26 (1993) 57–75. On the relationship of friendship and the Stoic theory of *oikeiōsis*, see M. W. Blundell, "Partial Nature and Stoic Oikeiōsis," *Ancient Philosophy* 10 (1970) 221–42. On *oikeiōsis* in early Stoicism, see esp. Troels Engberg-Pedersen, *The Stoic Theory of Oikeiosis: Moral Development and Social Interaction in Early Stoic Philosophy* (Studies in Hellenistic Civilization 2; Aarhus: Aarhus University Press, 1990).

[18] See *The Life of Secundus* 11: "What is a Friend? A desirable name, a person unseen, a rare commodity, an encouragement in difficulty, a refuge from misfortune, support in distress, an observer of life, a person inaccessible, a substantial treasure, inaccessible good fortune." The translation is that of David E. Aune, "Greco-Roman Biography," *Greco-Roman Literature and the New Testament: Selected Forms and Genres* (ed. D. E. Aune; SBLSBS 21; Atlanta: Scholars Press, 1988) 119, who also provides a helpful discussion of the work.

[19] See, for example, S. Y. Yuen, "Friendship in the Poetry of Catullus" (M.A. Thesis, Brown University, 1986), and M. F. Williams, "Catullus 50 and the Language of Friendship," *Latomus* 47 (1988) 69–73.

[20] See W. S. Maguinness, "Friends and the Philosophy of Friendship in Horace," *Hermathena* 51 (1938) 29–48; Karl Meister, "Die Freundschaft zwischen Horaz und Maecenas," *Gymnasium* 57 (1950) 3–38; Kl. Eckert, "Horazens Freundschaft mit Maecenas als eine Seite seiner Religiosität" (Ph.D. Diss., Freiburg, 1957); K. Gantar, "La préhistoire d' '*amicus sibi*' chez Horace," *EtClass* 44 (1976) 209–21; K. Buechner, "Dienst der Freundschaft, Horaz c. 3,29," *Studi di poesia latina in onore di Antonio Traglia* (2 vols.; Roma: Edizioni di storia e letteratura, 1979) 533–71; R. L. Hunter, "Horace on Friendship and Free Speech (Epistles 1.18 and Satires 1.4)," *Hermes* 113 (1985) 480–90; R. S. Kilpatrick, *The Poetry of Friendship: Horace, Epistles I* (Edmonton, Canada: University of Alberta Press); J. L. Moles, "Politics, Philosophy, and Friendship in Horace Odes 2,7," *QUCC* 54 (1987) 59–72; and L. F. Pizzolato, "L'amicizia con Mecenate e l'evoluzione poetica di Orazio," *Aevum Antiquum* 2 (1989) 145–82.

[21] R. Seager, "Amicitia in Tacitus and Juvenal," *AJAH* 2 (1977) 40–50, and R. A. LaFleur, "*Amicitia* and the Unity of Juvenal's First Book," *ICS* 4 (1979) 158–77.

[22] See L. Alfonsi, "L'amore-amicizia negli elegiaci latini," *Aevum* 19 (1945) 372–78. See also Peter White, "*Amicitia* and the Profession of Poetry in Early Imperial Rome," *JRS* 68 (1978) 74–92. See also his "The Friends of Martial, Statius, and Pliny, and the Dispersal of Patronage," *HSPh* 79 (1975) 265–300. On the whole issue of patronage and friendship, see esp. Richard Saller, "Patronage and Friendship in Early Imperial Rome: Drawing the Distinction," *Patronage in Ancient Society* (ed. A. Wallace-Hadrill; London: Routledge, 1989) 49–62. See also P. A. Brunt, "'*Amicitia*' in the Late Roman

early and later Christian writers and works.[23] The same is true for various clichés, proverbs, and phrases involving friendship, such as "friend of God" and "friend of the king."[24] And yet, while readily

---

Republic," *PCPhS* n.s. 11 (1965) 1–20, and David Konstan, "Patrons and Friends," *CP* 90 (1995) 328–42.

[23] For general surveys that treat both non-Christian and Christian authors, see F. Hauck, "Die Freundschaft bei den Griechen und im Neuen Testament," *Festgabe für Theodor Zahn* (Leipzig: Deichert, 1928) 211–28, K. Treu, "Freundschaft," *RAC* 8 (1972) 418–34, and esp. Luigi Pizzolato, *L'idea di amicizia nel mondo antico classico e cristiano* (Filosofia 238; Torino: G. Einaudi, 1993). For a brief discussion of Jesus as "friend," see K. O. Sandnes, *A New Family: Conversion and Ecclesiology in the Early Church with Cross-Cultural Comparisons* (Studies in the Intercultural History of Christianity 91; Bern: Peter Lang, 1994) 86–91. On the NT book of James, see L. T. Johnson, "Friendship with the World/Friendship with God: A Study of Discipleship in James," *Discipleship in the New Testament* (ed. F. Segovia; Philadelphia: Fortress Press, 1985) 166–83, and *The Letter of James: A New Translation with Introduction and Commentary* (AB 37A; New York: Doubleday, 1995) 243–44, 278–80, 338–39. For later patristic views of friendship, see Carolinne White, *Christian Friendship in the Fourth Century* (Cambridge: Cambridge University Press, 1992). For monastic friendship, see A. M. Fiske, *Friends and Friendship in the Monastic Tradition* (Cuernavaca, Mexico: Centro Intercultural de Documentacion, 1970), and B. P. McGuire, *Friendship and Community: The Monastic Experience 350–1250* (Kalamazoo, Michigan: Cistercian Publications, 1988). For other studies either on or relevant to early Christian friendship, see Albrecht Dihle, "Ethik," *RAC* 6 (1966) 658–59; Rosemary Rader, *Breaking Boundaries: Male/Female Friendship in Early Christian Communities* (Theological Inquiries; New York: Paulist Press, 1983); Otto Hiltbrunner, "Warum wollten sie nicht φιλάνθρωποι heissen?" *JAC* 33 (1990) 7–20; and John T. Fitzgerald, "Friendship," *Encyclopedia of Early Christianity* (ed. E. Ferguson; 2d ed.; New York: Garland, forthcoming). For friendship in later Christian history, see R. R. Edwards and S. Spector (eds.), *The Olde Daunce: Love, Friendship, Sex, and Marriage in the Medieval World* (SUNY Series in Medieval Studies; Albany: State University of New York Press, 1991), and Reginald Hyatte, *The Arts of Friendship: The Idealization of Friendship in Medieval and Early Renaissance Literature* (Brill's Studies in Intellectual History 50; Leiden: E. J. Brill, 1994). For a discussion of the role of friendship in contemporary pastoral theology, see Egon Mielenbrink, *Freundschaft in christlicher Erziehung und Seelsorge* (Würzburg: Echter-Verlag, 1967).

[24] For clichés and proverbs involving friends and friendship, see A. Otto, *Die Sprichwörter und sprichwörtlichen Redensarten der Römer* (Leipzig: Teubner, 1890) 19–23, and Karl Rupprecht, "παροιμία," PW 18:2 (1949) 1720. On friendship with God, see H. Rönsch, "Abraham der Freund Gottes," *ZWT* 16 (1873) 583–90; Erik Peterson, "Der Gottesfreund: Beiträge zur Geschichte eines religiösen Terminus," *ZKG* 42 (1923) 161–202; Richard Egenter, *Gottesfreundschaft: Die Lehre von der Gottesfreundschaft in der Scholastik und Mystik des 12. und 13. Jahrhunderts* (Augsburg: Dr. Benno Filser, 1928); and Maurice Vidal, "La *theophilia* dans la pensée religieuse des grecs," *RSR* 47 (1959) 161–84. On "friend of the king" and similar titles, see Arnaldo Momigliano, "Honorati amici," *Athenaeum* n.s. 11 (1933) 136–41; E. Bammel, "Φίλος τοῦ Καίσαρος," *TLZ* 77 (1952) 205–10; Herbert Donner, "Der 'Freund des Königs,'" *ZAW*

acknowledging the limits of this collection of essays, we hope that these studies will not only prove useful to those interested in the theory and practice of friendship in the ancient Mediterranean world but also prompt new investigations of this important topic.

Some additional studies of friendship by members of the Hellenistic Moral Philosophy and Early Christianity Group have already been completed. Readers who find the essays in this work helpful may wish to consult the companion volume, published by E. J. Brill in the Supplements to Novum Testamentum series. That volume deals with the topics of friendship (φιλία), flattery (κολακεία), and frankness of speech (παρρησία) in the New Testament and in the surrounding Greco-Roman world. These three topics were often related, with candor or frank criticism viewed as the trait that distinguished the genuine friend from the unscrupulous flatterer.[25]

Finally, I wish to thank Candice Ventra and Rita Sanchez for their help in preparing the indexes and the personnel at Scholars Press for their patience and assistance in guiding this volume through the process of publication.

John T. Fitzgerald

---

73 (1961) 269–77; and Gabriel Herman, "The 'Friends' of the Early Hellenistic Rulers: Servants or Officials?", *Talanta* 12/13 (1980–81) 103–49.

[25] John T. Fitzgerald (ed.), *Friendship, Flattery, and Frankness of Speech: Studies on Friendship in the New Testament World* (NovTSup 82; Leiden: E. J. Brill, 1996). Essays in this companion volume are divided into three parts. Part One deals with the triad in Greco-Roman authors and contains the following essays: David Konstan, "Friendship, Frankness and Flattery"; Clarence E. Glad, "Frank Speech, Flattery, and Friendship in Philodemus"; and Troels Engberg-Pedersen, "Plutarch to Prince Philopappus on How to Tell a Flatterer from a Friend." Part Two deals with Paul's use of friendship language in Philippians and contains the following four essays: John Reumann, "Philippians, Especially Chapter 4, as a 'Letter of Friendship': Observations on a Checkered History of Scholarship"; Ken L. Berry, "The Function of Friendship Language in Philippians 4:10–20"; Abraham J. Malherbe, "Paul's Self-Sufficiency (Philippians 4:11)"; and John T. Fitzgerald, "Philippians in the Light of Some Ancient Discussions of Friendship." Part Three examines the concept of παρρησία in the New Testament and contains the following four essays: David E. Fredrickson, "Παρρησία in the Pauline Epistles"; Sara C. Winter, "Παρρησία in Acts"; Alan C. Mitchell, "Holding on to Confidence: Παρρησία in Hebrews"; and William Klassen, "Παρρησία in the Johannine Corpus."

FRIENDSHIP IN THE GREEK WORLD PRIOR TO ARISTOTLE

John T. Fitzgerald

Greek friendship prior to Aristotle was a diverse phenomenon that included both affective and non-affective forms of close association. This essay provides an overview of friendship as depicted by Homer and discussed by Theognis and Hesiod, giving attention to the forms, problems, and vocabulary of friendship in the archaic and classical periods of Greek history.

Aristotle was apparently the first person in the Greek world to discuss friendship in a systematic manner, but he was by no means the first to comment on the theory and practice of Greek friendship. Indeed, from the very beginnings of Greek literature one finds evidence of the ancient understanding and practice of friendship. The purpose of the following essay is to provide a brief overview of some aspects of Greek friendship in the periods prior to Aristotle, paying particular attention to the earliest literary materials.

Of necessity, this discussion will be selective and introductory rather than comprehensive and detailed. A truly adequate analysis of Greek friendship in the archaic and classical periods would require a much fuller discussion than is possible here. Such an investigation—in the form of either an entire monograph or another collection of essays—would also need to indicate points of continuity and discontinuity in the understanding and practice of friendship between Homer and Aristotle. It would need, for example, to weigh the claim of A. W. H. Adkins that "[i]n essentials, the concept of φιλία [in Aristotle] remains as it was in Homer"[1] against the more likely thesis of David Konstan that

---

[1] See A. W. H. Adkins, "'Friendship' and 'Self-Sufficiency' in Homer and Aristotle,"

Aristotle's discussion of φιλία reflects the specific concerns and values of the democratic *polis* of the classical period.[2] To do that, however, would require a detailed examination of friendship not only in Homer and Aristotle but also in the authors who lived between them.[3] Instead of providing an exhaustive analysis of all pre-Aristotelian material, I shall focus my comments on Homer's depiction of friendship. In that connection, I shall begin by providing an overview of the ways in which philologists have treated the common Greek word for "friend," then turn to Homer himself. Following the discussion of Homeric friendship, I shall conclude by commenting selectively on aspects of friendship in the

---

CQ n.s. 13 (1963) 41. This claim is part of his more general thesis that "in essentials the conditions of life [between Homer and Aristotle] have not changed ... that the individual paterfamilias of fourth-century Athens is still in much the same position, and has much the same values, as the head of the Homeric οἶκος" (ibid.).

[2] See David Konstan, "Greek Friendship," *AJP* 117 (1996) 71–94. See also his "Friendship and the State: The Context of Cicero's *De amicitia*," *Hyperboreus* 1:2 (1994–95) 1–16. On friendship in Athenian politics, see L. G. Mitchell and P. J. Rhodes, "Friends and Enemies in Athenian Politics," *G&R* 43 (1996) 11–30.

[3] See the older study of Franz Dirlmeier, *Φίλος und φιλία im vorhellenistischen Griechentum* (Ph.D. Diss., Ludwig-Maximilians-Universität zu München; München: Druck der Salesianischen Offizin, 1931). For more comprehensive studies on friendship in the ancient world, see L. Dugas, *L'amitié antique d'après les moeurs populaires et les théories des philosophes* (Paris: Félix Alcan, 1894); Gottfried Bohnenblust, "Beiträge zum Topos Περὶ Φιλίας" (Inaug. Diss., Univ. Bern; Berlin: Gustav Schade [Otto Francke], 1905); J.-C. Fraisse, *Philia: La notion d'amitié dans la philosophie antique* (Bibliothèque d'histoire de la philosophie; Paris: Libraire philosophique J. Vrin, 1974); and Luigi Pizzolato, *L'idea di amicizia nel mondo antico classico e cristiano* (Filosofia 238; Torino: G. Einaudi, 1993). See also E. Klein, "Studien zum Problem der griechischen und römischen Freundschaft" (Ph.D. Diss., Freiburg, 1957), and Horst Hutter, "Friendship in Theory and Practice: A Study of Greek and Roman Theories of Friendship in Their Social Settings" (Ph.D. Diss., Stanford University, 1972), which is foundational for his *Politics as Friendship: The Origins of Classical Notions of Politics in the Theory and Practice of Friendship* (Waterloo, Ontario: Wilfrid Laurier University Press, 1978). For brief overviews of ancient Greek and Roman friendship, see St. George Stock, "Friendship (Greek and Roman)," *ERE* 6 (1914) 134–38, and John Ferguson, *Moral Values in the Ancient World* (London: Methuen, 1958) 53–75. For older histories of friendship in the West, see esp. A. V. Gleichen-Russwurm, *Freundschaft: Eine psychologische Forschungsreise* (Stuttgart: Verlag von Julius Hoffman, 1912), and Ruth Eglinger, *Der Begriff der Freundschaft in der Philosophie: Eine historische Untersuchung* (Ph.D. Diss., Basel; Basel: Buchdruckerei zum Basler Berichthaus, 1916). See also Edward Carpenter (ed.), *Iolaüs: An Anthology of Friendship* (2d ed.; London: Swan Sonnenschein, 1906).

period between Homer and Aristotle, giving attention primarily to Hesiod and Theognis.

Homer

Φιλία, the word which later became the standard Greek term for friendship, does not occur in Homer. One does find the word φίλος, the usual later Greek term for friend, though philologists have differed greatly in regard to its etymology as well as its meaning and use in Homer. Numerous etymologies for the stem φιλ- have been proposed, yet all remain problematic.[4] Similarly, philologists have long disagreed about the meaning of φίλος in the *Iliad* and the *Odyssey*. Most believe that Homer uses φίλος in two main ways. The first use is as a reflexive possessive pronoun (or possessive adjective) in the sense of "one's own" (= ἴδιος or ἑός). The second use is as an emotive adjective, usually in the passive sense of "dear, beloved," but occasionally in the active sense of "loving, friendly."[5] The word occurs in both the attributive and predicate position, and some have attempted to link the meaning of the term with its position in the sentence.[6] Those who admit both senses[7] have also differed as to which meaning was original,

---

[4] "A convincing and entirely unobjectionable etymology is lacking." So Hjalmar Frisk, *Griechisches etymologisches Wörterbuch* (3 vols.; 2d ed.; Heidelberg: Carl Winter, 1972–73) 2.1019. Similar judgments are expressed by both Pierre Chantraine, *Dictionnaire étymologique de la langue grecque: Histoire des mots* (4 vols. in 2; new impression; Paris: Éditions Klincksieck, 1983), 2.1206, who says the etymology is "unknown," and Gustav Stählin, "φιλέω, κτλ.," *TDNT* 9 (1974) 113, who terms it "uncertain." In addition to the etymological proposals given by Frisk, Chantraine, and Stählin, see also those mentioned by Manfred Landfester, *Das griechische Nomen "philos" und seine Ableitungen* (Spudasmata 11; Hildesheim: Olms, 1966) 34–41.

[5] The active sense is usually claimed for both *Il.* 24.775 and *Ody.* 1.313, though some scholars, such as A. W. H. Adkins, have argued that both of these are passive. See his "'Friendship' and 'Self-Sufficiency' in Homer and Aristotle," 31 n. 1. Others seek to remove the active sense by emendation; see, for instance, the discussion by S. West in A. Heubeck, S. West, and J. B. Hainsworth, *Introduction and Books I-VIII*, Vol. I of *A Commentary on Homer's Odyssey* (Oxford: Clarendon, 1988) 115.

[6] For example, Landfester in *Das griechische Nomen "philos"* argues that attributive φίλος is a reflexive possessive pronoun meaning "one's own." Predicative φίλος, on the other hand, is treated as a qualitative adjective meaning "beloved."

[7] Those who admit both senses are not always certain whether the term in a given passage is possessive, emotive, or both (indicating possessive affection).

with some preferring the possessive[8] and others the emotive.[9] Still others have functionally restricted the meaning of φίλος in Homer so that it is *only* possessive,[10] whereas at least one recent scholar has argued that φίλος in Homer is *never* possessive. The latter position entails a rejection of the claims of both ancient scholiasts and modern lexicographers that Homeric φίλος has a weak as well as a strong possessive force.[11]

This diversity of opinion on φίλος has important implications for the meaning of the word when Homer uses it as a substantive. Those who stress the priority of the possessive sense generally argue that substantive φίλος originally designates someone who is

---

[8] See, for instance, E. Curtius, "Die Freundschaft im Alterthume," *Alterthum und Gegenwart* 1 (1882) 187; Paul Kretschmar, "Griech. φίλος," *IF* 45 (1927) 267–71; Ferguson, *Moral Values*, 53; A. Heubeck, *Lydiaka: Untersuchungen zu Schrift, Sprache und Götternamen der Lyder* (Erlanger Forschungen A/9; Erlangen: Universitätsbund Erlangen, 1959) 69; K. Treu, "Freundschaft," *RAC* 8 (1972) 419; Stählin, "φιλέω," 114, 146; E. P. Hamp, "Φίλος," *Bulletin de la Société de Linguistique de Paris* 77 (1982) 251–62; and Ceslas Spicq, *Theological Lexicon of the New Testament* (3 vols.; Peabody, MA: Hendrickson, 1994) 1.10 n. 15.

[9] See, for example, Hermann Fränkel, *Early Greek Poetry and Philosophy* (New York and London: Harcourt Brace Jovanovich, 1973) 83, and James Hooker, "Homeric φίλος," *Glotta* 65 (1987) 44–65. On the emotive aspect of the term, see also Adkins, "'Friendship' and 'Self-Sufficiency' in Homer and Aristotle," 33, who says that "undoubtedly anyone who uses φίλος of a person or thing does so in virtue of an emotion which he feels for that person or thing, as does a man who uses the word 'friend'."

[10] As Hooker, "Homeric φίλος," 47, points out, H. B. Rosén virtually eliminates the emotive sense of φίλος in his discussion of the term. See Rosén's "Die Ausdrucksformen für 'veräusserlichen' und 'unveräusserlichen' Besitz im Frühgriech. (Das Funktionsfeld v. homerisch φίλος)," *Lingua* 8 (1959) 264–93, and *Strukturalgrammatische Beiträge zum Verständnis Homers* (Amsterdam: North-Holland, 1967) 12–41. He tries to prove that Homer uses attributive φίλος to designate inalienable possessions and predicative φίλος to indicate those properties and possessions that are alienable. For criticism of this distinction from two different perspectives, see Hooker, "Homeric φίλος," 47–51, and Landfester, *Das griechische Nomen "philos"*, 9–13.

[11] See David Robinson, "Homeric φίλος: Love of Life and Limbs, and Friendship with One's θυμός," *'Owls to Athens': Essays on Classical Subjects Presented to Sir Kenneth Dover* (ed. E. M. Craik; Oxford: Clarendon, 1990) 97–108. Robinson is by no means the first to reject a possessive sense for φίλος. Émile Benveniste, *Indo-European Language and Society* (Miami Linguistic Series 12; Coral Gables, FL: University of Miami Press, 1973) 288, asserts that the interpretation of φίλος as equivalent to a simple possessive is "a long-standing error, which is probably as old as Homeric exegesis, and has been handed down from generation to generation of scholars."

"one's own." Φίλοι are thus "those who belong to one," hence "one's kin," "one's nearest relatives," "those who belong to one's house(hold)," "one's group," and so forth. In this case, the term originally expresses relationship rather than affection; φίλοι may, of course, have affection for one another, but such affection is not part of the original meaning of the term.[12] "Φίλος, regardless of the etymological details, literally expresses not an emotional attachment, but belonging to a social group, and this usage is linked to the use of the word as a possessive in Homer."[13] Φίλος as "one's own" is thus an antonym of ξένος (ξεῖνος), "the stranger who does not belong to one's group" and thus is "not one's own."[14] Accordingly, the use of φίλος to indicate a "friend" or "loved one" is a later development,[15] as is the notion of the guest-friend.[16]

A key issue among those who posit an original possessive meaning of φίλος is whether this semantic development into the notion of friendship has already taken place by the time of Homer. For some, this development is essentially or entirely post-Homeric.[17] For others, Homeric φίλος can already designate

[12] Ferguson, *Moral Values*, 53: "It denotes a practical, not an emotional, relationship, and represents the stage of establishing social ties similar to those existing within the family, but extending more widely."

[13] Pierre Chantraine, *Études sur le vocabulaire grec* (Paris: Librairie Éditions Klincksieck, 1956) 15. The translation is that of J. D. Ernest in Spicq, *TLNT*, 1.10 n. 15, where Chantraine is cited with approval. See also Chantraine, *Dictionnaire étymologique*, 2.1204.

[14] H. J. Kakridis, *La notion de l'amitié et de l'hospitalité chez Homère* (Ph.D. Diss., University of Paris; Thessaloniki: 1963) 41, 86, and Spicq, *TLNT*, 1.10 n. 15.

[15] Landfester, *Das griechische Nomen "philos"*, 71–74, followed by, among others, Eldho Puthenkandathil, *Philos: A Designation for the Jesus-Disciple Relationship. An Exegetico-Theological Investigation of the Term in the Fourth Gospel* (European University Studies 23/475; Frankfurt am Main: Peter Lang, 1993) 9–10.

[16] For a discussion of this semantic evolution, see Kakridis, *La notion de l'amitié*, 86–108. Contrast Benveniste, *Indo-European Language and Society*, 278–88, who regards the practice of guest-friendship as the *original* social and institutional matrix for the meaning of φίλος. In his view, "the notion of *philos* expresses the behaviour incumbent on a member of the community towards a *xénos*, the 'guest-stranger'" (278; see also 284).

[17] For instance, Rosén, "Die Ausdrucksformen," 264–93 and *Strukturalgrammatische Beiträge*, 12–41, "purports to remove all notion of 'friendship' from Homeric φίλος" (so Hooker, "Homeric φίλος," 47). Similarly, Landfester, *Das griechische Nomen "philos"*, 71–72, claims that the meaning "friend" is not found in Homer, though he concedes that "φίλος in the vocative occasionally comes close to such a meaning and

someone who is a "friend."[18] In either case, the possessive origin of the term should not be given undue weight in attempts to explicate the Greek understanding of friendship. "The ... notion that 'strongly' possessive overtones hang about φίλος to the extent that we can declare all Greek friendship to have been selfishly motivated is ludicrous on any etymology of the word."[19]

As one would anticipate, those who believe that the original meaning of the term is emotive typically defend the position that substantive φίλος in Homer expresses affection and friendship.[20] David Robinson, for example, argues that the sense of φίλος in Homer is sometimes reciprocal, including both an active ("friendly, loving, hospitable") and a passive ("dear, beloved, valued") sense; in such cases, it indicates "'a friend', who is not merely a beloved person, since friends are those involved in a mutual and reciprocated relationship."[21] Interestingly, he also extends the notion of friendship to several of those passages where Homer applies φίλος to the bodily organs. These organs, he says,

> are subject to emotions with which usually one sympathizes, though occasionally one must resist them. One feels towards these organs as towards friends, often sharing their feelings and preserving one's friendship with them even when overriding their promptings.[22]

---

once (I 528) designates friends."

[18] See the passages listed in LSJ, s.v. φίλος (such as *Ody.* 2.333; 4.722; 15.22). On *Il.* 21.106, see Hooker, "Homeric φίλος," 49–50, and Nicholas Richardson, *Books 21–24*, Vol. VI of *The Iliad: A Commentary* (ed. G. S. Kirk; Cambridge: Cambridge University Press, 1993) 62, who notes "the juxtaposition of friendship and death" in the line.

[19] Robinson, "Homeric φίλος," 98. He goes on to say that "etymologies do not bind the development of meanings—still less of phenomena—in anything like that way."

[20] Not all scholars who deny the priority of the possessive sense believe that φίλος originally denoted affection. For instance, Benveniste, *Indo-European Language and Society*, 273–88, believes that the original meaning of the term was primarily social and institutional, not emotive. It was only later, when φίλος was "used with reference to relations within a family group," that emotional values became attached to the term (273).

[21] Robinson, "Homeric φίλος," 101. He also notes that "'friend' can often be represented as = φιλῶν τε καὶ φιλούμενος" (102).

[22] Ibid., 106–07. See also Fränkel, *Early Greek Poetry and Philosophy*, 83: "The organs are 'friendly' to the self; in general all the elements in a person—limbs, intellect, feeling—will cooperate sympathetically for practical ends, without conflict or complications."

The debate about the original and Homeric meaning of φίλος is far from settled, yet uncertainty about this issue should not obscure the fact that the *idea* of friendship is clearly present in the Homeric epics. This is seen above all in the famous friendship of Achilles and Patroclus.[23] Yet it is striking that Homer's primary word to designate their relationship is not φίλος but ἑταῖρος ("comrade"), the term that he uses elsewhere to describe a person's shipmates and comrades-in-arms. That term by itself, however, does not necessarily imply the existence of any friendly feelings between or among individuals who associate together in this relationship,[24] though it certainly does not exclude such feelings.[25] Therefore, to indicate that an affective relationship does exist between various companions, Homer combines the two words.[26] Patroclus is thus the "dear comrade" (φίλος ἑταῖρος) of Achilles (*Il*. 17.642; 18.80; 22.390; 23.178; 24.591; see also 18.114) and vice-versa (*Il*. 9.205; 11.616).[27] Yet, inasmuch as the other comrades of Achilles and Patroclus are also dear (*Il*. 18.233; 19.305; 23.77; 24.123; see also 9.630)—especially Phoenix, Telamonian Ajax, and Odysseus (9.204, 641–42)—Homer uses superlatives to describe the special bond that existed between these two men. Patroclus is "by far the

---

[23] On their friendship, see esp. D. S. Sinos, *Achilles, Patroklos, and the Meaning of Philos* (Innsbrucker Beiträge zur Sprachwissenschaft 29; Innsbruck: Institut für Sprachwissenschaft der Universität Innsbruck, 1980), and D. M. Halperin, *One Hundred Years of Homosexuality and Other Essays on Greek Love* (New York: Routledge, 1990) 75–87.

[24] See Kakridis, *La notion de l'amitié*, 47–77, and esp. Christoph Ulf, *Die homerische Gesellschaft: Materialen zur analytischen Beschreibung und historischen Lokalisierung* (Munich: C. H. Beck, 1990) 127–38.

[25] For the possibility of a comrade being a close friend, see esp. *Ody.* 8.585–86: a comrade "with an understanding heart can be quite as dear as a brother." The translation is that of D. C. H. Rieu in the revised edition of E. V. Rieu, *Homer: The Odyssey* (London: Penguin Books, 1991) 123. See also M. L. West, *Hesiod: Works & Days* (Oxford: Clarendon, 1978) 200, who notes that the term often indicates "a close, emotional relationship, in which mutual trust plays an important part."

[26] See, for example, *Il*. 5.695 (Sarpedon and Pelagon); 10.522 (Hippocoon and Rhesus); 16.491 (Sarpedon and Glaucus); 23.556 (Achilles rejoices in Antilochus because the young man is his dear comrade); 23.563 (Achilles and Automedon); and also 13.653; 15.650; and 23.695.

[27] Homer also describes Patroclus as Achilles' "trusty comrade" (πιστὸς ἑταῖρος), an idea that appears later in the form of the faithful friend. See *Il*. 17.557; 18.235, 460.

dearest" (πολὺ φίλτατος) of Achilles' comrades (*Il.* 17.411, 655; see also 19.315), a man whom he honored above all his other comrades and loved as much as his own life (18.80–82)—indeed, "*more* than his own life."[28] Similar combinations are used to express other affective relationships, such as that between a lord and his squire (see esp. *Il.* 13.249).[29] That Homer does this suggests that "a specific vocabulary of friendship" either does not yet exist in his time or is only in the process of being created.[30] The practice of friendship thus precedes its precise definition.

Not all aspects of Homeric friendship are necessarily affective. The most conspicuous example of a non-affective friendship in Homer is that of φιλοξενία, "guest-friendship."[31] The practice of extending friendship and hospitality (ξενία) to strangers created bonds that were trans-generational, forming alliances not only between the original host and guest but also between their descendants.[32] The impetus for this practice was practical, not

---

[28] The observation is that of M. W. Edwards, *Books 17–20*, Vol. V of *The Iliad: A Commentary* (ed. G. S. Kirk; Cambridge: Cambridge University Press, 1991) 155. Edwards also notes that the exegetical scholia link Achilles' willing acceptance of death in 18.98 with the maxim that a friend is willing to die for his friends: "a splendid example of friendship, when after not being persuaded by such magnificent gifts, he chooses even to die on behalf of his friend without them" (quoted by Edwards, *Books 17–20*, 161–62).

[29] On the θεράπων or squire in Homer, see Kakridis, *La notion de l'amitié*, 78–85.

[30] For several of the points in this paragraph I am indebted to the brief discussion of David Konstan, "Friendship, Frankness and Flattery," *Friendship, Flattery, and Frankness of Speech: Studies on Friendship in the New Testament World* (ed. J. T. Fitzgerald; NovTSup 82; Leiden: E. J. Brill, 1996) 7–8.

[31] For the Greek term, see the note of Robert Renehan, *Greek Lexicographical Notes* (Hypomnemata 45; Göttingen: Vandenhoeck & Ruprecht, 1975) 199. See also Hom. *Ody.* 6.121; 8.576; 13.202. For the phenomenon, see M. I. Finley, *The World of Odysseus* (rev. ed.; New York: Viking, 1978) 99–103, and O. Hiltbrunner, D. Gorce, and H. Wehr, "Gastfreundschaft," *RAC* 8 (1972) 1061–1123.

[32] In *Indo-European Language and Society*, Benveniste regards the social institution of guest-friendship as the *Sitz im Leben* for the development of the vocabulary of friendship: "The pact concluded in the name of *philótēs* makes the contracting parties *phíloi*: they are henceforth committed to a reciprocity of services which constitute 'hospitality'" (278). Furthermore, "the verb *phileîn* expresses the prescribed conduct of the person who welcomes a *xénos* to his hearth and whom he treats according to ancestral custom" (278). "The act of 'kissing' [*phílēma* = "kiss"]," moreover, "has its place in the deportment of 'friendship' as a mark of recognition between *phíloi*" (281). See notes 16 and 20 above.

emotional, and utility remained its hallmark. Mutual affection between the generous host and the grateful guest might, of course, result from this exercise of hospitality,[33] but human experience suggests that this would not always have been the case. Furthermore, among descendants who had never met, there could be at most an openness to a renewal of the pact of guest-friendship and to the possibilities that this relationship offered for mutual affection.[34]

Therefore, the sociology of Homeric friendship embraces a broad number of diverse relationships, some purely social and formal, others more personal and emotive.[35] In all cases, however, this nexus of relationships involves certain assumptions, expectations, and obligations. These include not only actions but also ideas about what friendship entails. In some instances, these ideas seem to anticipate sentiments about friendship that become widespread in the classical and hellenistic periods. For example, in later Greek thought friends are commonly said to "think the same thing." This later connection is already somewhat anticipated in Book 4 of the *Iliad*, where Agamemnon speaks amicably to Odysseus, telling him "that the temper in your dear (φίλοισιν) breast knows friendly

---

[33] For the guest as φίλος (dear) to the host, see *Ody.* 8.21; for the host as φίλος to the guests, see *Il.* 6.14–15. The latter reference assumes that φίλος in *Il.* 6.14 is passive in meaning: Axylus was beloved *because* he used to show hospitality to strangers. The sentiment is thus the product of the action; this is how, for example, Murray in the LCL, W. H. D. Rouse (*Homer: The Iliad* [New York: The New American Library, 1954], 74), and Adkins ("'Friendship' and 'Self-Sufficiency' in Homer and Aristotle," 34 n. 2) interpret the line. Others, however, regard φίλος in *Il.* 6.14 as active in meaning: Axylus was a friend to all humanity *in that* he used to entertain guests. For this understanding, see Robinson, "Homeric φίλος," 101, and the translations of Richmond Lattimore, *The Iliad of Homer* (Chicago: University of Chicago Press, 1951) 153, and Robert Fagles, *Homer: The Iliad* (with introduction and notes by Bernard Knox; New York: Penguin Books, 1991) 196.

[34] The most famous Homeric example of the trans-generational power of guest-friendship occurs in Book 6 of the *Iliad*, where Glaucus and Diomedes meet for the first time on the battlefield and discover that their grandfathers were guest-friends. They immediately acknowledge the validity of that same relationship for themselves and exchange armor so that others may know of their own guest-friendship (6.119–236).

[35] For the use of friendship language in treaties and pacts of non-aggression, see *Il.* 3.73, 256, 323, etc.

intentions (ἤπια), for you think the same things as I" (4.360–61).³⁶ Their agreement in thought is evidence that, despite his anger, Odysseus is well-disposed toward Agamemnon, and the latter's use of "dear" is evidence that the feeling is mutual.

The same basic idea also appears in Book 22, but with a twist. Here Achilles rejects Hector's offer of a pact between the two heroes. "As between lions and men there are no oaths of faith, nor do wolves and lambs have hearts of concord (ὁμόφρονα) but are evil-minded (κακὰ φρονέουσι) continually one against the other, even so it is not possible for thee and me to be friends (φιλήμεναι) . . . ." (22.262–65).³⁷ Because ὁμοφροσύνη does not exist between wolves and lambs, they are not friends;³⁸ similarly, says Achilles, there can be no truce or friendship between Hector and himself.

The presence or absence of "oneness of mind" is thus decisive for the existence of friendship, enabling it between Agamemnon and Odysseus but excluding it in the case of Hector and Achilles. The same is true in regard to the relationship of Telemachus and Peisistratus (*Ody*. 15.195–98). It is no wonder that Homer regards ὁμοφροσύνη as the greatest gift of the gods (*Ody*. 6. 180–85).³⁹

Homer uses the closely related phrase "having one spirit" (ἕνα θυμὸν ἔχοντες) to express the same idea of unity of mind and purpose that characterizes those who are friends (*Il*. 13.487; 15.710; 16.219; 17.267). When Telemachus, for instance, comes to see Nestor, his father's old friend, the latter repeatedly calls the young man "friend" (*Ody*. 3.103, 199, 211, 313, 375) and tells him that:

---

³⁶ The translation is that of Fränkel, *Early Greek Poetry and Philosophy*, 82–83, who notes that "community of interest is at once taken as evidence of a friendly attitude."

³⁷ The translation is that of A. T. Murray in the LCL. Unless otherwise indicated, all translations of ancient texts are those of the LCL, though the renderings sometimes have been slightly modified.

³⁸ Rouse, *Homer: The Iliad*, 260, correctly notes the basic idea when he renders *Il.* 22.263 with "wolves and lambs have no friendship."

³⁹ The specific reference in *Ody.* 6.180–85 is to unanimity in marriage. It should also be noted that the motif of "oneness of mind" appears here in connection with another widespread friendship motif, viz. the idea that friendship entails helping one's friends and harming one's enemies. This is the earliest appearance of this dual theme, which is discussed most fully by M. W. Blundell, *Helping Friends and Harming Enemies: A Study in Sophocles and Greek Ethics* (Cambridge: Cambridge University Press, 1989).

all the time that we were there [at Troy] goodly Odysseus and I never spoke at variance either in the assembly or in the council, but being of one mind advised the Argives with wisdom and shrewd counsel how all might be for the best (*Ody.* 3.126–29).

Their unanimity was not only a manifestation of their friendship but also stood in striking contrast to the strife caused by the two brothers Agamemnon and Menelaus, who spoke foolishly and harshly in the assembly (*Ody.* 3.130–50).[40] The brothers failed the friendship test, whereas Odysseus and Nestor passed it.

As might be expected, Greeks of a later period not only found some of their ideas about friendship anticipated in Homer, but they also read back into Homer some of their own concerns. For instance, during the Greco-Roman period writers on friendship became acutely concerned with the problem of the flatterer, who feigned friendship with the rich and powerful in order to secure his own advantage. Cicero (*Amic.* 88–100), Philodemus (*De libertate dicendi*), Plutarch (*Quomodo adulator ab amico internoscatur*), and Maximus of Tyre (*Or.* 14) all addressed the issue of how the flatterer could be distinguished from the genuine friend, with each presenting frankness of speech as a distinguishing mark of the friend.[41] In looking for examples of flatterers, some focused on Podes, the comrade of Hector. Homer says that Podes was Hector's "trusty comrade" and "a good man among the foremost fighters" (*Il.* 17.589–90). Furthermore, he was well-bred and wealthy, a comrade who served as Hector's beloved dining-and-drinking companion, a man whom Hector prized "above all the people" (*Il.* 17.576–77). In this entire description, there is nothing at all negative. Yet some later Greeks seized on the fact that Podes was Hector's "banqueting buddy" (εἰλαπιναστής: *Il.* 17.577). Athenaeus (6.236d-e) says that this description led some people to assert that Podes was a "parasite." "For when he speaks of a friend

---

[40] For strife and friendship as antonyms, see *Il.* 7.301–02.

[41] For an introduction to this Greco-Roman discussion, see Konstan, "Friendship, Frankness and Flattery," 7–19. For Philodemus and Plutarch, see the treatments by C. E. Glad, "Frank Speech, Flattery, and Friendship in Philodemus," and Troels Engberg-Pedersen, "Plutarch to Prince Philopappus on How to Tell a Flatterer from a Friend," both in *Friendship, Flattery, and Frankness of Speech: Studies on Friendship in the New Testament World* (ed. J. T. Fitzgerald; NovTSup 82; Leiden: E. J. Brill, 1996) 21–59 (Glad) and 61–79 (Engberg-Pedersen).

at the feast he means a friend when it came to eating. That is why [Homer] represents him as wounded by Menelaus in the belly [*Il.* 17.578], just as, Demetrius of Scepsis says, Pandarus for his perjury was wounded in the tongue.[42] And Podes was wounded by a man from Sparta [= Menelaus], who zealously practised frugality."

As this quotation indicates, the character of Podes has been transformed by interpreters from a later period, who have turned Homer's positive portrait into a negative one.[43] Their purpose in doing so was hermeneutical. The parasite or flatterer was not a chief concern in Homeric society, but it was in later periods of Greek history. By transforming Podes into a parasite, these interpreters were providing a means of allowing Homer to address the post-Homeric social problem of parasitic friendship, a problem particularly associated with friendship between those who were not social equals.

In contrast to this later Greco-Roman concern, one of the major friendship problems of Homeric society was the abuse of the guest-friend relationship. It was, after all, a breach of faith on the part of a guest that led to the Trojan War. When Paris seduced Menelaus' wife Helen, he violated the pact of guest-friendship that governed guest-host relations.[44] Paris' disregard of his obligations as guest stands in stark contrast to Odysseus' behavior in Book 8 of the *Odyssey*, where he refuses to compete with his host Laodamas. As Odysseus observes, only a foolish and worthless man would venture to do that (*Ody.* 8.209–11).

As an aristocratic institution, guest-friendship had a special code of conduct, and both hosts and guests were sensitive to possible

---

[42] On the Greek understanding of perjury, see John T. Fitzgerald, "The Problem of Perjury in Greek Context: Prolegomena to an Exegesis of Matthew 5:33; 1 Timothy 1:10; and *Didache* 2.3," *The Social World of the First Christians: Essays in Honor of Wayne A. Meeks* (Ed. L. M. White and O. L. Yarbrough; Minneapolis: Fortress Press, 1995) 156–77, and "Perjury in Ancient Religion and Modern Law: A Comparative Analysis of Perjury in Homer and United States Law," forthcoming in the *International Journal of Comparative Religion and Philosophy*.

[43] Compare the way in which Matthew transforms Mark's positive depiction of the scribe who is "not far from the kingdom of God" (Mark 12:28–34) into the negative one of a Pharisaic lawyer who seeks only to test Jesus (Matt 22:34–40).

[44] West, *Hesiod: Works & Days*, 199: "The most outrageous aspect of Paris' seduction of Helen was that it was a crime against his ξεινοδόκος (*Il.* 3.354, etc.)."

The Greek World Prior to Aristotle

violations of this code. The host, for instance, was expected not only to entertain his guest in grand and lavish fashion but also to do so for as long as the guest wished to stay. But when the guest wished to depart, the host was not to seek to detain him. As Menelaus tells his guest Telemachus,

> I will not keep you here long if you wish to get back. I disapprove of any host who is either too kind or not kind enough. There should be moderation in all things, and it is equally offensive to speed a guest who would like to stay and to detain one who is anxious to leave. Treat a man well while he's with you, but let him go when he wishes (*Ody.* 15.68–74).[45]

The guest, for his part, was not only expected to reciprocate when the opportunity arose but also to behave appropriately for as long as he was a guest. That meant, for instance, that, like Odysseus in regard to Laodamas (see above), he would refrain from agitating or embarrassing his host. It doubtless also meant that he would not unduly prolong his stay with a generous host.[46]

Two other major friendship problems in Homeric times were the deaths of friends and the alienation of friends from one another. These two problems are obviously perennial ones, faced by friends in all times and places, yet Homer pays inordinate attention to both of them in the *Iliad*. Indeed, the two problems are closely intertwined. The estrangement of Achilles from Agamemnon leads to Achilles withdrawing from the fray. When Patroclus is unable to persuade his intransigent friend to come to the aid of his Achaean comrades, he joins the battle in Achilles' stead. That leads in turn to Patroclus' death, which provides the impetus for Achilles to be formally reconciled with Agamemnon and return to the battlefield.

Therefore, in a very concrete sense, the *Iliad* is not so much about "the wrath of Achilles" (1.1) as it is about the loss and restoration of friendly relations between Agamemnon and Achilles. In the Patrocleia of Book 16, the Trojans see Patroclus in his

---

[45] The translation is that of Rieu, *Homer: The Odyssey*, 224–25.
[46] For the argument that the *Odyssey*'s tale of the suitors was originally a story about guests who had abused their host's generosity and impoverished him, see H. L. Levy, "The Odyssean Suitors and the Host-Guest Relationship," *TAPA* 94 (1963) 145–53.

friend's shining armor and assume that it is Achilles. At that moment,

> all their courage quaked, their columns buckled,
> thinking swift Achilles had tossed to the winds
> his hard rage (μηνιθμὸν) that held him back by the ships
> and chosen friendship (φιλότητα) toward the Argives now (16.280–82).[47]

When Achilles himself eventually returns to the fray, that is precisely what he has done. He has cast aside his wrath and chosen friendship with Agamemnon and the rest of the Achaeans. The result is just what Agamemnon knew it would be from the very beginning of their conflict, when he said, "Ah if the two of us could ever think as one (μίαν βουλεύσομεν), Troy could delay her day of death no longer, not one moment" (*Il.* 2.379–80).[48] "Wrath" and "friendship" in the *Iliad* are thus antonyms, so that the end of Achilles' rage marks his reconciliation and friendship with his fellow warriors.[49]

From Homer to Aristotle

In the period following Homer, friendship continued to play an important role in Greek life and thought. Many aspects of friendship remained essentially the same, but the massive changes

---

[47] The translation is that of Fagles, *Homer: The Iliad*, 421.

[48] The translation is again that of Fagles, *Homer: The Iliad*, 112. On the idea that friends are of one mind and think the same thing, see the discussion above.

[49] For Agamemnon's earlier attempt at reconciliation with Achilles, see *Il.* 9.120. Achilles and Agamemnon were, of course, never close friends, and Achilles' return to battle is an expression of his solidarity with his fellow Achaeans, not of any fondness for Agamemnon. Yet the contrast of "wrath" and "friendship" in *Il.* 16.280–82 indicates not only that these two terms are antonyms but also that "friendship" here, like "rage," has an emotive dimension. For a recent treatment of the connection between the themes of anger and friendship in epic poetry, see L. C. Muellner, *The Anger of Achilles: "Mênis" in Greek Epic* (Myth and Poetics; Ithaca: Cornell University Press, 1996), esp. 133–75.

"Strife" and "friendship" are also antonyms in the *Iliad*; see the way in which the end of strife between Hector and Telamonian Ajax marks the inception of their friendship in *Ody.* 7.301–02: "These two fought each other in heart-consuming hate, then joined with each other in close friendship, before they were parted" (trans. Lattimore, *The Iliad of Homer*, 176). Finally, for the contrast of enmity and friendship, see *Il.* 3.453–54.

that occurred during the later archaic and classical periods had important implications for the understanding and practice of friendship. As indicated at the beginning of this essay, a thorough study of friendship in the period between Homer and Aristotle lies far beyond the scope of this investigation. Indeed, in what follows I shall mention only one major change that occurred and discuss only two inter-related friendship problems that occupied writers of this period.

Of the many developments that occurred during the archaic period, none is more important than the rise of the *polis*. Aristotle's entire discussion of friendship presupposes the *polis*, an institution that either did not exist at the time of Homer or, as is more likely, was only in its incipient stage.[50] The emergence of the *polis* had important implications for the ethics of guest-friendship, which continued to be practiced throughout the archaic and classical periods. In certain situations, individuals' obligations as guest-friends came into sharp conflict with their duties as citizens of the *polis*.[51] The ethics that had governed guest-friendship in Homeric times were no longer self-evident in all situations, so that new problems in the practice of that kind of friendship arose. The history of Greek friendship is thus intertwined with Greek political history, and the one cannot be written without a knowledge of the other.[52]

Of the various friendship problems encountered by people during the archaic and classical periods, the one that is probably the most frequently mentioned is that of the disloyal and unfaithful friend. This stands in vivid contrast to friendship as

---

[50] The rise of the *polis* is a complex question, involving such related issues as the relationship of the *polis* to colonization and to hero cults. For a discussion of the latter issue and pertinent bibliography, see C. M. Antonaccio, *An Archaeology of Ancestors: Tomb Cult and Hero Cult in Early Greece* (Greek Studies: Interdisciplinary Approaches; Lanham, Maryland: Rowman & Littlefield, 1995) 245–68.

[51] See, for example, the perspective of Agesilaus on war and guest-friendship (Xen. *Hell.* 4.1.34–35), and Demosthenes' *synkrisis* of his own conduct (*Or.* 18.109) with that of Aeschines (*Or.* 19.248). For a discussion of these passages, see Gabriel Herman, *Ritualised Friendship and the Greek City* (Cambridge: Cambridge University Press, 1987) 1–5.

[52] On this whole topic, see esp. Herman, *Ritualised Friendship*, whose overall thesis is stated succinctly on page 6.

depicted by Homer. "In . . . the Homeric epics," as Walter Donlan points out, "the ties that bind men in friendship appear as strong and inviolable. It is taken for granted that friends (*philoi*) and companions (*hetairoi*) are loyal and trustworthy."[53] One apparent exception to this standard Homeric depiction is Achilles, who, his comrades allege, has shown no regard for their friendship by his staunch refusal to join the battle (*Il.* 9.630–31). Yet, as we have seen, the real problem is the breakdown of friendly relations between Achilles and Agamemnon, and his "dear comrades" are suffering the effects of that breakdown. By refusing to come to his companions' aid, Achilles shows that he attaches greater significance to Agamemnon's unfriendliness in taking Briseis from him than he does to his comrades' claims of friendship.[54] For Patroclus, by contrast, these claims of his comrades finally outweigh even those of his close friend Achilles, so that he, with Achilles' blessing, joins his comrades on the field of battle. In short, the issue in the *Iliad* is one of competing claims and codes of conduct. Caught in the web of multiple friendships, even the closest of friends, Achilles and Patroclus, choose different courses of action. The issue is thus not one of simple disloyalty; it is rather the much more complex and complicated problem of choosing between conflicting loyalties.[55]

---

[53] Walter Donlan, "*Pistos Philos Hetairos*," *Theognis of Megara: Poetry and the Polis* (ed. T. J. Figueira and G. Nagy; Baltimore: Johns Hopkins, 1985) 223.

[54] See Hugh Lloyd-Jones, *The Justice of Zeus* (2d ed.; Berkeley: University of California Press, 1983) 17. As Bryan Hainsworth, *Books 9–12*, Vol. III of *The Iliad: A Commentary* (ed. G. S. Kirk; Cambridge: Cambridge University Press, 1993) 143, points out, Achilles really has no reply to Ajax's devastating charge and can only promise that he will help his friends at a later stage of the conflict. Throughout his response to Ajax, Achilles is conciliatory, so that "in spite of [Ajax's] provocative language," he "is treated in a comradely manner" by Achilles.

[55] To be more precise, the issue is much broader than friendship proper. The claims of friendship not only compete with one another but also vie with other kinds of claims, such as those involving justice and loyalty, which differ from friendship but are also related to it (see Lionel Pearson, *Popular Ethics in Ancient Greece* [Stanford: Stanford University Press, 1962] 136–60). The result is an ethical dilemma of considerable complexity. For a different view, see Donlan, "*Pistos Philos Hetairos*," 224, who thinks that "Achilles' failure of friendship is temporary, an exception to accepted standards of the group."

The Greek World Prior to Aristotle

If Homer depicts the ideal of the faithful friend, the archaic poets discuss the reality of the unreliable companion. Nowhere is this problem lamented more than in the Theognidea, the corpus of some 1400 verses of poetry traditionally associated with Theognis of Megara.[56] "On internal grounds, the Theognidea can be dated to the period 640–479 B.C. Thus, the poetry is situated between the heroic age, depicted by Homer, and the classical age, which attained its apex in the second half of the fifth century B.C."[57]

The most extensive recent discussion of Theognidean friendship is that of Donlan, who conveniently organizes the evidence into the three categories of complaints, advice, and observations:

A. *Complaints.*

A 1. Poet complains that friends have betrayed him, deceived him, or acted duplicitously toward him: 253–254, 575–576, 599–602, 811–813, 851–852, 861–862, 967–970, 1097–1100, 1101–1102 = 1278a-b, 1243–1244, 1263–1266, 1311–1318, 1361–1362; cf. 271–278, 1241–1242, 1245–1246, 1377–1380.

B. *Advice.*

B 1. Poet advises not to betray a friend or not to be duplicitous toward a friend: 87–90 = 1082c-f, 323–324, 399–400, 1083–1084, 1151–1152 = 1238a-b, 1283–1294.

B 2. Poet warns against a duplicitous friend: 91–92, 93–96, 333–334, 963–966, 979–982, 1239–1240.

B 3. Poet advises to be a duplicitous friend: 63–65, 73–74, 213–218, 309–312, 1071–1074; cf. 301–302, 313–314.

B 4. Poet advises to trust no one or to trust only a few: 61–68, 75–76, 283–286.

B 5. Poet advises never to be a friend to, nor to trust, a *kakos* [evil, worthless] man: 69–72, 101–104, 105–112, 113–114, 305–308; cf. 1238a–1240.

---

[56] See T. Hudson-Williams, *The Elegies of Theognis and Other Elegies included in the Theognidean Sylloge* (London: G. Bell and Sons, 1910), and Jean Carrière, *Théognis, Poèmes élégiaques* (rev. ed.; Paris: Société d'Édition "Les Belles Lettres," 1975).

[57] Veda Cobb-Stevens, T. J. Figueira, and Gregory Nagy, "Introduction," *Theognis of Megara: Poetry and the Polis* (ed. T. J. Figueira and G. Nagy; Baltimore: Johns Hopkins, 1985) 1.

C. *Observations.*

C 1. Poet observes that trustworthy friends are few in difficult or trying circumstances: 77–78, 79–82, 115–116, 209–210, 299–300, 332a-b, 643–644, 645–646, 697–698, 857–860, 929–930; cf. 83–86, 97–100 = 1164a-d.

C 2. Poet comments that it is difficult to tell a false friend from a true one: 119–128, 641–642, 963–970, 1219–1220; cf. 117–118, 221–226, 571–572, 1016.

C 3. Poet asserts that he is a trustworthy friend (having been tested): 415–418 = 1164e-h, 447–452, 529–530, 869–872, 1104a–1106; cf. 237–254, 511–522, 1079–1080, 1087–1090, 1311–1318, 1363–1364.[58]

As this evidence suggests, the problem of the unreliable and duplicitous friend has become an immense one in the aristocratic circles that produced this poetry. The problem is so pervasive in the poems that it suggests a crisis, if not a virtual breakdown, in the practice of Greek friendship.[59] Archaic literature, of course, is often nostalgic about the heroic age, depicting it as a time when people were nobler and problems fewer. The current age, by contrast, is seen as filled with base and ignoble people, whose number is destined only to increase (Hes. *Op.* 174–201). The perception that friends are generally unreliable is part of this larger conviction about the breakdown of society as a whole. Families are not immune to this breakdown, so that as society continues to degenerate, relations within the family will be affected. As Hesiod puts it, no longer "will brother be friend (to brother),"[60] a conviction no doubt instilled and/or reinforced by the scandalous conduct of his own brother Perses.

---

[58] Donlan, "*Pistos Philos Hetairos*," 225. The prominence of friendship in the Theognidea is also reflected in Wiktor Steffen's claim that two of the ten elegies that he finds in the collection were devoted to friendship. See his "Die Elegien des Theognis," *Acta philologica aenipontana* 2 (1967) 68–70. See also Pizzolato, *L'idea di amicizia*, 21–24.

[59] Ibid., 228–29. Older scholarship tended to provide a psychological rather than a sociological explanation for Theognis' negative comments on friendship. See, for example, C. M. Bowra, *Early Greek Elegists* (New York: Barnes & Noble, 1960) 157: "He seems indeed to have had a curiously untrusting nature and often to have felt that Cyrnus was acting against him behind his back."

[60] Hes. *Op.* 184. The translation is that of West, *Hesiod: Works & Days*, 199. For a brief treatment of friendship in Hesiod, see Pizzolato, *L'idea di amicizia*, 16–18.

As Donlan correctly observes, the Theognidea are much more pessimistic than is Hesiod about society in general and the institution of friendship in particular. In his view, the Theognidea

> are a distillation of archaic aristocratic alienation in a time of flux, when the complexities of a society in change had rendered epic friendship a nostalgic and formal vision contained only in the poetic memory.... The obsessive and deeply pessimistic attitude toward friendship in the Theognidea ... appears to reflect the belief that the social universe once integrated by blood, affinal, and close personal ties (the kinship community) is now threatened with disintegration.[61]

The real culprits, in Theognis' view, were greed and factional discord, which prompted friends to betray one another and be disloyal.[62] Consequently, because of this moral, social and economic breakdown, the *polis* itself was in crisis, and, as a result, so was friendship.

The problem of the disloyal and duplicitous friend contributed to certain convictions about friendship. Two of these may be noted. The first is the view that one's friends will necessarily be few in number; a wide circle of reliable friends as in the Homeric epics was no longer seen as a realistic possibility.[63] The second is the belief that a friend is, above all else, loyal. Homer's occasional description of companions as "trustworthy" now becomes the paramount aspect of friendship.[64] Both of these convictions will continue to be held in the classical and hellenistic periods.[65]

Once the problem of the disloyal friend emerged as a topic of discussion in archaic thought, it raised other closely related

---

[61] Donlan, "*Pistos Philos Hetairos*," 228–29.

[62] Ibid., 239–43.

[63] One may justly doubt whether all of the "dear comrades" in Homer are truly "friends" in the narrower sense of the term. Indeed, it is precisely Homer's broad use of φίλος that becomes problematized in the Theognidea. As is often the case, the traditional linguistic terminology is conceptually flawed and has contributed to the social difficulties lamented in the Theognidea. One finds here some of the initial steps toward a more restrictive use and understanding of φίλος.

[64] See Bowra, *Early Greek Elegists*, 156: "The virtue which Theognis admired above all others was loyalty, and especially loyalty to friends."

[65] On the idea that the number of true friends will be small, see, for example, Arist. *Eth.Nic.* 8.6.2 (1158a10) and Plutarch's discussion of the issue in *On Having Many Friends*.

problems. One of these was the question of how the faithful friend was to deal with a friend whose words or deeds were incommensurate with his status as friend. Hesiod addresses this issue in the midst of offering the following advice on friendship:

> Do not make a friend on a par with a brother; and if you make one, do not do him ill unprovoked, or offer false tongue-favour. But if he is the one who gives you a disagreeable word or deed, make sure he pays for it double. And if he brings you back into his friendship and is willing to make amends, accept them. It is a worthless man who keeps changing his friends: let *your* disposition not disgrace your appearance (*Op.* 707–14).[66]

On the one hand, therefore, a person is never to be the first to inflict an injury. On the other hand, if injured, an individual is to retaliate two-fold.[67] Yet, if the offending party takes the initiative in wanting to restore the relationship and is willing to make atonement by offering reparations, the injured party should accept the offered compensation and welcome the friend back. In short, according to Hesiod, a person's moral obligation following injury was retaliation; the offending party must be paid back twice over. The responsibility for recompense and reconciliation, if it was to occur, resided with the offending party.

The Theognidea also address this issue but offer two different perspectives. One recalls Hesiod's desire for double compensation in case of injury, but here the basis for reparations is bad counsel:

> Castor and Pollux, you who live in divine
> Lacedaemon, by the lovely flowing stream
> Eurotas, if I ever give a friend
> Bad counsel, let me suffer his results.
> If he does it to me, let him pay twice (1087–90).[68]

The other is much more tolerant toward a friend's lapses:

> A man who's always angry with his friend

---

[66] The translation is that of M. L. West, *Hesiod: Theogony and Works and Days* (Oxford: Oxford University Press, 1988) 58.

[67] On two-fold retaliation/atonement, see also Aesch. *Ag.* 537.

[68] Translations of Theognis are those of Dorothea Wender, *Hesiod: Theogony, Works and Days. Theognis: Elegies* (New York: Penguin Books, 1973). It is noteworthy that double compensation is a factor only when Theognis receives bad counsel, not when he gives it!

For any fault will have no peace nor friends.
Along with mortals, Kurnos, come mistakes;
Only the gods will not put up with them (325–28).

Therefore, beginning in the archaic period, one finds discussions on how to respond to the failings of one's friends. This discussion, along with that of the unreliable friend, continued into the classical period. In that context, the faithless friend was generally seen as the fair-weather friend who failed to offer assistance in a time of crisis, particularly one of a financial nature.[69] In the latter Greco-Roman period, the false friend was frequently the flatterer, who, as we have seen, feigned friendship with an affluent and powerful person in order to advance his own interest. Along with these discussions of the false and unfaithful friend, there was also continuing reflection on how best to treat the failings of a friend (e.g., Cic. *Amic.* 78). All of these discussions, plus the painful experience of discovering that an individual's "one and only true friend" is actually an ungrateful wretch,[70] contributed to the ever-developing ancient understanding of what it meant to be a genuine and reliable friend.[71]

Conclusion

In conclusion, Greek friendship had a long history before Aristotle offered the first systematic analysis of it. As far as our

---

[69] Konstan, "Friendship, Frankness and Flattery," 8–10.

[70] For a poignant expression of the pain caused by an ungrateful friend, see the 73rd poem of Catullus:
Give up expecting that anyone ever will thank you
  for anything, or show you gratitude ever.
All are ungrateful, and doing a kindness is nothing,
  or rather worse than nothing: a damaging nuisance!
So it is now with me—whom no one has hurt quite so badly
  as one who once called me his one and only true friend.
The translation is that of Charles Martin, *The Poems of Catullus* (Baltimore: Johns Hopkins, 1990) 110.

[71] For the phrase "genuine friend," see Phoc. 2A (ed. Bergk, *PLG*) and the texts cited by C. Spicq in the *TLNT* 1.297. For the argument that "true yokefellow" in Phil 4:3 is a synonym for "genuine friend," see J. T. Fitzgerald, "Philippians in the Light of Some Ancient Discussions of Friendship," *Friendship, Flattery, and Frankness of Speech: Studies on Friendship in the New Testament World* (ed. J. T. Fitzgerald; NovTSup 82; Leiden: E. J. Brill, 1996) 149–51.

records indicate, Greek friendship was always an extremely diverse phenomenon that included both affective and non-affective forms. The history of Greek friendship included not only ruminations on the conceptual ideal of friendship but also complaints about the harsh realities of flawed and failed friendships. Greek friendship did not develop in a vacuum but was intimately related to Greek political and social history, which helped to shape both the theory and practice of friendship in all its various forms. This history and Aristotle's own historical situation influenced his perception of friendship,[72] and his discussion of it helped in turn to define the understanding of friendship throughout the Greco-Roman period.[73]

---

[72] For a brief comparison of Theognis and Aristotle on friendship, see Carrière, *Théognis*, 35–37.

[73] See the following essays in this volume. For helpful comments on an earlier version of this article, I wish to express my thanks to David Konstan. That I have not always heeded his sage counsel reflects my own intransigence on certain points.

FRIENDSHIP IN ARISTOTLE AND SOME PERIPATETIC PHILOSOPHERS

Frederic M. Schroeder

Aristotelian friendship, as shared activity, preserves immanence, and as shared activity in accordance with virtue, transcendence. Located in the social context of the polis, it cannot be sustained in the cosmopolitan milieu of the Hellenistic world that seeks a purely transcendent ground and a consequent universal extension of friendship.

Aristotle sets forth his theory of friendship (φιλία) in the eighth and ninth books of the *Nicomachean Ethics* and the seventh book of the *Eudemian Ethics*. There is also some treatment of the subject in the *Politics*, the *Rhetoric*, and the *Magna Moralia*. In general, the Aristotelian school treatises were not influential in the period that extends from the death of Theophrastus in 288 BC to the edition of Andronicus of Rhodes in the first century BC, although the "exoteric" works aroused interest. Before Aspasius, the *Eudemian Ethics* was the most widely known. Aspasius, in the second century AD, whose commentary on the *Nicomachean Ethics* includes the eighth book, provides us with the most extensive text on the subject of Aristotelian friendship which may be dependent upon earlier Hellenistic sources. We cannot exclude Aristotle's works on friendship from the list of texts that might have influenced the Hellenistic discussion of the subject.[1]

---

[1] The ethical treatise most commonly quoted was the *Eudemian Ethics* (cf. A. Kenny, *The Aristotelian Ethics: A Study of the Relationship between the Eudemian and Nicomachean Ethics of Aristotle* (Oxford: Clarendon Press, 1978) 1101 and n. 112). If we are to believe Kenny, the treatise Περὶ φιλίας, number 24 in the catalogue of Hermippus, librarian of the library in Alexandria *circa* 200 BC, corresponds to the seventh book of the *Eudemian Ethics*, which is a discussion of friendship (cf. Kenny, *Aristotelian Ethics*, 39–43; H. B. Gottschalk, "Aristotelian Philosophy in the Roman World from the Time of Cicero to the End of the Second Century A.D.," *ANRW* 2.36.2 (1988) 1090 and n. 49). Ptolemy's catalogue includes the *Eudemian Ethics* in eight books (including the

If we look to the proportion of the whole occupied by friendship in the *Nicomachean* and *Eudemian Ethics* (two of ten books in the former, one of eight in the latter), we may see that the subject maintains a much larger importance in Aristotle's ethics than it does in modern philosophy. Friendship in Greek, while it, of course, includes subjective feelings, extends beyond them to objective ties of kinship and alliance.² An understanding of Aristotelian friendship must pay attention to its social setting. While Aristotle is interested in friendship between individuals, all friendship finds its situation in the communal life of the classical polis. Thus the larger network of social obligation frames all of Aristotle's discussion of friendship.

---

books common to the *Nicomachean Ethics* and the *Eudemian Ethics*). Ptolemy lived in the third century AD. Arius Didymus, in the first century BC, refers to the tenth book of the *Nicomachean Ethics* (which does not treat of friendship). (Cf. Ar. Did. *ap.* Stob. *Ecl.* 2.7.52.10 Wachsmuth and Hense, and Gottschalk, "Aristotelian Philosophy," 1101 and note 111). Arius Didymus did, however, consider kinds of friendship mentioned in Aristotle (cf. P. Moraux, *Der Aristotelismus bei den Griechen: von Andronikos bis Alexander von Aphrodisias* [2 vols.; Berlin: de Gruyter, 1973–84] 2.400–1]). Atticus in the second century AD enumerates the *Nicomachean Ethics*, the *Eudemian Ethics*, and the *Magna Moralia* (cf. Atticus fr. 2.9 Des Places, and Gottschalk, "Aristotleian Philosophy," 1101 and n. 111). Aspasius in the second century AD writes a commentary on the *Nicomachean Ethics* 1, 2, 3, 7, and 8 (the eighth book deals with friendship). From this point forward, the commentors emphasize the *Nicomachean Ethics* at the expense of the *Eudemian Ethics.* Cf. Gottschalk, "Aristotelian Philosophy," 1101.

² Aristotle's treatment of friendship is descriptive, as well as prescriptive, and thus reflects normal Greek usage. Perhaps in English we tend to use the word "friendship" mostly of subjective feelings among individuals. In Greek, the word φιλία has, in addition to that sense, a larger, objective meaning. Thus Antigone's concern to bury the corpse of Polyneices is actuated by φιλία, in a sense of binding family obligation to which the sense of "liking" can even be irrelevant (cf. Soph. *Ant.* 10, 11, 73, 99, 847, 898–99, and M. Nussbaum, *The Fragility of Goodness* [Cambridge and New York: Cambridge University Press, 1986] 64 and note 40). In Xenophon, φίλοι may bear the sense, not so much of "friends," as of "allies" (*Mem.* 2.2.2). The Socratic care for the self or soul in Xenophon expands, as it were, in concentric circles from oneself, to the household, to one's friends, to the polis, in such a way that again φίλοι would rather bear the sense of "allies" in the political sense (cf. *Mem.* 3.7.9 and my "The Self in Ancient Religious Experience," *Classical Mediterranean Spirituality: Egyptian, Greek, Roman* [ed. A. H. Armstrong; World Spirituality 15; New York: Crossroads, 1986] 347).

Aristotelian Friendship and Altruism

Aristotle classifies friendship into three kinds, character friendship or friendship that is grounded in virtue, friendship grounded in pleasure, and friendship grounded in utility.[3] Character friendship is the true friendship, that with reference to which the other two kinds of friendship may be understood as friendship at all.[4]

Obviously, the two latter kinds of friendship cannot be truly altruistic because they are grounded in qualities other than love for the friend himself, i.e., pleasure and utility. We may yet ask whether character friendship is altruistic.

Vlastos states the problem thus:[5]

> His [Aristotle's] intuition takes him as far as seeing that (a) *disinterested affection for the person we love* - the active desire to promote that person's good "for that person's sake, not for ours" - must be built into love at its best, but not as far as sorting this out from (b) *appreciation of the excellence instantiated by that person;* (b), of course, need not be disinterested and *could* be egoistic. The limits of Aristotle's understanding of love show up in his failure to notice the ambiguity in "loving a person for himself."

Phrases that suggest that we love the friend for his own sake are ambiguous and may unpack as either (a) or (b).[6] Such a phrase may also unambiguously express (b).[7] Vlastos expresses it in these words: "'A and B are good men and A loves B for B's self' implies 'A loves B because B is a good man and in so far as he is a good man.'" We may, in addition to Vlastos' argument, observe that the view that friendship, even character friendship, is selfish seems to receive further support from Aristotle's doxastic observation that the self-sufficient man, who has all the good things of life already, will have no need of friends. The function of the friend, who is a

---

[3] *Eth.Nic.* 8.2.1155b17–8.3.1156b32; *Eth. Eudem.* 7.1.1234b29–7.2.1237a36.

[4] *Eth.Nic.* 8.3.1156b7–32; *Eth. Eudem.* 7 2.1236a15–35.

[5] G. Vlastos, "The Individual as Object of Love in Plato," *Platonic Studies* (2d ed.; Princeton: Princeton University Press, 1981) 33 n. 100.

[6] *Rh.* 2.4.1380b37: ἐκείνου ἕνεκα; *Rh.* 1.5.1361b37: δι' ἐκεῖνον.

[7] *Eth.Nic.* 8.4.1157b3: οἱ δ' ἀγαθοὶ δι' αὑτοὺς φίλοι· ᾗ γὰρ ἀγαθοί.

second self (ἕτερον αὐτόν), is to supply things we cannot procure for ourselves.[8]

We may surely see in Vlastos' argument the ghost of Nygren's attack on Platonic *erōs* (as distinguished from *agapē*) as selfish and evaluative. Indeed Nygren observes disparagingly that friendship in the eighth and ninth books of the *Nicomachean Ethics* "is built in the last resort, according to Aristotle, on self-love."[9] If by "building on self-love" we mean that friendship is merely the satisfaction of egotistical desires, then Nygren's reading is unfair. Rather, Aristotle presents self-love as a model for friendship, i.e., that one loves another as one loves oneself, or that self-love and friendship satisfy the same conditions. A friend is one who desires the real or apparent good of another for his own sake, the existence or preservation of the friend for the friend's own sake, one who shares another's life, desires, joys, or sorrows. Yet all these characteristics are marks of one's own desires for and relationship to oneself. Thus the good man wishes his own good, real or apparent, and seeks it actively for his own sake, desires his own preservation and security, desires his own company (as he is good), and is aware of his own joys and sorrows.[10] In a pregnant phrase, Aristotle declares that "the friend is another self" (ὁ φίλος ἄλλος αὐτός).[11] Notice that Aristotle does not commit himself to the claim that friendship is simply an extension of self-love. He rather stipulates that self-love is a *model* for love of another, i.e., both forms of love fulfill the same conditions.

Aristotle also requires that for friendship to exist, the disposition toward friendship must be reciprocated by the friend. Thus, although wine might be dear to us, it cannot be a friend, as there is no reciprocation of friendly disposition (ἀντιφίλησις). We may feel well disposed to a person whom we have never seen and who is unaware of our feelings. Such goodwill would not qualify as

---

[8] *Eth.Nic.* 9.9.1169b3–7.

[9] A. Nygren, *Agape and Eros* (London: S.P.C.K., 1957) 186.

[10] *Eth.Nic.* 9.4.1166a1–33.

[11] *Eth.Nic.* 9.4.1166a31–32; cf. *Eth. Nic.* 9.9.1169b6–7: ἕτερον αὐτὸν. The phrase is of Pythagorean provenance, cf. Porphyry *De Vita Pythagorae* 33: ἄλλος ἑαυτός and J.-C. Fraisse, *Philia. La notion d'amitié dans la philosophie antique. Essai sur un problème perdu et retrouvé* (Paris: Vrin, 1974) 65, note 25.

Aristotle and Some Peripatetic Philosophers

friendship in the absence of reciprocation.[12] The requirement for reciprocation should go some distance toward exonerating Aristotle of the narcissism with which Vlastos charges him. Aristotle's treatment of beneficence, even at the cost of one's life, also militates against the view that his friendship is an expression of pure egoism.[13]

Aristotle defines happiness or the good for humanity in terms of action:

> The good for man comes about as an activity of the soul in accordance with virtue (ἀγαθὸν ψυχῆς ἐνέργεια κατ' ἀρετήν), or if there were more than one virtue, in accordance with the best and most perfect among them. What is more, it must occupy a complete lifetime; for one swallow does not make a summer, or one day. Thus neither one day nor a short time make a person blessed or happy.[14]

Notice that the activity that is the good for humanity and constitutes happiness is not an isolated moment but extends over a lifetime. It also contains its end (unlike the end of the craftsman's activity) internally: it is an activity in accordance with virtue and thus needs no external justification. Aristotle specifies that happiness consists in this activity and is not to be regarded as a possession (κτῆμα) of some kind.[15]

In Plato's *Symposium*, *erōs* always expresses a lack of something that we do not have.[16] On this logic, if I love someone because he possesses a quality, X, my love of that person is grounded in my desire for this quality or possession that I lack. When I acquire that possession, the friend becomes dispensable.

Now since Aristotle specifically denies, in affirming that the good for humanity is an activity in accordance with virtue, that it is a possession, he is stepping outside the Platonic assumptions. For the Platonic analogy of the arts, the good is the external product of

---

[12] *Eth.Nic.* 8.2.1155b17–1156a5; cf. *Rh.* 2.4.1381a2.
[13] *Eth.Nic.* 9.8.1169a18–29; cf. *Eth.Nic.* 9.9.1169b8–13.
[14] *Eth.Nic.* 1.6.1098a16–20.
[15] *Eth.Nic.* 9.9.1169b28–30.
[16] Cf. *Symp.* 204a1–2; 199e6–201a7; cf. 200d2: κεκτῆσθαι and Aristotle *Eth.Nic.* 9.9.1169b28–30 where Aristotle specifies that happiness is not a κτῆμα; the *Lysis* 211e2–3, 7; 212a5 uses κτῆμα and κτᾶσθαι of possessing friends, but the passage is not relevant to the present argument.

action. For Aristotle, excellence is contained internally by the activity in accordance with virtue. The present difference between Plato and Aristotle suggests that the possession of happiness, as of a thing, is the completion of striving. On this model the friend, once his happiness is appropriated, is dispensable. Aristotle's model of non-productive action that contains its end internally would suggest that the *activity* of happiness, which extends over a lifetime, may be *shared*. If we share the life of another, it may be shared without loss, and indeed with enhancement, over a lifetime without its being selfish as Vlastos would have it. Virtuous activity *need* not be shared, of course. but that it may would disarm the argument that friendship resides alone in the appropriation of the friend's quality or qualities as if they were things the acquisition of which is the whole basis of interest in that person.

Indeed Aristotle argues that no one would prefer a life of isolation or prefer to have all good things on the condition that he have them in a state of solitude: "For the human being is a social being (πολιτικόν: a creature of the polis or city-state) and by nature designed to share his life (συζῆν πεφυκός)."[17] The good ruler will promote civic friendship on the grounds that it is more productive of justice than mere constitutional provisions.[18]

Aristotle avoids a foundationalist approach in his descriptive and doxastic approach to friendship. He does not deliberate about friendship as from an Archimedian point outside the social universe of the classical polis. He takes up the question from the horizon of a humanity already deeply immersed in social and political life, of people whose lives are from birth inexorably entwined with the lives of others, departing exponentially from the social givenness of the family.[19]

Obviously there are many activities that we may pursue either alone or in company. What are the advantages of pursuing such activities in company? To pursue an activity in isolation carries with it the disadvantage that I cannot see myself as engaged in the activity. Indeed, in some activities, such as putting, self-conscious-

---

[17] *Eth.Nic.* 9.9.1169b18–19.

[18] *Eth.Nic.* 8.1.1155a22–28.

[19] For familial friendship see *Eth.Nic.* 8.1.1155a16–19; 8.11.1161a15–1161a29.

ness can even be a hindrance. Yet if I pursue the activity in the company of a friend, I may see in my friend's enjoyment of the activity, as in a mirror, my own pleasure and happiness.[20]

Furthermore the pursuit of an activity in isolation can be one-sided, partial, and boring. If I feel that I am caught up in the work of a larger project (such as our present project in the exploration of Hellenistic value terms and the New Testament) I have the awareness that parts of the project are not addressed by myself, even parts that continue after my death, yet involve me and indirectly contribute to my happiness. This sense of involvement in a larger enterprise may explain why Aristotle says that the good person will, for the sake of the city or for his friends, be ready to sacrifice his possessions and honours, even his life. He will do all of this for his pursuit of the fine. Indeed he might even sacrifice the good of doing a fine action, e.g., sacrificing his life on behalf of the polis or for one of his friends, to allow a friend to perform it. In apparent paradox, such a sacrifice is still a love of self.[21] Aristotle affirms that actions in accordance with virtue (κατ' ἀρετὴν πράξεις) are fine and for the sake of the fine.[22] If such actions are defined in terms of internal goals and are social in character, then there need be no contradiction between the model of self-love and altruism.[23]

The Kinds of Friendship

In the *Nichomachean Ethics*, Aristotle says of the three friendships that they "differ in kind" (εἴδει), without explaining what he means by "kind." His account in the *Eudemian Ethics* is more rigorous. There are, for Aristotle, three possibilities. Either the kinds of friendship share generic similarities and participate in a common genus of friendship. Or they possess a non-generic focal meaning. Or they are merely homonymous, sharing only a name in common.

---

[20] *Eth.Nic.* 9.9.1169b30–1170a4.
[21] *Eth.Nic.* 9.8.1169a18–1169b2.
[22] *Eth.Nic.* 4.1.1120a23–24.
[23] The reader familiar with the literature on friendship in Aristotle will recognize my debt to J. M. Cooper, "Aristotle on Friendship," *Essays on Aristotle's Ethics* (ed. A. O. Rorty; Berkeley: University of California Press, 1980) 301–40 for this account of the social character and setting of friendship.

In the *Eudemian Ethics* Aristotle rules out mere homonymy and generic predication in favour of focal meaning. The kinds of friendship exhibit an ordered series so that knowledge of the friendships of pleasure and advantage and their respective goods presupposes a cognitive priority in which we know character friendship and its non-derivative good first.[24]

A major question in the literature is whether Aristotle's taxonomy of friendships in accordance with focal meaning will really stand up, or is in danger of lapsing into mere homonymy. To put the hard case, we may ask whether knowledge of character friendship really affords an insight into the friendship of utility. A friendship based solely on utility is hard to grasp. It would be at the very best a truncated version of friendship. I remarked above that friendship occupies a far larger place in Aristotelian ethics than it does in contemporary treatises on ethics. Perhaps the friendship of utility really covers ground that we would encompass with treatises on moral obligation that are independent of friendship.

In fact, the *Nicomachean Ethics* does not really spell out how focal meaning applies to the different kinds of friendships. The *Nichomachean Ethics* explores the friendships rather on the basis of function, resemblance, and analogy.[25] In the *Nichomachean Ethics*, the friendships bear to each other a relationship of resemblance. Thus both character friendship and the friendship of pleasure share pleasure as a common feature.[26] Associations based on pleasure and utility are friendships on the basis of resemblance, but Aristotle in addition suggests that they bear to each other the relationship of analogy, in saying that pleasure is the good to those who love pleasure.[27] We could fill out the analogy. Moral goodness, pleasure, and utility are functional goals of liking (φιλητά).[28] As moral good is the good sought by character friendship, so is

---

[24] *Eth. Eudem.* 7.2.1236a15–35.

[25] That we are not to seek focal meaning in the account of friendship provided in the *Nicomachean Ethics*, cf. W. W. Fortenbaugh, "Aristotle's Analysis of Friendship: Function and Analogy, Resemblance, and Focal Meaning," *Phronesis* 20 (1975) 51 n. 1 for bibliography on this question.

[26] *Eth.Nic.* 8.3.1156a35–8.4.1157a2; 8.6.1158b5–8.

[27] *Eth.Nic.* 8.4.1157a25–33.

[28] *Eth.Nic.* 8.2.1155b17–21.

pleasure the goal of the friendship of pleasure, and the useful the goal of the friendship of utility. Character friendship, which is perfect, possesses both moral goodness, pleasure, and utility and can thus mediate between the latter two friendships that are friendships in so far as they resemble character friendship.[29]

Another solution to the question of how friendship may be commonly predicated of the three kinds of friendship will again lie in the social and (in the Greek sense) political nature of friendship. It is significant that, where Plato collapses the individual into the household economy (the οἶκος), and the latter into the polis, Aristotle regards the polis as parasitic on the household, and the latter on the individual. It is thus easier for Plato to argue that the realm of good in the sense of utility may be understood from the absolute Good than for Aristotle.

Aristotle claims that the flourishing person has greater pleasure in life if he shares activities, because in this way his activity will be more continuous.[30] My feeling that a project is shared, that my activity both initiates and resumes the activity of others, renders my activity more continuous by the fact that it is sustained by collective effort, by my continuous involvement in the lives of others.

The friend of character friendship is loved for himself. As we have seen, the words "for himself" embrace the qualities that he possesses, qualities that, once acquired, are lasting and trustworthy.[31] In the friendship of pleasure, the friend is loved "because of pleasure" (δι' ἡδονήν) and in the friendship of advantage, "because of utility" (διὰ τὸ χρήσιμον).[32] In the case of character friendship, as virtue is established over time and is lasting, the ground of friendship is an antecedent causal condition. In the case of the latter two friendships, as they are more brief and tenuous,[33] it might be thought that the force of the preposition διά, which expresses the ground of friendship, would rather be

---

[29] *Eth.Nic.* 8.6.1158b1–11 (for the perfection of character friendship, see *Eth. Nic* 8.3.1156b6). For the above account of friendship in terms of resemblance, analogy, and function, see Fortenbaugh, "Aristotle's Analysis of Friendship."

[30] *Eth.Nic.* 9.9.1170a4–11; cf. 9.9.1170b10–14.

[31] *Eth.Nic.* 8.3.1156b11–12.

[32] *Eth.Nic.* 8.3.1156a10–12.

[33] *Eth.Nic.* 8.3.1156a19–20.

prospective, expressing a hope as to what the person may be in the future. Yet in all three friendships, friends love "in that respect in which they are friends" (ταύτῃ ᾗ φιλοῦσιν).[34] If the latter two friendships follow the paradigm of character friendship at all, then we should expect that they too look to an antecedent causal condition, pleasure or use in the past, as their ground.[35]

If such is the case, then we may see that even the friendship of utility, which presents the hard case, does not always seek immediate advantage. For example, in business I may be well disposed to a customer and take special care to see to his needs by looking to the whole history of the relationship: he is a "good customer." Thus the friendship of advantage, when viewed from the perspective of friendship as taking place in an established collectivity of lives and values, has more than an equivocal relationship to character friendship which Aristotle claims is its paradigm.

Aristotle argues that, even as justice is of two kinds, unwritten and written, so is the friendship of utility of two sorts, moral and legal.[36] The distinction reflects the difference between equity and law. Equity will look to general principles rather than to the minutiae of legal requirement.[37] Similarly, the moral friendship of utility, while it indeed looks to advantage, also respects the generality of the relationship, and does not insist upon the detailed phenomena of agreement.[38]

Even as the ideal of the legislator is to promote friendship among citizens, so does the existence of friendship render justice and legislation superfluous.[39] If we see the moral friendship of utility as transcending the mere calculation of immediate advantage and promoting the ends of justice, it must reflect the

---

[34] *Eth.Nic.* 8.3.1156a9–10.

[35] Cf. Cooper, "Aristotelian Friendship," esp. 310–11.

[36] *Eth.Nic.* 8.13.1162b21–23; cf. *Eth. Eudem.* 7.10.1242b31–32 and Fraisse, *Philia*, 215.

[37] *Eth.Nic.* 5.10.1137b11–1138a3.

[38] *Eth.Nic.* 8.13.1162b21–1163a8.

[39] For the legislator's promotion of friendship, cf. *Eth.Nic.* 8.1.1155a22–26; *Pol.* 2.1.1262b7–9; for the superfluity of legislation, cf. *Eth.Nic.* 8.1.1155a26–28.

friendship based on virtue at least to some extent so that its title to the name of friendship rests upon more than equivocation.[40]

While for Aristotle character friendship can exist properly only between equals, lesser friendships are classed as proportional with respect to mutual obligation. While friendship transcends the demands of law, it is still important to assess the gratidude owed for favour on the part of an unequal beneficiary.[41] In his account of proportional friendship, Aristotle paves the way for the obligation between patron and client and a redefinition of friendship along these lines in the postclassical period.[42]

Friendship and the Peripatetic Tradition

Friendship in Theophrastus

Theophrastus of Eresus, Aristotle's immediate successor, wrote a work *On Friendship* in three volumes.[43] Theophrastus, together with Eudemus, preserves the Aristotelian taxonomy of character friendship, the friendship of pleasure, and the friendship of utility. However, he asks whether the three kinds are preserved in friendships involving superiority. Character friendship may exist between persons of different degree but equal virtue, e.g., between father and son, or husband and wife. Persons of average character, but of differing degree, may observe the latter two kinds of friendship, *viz.*, the friendships of pleasure and utility. There remains the question of whether the friendship of utility may exist between father and son, where the father may be presumed to love the son only for himself.[44]

A vexatious and crucial question for Theophrastus was whether one ought to do injustice for the sake of a friend. He taught that

---

[40] Cf. Fraisse, *Philia*, 210–217.

[41] *Eth.Nic.* 8.12.1162a34–14.1163b28; *Eth. Eudem.* 7.7.1241a33–7.12.1246a25.

[42] See E. N. O'Neil, "Plutarch on Friendship," B. Fiore, "The Theory and Practice of Friendship in Cicero," and A. C. Mitchell, "'Greet the Friends by Name': New Testament Evidence for the Greco-Roman *Topos* on Friendship" in the present volume.

[43] W. W. Fortenbaugh *et al.* (ed. and trans.), *Theophrastus of Eresus. Sources for his Life, Writings, Thought, and Influence* (2 vols.; PhilAnt 54.1-2; Leiden: Brill, 1992) 2.352, fr. 532.

[44] Fortenbaugh *et al.*, *Theophrastus of Eresus*, 2.352, fr. 533.

this delicate issue should be resolved without undue scrupulosity.[45] Fortenbaugh successfully demonstrates that Theophrastus is in this principle faithful to Aristotle for whom practical wisdom will in certain instances prefer equity to positive law.[46] He generally urges that friendship is long-suffering in the absence of actual envy or ill-will.[47] Theophrastus took the view that friends shared in wealth, so that there was no true friendship if one party to the relationship remained poor.[48] The social realism that drives Aristotle to establish proportional friendship is obviously not at work in Theophrastus.

On one principle, of exclusion, the circle of friends should be limited. While one should show tolerance toward friends, one should also judge their character not after, but before entering into friendship.[49] On another principle, of inclusion, the community of friends should be expanded. If friends hold all things in common, they ought to hold friends in common.[50]

Simplicius seems to attribute to Theophrastus the view that friendship and goodwill can, like faultfinding, anger, and rage, differ in degree as well as in kind.[51] The baser emotions such as anger, can change in kind by an intensification of degree, e.g., anger can become savagery or bestiality. There is no suggestion that goodwill or friendship can become something else by an intensification in degree, e.g., friendship between child and parent is more pleasant and useful than friendship between persons who

---

[45] Fortenbaugh et al., *Theophrasuts of Eresus*, 2.354, fr. 534; see below under "Cicero" for further discussion of this material (Gell. *Noctes Atticae* 1.3.8–14, 21–9) and the relevant passages in Cicero where, according to Aulus Gellius, Cicero offers a trivial explanation of this subject.

[46] Cf. W. W. Fortenbaugh, "Theophrastus, fr. 534 FSH&G. On Assisting a Friend Contrary to the Law," *Synthesis Philosophica* 10 (1990) 457–68.

[47] Fortenbaugh et al., *Theophrastus of Eresus*, 2.364, fr. 540; 366, fr. 541; 366, fr. 542; 368, fr. 543.

[48] Fortenbaugh et al, *Theophrastus of Eresus*, 2.360, fr. 536; 360, fr. 537.

[49] Fortenbaugh et al., *Theophrastus of Eresus*, 2.362, fr. 538A; 362, fr. 538B; 362, fr. 538C; 362, fr. 538D; 364, fr. 538E; 364, fr. 538F.

[50] Fortenbaugh et al., *Theophrastus of Eresus*, 2.360, fr. 535.

[51] Fortenbaugh et al., *Theophrastus of Eresus*, 2.264, fr. 438 (= Simplic. *In Ar. Cat.*, *CAG* 8.235.3–13 Kalbfleisch); it is unclear whether friendship and goodwill are further examples beyond faultfinding etc. which Simplicius clearly ascribes to Theophrastus, or whether they are fresh examples supplied by Simplicius.

are unrelated.⁵² What is interesting about this passage is that friendship may here be treated as an emotion, rather than as an objectively founded relationship. There is precedent for this in Aristotle who in the *Rhetoric* classes friendship and goodwill as emotions.⁵³ In the *Nichomachean Ethics*, however, Aristotle distinguishes friendship (φιλία) from affection (φίλησις) on the grounds that the former is a disposition, the latter an emotion.⁵⁴

Cicero

Cicero, whose philosophical writings are eclectic, despite a basic predilection for Stoicism, is dissatisfied with the reduction of friendship in classical Stoicism to a universally extended benevolence. Cicero, in the *De Officiis*, teaches that duties to one's own circle of friends are not to be relativized by the larger cosmopolitan context and invites a concentration on the specific obligations of friendship in the narrower sense.⁵⁵

In the *De Amicitia*, Cicero defines friendship as "nothing other than agreement in all things, human and divine, together with goodwill and affection," and states that, as among divine gifts, it is exceeded in value only by wisdom.⁵⁶ Thus friendship, although it mirrors a kind of Pythagorean cosmic harmony, is of intrinsic value, apart from its connection with the wisdom of the Stoic sage. Cicero defies the Stoic teaching that virtue must, to be secure, avoid emotion, so that life without friendship is unthinkable.⁵⁷ He also allows friendship to be based, not only upon virtue, but upon pleasure and utility as well, additional grounds we have

---

⁵² *Eth.Nic.* 8.12.1162a7–9.

⁵³ *Rh.* 2.1.1378a18–19; on the Simplicius passage and friendship see W. W. Fortenbaugh, "Theophrastus on Emotion," *Theophrastus of Eresus. On His Life and Work* (ed. W. W. Fortenbaugh; Rutgers University Studies in Classical Humanities, 2; New Brunswick, N.J.: Transaction Books, 1985) 212–15.

⁵⁴ *Eth.Nic.* 8.5.1157b28–29.

⁵⁵ *Off.* 1.17.55–56 and Fraisse, *Philia*, 384–85.

⁵⁶ *Amic.* 6.20.

⁵⁷ *Amic.* 13.47–48 and K. Bringmann, *Untersuchungen zum späten Cicero* (Göttingen: Vandenhoeck & Ruprecht, 1971) 227–28, who sees at work here an influence from the Peripatetic view of emotion in its relation to virtue, e.g., the good man despises injustice.

encountered in Aristotle.[58] Before we see in this an illegitimate extension of the Stoic idea of friendship to include Aristotelian grounds, we should understand that the Stoic view of friendship accomodated these supplementary grounds in slightly altered terminology.[59] Cicero adopts the Peripatetic tag that the friend is "another self."[60] Yet the competitive character of the Roman political world in which he situates such friendship is inhospitable to it.[61]

The thoughts of Scipio on friendship that begin the third part of the *De Amicitia* are indebted to Theophrastus. Scipio dwells upon the precarious nature of friendship, unlikely to endure over a lifetime without both wisdom and good luck. In light of the tenuous longevity of friendship, the friend may be faced with the necessity of performing injustice for the sake of a friend. Aulus Gellius testifies that this latter question was thoroughly discussed by Theophrastus, to whom, he says, Cicero was indebted for his discussion of the subject in the *De Amicitia*.[62] He faults Cicero for offering only a truncated version of Theophrastus' more intricate and elaborate discussion (Cicero's example that one should not take up arms against one's fatherland is too extreme and what is really wanted is help with more difficult cases).[63] The Theophrastean character of the view put forth is perhaps also attested by the un-Stoic idea that the duration of friendship might depend on chance.[64] Cicero's concession that a friend might under certain circumstances have to do injustice for the sake of a friend contrasts with his views elsewhere in the *De Amicitia*.[65]

---

[58] *Amic.* 6.20–22 and Fraisse, *Philia*, 391–392.

[59] Cf. *SVF* 3.181.32–37 (§723) and Bringmann, *Untersuchungen*, 22 and n. 52.

[60] *Amic.* 21.80.

[61] Cf. E. W. Leach, "Absence and Desire in Cicero's *De Amicitia*," *CW* 87.2 (1993) 12–13.

[62] Gell. 1.3.10–11 and Cic. *Amic.* 11.36 and 17.61.

[63] Cf. Gell. 1.3.10–29; cf. specifically Gell. 1.3.10–18 and Cic. *Amic.* 17.61; Gell. 1.3.19–20 and Cic. *Amic.* 11.36 for the Ciceronian passages criticized; cf. Fortenbaugh, "On Assisting a Friend," 459.

[64] Cf. Fraisse, *Philia*, 397.

[65] For the concession, see *Amic.* 17.61; for his contrasting views elsewhere, see *Amic.* 12.40, 12.42 and 13.44. For the view that Cicero's philosophy of friendship reproduces the ideas of Panaetius, a Stoic who accomodates Peripatetic positions, see

Arius Didymus

Arius Didymus presents a doxographic account of Peripatetic ethics which conflates Peripatetic and Stoic positions and is preserved in the *Eclogae Physicae et Ethicae* of Stobaeus.[66] The treatise is a redaction of various anonymous Peripatetic sources.[67] A part of this work is devoted to friendship.[68] Arius Didymus identifies four classes of friendship: of comradeship (ἑταιρική), of kinship (συγγενική), of hospitality (ξενική), and erotic (ἐρωτική). Two dubious candidates which would require further rational consideration are friendships of beneficence (εὐεργετική) and admiration (θαυμαστική). The ground of comradeship is intimacy (συνήθεια), of kinship is nature (φύσις), of erotic friendship is passion (πάθος), of beneficence is gratitude (χάρις), of hospitality is need (χρεία), and of admiration is power (δύναμις).[69] The first three kinds of friendship are established in the ethical treatises of Aristotle, but the last three are resonated in those works, even if the same vocabulary is not used by Aristotle.[70] The grounds of friendship are not to be found in Aristotle.[71] The goals of all friendships are the ethically beautiful, the advantageous, and the

---

F.-A. Steinmetz, *Die Freundschaftslehre des Panaitios nach einer Analyse von Cicero's 'Laelius De Amicitia'* (Wiesbaden: F. Steiner, 1967) followed by Fraisse, *Philia*, 382–412; see, however, the cogent arguments of Bringmann, *Untersuchungen*, 206–28; 268–70 against the view that Panaetius contaminates his Stoicism in this respect. Bringmann, *Untersuchungen*, 209, argues persuasively (*pace* Steinmetz, *Freundschaftslehre*, 112–14) that the Theophrastean passage consulted by Aulus Gellius is mediated directly and not through Panaetius.

[66] Ed. C. Wachsmuth and O. Hense 2.7.116.19–152.25; on the question and history of fixing the reference of 57–152 to the *Epitome* of Arius Didymus, see C. H. Kahn, "Arius as Doxographer," *On Stoic and Peripatetic Ethics: The Work of Arius Didymus* (ed. W. W. Fortenbaugh; Rutgers University Studies in Classical Humanities, 1; New Brunswick, N.J.: Transaction Books, 1983) 3–13.

[67] Cf. H. Goergemanns, "*Oikeiōsis* in Arius Didymus," *On Stoic and Peripatetic Ethics* (ed. W. W. Fortenbaugh; Rutgers University Studies in Classical Humanities, 1; New Brunswick, N.J.: Transaction Books, 1983) 165–89.

[68] *Ap.* Stob. *Ecl.* 2.7.143.1–16 Wachsmuth and Hense.

[69] *Ap.* Stob. *Ecl.* 2.7.143.5–8 Wachsmuth and Hense.

[70] For the references in Aristotle, see H. von Arnim, "Arius Didymus' Abriss der peripatetischen Ethik," *Sitzungsberichte, Akademie der Wissenschaften in Wien, Philosophisch-historische Klasse* 204.3 (1926) 78–9; cf. Moraux, *Aristotelismus*, 2.400.

[71] Cf. Moraux, *Aristotelismus*, 1.400.

pleasing.⁷² These obviously correspond to the three kinds of friendship in Aristotle.

The first instance of friendship is friendship toward oneself (τὴν πρὸς ἑαυτὸν φιλίαν), the second friendship toward one's parents; then friendship extends toward all other kin and friends who are not relatives. For this reason, in friendship toward oneself, one should take care to avoid excess, and in friendship toward others to avoid coming short. The first carries with it the reputation of egotism (self-love in the bad sense), the second of miserliness.⁷³

Arius Didymus refers this account of friendship toward oneself and its social expansion to a previous collection.⁷⁴ Self-love is there drawn into the ambit of *oikeiōsis*, as the natural instinct toward self-preservation is extended to embrace one's parents, family, city, strangers, and finally the whole human race.⁷⁵ Since *oikeiōsis* is normally associated with Stoicism, it seems strange that Arius Didymus would ascribe the doctrine to the Peripatetics.

Alexander of Aphrodisias relates that Boethus and Xenarchus, predecessors of Arius Didymus, found the doctrine of *oikeiōsis* in the eighth and ninth books of Aristotle's *Nichomachean Ethics* which are, of course, the books devoted to friendship.⁷⁶ It is not in fact possible to derive this doctrine from these references which discuss only wishing the good for oneself and how self-love is a model for friendship.⁷⁷

Because the idea is attributed to the Peripatetics by Arius Didymus, it was earlier thought that it stemmed from

---

⁷² *Ap.* Stob. *Ecl.* 2.7.143.8–9 Wachsmuth and Hense; cf. Moraux, *Aristotelismus*, 1.400.

⁷³ *Ap.* Stob. *Ecl.* 2.7.143.11–16 Wachsmuth and Hense; cf. Moraux, *Aristotelismus*, 1.401.

⁷⁴ *Ap.* Stob. *Ecl.* 2.7.143.11 Wachsmuth and Hense. The part referred to is 118.11–119.4; 119.22–121.21.

⁷⁵ Cf. S. G. Pembroke, "Oikeiōsis," *Problems in Stoicism* (ed. A. A. Long; London: Athlone, 1971) 124; Moraux, *Aristotelismus* 1.401; Gottschalk, "Aristotelian Philosophy," 1125–26; Ar. Did. *ap.* Stob. *Ecl.* 2.7.119.22–121.21 Wachsmuth and Hense also owes a debt to Aristotle *Eth.Nic.* 8.1.1155a16–22: see below on Aspasius for further discussion of this passage and its debt to Aristotle.

⁷⁶ *De Anima Mantissa, Supplementum Aristotelicum* 2.1.151.7–13 Bruns.

⁷⁷ For wishing the good for oneself, see *Eth.Nic.* 8.2.1155b17–27; for self-love as a model for friendship, see *Eth.Nic.* 9.8.1168a28–1168b10.

Theophrastus, or even Aristotle. The current view is that it was originally Stoic and was imported into the first-century Peripatos by Antiochus of Ascalon.[78] Arius' material is from late Hellenistic Peripatetic authors who borrowed *oikeiōsis* from Stoicism.[79] The account is doubtless enriched by access to the text of the *Nichomachean Ethics* published by Andronicus of Rhodes.[80] In the previous section in which Arius claims to discuss friendship, he in fact discusses *oikeiōsis* and departs, not from the child's affection for the parent, but from the parent's affection for the child.[81] It is difficult to parallel the latter account of *oikeiōsis* in Stoic texts or to show by what process of analogy or metathesis that affection would be transferred. Arius' account of *philia* would be most interesting if it could be established that (in Pembroke's words) "the extension of *philia* set out by Arius really does represent a process of individual development beginning in infancy." As Pembroke observes, "The extension seems rather to be a purely logical one, flatly superimposed on an inherited doctrine of parental affection."[82]

Arius Didymus offers the following definition of the human being: The human being is an animal that engages in mutual affection and is social (φιλάλληλον γὰρ εἶναι καὶ κοινωνικὸν ζῷον τὸν ἄνθρωπον).[83] Although Arius, in a definition attributed to the Peripatos, here uses the word φιλάλληλος as part of the

---

[78] There is a reference to Theophrastus at *ap*. Stob. *Ecl.* 2.7.140.8 Wachsmuth and Hense within an account of moral virtue (137.13–142.13). Cf. Gottschalk, "Aristotelian Philosophy," 1117, 1128; Pembroke, "Oikeiōsis," 135; N. P. White, "The Basis of Stoic Ethics," *HSPh* 93 (1979) 143–78, sees in Aristotle's ethics an emphasis upon "developing, exploiting, and acting in accordance with what is peculiar to the human species," but misses the cosmic context of such self-realization that is to be found in Stoicism.

[79] Cf. Goergemanns, "*Oikeiōsis*," 181.

[80] For explicit reference to the text of the *Nicomachean Ethics* cf. Ar. Did. *ap*. Stob. *Ecl.* 2.7.140.12 ff. Wachsmuth and Hense, and O. Regenbogen, "Theophrastos," PWSup 7 (1940) 1492; cf. Pembroke, "Oikeiōsis," 135.

[81] *Ap*. Stob. *Ecl.* 2.7.120.8–20; cf. Pembroke, "Oikeiōsis," 124.

[82] Pembroke," Oikeiōsis," 125. Pembroke, "Oikeiōsis," 132 and note 88 cites Diogenes Laertius (*SVF* 3.183.22–25 [§731] = D.L. 7.120) as an indubitably orthodox Stoic witness that parental affection is natural only to the wise, but not to the base, i.e., it cannot be a universal point of departure for *oikeiōsis*.

[83] *Ap*. Stob. *Ecl.* 2.7.120.14 Wachsmuth and Hense.

definiens of the human being, he elsewhere attributes it to the Stoa, its more likely origin.[84] We may contrast this with Aristotle's definition of the human being as a political animal (πολιτικὸν ζῷον) in the *Politics*.[85] Aristotle, in the *Nichomachean Ethics*, sees friendship as the basis of the polis.[86] He also sees daily intercourse as a requirement of friendship and teaches that true friendship demands that one's circle of friends be small.[87] Arius Didymus, by contrast, argues that it does not matter whether our friendships are directed near or afar, as each true friendship is choiceworthy for itself and not for need.[88] He remarks: "If friendship toward fellow-citizens is choiceworthy for itself, it is necessary that friendship toward one's own people and race would be choiceworthy in itself, with the result that also friendship directed toward all human beings would be choiceworthy in itself."[89]

As we have seen, *philia* in Aristotle must always involve reciprocation.[90] *Oikeiōsis*, which is an asymmetrical relationship, does not require reciprocation and, for this reason, may be regarded (in Goergemann's words) as "more suitable than *philia* as a basis for an individualistic ethics."[91] Stoic ethics is, on the one hand, individualistic, but on the other looks to a wider community than that of the classical polis. While the requirement for reciprocation would limit the circle of *philia, oikeiōsis*, working outward from the individual, embraces all humankind.

---

[84] *Ap.* Stob. *Ecl.* 2.7.109.18 Wachsmuth and Hense (= *SVF* 3.172.14–173.3 [§686]); it occurs as well (again in the company of κοινωνικός) in Epict. *Dissertationes* 3.13.5 Schenkl; cf. 4.5.10; Iambl. *Protr.* 123.12 Pistelli where the word occurs in a Pythagorean context and Pembroke, "Oikeiōsis," 127 and note 62.

[85] 1.1.1253a3; cf. von Arnim, "Arius Didymus," 142: "Denn in φιλάλληλον liegt, dass unter allen Menschen als solchen, nicht nur als Bürgern des gleichen Staates, ein natürliches Gemeinschaftsgefühl besteht."

[86] 8.1.1155a22–23.

[87] For the requirement for daily intercourse, see *Eth.Nic.* 8.6.1158a7–10. and for the size of one's circle of friends, see *Eth.Nic.* 8.6.1158a10–18; 9.10.1170b20–1171a20.

[88] *Ap.* Stob. *Ecl.* 2.7.120.15–17 Wachsmuth and Hense.

[89] *Ap.* Stob. *Ecl.* 2.7.120.17–20 Wachsmuth and Hense.

[90] *Eth.Nic.* 8.2.1155b27–1156a5; cf. *Rh.* 2.4.1381a2.

[91] Cf. Goergemanns, "*Oikeiōsis*," 185 and his philological examination of *oikeiōsis*, 181–87.

Aristotle and Some Peripatetic Philosophers 53

Aristotelian friendship is political in the sense that it has its *locus* in the intertwining of lives and *praxis* in the ancient polis. Significantly, Arius Didymus directs friendship toward all of humankind universally. Although he attributes his views to the Peripatos and uses Peripatetic language, the sentiment is more in keeping with Stoicism, a philosophy that reflects the decline of the classical polis and the rise of the Hellenistic cosmopolis and individualism. Friendship becomes an expression of *humanitas*. Thus no-one would refrain from saving a fellow human being from being devoured by a beast, from pointing the way to a traveler, or from showing the way to water to a fellow wanderer in the desert.[92] He reasons: "All who thus save (τοὺς σῴζοντας) [themselves and others] act toward their neighbours (τοὺς πλησίον), so that not in accordance with desert, but in accordance to that which is choiceworthy in itself they do most things."[93] Thus cosmopolitan friendship becomes a concern for the salvation of one's neighbour.

Arius Didymus is of particular interest for the present volume, as his influence upon the household codes of the New Testament has been demonstrated.[94] Balch examines Arius *ap.* Stobaeus *Eclogae Physicae et Ethicae* 2.7.147.26–152.25 Wachsmuth and Hense and finds parallels with the eighth book of the *Nicomachean Ethics* whose subject is friendship. There are parallels between the treatment of the household and the nucleus of the state[95] and of the connection between the best constitution and virtue and the worst constitution and vice.[96] In none of these texts, however, is friendship as such thematized.

---

[92] *Ap.* Stob. *Ecl.* 2.7.121.3–8 Wachsmuth and Hense.

[93] *Ap.* Stob. *Ecl.* 2.7.120.20–121.3 Wachsmuth and Hense; we may compare Luke 10:27 where Jesus tells us to love our neighbor (τὸν πλησίον) as ourselves.

[94] Cf. D. L. Balch, "Household Codes," *Greek and Roman Literature and the New Testament: Selected Forms and Genres* (ed. D. E. Aune; Atlanta: Scholars Press,1988).

[95] *Ap.* Stob. *Ecl.* 2.7.148.5–8 Wachsmuth and Hense and Aristotle *Eth.Nic.* 8.12. 1162a15–33; cf. also Aristotle *Pol.* 1.1.1152a24–31; Ar. Did. *ap.* Stob. *Ecl.* 2.7.148.16–19 and Aristotle *Eth.Nic.* 8.10.1160b22–1161a9. Cf. Balch, "Household Codes," 43.

[96] *Ap.* Stob. *Ecl.* 2.7.151.3–5 and Aristotle *Eth.Nic.* 8.10.1160a35–1160b22; cf. *Pol.* 4.2.1289a26–1289b26. Cf. Balch, "Household Codes," 43.

Alcinous

Alcinous insists that the highest friendship, or friendship that is most deserving of the name, is based upon mutual goodwill and rests upon equality, specifically ethical equality.[97] The likeness that they share consists in the shared attribute of moderation, so that immoderate people cannot be friends. The latter observation invokes Plato's *Laws* 716c.[98] However, his view of friendship is also reminiscent of the Aristotelian view that the highest friendship involves shared virtue.[99] Natural, familial, and political friendships are inferior brands which do not quite deserve the term "friendship" and are not really based, as is true friendship, on reciprocity of goodwill.[100] The types of friendship classified here are also to be found in Aristotle.[101] While it is customary to class Alcinous as a Middle Platonist, it is obvious from these passages that there is also reference to Aristotle. In fact, it is not clear that Alcinous is a Platonist or, indeed, that he has any defined philosophical position, appearing to be merely a doxographer of others' opinions.[102]

Aspasius

Aspasius follows the account of the *Eudemian Ethics* (which he thinks to be by Eudemus, not Aristotle) in seeing the taxonomy of friendships in the *Nichomachean Ethics* in terms of focal meaning.[103] In seeking to base focal meaning merely upon the account of resemblance, Aspasius may be considered the author of

---

[97] *Didaskalikos* 33.187.7–13 and Moraux, *Aristotelismus*, 2.478; for the argument that we should now call this author "Alcinous" rather than "Albinus," cf. J. Whittaker, "Platonic Philosophy in the Early Empire," *ANRW* 2.36.1 (1987) 83–102.

[98] Cf. Moraux, *Aristotelismus*, 2.478.

[99] Cf. *Eth.Nic.* 8.4.1157a25–32; 8.6.1158b1; *Magna Moralia* 2.11.1209a8–9; 1209b11–15; 1210a7–9 and Moraux, *Aristotelismus*, 2.478–79.

[100] *Didaskalikos* 33.187.13–17 and Moraux, *Aristotelismus*, 2.479.

[101] Cf. *Eth.Nic.* 8.5.1157b23; 11.1161b11–13; 14.1163b24 and Moraux, *Aristotelismus*, 2.479.

[102] Cf. Whittaker, "Platonic Philosophy," 100–2.

[103] Cf. Aristotle *Eth. Eudem.* 7.2.1236a15–32 and Asp. *In Eth. Nic.*, *CAG* 19.163.27–164.11 Heylbut, and Moraux, *Aristotelismus*, 2.289–90.

subsequent confusion in finding focal meaning in the Nicomachean account.[104]

Aspasius, commenting on Aristotle's distinction between liking (φίλησις) as an affect and friendship (φιλία) as a disposition (ἕξις), remarks that friendship must embrace both rational and irrational elements.[105] Aspasius elsewhere, in exploring Aristotle's statement that virtue is concerned with pleasures and pains, polemicizes against the Stoic belief that all passions are contrary to reason and therefore irrational, teaching that not every passion is opposed to reason and may rather be brought into accord with reason.[106] Doubtless here too, in his account of friendship, he is criticizing the negative Stoic evaluation of emotion.[107]

Aristotle, in his introduction to his discussion of friendship, speaks of the natural friendship that parents have for their offspring, of the friendship among persons of the same race, and among human beings generally, when we praise lovers of humanity (καὶ μάλιστα τοῖς ἀνθρώποις, ὅθεν τοὺς φιλανθρώπους ἐπαινοῦμεν). The series seems to expand as the last term is introduced by the words καὶ μάλιστα ("and especially"), which would appear to mark an ascending climax. Aristotle illustrates the propensity to universal friendship by remarking on the affinity and friendly feeling that exist among travelers.[108]

Although there is no specific mention of *oikeiōsis* in Aspasius, in his commentary on this passage he does undertake a universal extension of friendship, in the manner we have encountered in Arius Didymus, beginning not from self-love, but from the love of parents, toward friendship.[109] Aspasius extends friendship from the relationship between parents and children, to fellows of the same

---

[104] Cf. Fortenbaugh, "Aristotle's Analysis of Friendship," 61.

[105] For the Aristotelian distinction, see *Eth.Nic.* 8.5.1157b28–29. For Aspasius' comment, see *In Ethica Nicomachea*, *CAG* 19.172.8–12 Heylbut, and Moraux, *Aristotelismus*, 2.289–90.

[106] For Aristotle's statement, see *Eth.Nic.* 2.3.1104b9. For Aspasius' polemic, see *In Eth. Nic.*, *CAG* 19.44.12–19 Heylbut, and Gottschalk, "Aristotelian Philosophy," 1157.

[107] Cf. Moraux, *Aristotelismus*, 2.290.

[108] *Eth.Nic.* 8.1.1155a16–22.

[109] Cf. Asp. *In Eth.Nic.*, *CAG* 19.159.26–160.7 Heylbut, and Ar. Did. *ap.* Stob. *Ecl.* 2.7.119.22–121.21 Wachsmuth and Hense..

race, to all humanity (πρὸς πάντας).[110] Arius extends friendship from parents and children, to fellow-citizens, to fellows of the same race, to all human beings (πρὸς πάντας ἀνθρώπους).[111] The rhetorical *exemplum* that illustrates the universal extension of friendship is the same: anyone would give a lost traveller direction.[112] Where Aristotle uses "human being," Arius and Aspasius say "*all* human beings," emphasizing the universality. The example of giving a lost traveler directions is also more specific than what we find in Aristotle. These considerations lead us to conclude either that Aspasius is following Arius, or that they are indebted to the same source or to a common exegetical tradition.[113]

Conclusions

Friendship in Greek philosophy is always constructed on the model of self-love and for this reason will be accused of selfishness and a lack of true regard for others. The ancient philosophy of friendship seeks its ground either, in transcendence, in some principle outside the relationship or, in immanence, within the relationship itself. A transcendent ground imperils altruism because it values a quality or characteristic other than the person. By its universality, it also extends the scope of friendship to cosmopolitan dimensions. An immanent account risks the failure of explaining the relationship satisfactorily. It also narrows the scope of friendship to the number of persons capable of sustaining it. Friendship occupies a much more prominent place in classical than in modern ethics, perhaps because it covers a larger set of obligations.

Friendship in Aristotle is fundamentally political, in the sense that its proper *locus* is in the intertwining of lives and deaths in the

---

[110] Asp. *In Eth. Nic.*, *CAG* 19.159.26–160.1.

[111] Ar. Did. *ap.* Stob. *Ecl.* 2.7.119.22–120.20.

[112] Asp. *In Eth. Nic.*, *CAG* 19.160.1–2 Heylbut; Ar. Did. *ap.* Stob. *Ecl.* 2.7.121.4–5 Wachsmuth and Hense.

[113] Cic. *Off.* 1.16.51 has the example of offering direction to the wanderer in the context of *oikeiōsis*, quoting Ennius. In 52, however, he undertakes a Panaetian qualification to the effect that universal liberality must still leave us with time for our friends (cf. Fraisse, *Philia*, 384).

classical polis. On the basis of this political reading of friendship in Aristotle the two cruces popular in the contemporary literature, the question of altruism, and the integrity of the Aristotelian taxonomy of friendship, may admit of a common solution. The virtual disappearance of the school treatises of Aristotle on the subject of friendship from after the death of Theophrastus until their publication by Andronicus of Rhodes severely limits their influence upon Hellenistic literature except for the continuing tradition of doxographic tags. In Arius Didymus and Aspasius we can see how Aristotelian friendship is pulled within the ambit of Stoic *oikeiōsis* and is extended in concentric circles emanating from love of self to the world as cosmopolis, a world whose anonymity and isolation of the individual from the social context of the classical polis prevents the existence of friendship in the Aristotelian sense of shared *praxis* and virtue in the contained world of the polis. Perhaps this absence of political character reflects merely the paucity of evidence. It might also bear witness to the collapse of the traditional polis in the Hellenistic civilization which may be thought, with such phenomena as New Comedy, the epyllion, and Epicurean friendship, to have given birth at once both to an intimacy and to a universality foreign to the transparency of life in the classical city.[114]

---

[114] I wish to thank Troels Engberg-Pedersen for his helpful comments on an earlier draft of this paper; of course, any continuing imperfections are my own responsibility. The reader is referred to my *Form and Transformation. A Study in the Philosophy of Plotinus* (Montreal and Kingston, London, Buffalo: McGill-Queen's Press, 1992) 91–113 for consideration of Platonic and Aristotelian friendship and their influence upon Plotinus. I received notice of S. Stern-Gillet, *Aristotle's Philosophy of Friendship* (New York: State University of New York Press, 1995) too late to take account of it.

THE THEORY AND PRACTICE OF FRIENDSHIP IN CICERO

Benjamin Fiore, S.J.

Cicero's theoretical treatment of friendship draws on sources from several philosophical traditions. The idealistic description in his *Laelius: de Amicitia* stresses the selfless union of spirit between carefully chosen friends. Cicero's practice of friendship in his political life reveals a more calculated pursuit of friends for his own advantage. This coincides well with the advice given in the *Commentariolum petitionis*, written perhaps by Cicero's brother Quintus.

"Friendship is the inexpressible comfort of feeling safe with a person having neither to weigh thoughts nor measure words." This quotation from the novelist George Eliot expresses a view of friendship which would meet with contemporary approval in United States society. It sets friendship within the realm of private relations and stresses personal values of feeling secure and free to speak one's mind in the company of a friend. In its classical form, friendship included some personal values like affection but was a public as well as a private relationship. As such, values like reciprocal obligation defined the friendship association. Feelings of security are one of the advantages of both sorts of friendship, but the security in classical friendship often derives from the friends' protection from external threats, be they political, economic or social. Moreover, the security and friendship are themselves maintained not by a free expression of unmeasured thoughts and words but, just the opposite, by a careful consideration of the expressions required by circumstances which affect the friends.

Cicero's Treatment of Friendship

Cicero's (106–43 BCE) treatise *Laelius: de Amicitia* presents a comprehensive view of friendship in the theory, if not always the practice of the philosopher/politician of the late Republic. Written in 44 BCE,[1] the treatise has been subjected to extensive source analyses. Such analyses have been inconclusive and the prevailing view is that Cicero cannot be tied to any particular sources or school of thought for his views on friendship but that the treatise rather represents an eclectic sampling of views as well as ideas prevalent in the popular culture of the day.[2] Cicero's interest in friendship was not merely theoretical, since his own participation in the politics of the late Republic led him to rely on friendship relations for his own advancement and security.

Since friendship whether for the patricians or the plebeians was part of the system of political relations in Rome, "solidarity in civic life" was a type of friendship (*Fam.* 5.7) although Cicero was critical of this facile type of friendship.[3] In the introduction to his treatise, he uses the word *familiaritas* for friendship, and the language he uses to describe friendship, e.g. *benevolentia* and *caritas* (*Lael.* 5.19–20),[4] indicates that he does not see friendship to be simply a reasoned relationship, as a Stoic might. On the other hand, he rejects the Epicurean idea of friendship as originating in necessity (8.26–9.32) and sees its origins rather in nature alone (5.19–20

---

[1] H. Faerber and M. Faltner, *M. Tulli Ciceronis Laelius De Amicitia* (Muenchen: Heimeran, 1961) 126.

[2] K. Bringmann, "Untersuchungen zum späten Cicero," *Untersuchungen zur Antike und zu ihrem Nachleben* (Hypomnemata 29; Göttingen: Vandenhoeck & Ruprecht, 1971) 223–25 and R. Harder, "Die Einbürgerung der Philosophie in Rom," *Das neue Cicerobild* (ed. K. Buechner; Darmstadt: Wissenschaftliche Buchgesellschaft, 1971) 32–33.

[3] J. Steinberger, *Begriff und Wesen der Freundschaft bei Aristoteles und Cicero* (Inaug. diss., Erlangen: Josef Steinberger, 1955) 47. Steinberger calls attention to the "solidarity in civic life" which serves as friendship in the according of the new status to Pompey's former enemies who are now his friends and also in Cicero's hope that his attachment to Pompey will be effected by interests of the state, if not by proofs of his devotion to Pompey. See *Fam.* 3.10.9 for the two types of friendship: private bonds (*domestica*) and public ties (*popularis*).

[4] Cicero uses the terms *amicus* and *familiaris* interchangeably in his letters *Ad familiares*, e.g. *Fam.* 3.1.3 and 4.12.2.

and 8.27).⁵ The impulse of *amor* is the original source (27.100) and to this Cicero subordinates *caritas* and *diligere* (27.100–101). Still in

---

⁵ Steinberger, *Begriff und Wesen*, 57, 60–61, and L. Dugas, *L'Amitié antique* (2d rev. ed.; Paris: Librairie Felix Alcan, 1914) 119, who cites Aristotle for the view that happiness is not independence or *autarkeia* but an act where one unites with others and acts on their behalf and where one senses another's happiness more than one's own (*E.N.* 9.10). Epicurus, as Dugas (128–30) notes, saw two classes of friendships: one based on self-interest, the other on attraction by the friend's charm (*D.L.* 10.120). From friendship flow comfort and security in the common life as well as happiness and pleasure (*RS* 27–28). While Cicero also considers pleasure as a derivative of friendship, as well as confidence and security, he enunciates the paradox that self-interest must be renounced and one must love the other as oneself (*Fin.* 1.20.67). The Stoics find *philia* to be part of *philanthrōpia*, a species of the genus, sought for itself and not for self-interest, for people are naturally sociable. Cicero reflects the Stoic view in *Fin.* 3.20 and *Lael.* 5.19; see also *Off.* 1.158; *Lael.* 8.26; and N. Wood, *Cicero's Social and Political Thought* (Berkeley: University of California, 1988) 79, 82. See also H. A. K. Hunt, *The Humanism of Cicero* (Melbourne: Melbourne University, 1954) 95, who cites *Fin.* 5.65–66 and describes the "chain" of solidarity starting with family and proceeding to kin, fellow citizens, political allies, and the whole human race; and see also p. 182, where he discusses *Off.* 3. The penchant to love what is like us starts out blind but becomes reflective and free as instinct becomes rational (Dugas, *L'Amitié antique*, 137–50). The Stoics also countenance and hold it to be a good to have a great number of friends, since friendship is an expression of basic *philanthrōpia* (*D.L.* 7.124: Zeno). Seneca, however (*Ben.* 6.34), taking a more personal view of friendship, follows Aristotle (*E.N.* 9.10) in stating that one cannot have many friends and be able to give oneself and to share one's life with them (Dugas, *L'Amitié antique*, 212–14). J.-C. Fraisse, *Philia: La notion d'amitié dans la philosophie antique. Essai sur une probleme perdu et retrouvé* (Paris: Librairie Philosophique J. Vrin, 1974) 338–55, explores the Stoic notion of *oikeiōsis*, appropriation, of which *philia* is the final stage, and asks how one moves to appropriate something essential for one's existence which is not oneself; or how to move from egocentric *philautia* to *philia*. He notes that the issue is a double one: first the movement from physical to moral appropriation, and second the movement from one form of pleasure to a fuller and purer one. The first is solved by seeing the *logos* in all things and so seeing a passage toward wisdom by a natural inclination. For the second, the friend is seen as contributing toward my own interest in our pursuit of common human goals. The pursuit of *philia* is connatural and essential, not just important. There is some question as to Stoic evaluation of friendship which falls below that among the sages, since there are varying degrees of friendship (*SVF* 3.181 [§723]). Also, friendship can exist only among the virtuous and not among the wicked (*D.L.* 7.124). At the same time, friends are useful for oneself and desirable in themselves, with a value attached to having many friends. Fraisse argues that in the Stoic view friendship is necessary due to the natural sociability of people and that it is irreducible, as is the pursuit of good. Moreover, the society of wise persons does not flee from or stand in opposition to the society of the wicked but is always open to enlargement. Cicero, as Fraisse notes (pp. 384–85, 394–95), focuses on the social rather than the natural order and describes the requirements within the circle of friends, which are the most specific and imperious of the demands placed on us as humans with respect to other humans (*Off.* 1.58). He also

the order of feeling, *benevolentia* is considered the underpinning (*conquiescit, stabilis*: 6.22), source (*fons*: 14.50), and bringer of good feeling (*jucundius*: 14.49; see also 15.52) for friendship.[6] Associated with friendship as cornerstones and tests are *constantia* (17.62–64), *fides* (18.65), and *veritas* (18.65–66 and 24.89–90). The latter serves as a norm for true friendship as opposed to flattery.[7] Friendship's main advantage is that it neither fades through absence nor through death, for the absent one is always present to his friend (7.23).[8] This true friendship, based on natural love, benevolence and probity, thus outlasts a friendship based on the exchange of goods, which passes when the goods are exchanged. In fact, there

sees that the sages are particularly given to friendship because they incarnate the force of the soul and its autonomy, and they are drawn into friendship relations with each other by the good qualities (*probitas, virtus*) of their character (*Lael.* 8. 27). Sages are also less responsive to the receipt of benefaction in friendship, not because they are self-sufficient but because they find more pleasure in giving than in receiving and enjoy the contest of sorts in magnanimity and liberality (*Lael.* 9.32: *honesta certatio*). Fraisse (p. 406–8) also finds that to the Stoic gauge of *pistis* in friendship, Cicero adds spontaneity, amiability and facilty of character. And while friendship facilitates the growth in virtue, it is not the same as the Stoic *agathon poiētikon* (*SVF* 3.25 [§106] and 3.26–27 [§112]), which disappears with the possession of the final goal. For Cicero, virtue—and not friendship—is ultimately the means (*Lael.* 22.84), and friendship is preferable to all other goods, virtue included (*Lael.* 23.86).

[6] Dugas, *L'Amitié antique*, 98–104, finds love of persons and wishing well of them to be the start of friendship in Aristotle (*E.N.* 8.2–9.5; *E.E.* 7.7), and they become actual friendship with the decision to act. The friendship becomes stronger as the reciprocal penetration of spirits grows in a psychological *syzēn* which complements their physical companionship (*E.E.* 7.12; *E.N.* 9.9).

[7] Steinberger, *Begriff und Wesen*, 62–79. Cicero's own adherence to the principles of constancy, loyalty and truth in the practical exercise of his friendship relationships fell short of the ideal. His relations with Caesar changed for the better after the latter's reconciliation with Cicero's friend Pompey at Luca. The same is true of his rapprochement with Clodius' family and his reconsideration of his views of Clodius his former enemy after the latter's death. Self-preservation as well as his maneuvers on behalf of the *respublica* caused shifts in his public friendships. Friendships in public life often rested on political benefit rather than on fellow feeling. P. A. Brunt in "*Amicitia* in the Late Roman Republic," *PCPhS* n.s. 11 (1965) 16–17, notes that one cannot be certain that political *amicitiae* were long lasting, powerful and cohesive.

[8] Dugas, *L'Amitié antique*, 267. Epicurus expresses this abiding spiritual presence of the absent friend in the epistle to Pythocles, as does Seneca in *Ep.* 55. One is to prepare for the absence of a friend, especially the absence of death, and when a friend dies one turns to others already friends or about to be made so, for to wallow in grief is an offence to one's surviving friends (Seneca *Ep.* 9 and 63; Epictetus *Diss.* 3.24).

is a greater utility from true friendship because of the friends' upright rivalry to do good for each other (9.32).

While friendship does not grow out of need, neither does it rest on the pursuit of pleasure (9.32; 13.46–15.54). In both of these ways, Cicero differentiates his views from those of the Epicureans.[9] Rather than contribute to a carefree life, friendship, as all virtuous activity, requires a life of care to keep its opposite away.[10] So friends bear the pain of others and do not seek to avoid them, at the risk of losing their humanity. One's heart grows with a friend's fortune and contracts with a friend's disgrace. This reciprocal love and joy in a virtuous person outweighs the pleasures of the world. Moreover, just as a pretended friendship will crumble under unfavorable circumstances, so too can good fortune threaten the stability of friendship. Rare indeed is the serious, stable, and constant friend, especially when called to bear the calamities of another (17.62–64).

---

[9] Fraisse, *Philia*, 294–98, 303–4, suggests that Epicurean materialism made pleasure something purely corporeal. "The principle and root of all good is the pleasure of the stomach and the things of the spirit and of the higher values lead to it" (Usener 409 after Athenaeus, *Deipnosophistes* 12.546). For Epicurus, friendship does not constitute a fundamental human need, a natural and necessary desire, the non-satisfaction of which results in sorrow while its satisfaction constitutes our good (*RS* 26 & 29). He finds that a friend's presence effects a change in a person and that friendship's usefulness lies in the fact that it leads on to a community of those enjoying the greatest pleasure (*D.L.* 10.120). Pleasure rests in having an awareness of oneself and in awareness of one like oneself, the friend. Epicurus' materialism stops short of allowing a common consciousness of human existence, which Cicero would maintain as possible. It at least allows the thought of a personal consciousness of oneself brought about by the regard a friend has of me. The regard of a friend helps wise persons enjoy their own existence. The pleasure consists in separating physical torments from the spirit, which is the key to the happy life (*RS* 18). Without reference to suffering, fear or sorrow, the person is carried to a realm untroubled by corporeal desires. Fraisse (p. 308) goes on to explain that perhaps the utility at the root of Epicurean friendship is not so much that of needing aid but rather the pleasure of being useful in a lived interchange and enjoyment of goodwill.

[10] In *Off.* 2 Cicero develops Panaetius' ideas on the compatibility of practical and expedient activity with moral conduct arising from virtue. Unlike the Stoics, Cicero attributes ethical significance to practical activity (Hunt, *The Humanism of Cicero*, 160). Nonetheless, Cicero had qualms about compromising his ideals of *honestum* in favor of *utile* in political associations (*Att.* 1.19.7; 1.20.2–3; 2.1.6–7; see also T. N. Mitchell, *Cicero: The Senior Statesman* [New Haven: Yale University, 1991] 94).

Self-interest in the form of active striving after glory or using friends in the pursuit of public office and advancement in public life (10.34, 17.64, 21.77) is a threat to friendship. Cicero corrects three opinions with regard to friendship and self-concern (16.56–17.61). To the opinion that "we ought to have the same affection for friends as we have toward ourselves," he says that we bear much ourselves which we do not put up with in the case of a friend. Rather, we attack, defend, and object on the friend's behalf. To the opinion that "our benevolence toward friends should match equally their benevolence toward us," he objects that friendship is greater than a calculus of equality. And to the opinion that "each one should be esteemed by friends to the extent that he esteems himself," he notes that we often think and hope less for ourselves and that friends should excite the spirit to hope and to better thoughts.[11] Cicero finds that in friendship it is necessary to treat as equal or superior friends of the lesser capability and to communicate good fortune with them and increase their dignity and position whenever possible (19.69–70). On the other hand, inferiors must not grieve at being surpassed in talent, fortune or dignity, just as superiors must see that they cannot raise everyone in fortune and self-esteem nor can everyone support higher honors (20.71–73).

Whereas self-interest damages friendship, sharing life with a friend enhances the bond and also creates the circumstance of a true enjoyment of honor and fame (22.83–84).[12] The commonality of possessions, counsel and will in friendship should exist without exception (16.56–17.61). Here Cicero reflects the Pythagorean maxim *koina ta tōn philōn* (*D.L.* 8.10), which became a

---

[11] Dugas, *L'Amitié antique*, 114–19, reports Aristotle's view that although love of self is the strongest human tendency, friends can love each other because the friend is another self. For Aristotle, love of self is the type of love of friends; it is stronger than and anterior to friendship, and it has all the elements which are experienced in love of others (*E.N.* 9.4, 8). Self-love and love of friends, which brings advantage, coincide because they spring from the same source, virtue and affection. What we love in others we love in ourselves, virtue.

[12] Steinberger, *Begriff und Wesen*, 97–99, and Dugas, *L'Amitié antique*, 18–19, who explains that community of life has traditionally been seen as an occasion for friendship (Aristotle *E.N.* 8.1), as well as a goal of friendship (Seneca *Ep.* 35).

commonplace in Greek and Roman thought.[13] Virtue and good moral habits are presuppositions for friendship (22.84; 26.100; 27.104; 17.62–63; 11.37) and virtue corrects and directs friendship toward truth and perfection (6.20).[14] Truth rather than obsequiousness is best in friendship, but warnings should come without bitterness and criticism without personal attack. Since giving admonition without bitterness and taking admonition patiently is proper to friendship, the biggest threats come from adulation, flattery and assent to vice. In the latter circumstances, there is none of the unity of spirit on which friendship stands, nor is there the constancy of character and virtue (24.89–26.100).

Friends should look to emending their friends' ways and should also go out of their way to help a friend, even at the risk of their own lives and reputations. Reputation and public benevolence are important "weapons" (*tela*) on which the friendship relation rests and serves to enhance (17.61). Perfect friends are an extreme rarity, akin to the divine (17.64), and so Cicero's ideal is remote from ordinary experience, possible only when virtue characterizes

---

[13] Dugas, *L'Amitié*, 11–18. Socrates extols the value of a friend as shelter from need because the friend will share his possessions (Xenophon *Mem.* 3.11.4; 2.4.6; 2.6.23). Plato expects that his friends will help Socrates get out of prison (*Crito* 45 A-B). Possession was still proprietary and individual (Seneca *Ben.* 7.12), although the neo-Pythagoreans might have pushed the maxim to an actual vowed renunciation and common ownership. On pp. 29–33 Dugas explains that Epicurus regularized and institutionalized the free *hetairia* of the Socratic association, with periodic meetings, mutual but not forced sharing of goods, commemorative banquets to reinforce free sharing, a hierarchy of succession to serve as depositories of his doctrine and continuators of his beneficence.

[14] Dugas, *L'Amitié antique*, 19–20: community of sentiment, *homonoia*, is not to be confused with *homodoxia*. It is not intellectual accord but sympathy and moral sentiment. He speaks (pp. 22–25 and 34–36) of the Socratic idea that the teacher is a friend of the pupil (Xenophon *Mem.* 1.2.14; 4.2.40; and Plato *Apol.* 31 B-C). Socrates ruled out paid, travelling teachers since they were strangers and guests, not friends of the youth, and persons whose salary eliminated the idea of moral beneficence and therefore made them unqualified to be the guides of the youth (Xenophon *Mem.* 1.2.7; Plato *Soph.* 233 D and *Gorgias* 420 C). Cicero agrees with the Stoics (Maximus of Tyre *Or.* 14, "How to Tell a Flatterer from a Friend") and the middle Platonists (Plutarch, "How to Tell a Flatterer from a Friend") who distinguish a friend from a flatterer. Frankness, if gentle, properly aimed, opportune and appropriate to the circumstances, aiming at averting or remedying a problem, was especially prized among friends across most of the popular philosophical schools (Dugas, pp. 218, 240–45, and see *D.L.* 6.69).

the whole person (5.18–19).¹⁵ Nonetheless, Cicero has Laelius offer his friendship with Scipio Africanus as an example. Laelius declares that their friendship is based on a mutual admiration of virtue and morals (9.30). He also cautions that one must choose friends carefully, selecting only those that are truly wise (11.38). He nonetheless admits that it is difficult to find friends among office holders and public officials, who tend to overlook friendship in their pursuit of power. Friends, on the other hand, will put a friend's career ahead of their own (17.63–64).[16]

One of the results of friendship is unlimited accord (*consensio*) among the friends (4.15; 6.20). Another consequence is advantage (*utilitas*: 6.22; 9.31; 14.51; 27.100). While Cicero decries friendships sought for the advantage they bring, he nonetheless sees it as one of friendship's valuable effects (6.22; 7.23; 9.31–32; 14.51; 27.100).[17] The *Commentariolum petitionis* (*Handbook on Electioneering*),[18] which is surveyed later in this essay, indicates how far advantage was counted on in political friendships.

In both the client-patron and the friend-friend relationships in Roman society,[19] a chain of obligations was established between the benefactor and beneficiary. The obligation to render appropriate honor and gratitude to one's benefactor was an essential factor in political and personal conduct. The reciprocal character of the obligation made the relationships dynamic and afforded them great social impact. Each benefaction led to the obligation of

---

[15] Steinberger, *Begriff und Wesen*, 120–25.

[16] Dugas, *L'Amitié antique*, 124–26, discusses the Epicureans' withdrawal from city, family and from public affairs (*lathe biōsas*) with friendship as their only refuge against the isolation of the individual. Friendship also supplied the Epicureans with the necessary affection and a circumstance where the need to love and to be loved is met, free from constraint of family and state. This perspective is quite different from Cicero's, especially where he refers to the role of friendship in public life and, as here, points to Laelius' political friendship with Scipio as a model.

[17] Steinberger, *Begriff und Wesen*, 132–37, 159–62.

[18] Wood, *Cicero's Social and Political Thought*, 184–85, suggests the book to be the work of Cicero's brother Quintus, written ca. 65–64 BCE in preparation for the consular elections in 63 BCE. He finds that the advice fits what is known of Cicero's and his peers' political activity.

[19] The former exists between unequals, the latter between equals (Wood, *Cicero's Social and Political Thought*, 183) although there is some blurring of the distinction, as the discussion below suggests.

reciprocity in the beneficiary. The latter's return, be it in gratitude, expressions of honor or another benefaction, led to an obligation in the initial beneficiary, which obligated him to an even greater benefaction. The usage functioned practically like a law and Cicero (*Off.* 1.47) declares that no duty is more important than that of returning gratitude and that nothing violates humanity as much as ingratitude (*Planc.* 81).[20]

This expectation of a return for an honor or gratitude bestowed in response to an initial benefaction gives a degree of power to the beneficiary over the original benefactor for "gratitude for one favor is the best method of securing another."[21] Priming the pump of benefaction by honorific expressions of gratitude was practiced among friends, between cities and their benefactors, and between social clubs and political assemblies and their donors. In the latter two cases, honors bestowed by the city or the association were considered greater than the gift and so further generosity from the initial donor/benefactor was obligated.[22] The gods were also depicted as benefactors and a reciprocal relation with them paralleled that among humans (*Fam.* 14.7.1; 13.4.1; 15.5.2;

---

[20] S. C. Mott, "The Power of Giving and Receiving: Reciprocity in Hellenistic Benevolence," *Current Issues in Biblical and Patristic Interpretation* (Festschrift Merrill C. Tenney; ed. G. F. Hawthorne; Grand Rapids: William B. Eerdmans, 1975) 60–62; see also T. A. Dorey, "Honesty in Roman Politics," *Cicero* (ed. T. A. Dorey; New York: Basic Books, 1965) 30–31, and H. H. Scullard, "The Political Career of a *Novus Homo*," *Cicero* (ed. T. A. Dorey; New York: Basic Books, 1965) 3, who describes the "nexus of personal obligations" and reciprocal duties which derived from political friendships or alliances and which could push an outsider up the political ladder. Dugas, *L'Amitié antique*, 136, finds that the Epicureans saw friendship not as a passive, mechanical habit but as a free decision and choice to make a personal gift of oneself, while at the same time they saw friendship go through a slow, natural course of development which preserves it from a quick dissolution. The freedom of association seems to constitute a relationship without the web of obligations that Cicero describes. While Cicero's own sometimes fickle and less than ideally motivated public friendships, as well as his expected dissimulations as a defense lawyer could raise questions about the sincerity of his remarks, his use of them attests an expectation of a favorable resonance in the popular consciousness with regard to the friendship ideals of his day.

[21] C. B. Welles, *Royal Correspondence in the Hellenistic Period: A Study in Greek Epigraphy* (New Haven: Yale University, 1934) 108, as quoted in Mott, "The Power of Giving and Receiving," 63.

[22] Welles, *Royal Correspondence*, 15.10–12; 22.15–17; 1; 14; 23; 45; 65–67, as cited in Mott, "The Power of Giving and Receiving," 63.

15.4.16).[23] Piety and religion were expressed in reverence and gratitude to them.[24]

Although there is an element of venality which was rightly criticized by the moralists[25] and while acting out of favor[26] was frowned on, nonetheless granting a benefit or expressing gratitude for a benefit received and thereby acquiring a favorable action from a political group or an individual was important in binding Roman society together, especially vertically among people of diverse power. Thus Cicero could cast in an unfavorable light utilitarian (Epicurean) friendship which seeks pleasure (*Lael.* 1.3; *Fin.* 2.82) and offer with the Stoics a definition focusing on benevolence even without receiving an advantage in return (*Fin.* 2.78; *Lael.* 6.22).[27] At the same time he could stress friendship's mutuality (*Planc.* 5 and *Lael.* 4.15), resting as it does on *fides* (*Lael.* 18.65), which is a relation of mutual confidence. In the end close, personal friendship issues into a unity of views and feelings (*Off.* 1.51 and 56; *Lael.* 18.65; 20.74; 21.80). Friendship's *caritas* and *benevolentia* (*Lael.* 6.20; *Part. or.* 78 and 88) are not just intellectual categories to him but rather express a complex communion, a lived and not just philosophical idea.[28] Thus, speaking for himself and others, Cicero could maintain (*Off.* 1.20) that *justitia* and *beneficentia* hold *societas* together. He could even see the practical sense in investing one's money in friends rather than hoarding it (*Planc.* 81 and *Lael.* 15.55).[29] For Roman politics and aristocratic society, which were based on reciprocal advantage and obligation, friendship was one of the decisive factors.[30]

---

[23] Seneca *Ep.* 95.48.
[24] Cicero *Planc.* 80 and Mott, "The Power of Giving and Receiving," 64.
[25] Seneca *Ben.* 4.20.3 and Cicero *Lael.* 5.19; 9.30–31; 15.53.
[26] *Charis* as "favor" is used by Cicero in *QF* 1.1.20 and 1.2.10.
[27] See also *Inv.* 2.166; *Fam.* 5.2.3; and *Pro S. Roscio Amerino* 111.
[28] J. Hellegouarc'h, *Le vocabulaire latin des relations et des partis politiques sous la république* (Paris: Société d'Édition "Les Belles Lettres," 1963) 43.
[29] Mott, "The Power of Giving and Receiving," 67–69.
[30] F. Lossmann, *Cicero und Caesar im Jahre 54: Studien zur Theorie und Praxis der römischen Freundschaft* (Wiesbaden: Steiner, 1962) 1, and Hellegouarc'h, *Le vocabulaire*, 41.
  Mitchell, *Cicero*, 92–94, describes Cicero's friendship with Pompey as a practical connection motivated by a good deal of self-interest. After his consulship and the

The *Commentariolum Petitionis*

Even when one takes into account P. A. Brunt's qualifications about the role of friendship in politics,[31] there can be no doubt that individuals relied heavily on friendship to secure a place in Roman political life. The *Commentariolum petitionis* gives evidence of this and its recommendations do not seem to diverge from what can be learned of Cicero's practical political outlook and practice.[32] The calculating use of friendship as a prop for political ambitions in the *Commentariolum* stands in interesting contrast to the rather idealistic discussion of friendship in *Laelius*. A closer survey of the former work will reveal how the ideals are bent to fit practical concerns. Pragmatism notwithstanding, however, the persistent presence of the higher ideals of friendship are apparent, even amid the compromises espoused in the electioneering suggestions.

---

disappointing weakness he found in the state, compounded by "floundering" leadership in the senate, Cicero moved toward friendship with Pompey and away from the optimate *principes* whom he had been cultivating. At the same time he began cultivating the upper class *juvenes* whom he had previously criticized. Pompey, for his part, needed a friendly college of Tribunes, loyal adherents of consular rank, and friends in the senate. Cicero claimed to be approaching Pompey in the interests of stabilizing the *respublica* while he saw Pompey as motivated by self-interest. Nonetheless, Cicero considered it a legitimate offer of friendship on Pompey's part, which in turn promised Cicero prominence and security through his association with an important and popular figure (*Att.* 1.18.6; 1.20.2; *Fam.* 1.8.1–4; 1.9.11). While Pompey did not help Cicero to prevent his exile, he later worked with Cicero's friends to have the exile lifted.

Other examples of Cicero's political friendships include what he sees as mutually beneficial relations with Crassus (*QF* 2.9.2; *Fam.* 1.9.20) and with Caesar (*Fam.* 1.9.12, 17–18; *QF* 2.12.5; *Att* 4.15.10; 4.19.2). See also the discussion in Scullard, "Political Career," 11–12, 16, 19.

J. P. V. D. Balsdon, "Cicero the Man," *Cicero* (ed. T. A. Dorey; New York: Basic Books, 1965) 188–89, distinguishes friendships in personal life from those in public or political life (*Lael.* 17.64). Friends in the latter circumstance are determined by one's vote pro or con. The circle of such friends constitutes a *societas* versus a *factio* of opponents; and the inner ring of friends would be considered *familiares* (*Att.* 2.3.3; *Fam.* 1.1.3; *QF* 2.2.2).

[31] Blunt notes in "*Amicitia* in the Late Roman Republic," 20, that the range of *amicitia* is vast, ranging from the "constant intimacy and goodwill of virtuous or at least of like-minded men to the courtesy that etiquette normally enjoined on gentlemen." Thus, political friendship ties had their place, but their importance cannot be assumed and private friendships could easily supersede them.

[32] Wood, *Cicero's Social and Political Thought*, 184–85.

The *Commentariolum* illustrates the role friendship was called upon to play in the political process. In the first place, the number of one's friends was itself an indication of the quality of the candidate, especially if the friends came from all ranks of the social order. This was particularly important for a person without an aristocratic family name (3: "for how many 'new men' have had as many as you have?"), who was trying to break into political circles which were treated as the preserve of the Roman aristocracy. More directly practical would be the service well-born friends could render in persuading other aristocrats that the candidate has always been sympathetic to their interests (5). While aristocratic support is crucial, "friends of every sort" must be secured for the particular service they can render; i.e., for show, men of illustrious career and name; to maintain legal rights, magistrates; for getting votes of the "centuries," persons of exceptional influence (18).

The friendship relationship presented a mechanism by which individuals could work through the highly stratified Roman society, as well as break into the formal and informal group structures upon which Roman society rested.[33] Ties of friendship could be fashioned on the basis of a variety of bonds; e.g., ties of blood, ties through marriage, fellowship in a sodality, or some other bond.[34] These associations offer "more genuine grounds" for friendship than do the practices of showing another goodwill, cultivating a person's society or calling upon a person regularly (16). Being affectionate and on pleasant terms with others will induce them to

---

[33] Wood, *Cicero's Social and Political Thought*, 182–83, finds that "informal political arrangements of influence and favor" bound the Roman political system together and enabled it to function. While *amicitiae* established a network of friends and associates giving cohesion to the upper classes and providing support for political candidates, *clientela* cemented the upper and lower classes and mobilized political backing for upper class candidates. See also Scullard, "Political Career," 2–3.

[34] Scullard, "Political Career," 5–12, surveys the climb of the outsider, *novus homo* Cicero through the *cursus honorum*. Although his family was one of the local gentry in Arpinum, his tutelage under Q. Scaevola pontifex brought him connections with his longtime friend T. Pomponius Atticus and with persons of influence such as Sulpicius Rufus, tribune in 88 BCE. His courtroom work put many under obligation to him (*In Verr.* 2.3.181). While his quaestorship in 76 BCE brought him into the senatorial ranks, his work in court continued and increased his *clientela*; e.g. his defense of *eques* Cluentius brought him the goodwill of equestrian families throughout Italy. Mitchell, *Cicero*, 1–8, complements this survey.

reciprocate and wish the political candidate every success. The effort must extend beyond those in one's close family circle to include fellow-tribesmen, neighbors, clients, and then freedmen and even one's slaves,[35] "for the talk which makes one's public reputation generally emanates from sources in one's own household" (17). Reputation comes not only from the words spoken about the person but from the crowd of friends in constant attendance upon the person (3). The service of these friends varies from those who call on the candidate at his home, those who escort him from his house to the public fora, and those who are his full-time attendants (36–38).[36]

The influence of friends expands the reach of the individual. Influential friends are valued for being able to secure the support of the masses in Italy's tribal system of social organization (29 and 32). Friends in small towns are counted on for securing support outside of Rome. Thus, the candidate is urged to canvas friends in the centuries, among the tribes, in one's home town and district, and in the *collegia* (31 and 32). The *Commentariolum* reminds the candidate that he has "four sodalities under obligation," and that he should remind them that they will not have another chance to thank him (19). The *equites*, as individuals and as an order, are

---

[35] Despite statements like this, it is debatable whether these affectionate relations with slaves could ever lead to any actual friendship. Wood, *Cicero's Social and Political Thought*, 79 and 90–92, reminds us that *humanitas*, the "brotherhood of men," is not a spiritual brotherhood involving the emotional feeling of universal love and fraternal intimacy. Rather, it implies relations and shared interests in a community of citizens, with all the inequalities of the traditional Roman social order. All humans, as endowed with reason, have a basic moral worth deserving of *reverentia* and can attain virtue. Cicero, however, condones a "proportionate equality" in the distribution of honors and offices according to the social worth of the person from lowest to highest among the legal social orders (*Rep.* 1.43, 69). As far as slaves are concerned, *Off.* 1.41 suggests they are human, though inferior. In the case of freedmen, *Fam.* 3.1.2 described how Cicero and the freedman Calix became *familiares*.

[36] While the title friend is not used explicitly in this listing of persons to whom affection should be shown, the comment flows without interruption from a discussion of those offering more genuine grounds for friendship in 16. Wood, *Cicero's Social and Political Thought*, 182–83, finds that while rich friends could provide their influential support, invite friends to their homes, plead for them in court, and offer surety for their word, it was the lower class clients who had the time daily to attend their patrons and benefactors at home or in public, vote for them, and provide other time-consuming personal services by which they fulfilled their obligations as clients (*Mur.* 70–71; *Rep.* 2.16.59). See also Mitchell, *Cicero*, 57.

singled out as particularly susceptible to overtures of friendship, since they are young and easily attached as friends (33). This is most likely because they have not yet obliged themselves in friendship ties and, as neophytes in public life, would be on the watch for persons to whose rising star they might attach themselves. Other young men are noted as having been drawn to the candidate by the pursuit of oratory, in which the candidate excelled (3).[37]

The political process in the *Commentariolum* as it relates to friendship is one in which the candidate wooes the support of new friends and calls in the debts of friends already obligated to him. To secure the active support of the latter, the *Commentariolum* advises the candidate to "hold on by admonitions, requests, or any other means of making it clear that there will never be another chance for those who owe you a debt to thank you or for the well-disposed to put you under obligation to themselves" (4). The last clause indicates the reciprocity of obligation which drives the whole system. A number of supporters can also be expected from those whom the candidate defended in court cases and the candidate is advised to apportion duty to each of those under obligation to him (20).

In order to attract new friends and their support, the *Commentariolum* has several suggestions. In the first place, the notion of "friend" in this context is broader than that in ordinary life, "for anybody who shows you some goodwill, or cultivates your society, or calls upon you regularly, is to be counted as a 'friend'" (16).[38] It goes on to explain that a candidate has an opportunity of making new friends in ways which in ordinary circumstances would be considered in poor taste and even a disgrace. Thus, if a person sees "that you value him highly, that you are sincere, that it is a good investment for him, that the result will not be a vote-catching friendship but a solid and permanent one," the candidate will not fail to win his friendly support. In a mode of expression that is odd

---

[37] Caesar put the young Curio and Aemilius Paullus on his staff in Gaul (Dorey, "Honesty," 32). Cicero gained similar attachment with the young C. Scribonius Curio (Scullard, "Political Career," 20).

[38] Perhaps the contemporary political term "connection" might more acurately reflect the range of the term *amicitia* in its broad, political usage here.

to the contemporary ear, the *Commentariolum* says that in a successful canvas of supporters "you cannot fail to induce someone to earn your affection and obligation to him by doing you a good turn." Once again, the notion of reciprocal obligation comes to the fore here whereby the pledge of support to a candidate virtually guarantees the supporter the friendship and obligation of the political hopeful (25-26). The disgrace and poor taste alluded to here would seem to be attached to the apparent venality of the friendship relationship, which Cicero contemns in his essay on friendship. Nonetheless, in politics such friendship is countenanced. For example, the candidate can expect to find friends and supporters in small towns if he appears to be anxious for their friendship, uses discourse appropriate to the purpose, knows them by name, and gives them to think that they will get protection for themselves in return for their support. For others also, the hope of "advantage and friendship" should win them over, with advantage seen as an immediate benefit and friendship as an association with future reciprocal obligations and benefits (31-32).

This calculating approach to friendship does not exclude real affection. "The endeavors of friends," the *Commentariolum* urges, "should be enlisted by kindness and observance of duties and old acquaintance and affability and natural charm." It goes on to say that "it is very useful to be on affectionate and pleasant terms with those who are friends on more genuine grounds" (16). Friendship is obviously a very elastic term which stretches to cover largely utilitarian relations of self-interest[39] and advancement as well as those bonds which spring from family ties or social relations of true affection and commonality of character. The reciprocal duty to pay honor and service to one's friend is the common element throughout and the dynamic force behind political, business and social relations.[40]

---

[39] The reclassification of former enemies as friends or the abandonment of old friendships in favor of cultivating new ones, while criticized in theory (*Lael.* 9.33-10.35), was part of Cicero's own practice, as he found himself driven by political requirements and opportunities (*Phil.* 1.10; 1.14; 5.19; 12.14; *Att.* 11.5.4; 14.13B.4; *Fam.* 1.9.19).

[40] Wood, *Cicero's Social and Political Thought*, 77-78, calls attention to the differential

The Practice of Friendship

In the realm of social relations, friends customarily gave advice as one of the institutional characteristics of friendship over and above bonds of affection. This practice of giving advice remained the case in the Empire, for even when the political influence of friends diminished, the social requirements and the function of protection remained in force.[41] The duty of mutual help and the requirement of a public acknowledgement for friendly service were common expectations.[42] This help, in the form of advice and instruction, was long institutionalized between young men and older, influential and experienced persons.[43] The friendly letter was a popular mechanism for such instruction.[44] Included in the advice was ethical instruction, not just in the form of handed-on traditional sayings, with or without embellishment, but actual paraenetic prescriptions.[45] Thus Cicero's letters are filled with the terminology of paraenetic direction. Not just for the young but for everyone, a friend was a useful guide since the friend was

---

generosity relative to one's own property and position. Accordingly, help should be given to persons of one's own station, starting with one's family and working outward to kin, friends, and associates. One's benevolence and support should be directed to clients and friends in gratitude rather than to the poor in general. Even the strength of friendship ties depends on the degree of proximity, beginning with family, kin, then friends, and finally all to whom fellow feeling is due (*Lael.* 5.19–20; *Off.* 3.69; and Wood, *Cicero's Social and Political Thought*, 82). Dorey, "Honesty," 30–31, summarizes Cicero's gratuitous acts and notes that Cicero performed them for his family or circle of friends, often as barrister. Among his beneficiaries were Sestius, Milo, Caelius, Archias, Lucullus, Plancius, and even Antonius.

[41] I. Hadot, *Seneca und die griechisch-römische Tradition der Seelenleitung* (Berlin: de Gruyter, 1969) 165–68.

[42] Cicero *Fam.* 12.26.1

[43] Cicero *Cato major* 9.28–29.

[44] K. Thraede, *Grundzüge griechisch-römischer Brieftopik* (Zetemata 48; München: C.H. Beck, 1970) 17–24, discusses the philophronetic letter, which was conceived to be a conversation, or half of one, between friends. The individuality of the writer was reflected in its style and the essence of this letter type was *philophronēsis*, with popular philosophical reflection an expected feature. Under Cicero's pen (Thraede, pp. 27–37), the letter style was finer than usual (*Fam* 6.10.4), although still a conversation at once playful and familiar (*Fam.* 2.4.1). The playful (*iocari*) conversation (*colloqui: QF* 1.1.45) was motivated by *benevolentia* and *amicitia* (*Fam.* 6.4.4; 7.1.6; see also *Att.* 7.15.1; 12.34.2).

[45] Cicero *Off.* 1.58 and *Fam.* 6.10.4–6; 6.6.1; 6.6.12–13.

considered an *alter ego* who helps the friend "know yourself" by proposing a mirror of the inner self.[46] The *alter ego topos* expresses an equality and identity between the friends, although not relative to rank and position.[47] Ideally the friend-advisor spoke not just out of affection and inner likeness but also with the authority of an incarnate paraenesis of the advice offered.[48]

Even the wise need friends as they come to know themselves and, in turn, they exemplify the high ethical ideals to their friends.[49] This setting of an example by the friend is done most directly by living in each other's company. The friendly letter, however, bridges the gap of physical separation and in it the writer addresses the friend as if the latter were actually present.[50] The promise of a future *parousia* by the letter-writer is an extension of this idea.[51]

On a more practical note, friends also helped their friends make contacts in new cities or among new social or business circles. The friend's letter of recommendation, the prized key to otherwise closed doors, was an integral part of the political and social structure of the Roman state. Through such letters, close and true relationships were forged. Not only was there a debt established between the person recommended and the one who

---

[46] Hadot, *Seneca*, 169 n. 33, refers to A.-M. Guillemin, *Pline et la vie littéraire de son temps* (Collections d'Études Latines, 4; Paris: Société d'Édition "Les Belles Lettres," 1929) 33–34, for these examples: *tecum ipse certa, perge, persevera* in *Fam.* 11.15.2 and 9.14.6; *persuade tibi* in *Fam.* 5.21.5; *fac animo fortis sis* in *Fam.* 6.5.4 and 5.21.5; and *moneo, hortor, rogo* in *Fam.* 5.13.4; 5.14.3; 5.17.3; and 5.18.1.

[47] Cicero *Off.* 1.56; *Lael.* 6.22; 7.23; 21.80; *Att.* 3.15.4; 4.1.7; 4.7.1; *Fam.* 2.15.4; 7.5.1; *Brut.* 1.15.2. See also Hadot, *Seneca*, 172–75, and Lossmann, *Cicero und Caesar*, 33–50.

[48] Cicero *De or.* 1.198.

[49] Hadot, *Seneca*, 93–94, and Cicero *Tusc.* 5.1–4. See also U. Knoche, "Der Gedanke der Freundschaft in Senecas Briefen an Lucilius," *Arctos* N.S. 1 (1954) 83–96, reprinted in G. Maurach, *Seneca als Philosoph* (Darmstadt: Wissenschaftliche Buchgesellschaft, 1975) 159–66.

[50] Thraede, *Grundzüge*, 39–46, notes the idea of presence, *videor* and not just *conloquor*, in *Fam.* 16.16.2; see also *Att.* 1.9; 12.53. The letter replaces real contact (*Fam.* 13.1.1; 15.4) and constitutes a spiritual presence (*Fam.* 5.3.5; 3.11.2; 15.16; 2.9.2). As the expression of *philophronēsis, eikōn psychēs*, and warm *lalein*, the letter's *iocari* refers more to the strengthening of bonds than to the transmission of facts.

[51] H. Koskenniemi, *Studien zur Idee und Phraseologie des griechischen Briefes bis 400 n. Chr.* (Helsinki: Suomalainen Tiedakatemia, 1956) 38–40, and Cicero *Att.* 8.14.1; 9.10.1; 12.53; 12.39.2; *QF* 1.1.45; *Fam.* 2.9.2.

receives the recommendation, but mutual obligations also sprang up between the recommender and the recommended as well as between the recommender and the one to whom the recommendation is addressed. Cicero found himself recommending others to his friend Julius Caesar (*Fam.* 13.70–71) and these recommendations would presumably cement the ties between Cicero and Caesar themselves.[52]

Conclusion

Unfortunately for Cicero, his reliance on friendship for advancement and security in the swirl of political life, rivalry, and civil war of the late Roman Republic did not protect him from being put to death as a supporter of the losing opposition. The social and political institutions, friendship included, which bound together and drove forward public life in the Roman Republic ran headlong into the ambitions of rival factions and were powerless to save those on the weaker side. Similarly, the high ideals of friendship enunciated in Cicero's theoretical works were tempered and changed by the reality of the public life in which those ideals were exercised. Nonetheless, the institution of friendship survived the conflict and continued to serve the society of the Roman Empire. Perhaps, with its interpersonal bonds and social network, it was even more important as persons worked to advance their interests and those of their societies in the far flung empire.

---

[52] Lossmann, *Cicero und Caesar*, 11–13. W. Glynn Williams in his introduction to Volume III of the Loeb edition of Cicero's *Letters to His Friends* (Cambridge: Harvard University Press, 1972) 2–5, calls attention to the preponderance of letters of recommendation (*litterae commendaticiae*) in book 13 of the letters (78 of 79 letters). Other letters of recommendation are found scattered throughout Cicero's correspondence. He attributes this concentration to Cicero's restored relations with Caesar and hopes for a reestablished *respublica*, to his happy marital and family situation, and to his literary and political eminence. The letters show him happily responding to the individuals and communities who appealed to him for his good word. They attest Cicero's unfailing readiness to do a friend, or even an acquaintance, a good turn; in short, they are evidence of that *humanitas* which was one of his dominant characteristics.

"HARMONIOUS EQUALITY": THE *TOPOS* OF FRIENDSHIP IN NEOPYTHAGOREAN WRITINGS

Johan C. Thom

> A survey is given of the various views on the *topos* of friendship found in four types of Neopythagorean sources: the Pseudopythagorean treatises, Pythagorean letters, Pythagorean sayings collections and the biographical traditions regarding Pythagoras and the Pythagorean life. Although these sources are heterogeneous, they all view friendship as an all-encompassing virtue transcending the limits of interpersonal relationships.

Pythagoras (ca. 570–490 BC) was the first to found a philosophical community based on friendship, and it was in his name that expressions like "Friends have everything in common" (κοινὰ τὰ τῶν φίλων), "Friendship is equality" (φιλότης ἰσότης), and "A friend is another I" (φίλος ἐστὶν ἄλλος ἐγώ) became commonplace.[1] It was still proverbial in late Antiquity to call good friends Pythagoreans (Iamblichus *VP* 230), which is an indication of the important and recognizable role friendship played in Pythagorean relationships throughout Antiquity.

In this paper we will consider the *topos* of friendship in the later, that is, Hellenistic and Neopythagorean tradition. Since the history of this later tradition is problematic, we need to take a brief look at the development of Pythagoreanism. After this a survey will be given of the Neopythagorean writings in which the *topos* of

---

[1] Kurt Treu, "Freundschaft," *RAC* 8.420; A. Delatte, *La vie de Pythagore de Diogène Laërce* (Mémoires de l'Académie royale de Belgique, Classe des Lettres et des Sciences morales et Politiques 2/17/2; Brussels: Lamertin, 1922) 168. The sayings were very often quoted; see the references cited by Delatte in his commentary on Diogenes Laertius 8.10 (*Vie de Pythagore*, 111, 168).

friendship is treated, followed by an analysis of the most important texts.

The Pythagorean Tradition

Pythagoras of Samos founded the philosophical and religious movement named after him in Southern Italy in the last quarter of the sixth century BC.[2] His followers practiced a communal life with a prescribed daily regimen, including strict ritual and dietary observances. They also had extensive political influence in Southern Italy, which eventually lead to their dispersion in the middle of the fifth century, after an adverse change in the political climate.

The subsequent history of Pythagoreanism is somewhat obscure.[3] It seems as if some groups managed to return to Southern Italy; in the first quarter of the fourth century, in any case, a remnant flourished under the guidance of Archytas of Tarentum. After his death around 380 BC, however, we have very little evidence for the continued existence of Pythagoreanism as a movement. Most important are the derisive references in Middle Comedy (4th–3d cent. BC) to the so-called "Pythagorists," who were ridiculed because of their slovenly appearance and sparse diet, but it is not clear how they relate to earlier Pythagoreans.[4] Despite the scarcity of evidence many scholars believe that there were individuals and maybe even small groups throughout the Hellenistic period who considered themselves Pythagoreans and who preserved the Pythagorean dietary and ritual regulations.[5]

---

[2] For the early history of Pythagoreanism see the excellent articles by Kurt von Fritz, "Pythagoras von Samos," PW 24.1 (1963) 171–209; "Pythagoreer, Pythagoreismus bis zum Ende des 4. Jhdts. v. Chr.," PW 24.1 (1963) 209–68. A brief survey of the Pythagorean tradition may be found in Johan C. Thom, "Pythagoreanism," ABD 5.562–63.

[3] Heinrich Dörrie, "Der nachklassische Pythagoreismus," PW 24.1 (1963) 268–77.

[4] The texts have been collected by Hermann Diels, *Die Fragmente der Vorsokratiker* (ed. Walther Kranz; 6th ed.; 3 vols.; Berlin: Weidmann, 1951–52) 1.478–80 (frg. 58E).

[5] Eduard Zeller, *Die Philosophie der Griechen in ihrer geschichtlichen Entwicklung* (4th–7th ed.; 3 vols.; Leipzig: Reisland, 1921–23) 3.2.95–97; Dörrie, "Nachklassische Pythagoreismus," 268–70; B. L. van der Waerden, *Die Pythagoreer: Religiöse Bruderschaft und Schule der Wissenschaft* (Zurich: Artemis, 1979) 269–71.

Be that as it may, from the Hellenistic period onwards a spate of Pseudopythagorean writings make their appearance, most of them under the name of some ancient Pythagorean.[6] These writings cover a wide variety of subjects and are heavily influenced by Academic, Peripatetic, and some Stoic doctrines. Many scholars date them at the very end of the Hellenistic period, that is, in the first century BC, or later,[7] although Thesleff has argued that some of them may be as early as the fourth century BC, and that few, if any, are later than the first century BC.[8]

In the first century BC a revival now known as Neopythagoreanism took place. The polymath Nigidius Figulus (100–45 BC), Publius Vatinius (b. ca. 95 BC), the philosophers Quintus Sextius (fl. under Augustus), Anaxilaus of Larissa (expelled from Rome by Augustus), Sotion the younger of Alexandria (a teacher of Seneca), Moderatus of Gades (end of 1st cent. AD), Nicomachus of Gerasa (fl. ca. AD 100), Numenius of Apamea (fl. ca. AD 150), and the wandering prophet and miracle worker, Apollonius of Tyana (1st cent. A D), were all considered Pythagoreans.[9]

---

[6] The texts have been collected by Holger Thesleff, *The Pythagorean Texts of the Hellenistic Period* (Acta Academiae Aboensis Ser. A, Humaniora 30/1; Åbo: Åbo Akademi, 1965), and introduced by the same author, *An Introduction to the Pythagorean Writings of the Hellenistic Period* (Acta Academiae Aboensis, Humaniora 24/3; Åbo: Åbo Akademi, 1961). See also B. L. van der Waerden, "Pythagoras: Die Schriften und Fragmente des Pythagoras," PWSup 10 (1965) 843–64.

[7] Zeller, *Philosophie der Griechen*, 3.2.123; Walter Burkert, "Hellenistische Pseudopythagorica," *Philologus* 105 (1961) 16–43, 226–46; "Zur geistesgeschichtlichen Einordnung einiger Pseudopythagorica," *Pseudepigrapha I: Pseudopythagorica, lettres de Platon, littérature pseudépigraphique juive* (Entretiens sur l'antiquité classique 18; Geneva: Fondation Hardt, 1972) 25–57.

[8] Thesleff, *Introduction*; see also his "On the Problem of the Doric Pseudo-Pythagorica: An Alternative Theory of Date and Purpose," *Pseudepigrapha I: Pseudopythagorica, lettres de Platon, littérature pseudépigraphique juive* (Entretiens sur l'antiquité classique 18; Geneva: Fondation Hardt, 1972) 59–87. For a brief survey of the secondary literature on the problem of dating the Pseudopythagorica, see David L. Balch, "Neopythagorean Moralists and the New Testament Household Codes," *ANRW* 2.26.1 (1992) 380–411, esp. 381–92.

[9] Zeller, *Philosophie der Griechen*, 3.2.109–14, 124–26, 164–75, with the additional note on Apollonius by Raffaello Del Re in E. Zeller and R. Mondolfo, *La filosofia dei greci nel suo sviluppo storico* 3.4 (Il pensiero storico 73; ed. Raffaello Del Re; Florence: La nuova Italia, 1979) 115–41. It is difficult to infer from the extant fragments of Nigidius' works that he was indeed a "Pythagorean"; see Holger Thesleff, review of *Nigidio Figulo*, by Adriana Della Casa, *Gnomon* 37 (1965) 44–48, esp. 47.

Neopythagoreanism as a philosophical movement was eventually absorbed by Neoplatonism, culminating in the "Pythagoreanizing program" of Iamblichus of Chalcis (ca. AD 240–325).[10]

During the Hellenistic and early Imperial period we find considerable interest in the legend of Pythagoras, even among non-Pythagoreans. The materials collected as a result of this interest eventually found their way into the later biographies of Pythagoras, the best known of which are those by Diogenes Laertius (Bk. 8), Porphyry, and Iamblichus. During the same period collections of Pythagorean sayings also make their appearance.

Neopythagorean Writings in Which Friendship Appears

We find the *topos* of friendship in four types of Neopythagorean writings.[11] The first type is the Neopythagorean treatises written in Doric and mainly extant as excerpts preserved by Stobaeus.[12] Surprisingly enough, our *topos* does not feature very prominently in these writings; it only occurs in three authors, Hippodamus, Callicratidas, and Zaleucus, and even in their writings it is only mentioned in passing. I find this unexpected for three reasons: (*a*) friendship is such an important Pythagorean *topos*; (*b*) it is also an important *topos* in Aristotle, and as we have seen, these writings were strongly influenced by Aristotelian ideas; and (*c*) related *topoi*, such as that of household ethical codes ("Haustafeln"), were indeed treated at length.[13]

A second type of writing in which the *topos* appears, is that of Pythagorean letters. I include here pseudonymous letters as well as the letters ascribed to Apollonius of Tyana, some of which may well

---

[10] Dominic J. O'Meara, *Pythagoras Revived: Mathematics and Philosophy in Late Antiquity* (Oxford: Oxford University Press, 1989).

[11] As a matter of expediency, I will henceforth refer to the Pythagorean writings from the Hellenistic period onwards simply as "Neopythagorean," without implying that their actual date is necessarily post- Hellenistic.

[12] References to these works are to page and line numbers in Thesleff's collection cited in n. 6 above.

[13] See Balch, "Neopythagorean Moralists."

be authentic.¹⁴ Once again, it is not a particularly significant *topos*; it is only mentioned cursorily in four letters, namely, the Letter of Theano to Nicostrate, and in three letters of Apollonius of Tyana: numbers 1, 47, and 52. (Incidentally, the *topos* does not appear at all in Philostratus' *Life of Apollonius.*)

A consideration of the third type of text, namely, various Pythagorean sayings collections, is more productive as far as the *topos* of friendship is concerned. It appears quite frequently in the *Sayings of Sextus*, the *Sayings of Clitarchus*, the collection known as the *Pythagorean Sayings*, as well as in the *Golden Verses*.¹⁵ The latter differs from the other three in being a unified composition in which a specific section of the poem is devoted to this *topos*; in the former three collections we only find individual sayings relating to friendship. For this discussion, we will leave aside the various sayings attributed to Pythagoras in other mixed gnomologies, because these attributions are very unreliable; the same saying, for example, may be ascribed to Pythagoras in one collection, and to Epictetus or Democritus in another.¹⁶ A special case is provided by the Pythagorean *akousmata*, also known as *symbola*. Many of them are very old sayings based on religious and cultic taboos; because the literal meaning was incomprehensible or offensive to later Pythagoreans, they soon became the subject of allegorical

---

[14] The pseudonymous letters are included in Thesleff's collection of Pseudopythagorean texts, but they have also been edited recently (with translation and commentary) by Alfons Städele, *Die Briefe des Pythagoras und der Pythagoreer* (Beiträge zur klassischen Philologie 115; Meisenheim am Glan: Hain, 1980). The letters of Apollonius are edited by Robert J. Penella, *The Letters of Apollonius of Tyana* (Mnemosyne Supplement 56; Leiden: Brill, 1979); see pp. 23-29 on the question of the authenticity of the letters ascribed to Apollonius of Tyana.

[15] For Sextus, see Henry Chadwick, *The Sentences of Sextus: A Contribution to the History of Early Christian Ethics* (Texts and Studies n.s. 5; Cambridge: Cambridge University Press, 1959); Richard A. Edwards and Robert A. Wild, *The Sentences of Sextus* (SBLTT 22; Chico, California: Scholars Press, 1981). The text of Clitarchus may be found in Chadwick, *Sentences of Sextus*, 76-83, that of the *Pythagorean Sayings*, in the same work, 84-94. For a text, translation, and commentary on the *Golden Verses*, see Johan C. Thom, *The Pythagorean Golden Verses: With Introduction and Commentary* (Religions in the Graeco-Roman World 123; Leiden: Brill, 1995).

[16] See on this problem Anton Elter, *Gnomica homoeomata I-V* (Programm der Rheinischen Friedrich-Wilhelms-Universität zur Feier des Geburtstages seiner Majestät des Kaisers und Königs am 27. Januar; Bonn: Georgi, 1900-1904).

interpretations. Collections of these interpreted *akousmata* were widely known from the Hellenistic period onwards.[17]

The most extensive treatment of our *topos* is to be found in the fourth type of text, namely, the biographical traditions concerning Pythagoras and the Pythagorean life.[18] Besides the extant biographies of Diogenes Laertius, Porphyry, and Iamblichus mentioned above, the *topos* also appears in a source used by Diodorus of Sicily. Although these authors were not Pythagoreans themselves (Iamblichus may perhaps be an exception), in many cases they rely on earlier Pythagorean sources, such as Nicomachus of Gerasa and Apollonius of Tyana,[19] or the anonymous *Pythagorean Memoirs* excerpted by Alexander Polyhistor and used by Diogenes Laertius.[20] Furthermore, the world view and way of life presented in these writings may, with some caution, be taken as a representation of contemporary Pythagorean thought, and as such

---

[17] The most important texts, but by no means all, are to be found in Diels, *Fragmente der Vorsokratiker* 1.462–66 (frg. 58C). A traditio-historical study under Rohde's guidance was done by Cornelius Hölk, "De acusmatis sive symbolis Pythagoricis" (Diss., Kiel, 1894). Friedrich Boehm collected comparative folkloristic material ("De symbolis Pythagoreis" [Diss., Friedrich-Wilhelms-Universität Berlin, 1905]). The most extensive discussion is by Armand Delatte, *Études sur la littérature pythagoricienne* (Bibliothèque de l'Ecole des Hautes Etudes 217; Paris: Champion, 1915) 269–312. More recently, a few valuable pages have been devoted to the *akousmata* by Walter Burkert, *Lore and Science in Ancient Pythagoreanism* (Cambridge, Massachusetts: Harvard University Press, 1972) 166–92. A chapter on the *akousmata* is also to be found in van der Waerden, *Pythagoreer*, 64–99. See also Kurt von Fritz, "Pythagoras," 192–97; Johan C. Thom, "'Don't Walk on the Highways': The Pythagorean *Akousmata* and Early Christian Literature," *JBL* 113 (1994) 93–112.

[18] For a valuable survey of the biographical tradition see John Dillon and Jackson Hershbell, trans., *Iamblichus, On the Pythagorean Way of Life* (SBLTT 29; Atlanta, Georgia: Scholars Press, 1991) 6–14.

[19] In a classic study of the sources used by Iamblichus, Erwin Rohde concluded that he mainly used the two sources named in the text ("Die Quellen des Iamblichus in seiner Biographie des Pythagoras," *RhM* 26 [1871] 554–76; 27 [1872] 23–61; reprinted in his *Kleine Schriften* [2 vols.; Tübingen: Mohr-Siebeck, 1901] 2.102–72). Although Rohde's theory has subsequently been revised, Nicomachus and Apollonius are still considered Iamblichus' main sources; see Burkert, *Lore and Science*, 98–101; Balch, "Neopythagorean Moralists," 381–84.

[20] The vexing problem concerning the date of the *Memoirs* need not detain us here; for the sake of this discussion I accept the Hellenistic dating proposed by A.-J. Festugière ("Les 'Mémoires pythagoriques' cités par Alexandre Polyhistor," *REG* 58 [1945] 1–65) and accepted and refined by Burkert ("Hellenistische Pseudopythagorica," 26; *Lore and Science*, 53).

it had an impact on the moral world of the period. This is especially true of Iamblichus' *On the Pythagorean Way of Life*; its intended function was an ethical preparation for the study of philosophy.[21]

We now turn to a more detailed analysis of the individual passages in which this *topos* appears.

Analysis of the Texts

The Pythagorean Treatises

Hippodamus (3d or 2d cent. BC?). A fragment of Hippodamus which may have formed part of his work *On Happiness* deals with the three types of friendship: "Some friendships, based on knowledge, are with the gods; others, based on mutual support, are with humans; still others, based on pleasure, are with animals" (τᾶν φιλιᾶν ἃ μὲν ἐξ ἐπιστάμας θεῶν, ἃ δ' ἐκ παροχᾶς ἀνθρώπων, ἃ δὲ ἐξ ἁδονᾶς ζῴων, 97.14–15 Thesleff = Clement *Strom.* 2.19.101.1).[22] A threefold division of friendship is of course Aristotelian (*Eth. Nic.* 8), but this typology differs from Aristotle's in two respects: (*a*) Aristotle has a descending hierarchy of friendships based on virtue, pleasure, and utility, while for Hippodamus the utilitarian type of friendship is more important than that based on pleasure. (*b*) Even more important, however, is that Aristotle only discusses human friendships; Hippodamus bases his typology not only on the grounds for friendship (knowledge, mutual support, pleasure), but also on the objects: gods, human beings, animals. As we shall see, Iamblichus also refers to friendships with gods and with animals.[23]

---

[21] See O'Meara, *Pythagoras Revived*, 39–40.

[22] An alternative translation may be "Some friendships are based on knowledge of the gods; others are based on mutual human support; still others are based on animal pleasure." This translation, though linguistically possible, seems less likely in view of the correspondence with Iamblichus referred to below. A summary of Hippodamus' extant fragments is given by Thesleff, *Introduction*, 14. A predilection for three-item series was characteristic of the real Hippodamus as well; cf. Diels, *Fragmente der Vorsokratiker*, 1. 389–91.

[23] Iamblichus *VP* 69 = *VP* 229; see the discussion of Iamblichus below. It is noteworthy that for Iamblichus as well, friendship with the gods is based on knowledge (ἐπιστημονικῆς θεραπείας), but he bases friendship with animals on "justice and

Callicratidas, On Household Happiness (3d or 2d cent. BC?). The fragments of Callicratidas *On Household Happiness* (pp. 102-7 Thesleff) belong to the same ideological sphere and date as that of the fragment of Hippodamus we have just discussed.[24] According to Callicratidas, "a family, being a system of kindred communion, consists of certain dissimilars, which are its proper parts; and is co-arranged with a view to one thing which is best, the father of the family, and is referred to a common advantage, unanimity" (103.28–104.3 Thesleff; trans. Balch, "Neopythagorean Moralists," 396). The parts of which the family consists, are both the family members and the household possessions (104.8). Callicratidas continues by suggesting that friends should be included among the parts constituting a family, since they contribute to the greatness of the family.

> If the good of friends is also attributed to the household [for thus it becomes greater and more magnificent by being manifold not only in possessions and in family ties, but also in the multitude of friends], since it is obvious that the companionship species of friendship also enhances the household, it should be counted among the things making a household complete. (*De dom. felic.* 104.19–24 Thesleff)

The specific form of friendship he has in mind, "the companionship species of friendship" (τὸ ἑταιρικὸν εἶδος τᾶς φιλίας), is a form we know from Aristotle (*Eth. Nic.* 8.1161a25, 1161b12–13, 1161b35). In Aristotle, this form of friendship is based on both pleasure and utility; here the aspect of mutual support, which characterizes the second type in Hippodamus' classification, is the most prominent.

Zaleucus, Preambles to the Laws (4th/2d cent. BC?). In a fragment from his *Preambles to the Laws*, Zaleucus states that "no one should consider anyone of the citizens whom the laws allow to participate in the rights of citizenship, an irreconcilable enemy. Such a person, whose anger prevails over his reason, could not rule nor

---

natural union and affability" (δικαιοσύνης καὶ φυσικῆς ἐπιπλοκῆς καὶ κοινότητος).

[24] Burkert, "Einordnung einiger Pseudopythagorica," 38. Callicratidas' work is summarized by Thesleff, *Introduction*, 14. For a discussion of parts of Callicratidas' fragments see Balch, "Neopythagorean Moralists," 393–407, *passim*.

judge well" (*Prooem.* 227.29–228.1 Thesleff).²⁵ A report of this fragment in Diodorus of Sicily runs as follows:

> They should consider no one of their fellow citizens as an enemy with whom there can be no reconciliation, but that the quarrel be entered into with the thought that they will again come to agreement and friendship; and that he who acts otherwise, should be considered by his fellow citizens to be savage and untamed of soul. (Diodorus Siculus 12.20.3 = Zaleucus *Prooem.* 226.18–21 Thesleff; trans. Oldfather in LCL)²⁶

Zaleucus expands the boundaries of friendship into the political sphere. The ideal relationship between all citizens is that of friendship; therefore, unchecked feelings of hostility endanger the social fabric and threaten to reduce society to the savagery of animals.

A little further on in the fragment Zaleucus warns rulers not to base their judgments on enmity or friendship, but on what is right (p. 228.10–12; cf. p. 226.21–22). He therefore distinguishes between a universal friendly feeling among members of the community, and personal friendly or hostile relations; the latter should not lead to favoritism or prejudice.

Pythagorean Letters

The Letter from Theano to Nicostrate. Theano, in a letter to Nicostrate (1st cent. BC/2d cent. AD?), advises the latter to bear patiently with her husband's infidelity; she supports the advice with the truism that "as times of physical suffering make the periods of rest more pleasant, so differences between friends make reconciliation more intimate" (*Pyth. Ep.* 6.5, p. 172.44–46 Städele = p. 199.29–31 Thesleff).²⁷ Of sole interest for our present purpose is the fact that Theano considers husband and wife to be "friends."

---

²⁵ For a brief summary of the *Preambles to the Laws*, see Thesleff, *Introduction*, 23.

²⁶ Zaleucus adapts the Greek proverb, "One should be friends as if one will later hate, and hate as if one will later be friends" (see Aristotle *Rhet.* 2.13; E. L. von Leutsch and F. G. Schneidewin, *Corpus paroemiographorum Graecorum* [2 vols.; Götting, 1839–51; reprinted, Olms Paperbacks 21–22; Hildesheim: Olms, 1965] 2. 359), in the same way Aristotle does: "It is a better practice that one should not, as they say, be friends as if one will later hate, but rather hate as if one will later be friends" (*Rhet.* 2.21).

²⁷ According to the editor, this letter could not have been written before the first

The Letters of Apollonius of Tyana (1st cent. AD). Apollonius mentions friendship only three times in his more than a hundred letters. In a letter to the Stoic philosopher Euphrates (*Ep.* 1), Apollonius states that he is friends with all philosophers, but not with "sophists or schoolmasters or any other such unfortunate type of men" (σοφιστὰς ἢ γραμματιστὰς ἤ τι τοιοῦτο γένος ἕτερον ἀνθρώπων κακοδαιμόνων), thus "scorning the whole of rhetorical culture."[28] In another letter to the same person (*Ep.* 52), Apollonius enumerates at length all the arts and virtues to be found in a Pythagorean; this includes friendship with both gods and *daimones*. Finally, in a letter to the council and people of Tyana (*Ep.* 47), Apollonius claims that he has in his travels gained the friendship and goodwill of famous cities and people for the city of Tyana. Although these are admittedly meager gleanings, we see that Apollonius excludes certain categories of people from his friendship (presumably on moral grounds), that he considers friendship with the gods possible (declared impossible by Aristotle [*Eth. Nic.* 8.1159a5]), and that he extends the notion of friendship to include that of diplomatic relations between cities.

We now turn to two types of textual traditions in which the *topos* of friendship plays a more prominent role, namely, sayings collections and biographical traditions.

Pythagorean Sayings Collections

The Sentences of Sextus, of Clitarchus, and the Pythagorean Sayings. Since the *Sentences* of Sextus and of Clitarchus, and the collection known as the *Pythagorean Sayings* consist of individual, unrelated sayings, it is best to discuss them together. The collection of sayings ascribed to Sextus is a Christianized reworking of originally Pythagorean sayings, and in its present form it probably dates from the second century AD.[29] The *Pythagorean Sayings* may come from

---

century BC, and some words even make a second century AD date probable (Städele, *Briefe des Pythagoras*, 308). On Theano in general, see Mary Ellen Waithe, *A History of Women Philosophers 1: Ancient Women Philosophers 600 B.C.–500 A.D.* (Dordrecht: Nijhoff, 1987), chap. 3.

[28] Penella, *Apollonius of Tyana*, 90.

[29] Chadwick, *Sentences of Sextus*, ix-xi; Edwards and Wild, *Sentences of Sextus*, 1.

the same period, while the date of the *Sentences* of Clitarchus is uncertain.[30]

Several strands of the friendship *topos* are encountered in these collections. (*a*) The first is that of *care in the selection of friends*: one should not make friends quickly (Clitarchus *Sent.* 88); it is better to have one worthy friend than many worthless ones (Clitarchus *Sent.* 141); the best friend is he who helps one to advance in wisdom (*Pythagorean Sayings* 33). At the same time one should beware of antagonizing those who do not pass the test for friendship (*Pythagorean Sayings* 76), and one should not consider anyone an enemy oneself (Sextus *Sent.* 105). (*b*) The second motif is that of *sharing*, already expressed in the ancient Pythagorean saying, "Friends have everything in common": one should yield everything to one's friends except one's freedom [of mind?] (*Pythagorean Sayings* 97); one ought to share in a friend's misfortune and let friends share in your own good fortune (Clitarchus *Sent.* 90). Since they may drastically alter the external conditions under which a friendship was formed, circumstances put friendship to the test (Clitarchus *Sent.* 92; *Pythagorean Sayings* 34). Sharing a friend's responsibilities continues even after his death: one should not mourn the death of a friend, but take care of his relatives (Clitarchus *Sent.* 91). (*c*) A further motif is implied in these sayings, namely, that *one should stay friends* regardless of the circumstances. (In a more realistic vein, Aristotle suggests that it is very difficult for friends to remain friends when circumstances alter their relative status or wealth [*Eth. Nic.* 8.1158b29–35].) (*d*) Finally, *friendship with God* is viewed as the ultimate goal of a pious life (Sextus *Sent.* 86b). This again differs from the Aristotelian view that it is impossible to be friends with people or beings that differ too much from oneself (*Eth. Nic.* 8.1158b35–1159a5), but as we shall see, Iamblichus too advocated an all-encompassing friendship between beings on different ontological levels.

The Golden Verses. The anonymous *Golden Verses* consist of moral and religious instructions, and it was probably used as an introductory teaching by some Pythagorean sect. Although recent

---

[30] See Luci Berkowitz and Karl A. Squitier, *Thesaurus Linguae Graecae: Canon of Greek Authors and Works* (3d ed.; New York: Oxford University Press, 1990) 103, 358.

scholarship has dated the poem in the late Hellenistic or even Imperial period (ca. 100 BC–AD 250),[31] I have elsewhere argued for a date in the early Hellenistic period.[32] The first part of the poem sketches the context in which the Pythagorean has to practice virtue: We first find a section on piety (vv. 1-4), that is, one's vertical relationships; it includes instructions to worship and honor the gods, heroes, *daimones*, parents, and other parental relatives. This section is followed by one on friendship (vv. 5-8), the virtue operative in horizontal relationships:

> Among others, choose as your friend him who excels in virtue.
> Yield to his gentle words and useful actions,
> and do not hate your friend for a small fault,
> for as long as you are able to do so. For ability lives near necessity.

The following points are made here regarding friendship:[33] (*a*) In the first place, friendship should result from a deliberate *choice*, based on the *criterion* of virtue. This criterion, as we have seen, is also the Aristotelian prerequisite for a perfect friendship.

(*b*) The next two aspects relate to positive and negative actions by friends. First the *positive*: one should yield to a friend's gentle words and useful actions, that is, allow oneself to be guided by his admonishments and advice, and to benefit from his help. "Gentle words" should not be confused with "weak words" or "flattery"; it rather refers to words of advice or admonition used by a well-meaning friend. Ancient authors often emphasized that such advice or criticism should be coached in "gentle words."[34] "Yield to gentle words" thus means "Pay heed to, do not become angry at, your friend's advice."[35] If such is the meaning of the first half of

---

[31] Cf., e.g., van der Waerden, "Schriften und Fragmente," 851-52, 863-64.

[32] Thom, *Golden Verses*, chap. 5.

[33] For a detailed analysis of this section, see ibid., 119-25.

[34] Cf. Plato *Leg.* 10.888A; Cicero *Amic.* 24.88-25.91; Horace *Ep.* 1.18.44-45; Iamblichus *VP* 101 = *VP* 231; also *Vita Aesopi* (W) 109, p. 101.34 Perry; Gal 6:1 (with the commentary by Hans Dieter Betz, *Galatians: A Commentary on Paul's Letter to the Churches in Galatia* [Hermeneia; Philadelphia: Fortress, 1979] 295-98); 2 Tim 2:25. For Paul's practice in general, see Abraham J. Malherbe, "'Gentle as a Nurse': The Cynic Background to 1 Thessalonians 2," *Paul and the Popular Philosophers* (Minneapolis: Fortress, 1989) 35-48.

[35] As we shall see, Iamblichus *VP* 101 = *VP* 230-31 also underlines the necessity of yielding and controlling anger in friendship, particularly in the case of a younger

verse 6, "useful actions" in the second half can only refer to a friend's guidance. The sentence as a whole therefore prescribes an openness, a willingness to benefit from a friend's *benevolent criticism and guidance*; it also indicates *the kind of friend* by whom one should allow oneself to be influenced.[36] That one should derive benefit from friendship is a commonplace in ancient thought (cf. Xenophon *Mem.* 2.9–10; Cicero *Amic.* 14.51; Plutarch *De amic. mult.* 3.94*B*). In fact, as Albrecht Dihle points out, although the strict individualism of Greco-Roman ethics seems to relent as far as friendship is concerned, this is not the case: even in friendship the emphasis is on mutual support for personal ethical progress; the ultimate value of friendship lies in the personal benefit derived from it which enables one to advance on the road to virtue.[37] Yielding to a friend, as understood here, is therefore very different from the Christian notion of self-denial which entails "a moment of surrender, of not insisting on one's own worth or claims,"[38] since the motivation for yielding here remains self-interest.

(*c*) Having laid down a rule for the correct attitude toward a friend's beneficial actions, the author turns to the *negative* side of the coin, namely, a friend's *faults and mistakes*: one should not hate a friend, that is, become his enemy, for a minor mistake. What is emphasized here, is *tolerance*, in order that a friendship may *endure*.[39] Tolerance, as an essential aspect of friendship, is also stressed by other Pythagorean authors.[40] The only justifiable reason

---

friend in his relation to an older one. See also the discussion, with references, on the problem of accepting advice without becoming angry, by Abraham J. Malherbe, "'Pastoral Care' in the Thessalonian Church," *NTS* 36 (1990) 375–91, esp. 384–85.

[36] According to Iamblichus *VP* 101 = *VP* 230–31 this would be friends superior to oneself: fathers, elders, and benefactors. In this context the latter would include teachers. Cf. also Democritus frg. 47 (Diels, *Fragmente der Vorsokratiker*, 2.156): one should yield to the law, rulers, *and to someone wiser*.

[37] Albrecht Dihle, "Ethik," *RAC* 6.658–59.

[38] Dihle, "Ethik," 658.

[39] Cf. Plato *Phdr.* 233C: ". . . not taking up violent enmity because of small matters, but slowly gathering little anger when the transgressions are great, forgiving involuntary wrongs and trying to prevent intentional ones; for these are the proofs of a friendship that will endure for a long time" (trans. H. N. Fowler in LCL); also Aristotle *Eth. Nic.* 9.3.3–5; Plutarch *De frat. amor.*, *passim*; Iamblichus *VP* 232. Very similar is Matt 18:21–22.

[40] Sextus *Sent.* 293; Iamblichus *VP* 101–2; also *VP* 230. For a somewhat different

for breaking off a friendship, is a great transgression or unrectifiable fault; we should therefore endure a friend's mistakes *as long as we can* (v. 8a). This is underlined by means of a gnome, "Ability lives near necessity" (v. 8b), which supports the command in the previous sentence by deducing an imperative ("You must not hate your friend") from the indicative ("You are able not to hate your friend").

The Akousmata. The *akousmata* come in two forms: definitions and prescriptions. Friendship is defined in the following manner: "Friendship is equality."[41] We also have a question-and-answer definition: "What is a friend? Another I."[42] Both these definitions emphasize the equality that constitutes true friendship (cf. Aristotle *Eth. Nic.* 8.1158b1–1159a12). Two other prescriptive *akousmata* also deal with friendship. "Do not give the right hand to everyone" is interpreted to mean "Do not become friends with everyone."[43] Here again care in the selection of friends is underlined. Finally, one of the interpretations given to the obscure *akousma,* "Do not break bread," is that friendship should not be dissolved,[44] stressing the importance of the duration of friendships.

---

approach to the same problem, cf. Matt 5:21–26; *Did.* 1:3–5.

[41] Timaeus of Tauromenium in Diogenes Laertius 8.10; Iamblichus *VP* 162; Olympiodorus *In Plat. Alcib.* p. 31.18 Westerink; cf. also Alexander Polyhistor in Diogenes Laertius 8.33 (discussed below).

[42] Aristotle *Eth. Nic.* 9.1166a31; [Aristotle] *Magn. mor.* 2.15; Cicero *De off.* 1.56; [Plutarch] *Vit. Hom.* 151; Antonius Diogenes in Porphyry *VP* 33; Iamblichus *In Nicom. arithm.* p. 35.6 Pistelli; Synesius *Ep.* 100.17; Eustathius *In Il.* 4.54.22 Stallbaum; Schol. *Il.* 18.82. This saying and the previous one are discussed by Delatte, *Vie de Pythagore,* 168. Both were popular proverbs, but even though it is not certain that they indeed originated with the Pythagoreans, the latter did appropriate them as fitting expressions of their views on friendship.

[43] [Plutarch] *De liber. educ.* 12E; cf. Plutarch *De amic. mult.* 96A; Diogenes Laertius 8.17; Iamblichus *Protr.* 21, p. 108.2, 122.15–21 Pistelli. A different interpretation is "Do not easily become reconciled" (*Mantissa proverbiorum* 2.13 in Leutsch and Schneidewin, *Corpus paroemiographorum Graecorum* 2.760), but this does not fit the literal meaning of the command.

[44] Aristotle in Diogenes Laertius 8.35 (= Aristotle frg. 195 Rose), who mentions this among other interpretations; for still different interpretations cf. Aristotle in Iamblichus *VP* 86; Hippolytus *Ref.* 6.27.5.

Pythagorean Biographical Traditions

Anonymus Diodori. Diodorus of Sicily, in his description of the Pythagorean way of life (Diodorus Siculus 10.3–11), makes use of a source that post-dates Callimachus (4th–3d cent. BC).[45] He lifts out two aspects of Pythagorean friendship: *sharing* and *constancy.* As to the first aspect, it consists in the first place in sharing one's property with friends in need:

> Whenever any of the companions [συνήθων] of Pythagoras lost their fortune, the rest would divide their own possessions with them as with brothers. Such a disposition of their property they made, not only with their acquaintances [γνωρίμων] who passed their daily lives with them, but also, speaking generally, with all who shared in their concerns. (Diodorus Siculus 10.3.5 = 230.10–13 Thesleff; trans. Oldfather in LCL, slightly adapted)

The *Anonymus* continues by adducing the example of

> Cleinias of Tarentum, who ... learning that Prorus of Cyrene [a fellow Pythagorean] had lost his fortune because of a political upheaval, ... went over from Italy to Cyrene with sufficient funds and restored Prorus to his fortune, although he had never seen the man before. (Diodorus Siculus 10.4.1 = 230.14–18 Thesleff; trans. Oldfather)

However, as we have seen in previous authors, sharing entailed more than just material goods: "And it was not only in giving away money that they showed themselves so devoted to their friends [γνωρίμοις], but they also shared each others' dangers on occasions of greatest peril" (Diodorus Siculus 10.4.2 = 230.19–21 Thesleff; trans. Oldfather). To illustrate this principle, the author recounts the well-known anecdote of the Pythagoreans Phintias and Damon (Diodorus Siculus 10.4.3–6 = 230.21–35 Thesleff).[46] Phintias was involved in a plot against Dionysius, tyrant of Syracuse (405–367 BC), and was condemned to death. He then asked

---

[45] Burkert, *Lore and Science*, 104 n. 36.

[46] The story is also found in Cicero *De off.* 3.45, *Tusc. disp.* 5.22; Porphyry *VP* 59–61; Iamblichus *VP* 234–36; Hyginus *Fab.* 257. For more references see Edouard des Places, ed. and trans., *Porphyre, Vie de Pythagore, Lettre à Marcella* (Collection des universités de France; Paris: Les Belles Lettres, 1982) 65 n. 3. Porphyry and Iamblichus' version (summarized below) is based on Aristoxenus and is probably the oldest; see Burkert, *Lore and Science*, 104 n. 36.

Dionysius for time to settle his affairs, and offered to leave a friend as guaranty of his return. When Dionysius granted his request, skeptical that any friend would be willing to go to such lengths, Phintias' friend Damon came forward as security. Just before the time of his execution arrived, Phintias returned. Dionysius was so amazed at such a loyal friendship that he remitted Phintias' punishment and urged them to admit him as a third into their friendship.

The second aspect of Pythagorean friendship that *Anonymus Diodori* discusses, is that of their *steadfastness* in friendship: "The Pythagoreans took the greatest care to ensure constancy [βεβαιότητος] towards one's friends [φίλους], believing as they did that the goodwill [εὔνοιαν] of friends is the greatest good to be found in life" (Diodorus Siculus 10.8.1 = 232.15-17 Thesleff; trans. Oldfather, adapted). How they achieved this constancy remained a secret to outsiders (Diodorus Siculus 10.8.2-3 = 232.18-25 Thesleff).

Diogenes Laertius Bk. 8. Diogenes Laertius (end of 3d cent. AD?) devotes the major part of Book 8 (sec. 1-50) of his *Lives of Eminent Philosophers* to Pythagoras.[47] In his description of Pythagoras and the Pythagorean life he makes use of a variety of sources, including the historian Timaeus of Tauromenium (4th-3d cent. BC), Aristoxenus (4th cent. BC), a student of Aristotle, and the polymath Alexander Polyhistor (100-ca. 40 BC). According to Timaeus, Pythagoras coined the phrase "Friends have everything in common" (κοινὰ τὰ τῶν φίλων); the Pythagoreans as a result put all their possessions into one common stock (Diogenes Laertius 8.10). In another passage (8.23) ascribed to Timaeus by Delatte, we find the precept that Pythagoreans "had to consider nothing their own."[48] This is preceded by the command "to behave to one another in such a manner as not to make friends into enemies, but to turn enemies into friends" (trans. Hicks in LCL, adapted). These ideas have all been encountered before: the notion of

---

[47] Delatte, *Vie de Pythagore*, gives a critical text, introduction, and extensive commentary of Diogenes Laertius 8.

[48] Delatte, *Vie de Pythagore*, 196. Thesleff, *Texts*, 162-63, includes it among the fragments of a *Sacred Discourse* (Ἱερὸς λόγος) ascribed to Pythagoras.

sharing property among friends, of avoiding enmity, and of acting in such a manner vis-à-vis enemies that it does not preclude subsequent friendship.[49]

Aristoxenus states that Pythagoras "was a great practitioner of friendship [ἱκανός τε ... ἦν φιλίας ἐργάτης], and ... when he found his own *symbola* [= *akousmata*] adopted by anyone, he would immediately take to that man and make a friend of him" (Diogenes Laertius 8.16; trans. Hicks, adapted). For Pythagoras therefore, friendship was a way of life, while friendship itself was based on professing and practicing the same doctrines.

In the *Pythagorean Memoirs* excerpted by Alexander Polyhistor there is a passage that revolves around the notion of *harmony*.

> Virtue is harmony, and so are health, and all good and God himself; this is why they say that all things are constructed according to the laws of harmony. Friendship also is harmonious equality [ἐναρμόνιον ἰσότητα]. (Diogenes Laertius 8.33; trans. Hicks, adapted)

The definition of friendship is of course a variation of the one we encountered among the *akousmata*. What is of interest here, is that friendship is identified with the harmonious relationships underlying reality. The same idea is present in a source used by Iamblichus (*VP* 69 = *VP* 229). (Other traditions regarding Pythagorean friendship in Diogenes Laertius 8.35 that are related by Aristotle have already been discussed above in connection with the *akousmata*.)

Porphyry, Life of Pythagoras (AD 234–301/304). In Porphyry's *Life of Pythagoras* a few aspects are mentioned that we have already encountered, but there are also some new ideas.[50] Among the criteria for selecting friends, Porphyry refers to Pythagoras' practice of not making a friend of anyone before he had judged his character by his features (φυσιογνωμονῆσαι; Porphyry *VP* 13). Porphyry derives this passage from Antonius Diogenes (1st cent.

---

[49] For the latter, cf. Zaleucus in Diodorus Siculus 12.20.3, discussed above.

[50] An edition of the text and a French translation of the *Life of Pythagoras* by Edouard des Places may be found in *Porphyre, Vie de Pythagore* (see n. 46 above). On the sources used by Porphyry and Iamblichus, see the summary of recent scholarship in Balch, "Neopythagorean Moralists," 381–84.

AD).⁵¹ From the same source we hear about Pythagoras' concern for his friends:

> He loved his friends very much, having been the first to say that friends have everything in common, and that a friend is another I. When they were in health, he did not cease spending time with them; when their bodies were ill, he used to care for them; when their souls were ailing, he used to encourage them . . ., sometimes with magical incantations, sometimes with music. (*VP* 33)

Pythagoras is thus upheld as an exemplum for true friendship.

Another passage (*VP* 59–61) derived from Nicomachus (fl. ca. AD 100) refers to two principles of Pythagorean friendship: they actively shunned friendship with outsiders (τὰς ἀλλοτρίας φιλίας, i.e., friendship with non-Pythagoreans), but they guarded and kept unwavering friendship (τὸ φιλικὸν . . . ἀνένδοτον) with one another for many generations. These principles are illustrated by means of two anecdotes: The first is that of Phintias and Damon which we have already met in Diodorus of Sicily, the only difference being that Dionysius' desire to put the friendship to a test is here given as reason for Phintias' condemnation. Despite Dionysius' insistence to be included in their friendship, Phintias and Damon determinedly refused.⁵² The second anecdote (derived from Hippobotus [end of 3d cent. BC?] and Neanthes [ca. 200 BC]) is that of Myllias and his wife Timycha. At this point Porphyry's text breaks off, but the same story is also preserved by Iamblichus (*VP* 189–94), and may be briefly summarized here: During a period of persecution, Myllias and Timycha were captured by the tyrant Dionysius, who offered them a great reward—even to share his rule—if they would reveal to him the Pythagorean secret relating to beans; if they refused, however, he threatened them with severe punishment. As may be expected, they adamantly refused. The moral drawn from this story is that the Pythagoreans were

---

⁵¹ Des Places, *Porphyre, Vie de Pythagore*, 15–16.

⁵² Following Cobet and Nauck, Burkert argues that this version, which is also found in Iamblichus *VP* 234–36 and which ultimately depends on Aristoxenus (frg. 31 Wehrli), is older than the one we find in Diodorus Siculus 10.4.3, since it is unlikely that Dionysius would have requested to become part of the friendship if Phintias had really plotted against him (*Lore and Science*, 104 n. 36).

relentless regarding friendship with an outsider (τὰς ἐξωτερικὰς φιλίας), even if he happened to be a king.

Despite their admitted goal of even turning enemies into friends, we see that the Pythagoreans had difficulties in extending the circle of friendship beyond that circumscribed by shared beliefs. This problem will be encountered again in the next author.

Iamblichus, On the Pythagorean Way of Life (ca. AD 240–305). We find the most material on Pythagorean friendship in Iamblichus' book *On the Pythagorean Way of Life*, although some of this is simply a repetition of what we have had already and we will therefore not discuss it again.[53] For Iamblichus, friendship is a very important virtue, if not the most important. Even if he often copies his sources almost mechanically, it is still possible to determine his own views by analyzing his redactional and compositional activity. Thus he arranges his discussion of the cardinal virtues in such a manner that the importance of friendship is emphasized: He first discusses piety (chap. 28 = sec. 134–56), then wisdom (chap. 29 = sec. 157–66), justice (chap. 30 = sec. 167–86), prudence (chap. 31 = sec. 187–213), and courage (chap. 32 = sec. 214–28). The discussion culminates in friendship (chap. 33 = sec. 229–40), which therefore appears as the summation of Pythagorean virtue. This impression is reinforced by the fact that the part on the virtues forms the climax of the book; the three chapters that follow are in the nature of appendices.[54]

---

[53] E.g., Iamblichus *VP* 32: "Friends have everything in common"; *VP* 86: the explanation of the *akousma*, "Do not break bread"; *VP* 162: "Friendship is equality"; *VP* 189–94: the story of Myllias and Timycha. The standard edition of *On the Pythagorean Way of Life* is by Ludwig Deubner (Iamblichus, *De vita Pythagorica liber* [ed. U. Klein; Bibliotheca scriptorum Graecorum et Romanorum Teubneriana; Stuttgart: Teubner, 1975]). A convenient new translation with the Greek text of the Deubner edition on facing pages has recently been published by John Dillon and Jackson Hershbell (see n. 18 above). All translations of the *Pythagorean Way of Life* are from this work.

[54] Michael von Albrecht, ed. and trans., *Iamblichos, Pythagoras: Legende, Lehre, Lebensgestaltung* (Bibliothek der Alten Welt, Reihe Antike und Christentum; Zurich: Artemis, 1963) 9; "Das Menschenbild in Iamblichs Darstellung der pythagoreischen Lebensform," *Antike und Abendland* 12 (1966) 57–58. Von Albrecht has been criticized by Walter Burkert for underplaying the importance of sources in the composition of the *De vita Pythagorica* (review of *Iamblichos, Pythagoras: Legende, Lehre, Lebensgestaltung*, ed. and trans. Michael von Albrecht, *Gnomon* 37 [1965] 24–26), but I

Before we turn to the chapter on friendship, let us first take a look at two other passages in the book. The first is Pythagoras' speech to the young men in Croton (Iamblichus *VP* 37–44 = Pythagoras *Orat. I*, pp. 178–80 Thesleff). Iamblichus' source for this speech is probably Apollonius of Tyana, who in turn may have used Timaeus of Tauromenium.[55] Among the instructions given to the young men, we find the following:

> He also directed them to be so disposed in their associations [ὁμιλίαις] with one another, that they never become enemies to their friends, but become, as quickly as possible, friends to their enemies. Also they should practice, on the one hand, in decency [εὐκοσμίᾳ] toward those older, the good will [εὔνοιαν] due their fathers, and, on the other hand, in benevolence [φιλανθρωπίᾳ] towards others, the fellowship [κοινωνίαν] due their brothers. (Iamblichus *VP* 40 = 178.32–179.4 Thesleff)

The first sentence reiterates the theme of friendship towards all that we have encountered in Zaleucus and Diogenes Laertius; this principle of universal friendship, as we shall see shortly, fits in with the Pythagorean doctrine of cosmic harmony.[56] In the second part of the passage, the universal friendly feeling is concretized by being rooted in the affection and respect characterizing family ties: all men become fathers and brothers.

Evidence for a negative aspect of Pythagorean friendship is found in the report of a fraudulent *Sacred Discourse* (Ἱερὸς λόγος) counterfeited by Cylon to malign the Pythagoreans, whom he considered political opponents (Iamblichus *VP* 259). According to this purportedly Pythagorean writing, "One should reverence friends like the gods, but subdue others like beasts." Although this is obviously a misrepresentation, it indicates some of the

---

do not think one can ignore the important structural position occupied by the chapter on friendship. The passages on friendship in Iamblichus *VP* have been analyzed by C. J. de Vogel (*Pythagoras and Early Pythagoreanism: An Interpretation of Neglected Evidence on the Philosopher Pythagoras* [Assen: Van Gorcum, 1966] 150–59) and by Jean-Claude Fraisse, who follows de Vogel in claiming that the Iamblichus material may be used as evidence for early Pythagoreanism (*Philia: La notion d'amitié dans la philosophie antique* [Diss., Université de Paris IV = Paris: Vrin, 1974] 57–67, esp. 58).

[55] Burkert, *Lore and Science*, 100 n. 12, 104 n. 37; see also Thesleff, *Texts*, note on p. 177 line 18.

[56] See de Vogel, *Pythagoras*, 81.

antagonism experienced by people who have been excluded from the Pythagorean circle.⁵⁷ The theoretical universality of Pythagorean friendship was counterbalanced by an exclusiveness based on initiation, a common way of life, and shared doctrines.⁵⁸ Such tension is probably unavoidable in highly idealistic groups.⁵⁹

We come now to Iamblichus' chapter on friendship. There are two extensive parallel passages to this chapter: sections 69–70 (p. 39.8–25 Deubner) are (with the exception of a few words) the same as sections 229–30 (p. 123.7–24 D.), while sections 101–2 (pp. 58.15–59.13 D.) are repeated verbatim in sections 230–32 (p. 124.1–25 D.). It will therefore not be necessary to discuss them separately. The source for the first part of the chapter (Iamblichus *VP* 229–30, p. 123.7–24 D.) is unknown, but most of the rest derives from Aristoxenus, whether directly or indirectly.⁶⁰

The chapter starts out (Iamblichus *VP* 229 = *VP* 69) by stating once again, "Friendship of all with all, Pythagoras taught in the clearest manner," but here the universality transcends the limits of interpersonal relations and becomes truly cosmic.⁶¹ Friendship viewed in this manner encompasses several ontological levels: (*a*)

---

⁵⁷ In commenting on my paper, David Balch points out that political opponents were often described as "beasts" to justify destroying them (citing, e.g., Dionysius of Halicarnassus *Ant. Rom.* 3.21.6, 6.36.1); see also his own paper elsewhere in this volume. Dehumanizing people as a polemical procedure seems a *topos* worth pursuing; cf. in the NT Matt 12:34, 23:33, Luke 13:32, Acts 20:29, Phil 3:2, Titus 1:12 (discussed in Johannes P. Louw and Eugene A. Nida, *Greek-English Lexicon of the New Testament Based on Semantic Domains* [2 vols.; New York: United Bible Societies, 1988] 1. 755–56, sec. 88.119–23).

⁵⁸ Because of the highly apologetic and idealistic nature of our sources on Pythagoreanism, it is difficult to determine what the actual position of Pythagoreans within society was, i.e., how separate or alienated they were. There is nothing to suggest that they deliberately withdrew from society; if they met with opposition, it was rather because of their conservative and elitist views of society, and their high moral requirements.

⁵⁹ We find a similar inclusion-repulsion tension in the depiction of the first Christian community; cf Acts 5:13–14.

⁶⁰ See Diels, *Fragmente der Vorsokratiker* 1.471–73, 477–78 (frg. 58D7, 9). Iamblichus *VP* 233–36 (pp. 125.13–127.11 D.) is included in Aristoxenus frg. 31 by Fritz Wehrli (*Die Schule des Aristoteles 2: Aristoxenos* [2d ed.; Basel: Schwabe, 1967]). Rohde's theory that Iamblichus only made use of two sources, viz., Nicomachus and Apollonius, is too restrictive: "Iamblichus could have read personally, as Stobaeus did, the Πυθαγορικαὶ ἀποφάσεις of Aristoxenus" (Burkert, *Lore and Science*, 100–1).

⁶¹ Iamblichus *VP* 229 is discussed by de Vogel, *Pythagoras*, 151–52.

In the first place, there is the friendship between *gods and human beings* "through piety [εὐσεβείας] and scientific worship [ἐπιστημονικῆς θεραπείας]." (*b*) Next there are *interpersonal relationships*: this includes friendship with fellow citizens "through sound observance of law," and with "those of another race through correct inquiry into natural laws [διὰ φυσιολογίας ὀρθῆς]," as well as family ties between a husband and a wife or children, brothers and relatives "through an unperverted spirit of community [διὰ κοινωνίας ἀδιαστρόφου]." (*c*) Thirdly, there is the relationship between *human beings and "certain irrational animals* through justice and natural union and affability [τῶν ἀλόγων ζῴων τινὰ διὰ δικαιοσύνης καὶ φυσικῆς ἐπιπλοκῆς καὶ κοινότητος]."[62] (*d*) In the fourth place, friendship also extends to *intrapersonal relations*, such as that between body and soul, that between "the rational part of the soul" and "all forms of the irrational through philosophy and contemplation in accord with this," and that within "the mortal body . . . , by reconciliation and conciliation of the opposite powers concealed in it, accomplished through health and a way of life [διαίτης] conducive to this and temperance [σωφροσύνης] conducive to this, in imitation of the efficient functioning of the cosmic elements."[63] (*e*) Finally, the notion of friendship includes the harmony, coherence, and consistency that have to exist among the *various sciences* (δογμάτων).[64] The source concludes that Pythagoras was rightly considered a culture hero and a legislator

---

[62] "However, the text also permits another interpretation: it is not necessary to have the words τῶν ἀλόγων ζῴων τινά after προσέτι depend on an understood πρός, but one may construe as follows: καὶ προσέτι (παρέδωκε) τῶν ἀλόγων ζῴων τινα (sc. φιλίαν εἶναι). 'And moreover he taught that a certain friendship exists among animals': they have some kind of justice, natural ties and solidarity amongst themselves" (de Vogel, *Pythagoras*, 152). This interpretation seems less plausible. Elsewhere in Iamblichus we find anecdotes about Pythagoras' friendly treatment of animals (*VP* 60–62 ˜ Porphyry *VP* 23–25) and statements to the effect that Pythagoras taught humans to practice justice towards animals (*VP* 107–8) and that he established friendly relations between humans and animals (*VP* 168).

[63] The theme of "inner conflict" is an ancient one, with many ramifications; see Gerd Theissen, *Psychological Aspects of Pauline Theology* (Philadelphia: Fortress, 1987) 211–21 (on Romans 7, with references to Greco-Roman authors).

[64] This interpretation of friendship "between the doctrines" (δογμάτων δὲ πρὸς ἄλληλα) is a combination of the views of de Vogel, *Pythagoras*, 151, and von Albrecht, "Menschenbild," 58.

(εὑρετὴς καὶ νομοθέτης) for classifying all these relationships together under the name *friendship* (Iamblichus *VP* 230 = *VP* 70).[65]

It is important to note that in the analysis of friendship found in this passage, friendship results from the activity of various cardinal virtues.[66] The relationship between gods and humans is based on *piety*, that between human beings, on *justice* and *wisdom* based on a sound knowledge of nature, that between humans and animals is again founded on *justice*, while sound relations on the psychic-somatic level are due to *wisdom* and *temperance*.[67] We see further that the ethical dimension of friendship is interwoven with the rational order or harmony underlying the cosmic unity.[68]

This first, theoretical part (*VP* 229–30) functions as the introduction to Iamblichus' chapter on friendship. The main body of this chapter, as we have seen, derives from Aristoxenus, and is more practical. It contains the following injunctions (I cannot do better than quote the summary by Cornelia de Vogel, *Pythagoras*, 155–56):

> (1) With the Pythagoreans the injunction was in force to do away with rivalry and discord (ἀγῶνα καὶ φιλονεικίαν) in friendship, preferably in *all* forms of friendship, but in any case towards fathers, older people and those towards whom one has obligations [i.e., benefactors; *VP* 230 = *VP* 101].
>
> (2) They said that in friendly relationships there must be as few wounds and sores as possible. Hence both parties must know how to give in and

---

[65] De Vogel argues that Pythagoras himself was indeed the origin of this conception of friendship (*Pythagoras*, 153–55). Our sources do not allow us to go back earlier than the 4th century BC, however. Franz Dirlmeier points out that the word φιλία is a relatively late form, and that it was not yet used in the 6th century. He is therefore skeptical of this attribution to Pythagoras ("ΦΙΛΟΣ und ΦΙΛΙΑ im vorhellenistischen Griechentum" [Diss., Ludwig- Maximilians-Universität, Munich, 1931] 32). For a similar comprehensive view of friendship, see already Plato *Gorg.* 507EF; the "wise" to whom he attributes this notion are usually identified as Pythagoreans.

[66] Von Albrecht, "Menschenbild," 57.

[67] Cf. also Iamblichus *VP* 167–68, where justice is described in the same terms used elsewhere for friendship.

[68] "The notion of *philia* is here synonymous with that of *harmonia*. Furthermore, to speak of a rational order by no means excludes the ethico-religious meaning of this order, as is witnessed in other passages [i.e., Iamblichus *VP* 45–46] by the connection between *harmonia*, *homonoia*, and *dikē*" (Fraisse, *Philia*, 60).

control their tempers, especially young people with respect to older people, etc. [*VP* 231 = *VP* 101].

(3) Reprimands and admonishments ... must ... be addressed very gently and cautiously by older people to younger people—μετὰ πολλῆς εὐφημίας τε καὶ εὐλαβείας. In doing so one must clearly show fatherly care [*VP* 231 = *VP* 101].

(4) In friendship one must always, whether in jest or in earnest, remain loyal (i.e. never betray each other, always keep promises and appointments, etc.) ... [*VP* 232 = *VP* 102].[69]

(5) Friendship should not be given up because of a misfortune or any other predicament which may suddenly occur in life. (What is meant here is, for instance, sudden illness or loss of freedom or possessions for political reasons.) The only acceptable ground for ending a friendship is a serious and irreparable moral defect in the other [*VP* 232 = *VP* 102].

(6) Never start enmity against people who are not completely depraved, and if there is enmity then act nobly in the conflict [*VP* 232].

(7) Do not fight with words but with deeds. (What is meant here is undoubtedly: do not use terms of abuse or slander.) An enemy is justified by human and divine law (νόμιμον καὶ ὅσιον) if he fights as man to man (i.e. if in the conflict he is able to preserve human dignity) [*VP* 232].

(8) In true friendship as much as possible must be ordered and regulated, and this should depend on good judgement and should not be just arbitrary [*VP* 233].[70]

Much of this is of course a repetition of previously encountered ideas. What is made very clear, however, is the need for *judgment* within the framework of friendship. Not all friendly relations are the same; one has to differentiate between one's relationships with older people and with younger people. Changes relative to a friend are not on an equal footing either: material changes have to be handled differently from moral changes. Similarly, not all enemies are the same, and different stances are possible in hostile

---

[69] There is a curious story about Lysis and Euryphamus in Iamblichus *VP* 185 that illustrates how seriously Pythagoreans kept appointments; see de Vogel, *Pythagoras*, 157-58.

[70] De Vogel adds a ninth point, "(9) Friendship with aliens [τὰς ἀλλοτρίας φιλίας] was avoided deliberately, but ties of friendship amongst themselves were preserved for generations," but in fact this forms the introduction to the following section based on a different fragment from Aristoxenus which contains various anecdotes (frg. 31 Wehrli).

relationships. All of this is summarized in the conclusion to this section (item [8] in the summary): all relationships should be entered into with circumspection and in a rational and orderly manner; they should not be left to chance.[71]

The next section (*VP* 234–39) of the chapter recounts the anecdotes we know that illustrate the loyalty of Pythagorean friendship, namely, the story of Phintias and Damon (*VP* 234–36), and of Cleinias and Prorus (*VP* 239). To the latter account a similar episode relating to Thestor of Posidonia and Thymaridas of Parus is added. In this fragment of Aristoxenus we do hear another charming story, however, to prove the point that Pythagoreans helped one another even though they had not met: A Pythagorean who was travelling fell ill in an inn and the innkeeper went to a lot of expense caring for him. When the man was finally dying, he wrote a secret sign (σύμβολον) on a tablet and told the innkeeper to put it in a conspicuous place outside the inn. Long afterwards another Pythagorean passed by, saw the sign, and when he heard from the innkeeper what had happened, he repaid him much more than he had spent (*VP* 237–38).[72]

The conclusion to this chapter is from Iamblichus' own hand:

> These [sc. stories], then, are noble and fitting proofs of their friendship. Much more wonderful than these, however, were what they established about partnership in divine goods, and about unity of intellect and the divine soul. For they often encouraged one another not to disperse the god within themselves. At any rate, all their zeal for friendship, both in words and deeds, aimed at some kind of mingling [θεοκρασίαν] and union with God, and at communion with intellect and with the divine soul. (*VP* 240)

Von Albrecht points out that the highest virtue in Iamblichus' Neoplatonic system is the hieratic virtue, which is intent on the one, the ἕν. In this passage it becomes clear that Iamblichus considers friendship, which unites all things, to be a reflection of this virtue.[73] Even though this passage is couched in Neoplatonic

---

[71] The role of judgment has been stressed by Fraisse; cf. the subtitle to his chapter on Pythagorean friendship: "Le pythagorisme: Ordre universel et jugement humain" (*Philia*, 57–67 and esp. 61–65).

[72] All these stories are summarized by de Vogel, *Pythagoras*, 156–57.

[73] Von Albrecht, "Menschenbild," 58. He also refers to Plotinus' notion of the

terms, the underlying idea of union with God fits in very well with the Pythagorean ideal "to follow God" (ἕπου θεῷ), which was later assimilated to the Platonic ideal of "likeness to God" (ὁμοίωσις θεῷ).[74] Iamblichus may therefore well be expressing a Neopythagorean sentiment in concluding, "I think that all the goods of friendship are embraced by it [i.e., union with God]."

Conclusion

Although the sources we have discussed do not represent a homogeneous tradition, it is remarkable to what extent there is agreement on the *topos* of friendship. We find very little theoretical discussion of the topic; most material is either prescriptive or anecdotal. Friendship is viewed comprehensively, to include most relationships affecting human beings. As regards interpersonal relationships, an openness to all, a universal friendliness, is advocated. This does not mean that anybody is acceptable as a friend, however. Strict criteria are applied in selecting friends; they have to be worthy and wise and virtuous. Once one has become friends, great emphasis is placed on remaining friends, that is, on friendship as an enduring relationship. This requires discretion and judgment, and a sharing of all things and circumstances with one's friend. The obverse side of the coin of selection is exclusion: tact is needed in dealing with people not worthy of one's friendship. At the same time, one should not be disloyal to one's principles and beliefs to accept somebody as a friend, no matter how important he may be.

Friendship transcends the limits of interpersonal relationships, however. Taken in this all-encompassing sense of a universal *relatedness* ("Zusammengehörigkeit"),[75] friendship becomes synonymous with the harmonious relations the Pythagoreans discovered in nature and in which they required their members to participate. Most important of these relationships is friendship with

---

intelligible, unity-producing ἐν τῷ παντὶ φιλία.

[74] For references, see Thom, *Golden Verses*, 170 nn. 336, 337.

[75] Von Albrecht, "Menschenbild," 57.

God, which is also reflected within as an integration of one's person. In friendship macro- and microcosm meet.[76]

---

[76] See also von Albrecht, "Menschenbild," 57–58. I am grateful to David Balch for a number of valuable suggestions to improve my paper. He is of course not responsible for any remaining shortcomings.

PLUTARCH ON FRIENDSHIP

Edward N. O'Neil

Friendship was a favorite topic of discussion in older Greek treatises. Plutarch, who was an avid reader, collected in his notebooks (ὑπομνήματα) many of these discussions and used them in his own treatment of the subject. For examples he often referred to the same contemporary Roman conditions which the Roman satirist Juvenal attacked.

Plutarch's composition Πῶς ἄν τις διακρίνειε τὸν κόλακα τοῦ φίλου ("How to Tell a Flatterer from a Friend" [48E–74E])[1] is generally considered his most comprehensive treatment of the subject of friendship, though his essay Περὶ πολυφιλίας ("On Having Many Friends" [93A–97B]) may be equally important. And these two are far from his only discussions of the subject. There are several others which deal with some special perspective of friendship; for example:

Πῶς ἄν τις ὑπ' ἐχθρῶν ὠφελοῖτο ("How One Can Profit from his Enemies") [86B–92F]
Γαμικὰ παραγγέλματα ("Conjugal Precepts") [138A–146A]
Περὶ φιλαδελφίας ("On Brotherly Love") [478A–492D]
Περὶ τοῦ ἑαυτὸν ἐπαινεῖν ἀνεπιφθόνως ("On Praising Oneself without Offense") [539A–547F]

And still other compositions of his at least touch upon some aspect of the subject, among them

Περὶ τῆς εἰς τὰ ἔκγονα φιλοστοργίας ("On Love of Offspring") [493A–497E]

---

[1] In connection with "How to Tell a Flatterer from a Friend," it is worthwhile to look at the "Life of Alcibiades." Plutarch considered this fifth century Athenian a good example of a flatterer because of the way in which he acted both in private and in public life. For an analysis of this *Life* see D. A. Russell's *Plutarch* (London: Gerald Duckworth & Co., 1972) ch. 7 (pp. 117–29): "Alcibiades, or the Flatterer: An Analysis."

Περὶ φθόνου καὶ μίσους ("On Envy and Hate") [536E–538E]
Πολιτικὰ παραγγέλματα ("Precepts of Statecraft") [798A–825F]

Numerous other passages in many of his so-called ethical treatises (*Moralia*) contain references to some aspect of friendship and in doing so occasionally make use of one or another of its τόποι. In addition, many passages in the *Lives* — of both the Greeks and the Romans — deal with the subject. And finally, there are some 13 fragments of a document entitled Περὶ φιλίας ἐπιστολή ("An Epistle on Friendship").[2] Unfortunately, however, these fragments are too brief and from apparently scattered places in the epistle to afford very much insight into the epistle's treatment of the subject.

F. H. Sandbach, the translator of the Fragments in Vol. XV of the *Loeb Classical Library*'s edition of Plutarch's *Moralia*,[3] makes the comment (p. 299) that

> The extracts have little to do with "friendship" in the narrow sense of the word. Several are concerned with goodwill[4] and concord in social or political fields. This is a possible meaning of the Greek word (i.e. φιλία) and it may be that the letter was directed to such aspects of the subject.

If this epistle did *not* address "such aspects of the subject," it would surely be Plutarch's only major discussion of friendship that failed to do so.

Plutarch's Understanding of Friendship

In Plutarch's mind, φιλία embraced several areas of thought and activity. Thus, for example, kinship is a type of friendship,[5] and our author clearly points up this connection when he says in the Περὶ φιλαδελφίας (ch. 3 [479 C-D]):

---

[2] Frags. 159–171 Sandbach.

[3] Sandbach is also editor of the Teubner edition of the same material in vol. VII.

[4] εὔνοια is a regular term in discussions of friendship's aspects and properties. It is discussed below (pp. 113–114).

[5] As the lists given above show, Plutarch devotes three separate essays to various aspects of kinship/friendship: "On Love of Offspring," "Conjugal Preceps," and "On Brotherly Love."

σκιαὶ γάρ εἰσιν ὄντως αἱ πολλαὶ φιλίαι καὶ μιμήματα καὶ εἴδωλα τῆς πρώτης ἐκείνης, ἣν παισί τε πρὸς γονεῖς ἡ φύσις ἀδελφοῖς τε πρὸς ἀδελφοὺς ἐμπεποίηκε.

Most friendships are actually shadows, imitations, and images of that first friendship which Nature has implanted in children toward parents and in brothers toward brothers.[6]

And, of course, Plutarch goes on to discuss this idea at length in the treatise.

Friendship[7] also embraces a social relationship. Here, however, equality of those who share in it is an added requirement because this φιλία, which philosophers in general, and Plutarch in particular, consider cannot be concerned with the relationship between persons of different social levels.[8] On the other hand, as we will discuss later, the traditional pairs of friends which many writers list and hold up as models are usually not equal partners. In this respect, they may have originated in a type of patron-client or ruler-adviser relationship.[9] From the early days of Greek literature there was a φιλία styled ἑταιρική, and these unequal partners may have shared such a φιλία. For Plutarch, however, as for most later Greek authors, the phrase φιλία ἑταιρική carries the nuance of a sexual relationship with an hetaira. In only a few places does Plutarch use ἑταιρικός with the meaning "of a companion," e.g. Περὶ φιλαδελφίας ("On Brotherly Love"), ch. 16 [487A]):

---

[6] Note that Plutarch omits any reference to affection of sister for sister, sister for brother and vice versa.

[7] The chief word for friendship is of course φιλία, but there are other terms. Indeed, in one composition the rhetor Libanius employs four terms for "friend," and often there appears to be little, if any, appreciable difference in their significance; i.e. φίλος, συνήθης, ἐπιτήδειος, γνώριμος, and Plutarch himself uses still other words, e.g. ὅμοιος, ἑταῖρος. In the case of the latter word, however, he may do so in one passage only for the sake of a play on words: προσαγορεύειν ἑταῖρον ὡς ἕτερον ("On Having Many Friends," (Ch. 2 [93E]). F. C. Babbitt, the Loeb translator, renders the phrase with "to call him 'brother' as though to suggest 'th'other.'"

[8] Generally the persons involved in the friendship relationship belong to the aristocratic class. Few ancient authors considered the lower classes worthy of such studies.

[9] As we will point out later, the terms "friend" and "friendship" were regularly used to designate relationships between two states, whether they were considered equal or unequal partners.

ἐπεὶ δὲ τῷ μὲν πρεσβυτέρῳ τὸ κήδεσθαι καὶ καθηγεῖσθαι καὶ
νουθετεῖν προσῆκόν ἐστι, τῷ δὲ νεωτέρῳ τὸ τιμᾶν καὶ ζηλοῦν καὶ
ἀκολουθεῖν, ἡ μὲν ἐκείνου κηδεμονία τὸ ἑταιρικὸν μᾶλλον ἢ τὸ
πατρικὸν ἐχέτω καὶ τὸ πεῖθον ἢ τὸ ἐπιτάττον ....

And since it is fitting for the older brother to be solicitous about the younger and for him to lead and admonish, and for the younger brother to honour, emulate and follow, let the solicitude of the former be that of a comrade rather than of a father, and of one who would persuade rather than command ....

In "On Having Many Friends" Plutarch discusses the aim of true friendship and says (ch. 3 [94B]):

... ἡ ἀληθινὴ φιλία τρία ζητεῖ μάλιστα, τὴν ἀρετὴν ὡς καλόν, καὶ
τὴν συνήθειαν ὡς ἡδύ, καὶ τὴν χρείαν ὡς ἀναγκαῖον.

... true friendship seeks after three things above all else: virtue as a good thing, intimacy as a pleasant thing, and usefulness as a necessary thing.[10]

Plutarch then goes on to point out that "Having Many Friends" (πολυφιλία) renders these aims impossible.

In Rome of the 1st and 2nd centuries after Christ at least,[11] the patron-client relationship filled the need for formal associations among individuals of unequal rank.[12] Here custom set out definite modes of conduct and responsibilities for both the patron and the client[13] and made clear the existence of different levels of society.

---

[10] The three terms here, ἀρετή, συνήθεια, and χρεία, are of course three of the standard terms in the language of friendship. They will be discussed below.

[11] Such practices are, of course, to be found at Rome as early as the second century BC and perhaps even earlier. According to Ludwig Friedländer, *Roman Life and Manners under the Early Empire* (4 vols.; London: Routledge & Kegan Paul, 1908–13) 4.59, *amici* at Rome were separated into two classes. See also 1.70–85 for a discussion of "The Friends and Companions of the Emperor."

[12] Yet such relationships can hardly be termed "friendships."

[13] One convention which developed from the reciprocal duties of patron and client was the *sportula*, a daily dole given by a patron to his clients; cf., for example, Juvenal's *Satires* 1.95–126; 10.43–46. In turn, the patron's social position was often marked by the number of clients that gathered around him. It is particularly apt to cite Juvenal in any study of Plutarch, for the two men were contemporaries, and for much of the time both men were in Rome and concerned with the same problems. For a discussion of the *sportula* cf. Friedländer, *Roman Life and Manners*, Appendix xiv (4.77–81); cf. also 1.195–202.

It is perhaps this sort of relationship that Plutarch has in mind when he says in "On Having Many Friends" (ch. 3 [94 A-B]),

ἐν δὲ ταῖς τῶν πλουσίων καὶ ἡγεμονικῶν οἰκίαις πολὺν ὄχλον καὶ θόρυβον ἀσπαζομένων καὶ δεξιουμένων καὶ δορυφορούντων ὁρῶντες εὐδαιμονίζουσι τοὺς πολυφίλους. καίτοι πλείονάς γε μυίας ἐν τοῖς ὀπτανίοις αὐτῶν ὁρῶσιν· ἀλλ' οὔθ' αὗται τῆς λιχνείας οὔτ' ἐκεῖνοι τῆς χρείας ἐπιλιπούσης παραμένουσιν.

In the houses of rich men and those in authority people see a noisy throng of visitors greeting and shaking hands and playing the part of armed retainers, and they suppose that those who have so many friends are happy. Yet they can see a far greater number of flies in those persons' kitchens. But the flies do not stay on after the good food is gone, nor do the retainers after their patron's usefulness is gone.[14]

These hangers-on are undoubtedly the flatterers whom Plutarch points to in "How to Tell a Flatterer from a Friend" (ch. 2 [49C]):

... τὴν κολακείαν ὁρῶμεν οὐ πένησιν οὐδ' ἀδόξοις οὐδ' ἀδυνάτοις ἀκολουθοῦσαν, ἀλλ' οἴκων τε καὶ πραγμάτων μεγάλων ὀλίσθημα καὶ νόσημα γιγνομένην, πολλάκις δὲ καὶ βασιλείας καὶ ἡγεμονίας ἀνατρέπουσαν.

... we observe that flattery does not attend upon poor, obscure, or unimportant persons, but is rather a stumbling-block and a pestilence in great houses and great affairs, and often overturns even kingdoms and principalities.[15]

From the early days of the Roman Empire a similar type of relationship existed between Rome and other states and was one of the chief factors in the creation of the Roman Empire where the terms *amicus* and *amicitia*[16] were officially applied to the "satellite" states, and neither the Roman Senate nor the leaders of the other state had any illusion (or delusion) about the role of each state in the relationship. And even though both individual and international associations of this type involved members of unequal

---

[14] Juvenal's brilliant vignette in *Satire* 1.95–126 reflects a situation similar to the one Plutarch describes here.

[15] Cf. Juvenal, *Sat.* 10.12–18.

[16] And of course for a Greek the corresponding terms were usually φίλος and φιλία.

rank, the ancients considered these associations to be aspects of friendship.

As a sort of image of — or is it a development from? — the social aspect of friendship, there is what we may term the political phase of the relationship; that is, between a ruler and his "friends."[17] Plutarch, like others who deal with friendship, discusses this association which may involve one of the oldest uses of the terms φίλος and φιλία. It is to this subject that Plutarch in part directs his treatise "How to Tell a Flatterer from a Friend," but not far removed is his other treatise "On Having Many Friends," for the general consensus is that a person cannot have many real friends: Many friends = many flatterers.

Many treatises on friendship use many of the same τόποι, and of course many authors, such as Plutarch, have used, if not copied, the works of their predecessors.[18] Authors like Plutarch, who depended a great deal on earlier compositions, often kept notebooks in which to jot down ideas which they might want to use at some later time. On two occasions Plutarch mentions his notebooks (ὑπομνήματα), and on one says in response to a friend who has requested an essay on the subject of εὐθυμία:[19]

μήτε δὲ χρόνον ἔχων, ὡς προῃρούμην, γενέσθαι πρὸς οἷς ἐβούλου μηθ' ὑπομένων κεναῖς παντάπασι τὸν ἄνδρα χερσὶν ὀφθῆναί σοι παρ' ἡμῶν ἀφιγμένον, ἀνελεξάμην περὶ εὐθυμίας ἐκ τῶν ὑπομνημάτων ὧν ἐμαυτῷ πεποιημένος ἐτύγχανον . . . .

---

[17] For a discussion of this subject see Friedländer, *Roman Life and Manners*, 1.70–82.

[18] In connection with this idea, Elizabeth L. Eisenstein (*The Printing Press as an Agent of Change* [2 vols.; New York: Cambridge University Press, 1979] and *The Printing Revolution in Early Modern Europe* [New York: Cambridge University Press, 1983]) points out that one of the ancient scholar's duties, without a means of easy reproduction of texts, or easy access to them, was to preserve the writings of his predecessors and only then to offer new ideas of his own.

[19] Περὶ εὐθυμίας ("On Tranquility of Mind") ch. 1 (464F). The other reference is at Περὶ ἀοργησίας ("On Control of Anger"), ch. 9 (457D): διὸ καὶ συνάγειν ἀεὶ πειρῶμαι καὶ ἀναγινώσκειν οὐ ταῦτα δὴ μόνον τὰ τῶν φιλοσόφων, οὕς φασι χολὴν οὐκ ἔχειν οἱ νοῦν οὐκ ἔχοντες, ἀλλὰ μᾶλλον τὰ τῶν βασιλέων καὶ τυράννων ("Therefore I always try to collect and read not only these sayings of philosophers, whom senseless people claim to have no guts, but even more so those of kings and rulers.") The key word here of course is συνάγειν.

> But since I neither had the time I might have wanted to meet your wishes, nor could I allow the friend who left me to be seen arriving at your home with empty hands, I collected from my notebooks those observations on tranquility of mind which I happened to have made for my own use . . . .

And that he did fill many ὑπομνήματα with copious notes on numerous topics is quite clear from, for example, the collections which are contained on Frankfurt pages 172A–242D and which pass under the titles of Ἀποφθέγματα βασιλέων καὶ στρατηγῶν ("Sayings of Kings and Commanders"), Ἀποφθέγματα Λακωνικά ("Sayings of Spartans"), Τὰ παλαιὰ τῶν Λακεδαιμονίων ἐπιτηδεύματα ("The Ancient Customs of the Spartans"), and Λακαινῶν ἀποφθέγματα ("Sayings of Spartan Women"). These pieces contain little, if anything, that is new. Rather they are apparently some of Plutarch's notebooks which were left among his belongings at the time of his death. Someone[20] mistook them for compositions, completed or otherwise, and had them published. Many passages of these "sayings" appear elsewhere in the various treatises of the *Moralia* and/or in the *Lives*, thus suggesting that they had been collected for his use in these compositions, as he himself says in the passage from Περὶ εὐθυμίας quoted above .

If we possessed all his notebooks, we would undoubtedly find in them many quotations from earlier authors on numerous subjects, including that on friendship. This practice of Plutarch was also followed by other authors. See, for example, the remark of Seneca (*Ep.* 33.7):

> Certi profectus viro captare flosculos turpe est et fulcire se notissimis ac paucissimis vocibus et memoria stare; sibi iam innitatur. Dicat ista, non teneat. Turpe est enim seni aut prospicienti senectutem ex commentario sapere.
>
> It is disgraceful for a man whose progress is assured to grab after choice passages and to prop himself up by means of the best known and concise sayings and to depend on memory. He should lean on himself. He should be making those sayings, not memorizing them. For it is

---

[20] That "someone" is probably Plutarch's son Lamprias who is credited with compiling the Catalogue named after him.

disgraceful for an old man, or one who is in sight of old age, to be wise from a notebook.

Clearly, the use of such notebooks was a common practice among numerous writers, though looked down on by others. In the case of Seneca, of course, although he may voice opposition to the practice, even a casual inspection of his *Moral Essays* and *Moral Epistles* shows apophthemata of all kinds in a plentiful amount.

Such notebooks apparently had their inception in Alexandria perhaps as early as the fourth century BC. As a result, down through the succeeding centuries authors of various subjects made use of the information which these compositions provided. Often a writer copied from the notebook *verbatim*, often he paraphrased his source, and often he thought he had an accurate remembrance — but did not. In any case, the existence of such handbooks, and the regular repetition of the same idea culled from them, have had a pronounced influence on the number and nature of τόποι in almost every area of ancient thought, including friendship.[21]

Therefore, in what follows here, it is generally impossible to identify the original author of various ideas on friendship, though those of Aristotle in the *Nicomachean Ethics* seem prevalent. Indeed, for our purposes, such identification is not important. What is important is taking note of the widespread repetition of certain words and ideas[22] and ascertaining which of them appear in Plutarch's writings. Here, then, are some (but not nearly all) of the τόποι on friendship and some (but not nearly all) of those which appear in Plutarch,[23] for the present study is admittedly only a

---

[21] For a brief discussion of such notebooks, see W. C. Helmbold and E. N. O'Neil, *Plutarch's Quotations* (APA Philological Monographs, 19; Baltimore: American Philological Association, 1959) vii-x. Incidentally, the reference on p. ix to Vol. VI, p. 163 should be Vol. VI, p. 167. As everyone knows, Plutarch quoted more frequently and from a greater number of authors than almost any ancient author (Athenaeus perhaps excepted).

[22] Indeed, this very repetition of an idea in similar wording is one feature that constitutes a τόπος.

[23] Among other things, Gottfried Bohnenblust's Inaugural Dissertation from the University of Bern entitled "Beiträge zum Topos Περὶ Φιλίας" (Berlin: Gustav Schade [Otto Francke], 1905) has been especially helpful. There is also the useful article on φιλία and kindred terms by Gustav Stählin in *TDNT* 9 (1974) 146–54, though it is a rather brief and general treatment of the subject. Also helpful has been K. Treu's article entitled "Freundshaft" in *RAC* 8 (1972) 418–34.

preliminary evaluation, a *prolegomenon*, as it were, of the subject of friendship. The key words which appear below are listed in a more or less alphabetical order.

Τόποι on Friend and Friendship in Plutarch

1. ἔπαινος καὶ ψόγος (or μέμψις) occur especially in chapters 12-17 (55E-60B) of "Flatterer"[24] and also in several other places in the same treatise, e.g. ch. 8 (53B), and ch. 9 (53C). Throughout this composition, Plutarch concentrates on the words and actions of the flatterer (κόλαξ), and the general sense is that a friend praises or blames the *action* of a friend, while the flatterer heaps praise or blame on the *person*. This subject is obviously a part of, or at least akin to, the concept of παρρησία ("frankness"), a topic which will appear later (#5, pp. 116-17) in this discussion.

2. εὔνοια or "goodwill" is a common ingredient in friendship literature. Plutarch's numerous references to the term are at times reminiscent of Aristotle's statements at *EN* 1155b32 and 1166b30ff. See, for example, Plutarch, "Flatterer" (ch. 12 [56A]):

> ὅταν δ' ἁμαρτάνωσι καὶ πλημμελῶσιν, ὁ μὲν ἐλέγχῳ καὶ ψόγῳ δηγμὸν ἐμποιῶν καὶ μετάνοιαν ἐχθρὸς δοκεῖ καὶ κατήγορος, τὸν δ' ἐπαινοῦντα καὶ κατευλογοῦντα τὰ πεπραγμένα ἀσπάζονται καὶ νομίζουσιν εὔνουν καὶ φίλον.

> Whenever these people are guilty of mistakes and blunders, the man who, by chiding and blaming them, implants the sting of repentance, and so appears to be an enemy and an accuser; whereas they welcome the man who praises and extols what they have done, and they regard him as kind and friendly.

See also "Friends" (ch. 5 [95B]):

> ἡ δὲ πολυφιλία διίστησι καὶ ἀποσπᾷ καὶ ἀποστρέφει, τῷ μετακαλεῖν καὶ μεταφέρειν ἄλλοτε πρὸς ἄλλον οὐκ ἐῶσα κρᾶσιν οὐδὲ κόλλησιν εὐνοίας ἐν τῇ συνηθείᾳ περιχυθείσῃ καὶ παγείσῃ γενέσθαι.

> Having many friends breaks up, separates, and scatters, since by calling one here and there and transferring one's attention first to this person, now to that, it does not permit any blending or close attachment of

---

[24] For the sake of brevity in what follows "Flatterer" = "How To Tell A Flatterer From A Friend" and "Friends" = "On Having Many Friends."

goodwill to occur in the intimacy that moulds itself around and assumes enduring form.

Indeed the words εὔνοια and εὔνους appear frequently in Plutarch's various compositions: in the *Moralia* εὔνοια 114 times, εὔνους 24 times; in the *Lives* εὔνοια 128 times, εὔνους 22 times.[25]

3. ἡδύς (ἡδονή) is a word used frequently of a friend or of friendship itself. For example in "Flatterer" (ch. 2 [49F]):

ἀλλ' οὐδὲν ἧττον τοῖς ἀγαθοῖς ἡδονὴν ἐπιφέρουσα καὶ χάριν[26] ἢ τῶν κακῶν ἀφαιροῦσα τὰς λύπας καὶ τὰς ἀπορίας παρέπεται.

When friendship attends us, it brings pleasure and delight to our prosperity no less than it takes away the pains and the feeling of helplessness from adversity.

And a little later in "Flatterer" (ch. 5 [51A-B]) there is this description of friendship:

Ὅτι μέντοι γε πάντων ἥδιστόν ἐστιν ἡ φιλία καὶ οὐδὲν ἄλλο μᾶλλον εὐφραίνει, διὰ τοῦτο καὶ ὁ κόλαξ ἡδοναῖς ὑπάγεται καὶ περὶ ἡδονάς ἐστιν.

For the very reason that friendship is the most pleasant thing in the world, and because nothing else gives greater delight, the flatterer allures by means of pleasures and concerns himself with pleasures.

And again in "Flatterer," ch. 11 (54 D-E):

Ἐπεὶ δ' ὥσπερ εἴρηται καὶ τὸ τῆς ἡδονῆς κοινόν ἐστι (χαίρει γὰρ οὐχ ἧττον τοῖς φίλοις ὁ χρηστὸς ἢ τοῖς κόλαξιν ὁ φαῦλος), φέρε καὶ τοῦτο διορίσωμεν. ἔστι δὲ διορισμὸς ἡ πρὸς τὸ τέλος ἀναφορὰ τῆς ἡδονῆς.

Since the element of pleasure is common to both friendship and flattery (for the good man takes no less delight in his friends than the bad man does in his flatterers), let us now draw the distinctions between them in this respect. The distinction lies in referring the pleasure to its end.

---

[25] All such figures are according to the unpublished *Critical Index Verborum Plutarcheus* of W. C. Helmbold and E. N. O'Neil.

[26] χάρις, too, is an important word in friendship literature and will be discussed later (#7 below, pp. 118–19). It is the delight which "gratification" for favors brings.

And as a final example, still in ch. 11 (55A), which by no means exhausts the subject:

συνελόντι δ' εἰπεῖν ὁ μὲν ἵν' ἡδὺς ᾖ πάντα δεῖν οἴεται ποιεῖν, ὁ δ' ἀεὶ ποιῶν ἃ δεῖ πολλάκις μὲν ἡδὺς πολλάκις δ' ἀηδής ἐστιν, οὐ τοῦτο βουλόμενος, εἰ δὲ βέλτιον εἴη, μηδὲ τοῦτο φεύγων.

To put it in a few words, the flatterer thinks he ought to do anything to be agreeable, while the friend, by doing always what he ought to do, is often times agreeable and often disagreeable, not from any desire to be so, but not attempting to avoid even this if it should prove to be better.

4. ὁμοιότης, ὅμοιος with its related words is a common feature of friendship. For example, "Flatterer" (ch. 5 [51B]):

ἐπεὶ δὲ τὸ μάλιστα φιλίας ἀρχὴν συνέχον ὁμοιότης ἐστὶν ἐπιτηδευμάτων καὶ ἠθῶν, καὶ ὅλως τὸ χαίρειν τε τοῖς αὐτοῖς καὶ τὸ ταὐτὰ φεύγειν πρῶτον εἰς ταὐτὸ συνάγει καὶ συνίστησι διὰ ὁμοιοπαθείας, τοῦτο κατιδὼν ὁ κόλαξ αὐτὸν ὥσπερ ὕλην τινὰ ῥυθμίζει καὶ σχηματίζει, περιαρμόσαι καὶ περιπλάσαι ζητῶν οἷς ἂν ἐπιχειρῇ διὰ μιμήσεως, ...

And since that which most especially cements a friendship begun is a likeness (ὁμοιότης) of pursuits and characters, and since to take delight in the same things and avoid the same things is what generally brings people together in the first place and gets them acquainted through the bond of having similar experiences, the flatterer takes note of this fact and adjusts and shapes himself, as though he were some inert matter, seeking to adapt and mould himself to fit those whom he attacks through imitation . . . .

The same general idea appears in "Friends" (ch. 9 [96F–97A]), where, after a discussion of the changes that a πολύπους makes in order to avoid capture, Plutarch says:

καίτοι τοῦ πολύποδος αἱ μεταβολαὶ βάθος οὐκ ἔχουσιν, ἀλλὰ περὶ αὐτὴν γίγνονται τὴν ἐπιφάνειαν, στυφότητι καὶ μανότητι τὰς ἀπορροίας τῶν πλησιαζόντων ἀναλαμβάνουσαν· αἱ δὲ φιλίαι τὰ ἤθη ζητοῦσι συνεξομοιοῦν καὶ τὰ πάθη καὶ τοὺς λόγους καὶ τὰ ἐπιτηδεύματα καὶ τὰς διαθέσεις.

However, the changes in the cuttle-fish have no depth but are wholly on the surface, which, owing to its closeness or looseness of texture, takes up the emanations from objects which come near it; whereas friendship seeks to effect a thorough-going likeness in characters, feelings, language, pursuits, and dispositions.

And finally, here is an example involving the adjective ὅμοιος, in "Flatterer" (ch. 7 [52A]):

Πῶς οὖν ἐλέγχεται καὶ τίσιν ἁλίσκεται διαφοραῖς, οὐκ ὢν ὅμοιος οὐδὲ γιγνόμενος ἀλλὰ μιμούμενος ὅμοιον;

What is the method of exposing him (i.e. the flatterer), and by what differences is it possible to detect that he is not really like-minded (ὅμοιος) or even likely to become so, but is imitating the trait of being like-minded (ὅμοιον)?

Again, these three examples by no means exhaust the topic, but three should suffice to indicate its role in friendship literature.

5. παρρησία occurs 103 times in the *Moralia* and 57 times in the *Lives*; in addition, the verb παρρησιάζομαι occurs 39 times in the *Moralia* and 20 times in the *Lives*. The noun παρρησιαστής occurs once (said of the orator Lycurgus, at *On the Ten Orators* 842D). This word-group may be the most commonly used one in Plutarch's (as well as other authors') discussions of friendship. In many ways the idea may be considered the very foundation of the relationship, for proper use of παρρησία is the surest mark of a true friend, whereas improper use points to a flatterer or an enemy.[27] In "Flatterer" Plutarch devotes so much space to παρρησία (Chs. 12–20 [55E–62B] and 25–37 [65E–74E]) that Frank Babbitt, the Loeb translator, supposes that this discussion could have formed a separate treatise[28] but yet is naturally a part of distinguishing the affection of a true friend from the affectation of a flatterer. One important aspect of παρρησία occurs in "Flatterer" (ch. 32 [70E]):

εὐλαβητέον ἐστὶν ἐν πολλοῖς παρρησίᾳ χρῆσθαι πρὸς φίλον.

We must be very careful about the use of frankness toward a friend in public.

This discussion is very similar to what Seneca says (*De moribus*, frag. 13) in his usual epigrammatic fashion: *mone in privato, palam lauda*.

---

[27] See in particular the insightful article by Heinrich Schlier, who outlines the history of the meaning of παρρησία in *TDNT* 5 (1967) 871–86, esp. 871–75.

[28] As it does in the writings of the first century BC Epicurean Philodemus.

One final passage on παρρησία is in order, "Flatterer" (ch. 36 [73C–D]):

ὥσπερ ὁ σίδηρος πυκνοῦται τῇ περιψύξει καὶ δέχεται τὴν στόμωσιν ἀνεθεὶς πρῶτον ὑπὸ θερμότητος καὶ μαλακὸς γενόμενος, οὕτω τοῖς φίλοις διακεχυμένοις καὶ θερμοῖς οὖσιν ὑπὸ τῶν ἐπαίνων ὥσπερ βαφὴν ἀτρέμα τὴν παρρησίαν ἐπάγειν.

Just as steel is made compact by cooling and takes on a temper as the result of having first been relaxed and softened by heat, so when our friends have become mollified and warmed by our commendations, we should give them an application of frankness like a tempering bath.

6. συνήθεια and συνήθης (the adjective is also used as a substantive on several occasions) are two of the more frequent words in the Plutarchan corpus. συνήθεια occurs some 135 times, συνήθης 243 times. Therefore it is with some surprise to find that neither word appears with any great frequency in Plutarch's discussions of friendship: συνήθεια 14 times and συνήθης 22 times. In spite of its scarcity in such a context, there is still enough evidence to show that the concept was an important one in the friendship relationship. Indeed the term often appears in conjunction, not only with φίλος, with which it is a synonym, but also with ὁμοιότης and related words. For example, in "Flatterer" (ch. 7 [52A]):

πρῶτον μὲν ὁρᾶν δεῖ τὴν ὁμαλότητα τῆς προαιρέσεως καὶ τὸ ἐνδελεχές, εἰ χαίρει τε τοῖς αὐτοῖς ἀεὶ καὶ ταὐτὰ ἐπαινεῖ καὶ πρὸς ἓν ἀπευθύνει καὶ καθίστησι παράδειγμα τὸν ἑαυτοῦ βίον, ὥσπερ ἐλευθέρῳ φιλίας ὁμοιοτρόπου καὶ συνηθείας ἐραστῇ προσήκει. τοιοῦτος γὰρ ὁ φίλος.

In the first place, it is necessary to observe the uniformity and permanence of his tastes, whether he always takes delight in the same things and commends the same things, and whether he directs and ordains his own life according to one pattern, as becomes a free-born man and a lover of congenial friendship and intimacy; for a friend is like this.

And in "Friends" (ch. 2 [93D]), while pointing out the disadvantages of having many friends, Plutarch says:

οὕτως ἕκαστον ἡμῶν διὰ τὸ φιλόκαινον καὶ ἀψίκορον ὁ πρόσφατος ἀεὶ καὶ ἀνθῶν ἐπάγεται, καὶ μετατίθησι πολλὰς ὁμοῦ καὶ ἀτελεῖς ἀρχὰς πράττοντας φιλίας καὶ συνηθείας, ἔρωτι τοῦ διωκωμένου παρερχομένους τὸ καταλαμβανόμενον.

Thus, because of our love of novelty and our fickleness the recent and blossoming friend always attracts, and changes our mind as we busy ourselves with many ineffectual beginnings of friendship and intimacy at the same time, since in our longing for the person we are pursuing, we pass over what is in our grasp.

And in the concluding chapter of his brief essay, "On Envy and Hate"[29] (ch. 8 [538E]), we read:

πολλοὺς ⟨γὰρ⟩ οἱ φθονοῦντες τῶν συνήθων καὶ οἰκείων ἀπολέσθαι μὲν οὐκ ἂν ἐθέλοιεν οὐδὲ δυστυχῆσαι, βαρύνονται δ' εὐτυχοῦντας·

for there are many of their intimates and connections that the envious would be unwilling to see destroyed or suffer misfortune, although tormented by their good fortune.

7. χάρις (which has been cited above in connection with other standard terms) is another important attribute of friendship. In particular it is often coupled with χρεία.[30] For example, in addition to "Flatterer," ch. 2 (49F)—quoted above (p. 114)—see especially ch. 5 (51B):

ὅτι δ' ἡ χάρις καὶ ἡ χρεία τῇ φιλίᾳ παρέπεται (καθ' ὃ δὴ καὶ λέλεκται πυρὸς καὶ ὕδατος ὁ φίλος ἀναγκαιότερος εἶναι), διὰ τοῦτο ἐμβάλλων εἰς τὰς ὑπουργίας ἑαυτὸν ὁ κόλαξ ἁμιλλᾶται σπουδαστικὸς ἀεὶ φαίνεσθαι καὶ ἄοκνος καὶ πρόθυμος.

And because graciousness and usefulness go with friendship (which is the reason why they say that a friend is more indispensable than fire and water), the flatterer thrusts himself into services for us, striving always to appear earnest, unremitting and diligent.

---

[29] According to Phillip De Lacy and Benedict Einarson, the Loeb translators, in this essay Plutarch used Aristotle's discussion of friendship in *Rhetoric* 2.4.1–29 (1380b34–1381b37); there are indeed many similiarities of thought in Aristotle's discussion of friendship and envy/hatred and that of Plutarch in Περὶ φθόνου καὶ μίσους ("On Envy and Hate").

[30] Of course one reason for the coupling of these two words, in addition to their meaning, may be the assonance that they produce.

As we have already seen, χάρις is also paired with ἡδονή ("Flatterer," ch. 2 [49F]). Moreover, in "Friends," ch.2 (93F) it appears with both εὔνοια and ἀρετή:

οὔτε γὰρ δούλους οὔτε φίλους ἔστι κτήσασθαι πολλοὺς ἀπ' ὀλίγου νομίσματος. τί οὖν νόμισμα φιλίας; εὔνοια καὶ χάρις μετ' ἀρετῆς, ὧν οὐδὲν ἔχει σπανιώτερον ἡ φύσις.

For it is impossible to acquire either many slaves or many friends with little coin. What then is the coin of friendship? It is goodwill and graciousness combined with virtue; Nature has nothing more rare than these.

8. ὠφέλιμος, along with χρεία and other words denoting the idea of utility, is another standard idea which is associated with the subject (it appears some 15 times in these treatises on friendship). For example, in "Flatterer" (ch. 5 [51C-D]):

ὥσπερ οἱ δεινοὶ τῶν ὀψοποιῶν τοῖς πικροῖς χυμοῖς καὶ αὐστηροῖς ἡδύσμασι χρῶνται, τῶν γλυκέων ἀφαιροῦντες τὸ πλήσμιον, οὕτως οἱ κόλακες οὐκ ἀληθινὴν οὐδ' ὠφέλιμον ἀλλ' οἷον ἐπιλλώπτουσαν ἐξ ὀφρύος καὶ γαργαλίζουσαν ἀτεχνῶς παρρησίαν προσφέρουσιν.

Just as clever cooks employ bitter extracts and astringent flavorings in order to remove the cloying effect of sweet things, so flatterers apply a frankness that is not genuine or beneficial, but which, so to speak, winks while it frowns, and does nothing but tickle.

Again, in "Flatterer" (ch. 11 [54F]):

... αἱ μὲν τῶν φίλων χάριτες ἐπὶ καλῷ τινι ὠφελίμῳ τὸ εὐφραῖνον ὥσπερ ἐπανθοῦν ἔχουσιν,

... the graciousness of friends, in addition to a certain goodness and utility, possesses also the power of giving pleasure as a sort of flowering.

And still in ch. 11 of "Flatterer" (55D) the word appears with several other standard terms:

ὥσπερ ἁρμονικὸς ὁ φίλος τῇ πρὸς καλὸν καὶ συμφέρον μεταβολῇ τὰ μὲν ἐνδιδοὺς ἃ δ' ἐπιτείνων πολλάκις μὲν ἡδὺς ἀεὶ δ' ὠφέλιμός ἐστιν. ὁ δὲ κόλαξ ἀφ' ἑνὸς διαγράμματος ἀεὶ τὸ ἡδὺ καὶ τὸ πρὸς χάριν εἰωθὼς ὑποκρέκειν οὔτ' ἔργον οἶδεν ἀντιτεῖνον οὔτε ῥῆμα λυποῦν, ἀλλὰ μόνῳ παρέπεται τῷ βουλομένῳ, συνᾴδων ἀεὶ καὶ συμφθεγ-γόμενος.

A friend, like a skilled musician, in effecting a transition to what is noble and beneficial now relaxes and now tightens a string, and so is often pleasant and always profitable, but the flatterer, being accustomed to play his accompaniment of pleasantness and graciousness in one key only, knows nothing either of acts of resistance or words that hurt, but is guided only by what the other person wants.

These, then, are a few of the terms which form the basis of many τόποι in friendship literature and in the compositions of a man who had read widely on the subject and compiled works that must be considered derivative at best. Yet the ideas which Plutarch has set forth represent the point of view of the man of letters in the second century AD of the Roman Empire.[31]

Plutarch also borrowed from predecessors numerous sayings and platitudes as well as other standard expressions about friendship. For example, one of these platitudes is expressed in this way: ἡ φιλία ἐστιν τὸ ἄλλον αὐτὸν ἡγεῖσθαι τὸν φίλον ("friendship is considering one's friend another self" ("Friends," ch.2 [93E]). Another platitude appears in "Flatterer" (ch. 24 [65A]): κοινὰ τὰ φίλων ("Friends' possessions are held in common").[32]

There are also numerous similies and metaphors that appear regularly in friendship literature, so numerous, however, that only a couple can be singled out.

There is, for instance, κολακεία = νόσημα in "Flatterer" (ch. 2 [49C-D]); and, as a counterbalance, in the same treatise, φιλία = ἰατρός (ch. 11[55A]).

---

[31] The frequent similariry between numerous passages in Plutarch's various compositions and Juvenal's *Satires* points up another fact about this Greek author. He is Greek mainly in his language. In his ideas, beliefs and observations he is a man of the Roman Empire of the second century AD. Many of his examples came from what he observed in the daily public and private life around him. Juvenal observed the same scenes and lashed out at those of which he disapproved. He was, after all, a satirist. Plutarch was no less disturbed by these events, but his gentler nature did not allow him to attack them quite so viciously.

[32] This saying appears elsewhere in Plutarch's writings. In "On Brotherly Love" (ch. 20 [490E]) Plutarch attributes it to Theophrastus, while in the essay "It is Impossible to Live Pleasantly by Following Epicurus" (ch. 22 [1102F]) he assigns the saying to the Cynic Diogenes. In short, it appears that by the time of Plutarch the saying was traditional, and anyone who used it simply attributed it to some apt predecessor, much as was done with chreiai and other traditional sayings.

In "Flatterer" (ch. 19 [61B]) a flatterer's παρρησία ("frankness") ἔοικε τοῖς τῶν ἀκολάστων δήγμασι γυναικῶν ("is like the love bites of lascivious women").

And in "Friends" ch. 2 (93C) ἡ τῆς πολυφιλίας ὄρεξις ("the appetite for many friends") is like an ὄρεξις ἀκολάστων γυναικῶν ("an appetite for lascivious women").

νόμισμα = φίλος is found in "Flatterer" (ch. 2 [49D-E]) and later (ch. 24 [65B]) there is νόμισμα παράσημον ("a counterfeit coin") = ὁ κόλαξ.

And finally, every study of friendship manages to include the "canon" of traditional pairs of friends (ζεύγεα φιλίας). Here is Plutarch's list which he gives in "Friends," ch. 2 (93E):

1. Theseus and Peirithoüs
2. Achilles and Patroclus
3. Orestes and Pylades
4. Phintias and Damon
5. Epameinondas and Pelopidas

To this list other pairs have been added by various writers, but this is Plutarch's list. There are some interesting points to these pairs: Only the last is certainly historical, and at least the first 3 pairs belong to the world of mythology. Then, as Stählin observes,[33] there seems to be a regular inequality between the members of each pair. Patroclus, for example, is by no means near to being the equal of Achilles; and Pylades, in the three so-called "Electra plays" (i.e. the *Choephori* of Aeschylus and the *Electra* of both Sophocles and Euripides), has only a single line to speak in Aeschylus' play. In the rest of that play and in the other two, he is always on stage when Orestes is, but his role is played by a mute. Dramatically, he is "excess baggage," but tradition was firm that Pylades simply must be at Orestes' side at all times.[34]

---

[33] *TDNT* 9.153.

[34] For some reason, Euripides chose to give Pylades a speaking part in the *Orestes*. Of course Euripides was a rebel of sorts and more often than not broke with tradition, thereby frequently earning the wrath of the Athenian people. The trouble here is that the *Orestes* may have been composed and produced earlier than his *Electra*, so if Euripides did break with tradition in the *Orestes*, he returned to the fold, so to speak, in his *Electra*.

One might make a case for the equality of Theseus and Peirithoüs, for the two heroes shared many dangers in several adventures, but by reputation at least the Athenian remains dominant over his Phocian partner.

Finally, all the characters on this list are from the world of the Greeks, for at this point in "Friends" Plutarch is, for whatever reason, limiting his discussion to Greek history.[35] As is readily apparent, however, from the discussion above, Plutarch often discusses Greek ideas of friendship but just as often has his eyes on Roman ideas. It is usually the theme of each composition that determines which aspect of friendship he considers.

Conclusion

There were basic differences between Greek and Roman views on friendship just as there were differences between many aspects Greek and Roman cultures in general, and Plutarch made use of both views in the *Moralia* as well as in the *Lives*. He often made use of the ideas of Greek writers while at the same time he recorded many of the conditions which he observed in Rome. Thus he represents both traditional Greek points of view and current Roman customs.

---

[35] So F. C. Babbitt in the *Loeb Classical Library*, 2.49.

POLITICAL FRIENDSHIP IN THE HISTORIAN DIONYSIUS OF HALICARNASSUS, *ROMAN ANTIQUITIES*

David L. Balch

Friendship in Dionysius is a political category, as in Cicero. I discuss four stories of relationships between "friends": *Ant. Rom.* 3 narrates war between Rome and its mother city, Alba. *Ant. Rom.* 6 describes internal civic conflict between patricians and plebeians, rich and poor. *Ant. Rom.* 7 records conflict between the plebeians and Coriolanus, the most sucessful commander of the Roman army. *Ant. Rom.* 8 analyzes conflicting views of friendship between Coriolanus and his mother, Veturia, with consequences for foreign affairs.

Many of the thousand instances of the root φιλ- in Dionysius[1] dramatically present diverse forms of love and the conflicts between them, for example, between love of family and country, alternative loves that force choices. I will narrate four friendship stories and the conflicts involved from the *Roman Antiquities*, books 3 (war between friends: Romans and Sabines), 6 (sedition among friends: patricians and plebeians), 7 (Coriolanus, lover of his country and hater of its poor plebeians?), and 8 (Coriolanus, a just enemy of former Roman friends?).[2]

---

[1] See Emilio Gabba, *Dionysius and the History of Archaic Rome* (Berkeley: University of California Press, 1991). I shall cite the text and translation of Dionysius, *Roman Antiquities*, by E. Cary (LCL; 7 vols.; Cambridge: Harvard University Press, 1937–50).

[2] For this paper I will not examine Dionysius' outline of Romulus' constitution instituting the patron-client relationship, for which he also employs friendship terminology (*Ant. Rom.* 2.8–11). See Emilio Gabba, "Studi su Dionigi da Alicarnasso: la costituzione de Romolo," *Athenaeum* 38/III–IV (1960) 175–225, esp. 181–84, 207–16.

War between Friends: Romans and Sabines (*Ant. Rom.* 3)

The first of Dionysius' four stories narrates an early conflict between friends, the Roman and Alban peoples; patriotic love of country, of Rome, is the primary value promoted in the story. A "converging narrative"[3] tells of the conflict of both peoples with the Veientes and Fidenates. The Alban king, Cluilius, Dionysius informs the reader, decided to go to war with Rome whose new king was Tullus. According to the treaty between them, neither was to begin a war, but if one complained of an injury, that city could demand satisfaction from the city doing the injury, and failing to obtain it, had the right to go to war (*Ant. Rom.* 3.3.1 [all the following references are also to book 3]; cf. Livy 1.22–26). The Sabines sent ambassadors to complain, but Tullus, suspecting this, had them entertained royally while he sent distinguished Romans to Alba to complain first. He then declared a "just war" (3.5), during which Cluilius died. Those who "were not influenced by either friendship or enmity"[4] considered his death the result neither of envy nor of despair, but of fate (5.2).

Fufetius was then chosen general by the Albans. During this war the Veientes and Fidenates decide to revolt and "were to regard neither side as friends, but whether the Romans or the Albans had won, were to slay the victors" (6.3). But some friends of the Roman

---

[3] Robert L. Brawley, *Centering on God: Method and Message in Luke-Acts* (Louisville: Westminster/John Knox, 1990) 65: a converging narrative integrates one elementary narrative into another as part of the narrative development.

[4] At the beginning of his *Histories*, Polybius both criticizes earlier historians and explains why he devotes such attention to the wars between Rome and Carthage: "Philinus will have it that the Carthaginians in every case acted wisely, well, and bravely, and the Romans otherwise, whilst Fabius takes the precisely opposite view. In other relations of life we should not perhaps exclude all such favouritism; for a good man should love his friends and his country, and he should share the hatreds and attachments of his friends; but he who assumes the character of a *historian* must ignore everything of the sort, and often, if their actions demand this, speak good of his enemies and honour them with the highest praises while criticizing and even reproaching roundly his closest friends, should the errors of their conduct impose this duty on him" (1.14.3–5, trans. Paton in LCL). Dionysius falls into the error of Fabius, always portraying Rome as right and just.

king in Fidenae informed him of the plot, and the Albans learned of it also, which made both willing to accommodate.

Fufetius and Tullus embrace, exchanging greetings usual among friends (7.1). Fufetius gives a speech urging that the banditry has been "trivial and petty and of too little consequence to dissolve so great a friendship and kinship" (7.3). In a second speech, the Alban general sets forth two alternatives:

> I hold that mutual reconciliation (διαλλαγὰς) is the best and the most becoming to kinsmen and friends (φίλοις), in which there is no rancour nor remembrance of past injuries, but a general and sincere remission of everything (ἀφέσεως ἅπασι πρὸς ἅπαντας) that has been done or suffered on both sides; less honourable than this form of reconciliation is one by which, indeed, the mass of the people are absolved of blame, but those who have injured one another are compelled to undergo such a trial as reason and law direct. Of these two methods of reconciliation, now, it is my opinion that we ought to choose the one which is the more honourable and magnanimous, and we ought to pass a decree of general amnesty. (8.4–5)[5]

He proposes settling "our mutual hatreds."

Tullus responds by agreeing to the reconciliation, "forgiving every injury and offense" (πᾶν ἀδίκημα καὶ πᾶν ἁμάρτημα ... ἀφιέντες; 9.2). But he wants not only to prevent war, the present enmity, but to be friends now and for all time. The Albans should cease to envy the Romans. "You hate us for this reason alone, that we seem to be better off than you." And the Romans suspect the Albans of plotting against them and regard them as enemies, "for no one can be a firm friend to one who distrusts him" (9.4) even if one puts it into a treaty and swears over sacrificial victims. Therefore, Tullus places the advantages of the Romans at the disposal of the Albans, who are then to move to Rome and live in the same city. "We shall then be lasting friends; whereas, so long as we inhabit two cities of equal eminence, . . . there never will be harmony between us" (9.7).

Fufetius rejects this proposal, and the two then debate about which city deserves to rule the other (10–11). They discuss again how to settle the dispute, the Roman wanting to decide the matter

---

[5] Cilliers Breytenbach, *Versöhnung: Eine Studie zur paulinischen Soteriologie* (WMANT 60; Neukirchen-Vluyn: Neukirchener Verlag, 1989) 57 n. 37, cites this passage.

in a David and Goliath manner by single combatants, the Alban by three men on each side. Divine providence, however, had prepared six cousins. Twin daughters of an Alban had married, one to Horatius a Roman, and the other to Curiatius an Alban; each sister became pregnant and bore triplets at the same time (13.4). Fufetius suggests that these cousins, who "love one another" (ἀλλήλους ... φιλοῦσιν; 15.2)[6] no less than their own brothers, fight for their countries. Tullus asks the Horatii whether they are willing to give their lives for their country (τὰ σώματα τῇ πατρίδι; 16.2), whether they rate their country more highly than kinship (16.3). They dutifully ask their father, affirming to him that "if the Curiatti esteem kinship less than honour, the Horatii also will not value the ties of blood more highly than valour" (17.5). Dionysius draws out the pathetic story of the subsequent conflict (18–20), but finally one Roman is victorious. The Roman people stream out to him; his sister, too, "overpowered by love" (ἔρωτι) deserts her household tasks (21.3; cf. 8.44.2). At this point the reader learns that she had been engaged to one of the Alban cousins killed by her brother. She tears her clothes, beats her breast, laments, and calls her brother a wild beast. He responds claiming to be a citizen "who loves his country (φιλοῦντος ... τὴν πατρίδα) and punishes those who wish her ill (21.6). Calling her a pretender to virginity, a hater of her brothers, a disgrace to her ancestors, one who dishonors her father and her brothers, he kills her. The father does not permit her to be buried and that night gives a splendid banquet to celebrate victory.[7]

The story of the Fidenates' revolt converges with that of the Roman-Sabine war, but I break off my retelling. The story enables several conclusions about political "friendship" in the Greco-Roman world. Unless there is equality, one city will envy the other, and the second will be suspicious of revolt. Other cities either go to war with or they submit to their "friends" the Romans.[8]

---

[6] Compare the language and contrast the thought of 1 John 2:10.

[7] "The Oath of the Horatii" painted in 1784 by Jacques Louis David, regarded by many as foreshadowing the French revolution, hangs in the Louvre.

[8] Cf. Peter Marshall, *Enmity in Corinth: Social Conventions in Paul's Relations with the Corinthians* (WUNT 2.23; Tübingen: J.C.B. Mohr [Paul Siebeck], 1987) 36, quotes L. Pearson: "the sharp distinction of friend and enemy as though the relation of enmity

When war between friends does occur, there is a moralistic concern to blame one's enemy and declare oneself "just." Acceptance of submission and friendship with the Romans may include being forced to give up ancestral homes and emigrating. The Romans are willing to forgive everything—if others submit. Love of Rome is the supreme value in this story, more valuable than family ties to uncles, aunts, cousins, brothers,[9] or to a sister, and a Roman father approves this hierarchy of values. A sister's rejection of this ethic motivates her brother to protect the family honor by killing her. Roman mothers appear only as those who bear soldiers. This is not the kingdom of God but of Patriotism.

Sedition among Friends: Patricians and Plebeians (*Ant. Rom.* 6)[10]

The second of Dionysius' stories that I retell concerns the first sedition (*Ant. Rom.* 6.22–92; cf. Livy 2.21–25), and it narrates conflict between "friends" within the state rather than primarily with foreign enemies. [All the following references are to book 6.] There is civil strife in Rome (22.1), so one of the consuls, Appius Claudius, diverts attention to a war with the Volscians (23.1). Altercations, quarrels (φιλονεικίες; 24.3; 28.1) continue, intensified by the appearance in the Forum of an old soldier (26.1). He was born free, had fought in twenty-eight battles, was often awarded prizes for valor, but had been forced to contract a debt and was

---

was natural and permanent, is a remarkable feature of Greek literature."

[9] Cf. the story of the seven brothers and their mother in 4 Maccabees and Hans-Josef Klauck, "Brotherly Love in Plutarch and in 4 Maccabees," *Greeks, Romans, and Christians: Essays in Honor of Abraham J. Malherbe* (ed. David L. Balch, Everett Ferguson, and Wayne A. Meeks; Minneapolis: Fortress, 1990) 144–56. Some stories present friendship as more important than public order; cf. Lucian, *Toxaris* 12–18, a tale discussed by David Konstan, "Friends and Lovers in Ancient Greece," *Syllecta Classica* 4 (1993) 1–12. Cf. nn. 32 and 34 below, but contrast Luke 14:26 and 20:34–35, where being Christ's disciple is more important than family (father, mother, wife, children, brothers, sisters) or one's own life. See David L. Balch and Carolyn Osiek, *Families in the New Testament World* (Louisville: Westminster/John Knox, forthcoming).

[10] See the reflections in Cicero, *Amic.* 13.46. Cf. *Social Struggles in Archaic Rome: New Perspectives on the Conflict of the Orders* (ed. Kurt A. Raaflaub; Berkeley: University of California, 1986). See also G. E. M. de Ste. Croix, *The Class Struggle in the Ancient Greek World from the Archaic Age to the Arab Conquests* (Ithaca: Cornell University Press, 1981).

then carried away as a slave by a money-lender and lashed with a whip. When he showed his wounds, the Forum was filled with other such debtors (26.2-3).

A speaker recognizes that Rome cannot give security to its friends and generate fear in its enemies in this state of discord (35.2):

> For we are living apart from one another . . . and inhabit two cities, one of which is ruled by poverty (πενίας) and necessity, and the other by satiety and insolence; but modesty, order and justice, by which alone any civil community is preserved (πολιτικὴ κοινωνία σώζεται), remain in neither of these cities. For this reason we already exact justice from one another by force and make superior strength the measure of that justice, like wild beasts choosing rather to destroy our enemy though we perish with him, than, by consulting our own safety, to be preserved together with our adversary (36.1).

In this situation the senate appoints Manius Valerius, a great friend of the people (φιλοδημοτάτος; 40.3; 71.2), dictator, and he advises them to turn their anger from their friends to their enemies, for the power of Rome, weakened by sedition, is superior to any other when there is harmony (41.1). The plebs should take revenge on its foreign enemies; then the senate will reward them by settling the controversies (φιλονεικίας) concerning their debts (41.2), although the senate fears that the poor (οἱ ἄποροι) will demand the fulfillment of these promises (43.1). It is the task of good men in the senate to promote peace and friendship in the city (47.4).

One of the moderates among them, Agrippa Menenius, urges the senate to a reconciliation (49.2). The Roman army within the walls consists of plebeians—laborers, clients, and artisans[11]—not trustworthy guardians for the tottering aristocracy (51.1) in a situation where poverty revolts against wealth, the humble against the eminent, who act arrogantly, as in nearly all states (54.1). Menenius asks the senate:

---

[11] *Ant. Rom.* 7.58.3 names them small farmers and the poor, who spend the seven days between markets in the country. They participate politically according to property rating (7.59.3-6). Coriolanus later vilifies them as the working class and vagabonds, haters of the virtuous (8.6.2-3).

will you who spare your [foreign] enemies make war upon your friends? ... Will you, who offer your own city as a safe refuge for all who stand in need of it, bring yourselves to drive out of that city the natives with whom you have been reared and educated ... ? (6.55.3)

The ailing part of the body ought not to be cut off (54.2; cf. esp. 86.1). The people hear words from the senate, but see no act of kindness (φιλάνθρωπον; 56.3),[12] and those of humble condition love to be enraged against those who treat them haughtily (56.5).

Appius Claudius, an enemy of the people (μισόδημον; 58.3; 60.1) who sets great value upon himself (ἀνὴρ μέγα φρονῶν ἐφ' ἑαυτῷ; 59.1),[13] responds denying that he has enslaved any for their debts or deprived any of their country by his avarice (φιλοχρηματία; 59.3). Rather, none of those who defrauded him were enslaved or disenfranchised, but all are free and grateful (χάρις), his friends and clients. Claudius refers sarcastically to Menenius as a "lover of his country" (φιλοπόλιδος; 60.3) who promotes the worst government, democracy. Dionysius writes ironically; Claudius speaks more truth than he realizes. The consul considers granting an abolition of debts (ἄφεσιν ... χαρισώμεθα τῶν χρεῶν) not to all collectively, to enemies, but to his friends individually, who would understand him to be bestowing favors, not by compulsion but by persuasion (χάριτας; 63.3). In this conflict the younger senators claim that they are not contending (φιλονεικεῖν) with the older ones, but are of one mind (66.1; 69.2).

They finally send Manius Valerius, a great friend of the people, to urge reconciliation, but Sicinius, a leader of the poor and humble (45.2-3), wants to know the terms of justice and humanity (φιλανθρώποις) on which the senate proposes this reconciliation (73.1; 78.1; 83.3). They do not want promises, but ask what kind of friendship and good faith is being offered (78.4); later,

---

[12] B. Fiore, "The Theory and Practice of Friendship in Cicero" (chap. 3 above), observes that Stoics find *philia* to be part of *philanthrōpia*, a species of the genus, sought for itself and not for self-interest (Marcus Aurelius 7.13.55). The term never occurs in the books translated from Hebrew into the Greek Bible (LXX) nor in the New Testament gospels or epistles; however, it is emphasized at the close of Acts (27:3; 28:2). See Otto Hiltbrunner, "Warum Wollten Sie Nicht ΦΙΛΑΝΘΡΩΠΟΙ Heissen?" *JAC* 33 (1990) 7-20: "philanthropy" was the hated slogan of those who violently introduced Greek customs into Judaism (cf. e.g. 2 Macc 6:20).

[13] Cf. *Ant. Rom.* 7.34.1; 8.1.4; and Paul's epistle, Rom 12:3.

accusations, jealousies, hatreds, and struggles may ensue (78.4) since the senators are not willing to cure the causes of the sedition (83.3), harsh exaction of debts.

One of the plebeians, Lucius Junius Brutus, says the senate offers them no honors, no magistracies, no relief of their poverty (ἀπορίας; 78.1). They are being driven out of Rome by their friends (80.2), since the senators are "unwilling to associate as fellow-citizens and to share their blessings with those of humbler estate" (ἀπολίτευτα καὶ ἀκοινώνητα πρὸς τοὺς ταπεινοτέρους φρονοῦντες; 80.4; cf. 7.65.1).

New Roman officials, tribunes, including Brutus, are then appointed to protect the plebeians. And Agrippa Menenius gives his famous speech in which he employs the "myth" describing the state as a human body consisting of many parts (83.2; 86.1). He also proposes that debts be forgiven (πάντας ἀφεῖσθαι τῶν ὀφλημάτων)[14] and that debtors in prison be freed (83.4). After the tribunes are appointed and Menenius has spoken, the people are willing to go to war and defeat the Volscians.

This story narrates conflict between the patricians and plebeians in Rome. Some in each class are unwilling to compromise with the other social group: the aristocrat Appius Claudius hates the people, and the plebeian Sicinius likewise opposes reconciliation with the senate (82.1–3). An old soldier, a poor plebeian who has been enslaved and imprisoned for his debts (26), is a contrast to the consul and general, Appius Claudius, who hates the people (58.3). The two social groups inhabit the same city like wild beasts, without community. But in their speeches some moderates on both sides propose compromise. Menenius chides the senate about their treatment of the humble poor. The plebeian Brutus, speaking to the ambassadors from the senate, asks what the new terms of friendship will be and demands magistrates for protection. In response Menenius does propose new officials to protect the people, tribunes, and agrees to the cancellation of their debts.

---

[14] Cf. *Ant. Rom.* 6.23.3; 6.81.3; 7.8.1 and the Lord's Prayer (Luke 11:4). See David L. Balch, "Rich and Poor, Proud and Humble in Luke-Acts," *The Social World of the First Christians: Essays in Honor of Wayne A. Meeks* (ed. L. Michael White and O. Larry Yarbrough; Minneapolis: Fortress, 1995) 214–33.

Dionysius writes of desperate poverty, of plebeians driven into exile, of the intransigence of the rich, and the potential for violence. He stresses how close society is to a breakdown of the social order, yet one of Dionysius' major theses is that, unlike the Greeks, the Romans avoid chaos.[15] Instead of the evils of Greece, actions in Rome are not "beyond remedy" (ἀνήκεστον); in Rome there is a different and surprising outcome, harmony (ὁμόνοια). Rich and poor, eminent and humble, different social classes, listen to each others' speeches (cf. esp. 7.66.3, 5) and accept being parts of one body, friends.

Coriolanus, Lover of his Country and Hater of its Poor Plebeians? (*Ant. Rom.* 7)[16]

Gaius Marcius, surnamed Coriolanus, "became the most illustrious man of his age" (*Ant. Rom.* 6.94.2), so Dionysius begins the story. He concludes by observing that both the Romans and their enemies, the Volscians, mourned his death for a year. "And though nearly five hundred years have already elapsed since his death down to the present time, his memory has not become extinct, but he is still praised and celebrated by all as a pious and just man" (8.62.3). Nevertheless, this lover of his country falls from eminence because he hates the poor and humble. The Coriolanus story fills two of Dionysius' books (6.92–8.62; cf. Livy 2.33–35), taking vastly disproportionate space within his history of archaic Rome. Schultze characterizes it as "virtually Dionysius' history in miniature, having an episode of every important type except a major battle."[17] It was conceived as an independent entity and includes numerous reflections on second- and first-century

---

[15] Clemence Elizabeth Schultze, "Dionysius of Halicarnassus as a Historian: An Investigation of his Aims and Methods in the *Antiquitates Romanae*" (Ph.D. Dissertation, Oxford University, 1980) 48, 168, 175, 181, 221, and esp. chap. 10 on Dionysius' narrative and Rome. Cf. Schultze, "Dionysius of Halicarnassus and His Audience," *Past Perspectives: Studies in Greek and Roman Historical Writings* (ed. I. S. Moxon *et al.*; Cambridge: Cambridge University Press, 1986) 1–41.

[16] See Eralda Noè, "Ricerche su Dionigi d'Alicarnasso: la prima stasis a Roma e l'episodio de Coriolano," *Ricerche de storiografia Greca di età Romana* (ed. Emilio Gabba; Ricerche di storiografia antica I; Pisa: Giardini Editori e Stampatori, 1979) 21–116.

[17] Schultze, "Dionysius of Halicarnassus as a Historian," 216.

phenomena and issues, e.g. the corn shortage. It is centrally concerned with justice in society and the apportionment of rights, responsibilities, and accountability.[18] I will cite a few passages that show how Dionysius portrays this friendship between patricians and plebeians.

The mother city of the Volscians was defeated. Marcius distinguished himself in these battles, but refused any booty, for which he was known as Coriolanus (6.92.3–93.3). Intense rivalry continues between the aristocracy and the people (*Ant. Rom.* 7.4.4 [the following references are all to book 7]). The tribune Brutus stirs up the people because of the dearth of corn, but he is opposed by Appius (15). The senate does not find acceptable (φίλον) anything the people determine, but their mutual hatred (τὸ μῖσος αὐτῶν) does not lead to irreparable mischief (ἀνήκεστον; 18.1).[19] Some of the more arrogant oligarchs, including Coriolanus and his large group of clients (21.3), seek to oppress the plebeians, whom they hate (μισεῖν τοὺς δημοτικούς; 21.1), by making corn as costly as possible (20.4), and they speak against letting the power of the new magistrates, the tribunes, grow (22.1; 23.4). Later the tribunes inveigh against Marcius and demand that he defend himself (27.1–2), despite which the senate is inclined to humane (φιλανθρωπότερα) rather than to stubborn opinions (27.3).

Minucius, the elder consul, tells the people that Marcius/ Coriolanus is a lover of his country (φιλόπολις; 30.1) and pleads:

> His speech has done you no harm, whereas his actions have done you great service.... Be reconciled to us and cause the commonwealth to be united as it was in the beginning. But if you do not yield to our persuasions, be assured that we shall not yield to your violence either; but this testing (πεῖρα) of the populace will be either the source of a sincere friendship (φιλότητος ἀδόλου) and of still greater benefits for all, or the fresh beginning of civil war and irreparable evils (32.3).

The plebeians were moved by the humanity of this speech (33.1), but Coriolanus himself in a proud, arrogant, contemptuous spirit reprimands the people with the wrath of an enemy (ἐχθροῦ;

---

[18] Ibid., 221.

[19] Contrast *Ant. Rom.* 2.11 on Gaius Gracchus.

34.2–5). The college of tribunes condemn him to death (35.3), following which there is a riot.

Decius, who had persuaded the senate to pass a decree for the trial of Coriolanus, accuses him of trying to dissolve the bonds between the senate and the people, which are unlawful to loose as long as the city is inhabited (44.1). "Giving to the liberty of the poor (πενήτων) the name of insolence, and to equality that of tyranny, he [Marcius] advised you to deprive us of them" (44.2). But if the poor lack the necessities of life, they will either leave the city and perish or, calling on the divinities to witness their sufferings, attack those who keep the price of corn high, no longer regarding them as friends (44.3–4). He advises Coriolanus to descend from his haughtiness (ὑπερηφάνων),[20] to assume the humble and piteous demeanour (σχῆμα ταπεινὸν καὶ ἐλεεινόν) of one who has erred (ἡμαρτηκότος) and is asking pardon (45.4; cf. 63.1).

> For if you will learn from the example (παραδείγμασι) afforded by Marcius and from history . . . , you will know that tyranny fostered against the people is fostered against the whole commonwealth, and that, though it begins at present with us, yet after it has gained strength it will not spare you either (46.6).

Appius Claudius, again named the greatest enemy of the plebeians (μισοδημότατος; 47.2), defends Coriolanus as one who did not exclude from humanity (φιλανθρωπία) even enemies who had fled to Rome for refuge (53.3). And Appius threatens the plebeians that, if they do not acquit Marcius, the senators will invite their slaves to liberty, their enemies to friendship, and all mankind to their hopes of victory (53.6).

Then even Manius Valerius advises the patricians to bring their clients and friends, as well as plebeians attached to them by benefits, for which they would show gratitude, to defend Marcius, for there are many in the people who love right and hate wrong and know how to feel compassion (ἐλεεῖν) for men in honorable positions when their fate has been reversed (54.3–4). But most of Valerius' speech is addressed to Coriolanus himself,

---

[20] Cf. Cic. Amic. 20.71.

in which he joined exhortation to admonition (παράκλησιν ἔχων νουθετήσει) ... that he would not make true and valid the accusations against himself by persevering in his invidious way of life, but would change it to an humble deportment (σχῆμα ταπεινὸν μεταλαβεῖν) .... (54.5)[21]

This is the way to unity and harmony (55.2).

Finally the vote comes, "the first time the Romans ever met in their tribal assembly to give their votes against a man" (59.2; cf. 65.1). After the first hundred and ninety-two centuries split their votes, the decision came down to the last century consisting of the poorest citizens (ἀπορωτάτων; 59.8), to whom Minucius speaks:

> First, he reminded the populace of all the benefits (εὐεργεσίας) they had received from the patricians; and next he asked that in return for so many good offices they should grant at their request one necessary favor (χάριν) in the interest of the public welfare. In addition to this he praised harmony and peace .... (60.1-2; cf. 62.2).

They should acquit Marcius. Marcius himself speaks, rending his garments to show his body full of wounds received in battles for Rome (62.3).

Decius responds, charging Marcius with taking the spoils of war and distributing them, not to the commons, but to his own friends (63.3). The vote is for Marcius' perpetual banishment (64.6).

Dionysius then approves of the people's rising to power and the patricians sharing (κοινωσαμένη) their prerogatives with all the citizens (65.1), except when avaricious men (φιλοκερδεῖς) gain power as tribunes and destroy others, not the case when good men become protectors of the people (65.5).[22] Marcius goes into exile, not showing signs of tenderness (φιλοφρονησάμενος) to his mother, wife, or children (67.3; cf. 8.41.6).

Dionysius' paradigmatic story of Coriolanus, the greatest soldier and general of his age whose aristocratic values nevertheless led

---

[21] In the New Testament see Luke 1:51-52 and Phil 2:6-8.

[22] Astoundingly, just after narrating how the plebeians for the *first* time had tried and condemned a patrician (7.59.2), Dionysius inserts a long excursus claiming that the Romans have never made any innovations in their institutions (7.70-73)! For other examples of this paradox, see my article on "The Greek Political Topos Περὶ νόμων and Matthew 5:17, 19, and 16:19," in *Social History of the Matthean Community: Cross-Disciplinary Approaches* (ed. David L. Balch; Minneapolis: Fortress, 1991) 68-84.

him to hate the plebeians, prefers the harmony of the state to the honor of this brilliant, successful tyrant. Plebeians bring this haughty "lover of his country" to trial and banish him for denying the poor the necessities of life by keeping the price of corn high. Neither the threats of the patricians and their clients nor Marcius' exhibiting the wounds he received in many battles persuades them to acquit him. The senate was fittingly forced to "share" their power with all the citizens. Tyranny against the poor, it is *persuasively argued* (cf. 46.6 and again, 66.3, 5), ultimately destroys the whole commonwealth.

Coriolanus, a Just Enemy of Former Roman Friends? (*Ant. Rom.* 8)[23]

Marcius Coriolanus, wanting to avenge himself on his enemies (*Ant. Rom.* 8.1.2 [all the following references are to book 8]), goes to Tullus Attius in Antium, the chief city of the Volscians, and becomes his suppliant, asking him not to use his strength against the humbled (τεταπεινωμένους):

> For though I was once looked upon as the most powerful of all men in the greatest city, I am now cast aside, forsaken, exiled, and abased [humble], and destined to suffer any treatment you, who are my enemy, shall think fit to inflict upon me. But I promise you that I will perform as great services for the Volscians, if I become their friend (φίλος), as I occasioned calamities to them when I was their enemy (ἐχθρός; 1.5-6).

Marcius asks the Volscians what kind of man he should be if, driven from country, family, friends, the gods and sepulchers of his ancestors, and if

> finding all these things among you against whom I made war for their sake, I should not become harsh toward those whom I have found enemies instead of fellow citizens, and helpful to those whom I have found friends instead of enemies? .... I regard as my fatherland not that state which has renounced me, but the one of which I, as an alien, have become a citizen; and as a friendly land, not the one in which I have been wronged, but that in which I find safety (7.1).

---

[23] Cf. the parallel treatment in Cicero, *Amic.* 11.36; Livy 2.36-40; and P. A. Brunt, "'*Amicitia*' in the Late Roman Republic," *PCPhS* n.s. 11 (1965) 1-20, at p. 12.

He charges that Rome deludes the Volscians with the hope of friendship (7.3), so he seeks to counteract their designs (7.3). Having decided on war, the Volscians send ambassadors to Rome saying

> they should be friends and allies without fraud or deceit. And they declared that it would be a sure pledge of friendship if they received back the lands and the cities which had been taken from them by the Romans; otherwise there would be neither peace nor secure friendship between them (9.3).

The Romans recognize that they want war, not friendship (10.1). With a Volscian army Coriolanus attacks several cities, and the Latin League sends to Rome to ask for assistance. The Roman senate then gives the Latins permission to enroll their own army and to send out their own generals in command, both of which had been forbidden by the treaty of friendship between them (15.2). After losing several cities, the senate sends its oldest members, who were Marcius' closest friends, to ask for reconciliation and friendship (22.4). Marcus Minucius, who had been most opposed to the plebeians, both persuades and accuses Marcius:

> Common to the nature of all men is this law—that the injured party is an enemy to the aggressor. But that you . . . class together the innocent with the guilty and friends with enemies, that you violate the inviolable laws of Nature, confound the duties of religion, and, even as to yourself, no longer remember from whom you are sprung and what sort of man you are—that has seemed strange to us (23.2).

> I should have refused to believe that a man who has the least regard for virtue would either destroy his friends along with his enemies or show himself harsh and inexorable in his anger . . . . (25.2).

> While your power is greatest and heaven still assists you, we advise you to act with moderation and to husband your good fortune, bearing in mind that all things are subject to change and that nothing is apt to continue long in the same state. All things that wax too great when they reach the peak of eminence, incur the displeasure of the gods and are brought to naught (εἰς τὸ μηδέν) again. And this is the fate which comes especially to stubborn and haughty spirits and those that overstep the bounds of human nature (25.3; cf. 33.3).

Dionysius of Halicarnasus 137

> Come now, if you do succeed, . . . it will be your fate to be deprived of those who are dearest (φιλτάτων)[24] and nearest of kin to you—of an unhappy mother, . . . of a faithful wife, . . . of two sons (28.1).

> [You will be] destitute of friends and living in a foreign land (28.4).

Marcius replies:

> To you Minucius . . . I am a friend . . . . [You] assisted me in times of need, but also after my banishment you did not turn from me in contempt of my then unhappy fate, as if I were no longer able either to serve my friends or to hurt my enemies, but you continued to show yourselves good and staunch friends by taking care of my mother, my wife and my children, and alleviating their misfortune by your personal attentions.[25] But to the rest of the Romans I am as hostile as I can be and am at war with them, and I shall never cease to hate them (29.1-2; cf. 3.11.9).

> For you, Romans, on whose account I was an enemy to these men, deprived me of all my possessions, and making a nobody (τὸ μηδέν) of me, cast me off; while they, who had suffered those dire evils at my hands, received me into their cities, the resourceless, homeless, humbled outcast (ταπεινὸν . . . ὑπεδέξαντο; 32.3).

> Who would not praise me on hearing that when I found my friends, from whom I had the right to expect kindness, to be my enemies, and my foes, by whom I should have been put to death, to be my friends,

---

[24] David Konstan, "Greek Friendship," *AJP* 117 (1996) 72–73, argues that "in Greek usage of the classical period and later, just as in English today, kin . . . were not normally spoken of as friends or *philoi*, and that the two categories were in fact distinct and, in general, exclusive," so he too translates such adjectives by "dear." However, K. Treu, "Freundschaft," *RAC* 8 (1972) 418–34 at col. 421 cites Plutarch, *Amatorius,* as different from the earlier erotics. In this work Protogenes praises pederasty because it includes friendship (750D), but denounces the housebound love of women as devoid of it (ἄφιλοι; 751B). Daphnaeus argues the contrary, that love between men and women is natural and conducive to friendship (751CD). Plutarch himself (766D–771C, esp. 769A,CD, and also 767E, 768E, 770AB) argues against older views of friendship with boys and men that a wife is a suitable, more graceful, pleasurable, continuous and constant friend (cf. also 752C, 756E, 757C–E, 758C). Plutarch illustrates Paul Veyne's thesis (*A History of Private Life* (ed. Veyne; [Cambridge: Harvard University Press, 1987] 36–37, 42–45) that there was a domestication of morals in the early empire (see the review article by Averil Cameron in *JRS* 76 [1986] 266–71). Therefore, instead of "dearest" in the above text of Dionysius, I would translate with a stronger superlative, "most beloved."

[25] Cf. Cic. *Amic.* 15.53 and 17.64.

instead of hating (μισεῖν) those who hate me and loving (φιλεῖν) those who love me, I took the opposite view! (32.5; cf. 34.1 and 50.3)

When you call those still my friends, Minucius, who banished me and that nation my country which has renounced me, when you appeal to the laws of Nature and discuss the obligations of religion, you seem to me to be ignorant of the most common facts, . . . namely, that a friend or an enemy is not determined either by the lineaments of a face or by the giving of a name, but both are made manifest by their services and by their deeds, and that we all love those who do us good and hate those who do us harm. . . . For this reason we renounce our friends when they injure us and make friends of our enemies when some kindly service (χάρις) is done for us by them; and we cherish the country that gave us birth when it helps us, but abandon it when it harms us, since our affection (ἀγαπῶντες) is based, not on the place, but on the benefit it confers. These are the sentiments, not merely of individual persons in private life, but of whole cities and nations . . . . I, therefore, . . . am doing what is just, advantageous and honourable, and at the same time what is most holy in the eyes of the gods (34.1-3).

Still, if Rome will enter into a pledge of perpetual friendship with the Volscians and give them equal rights of citizenship, he will end the war. Although the Romans could be just, they hazard all by their continual fondness for the possessions of others (φιλοχωροῦντες τοῖς ἀλλοτρίοις; 35.4; cf. 47.3).

In this crisis Valeria, sister of Publicola, one of the men who freed the commonwealth from the kings, moved by divine inspiration, called the other wives, comforted and encouraged them, and asked, "What can we women do to save our country when the men have given it up for lost?" (39.3) She suggests going to the house of Veturia,[26] mother of Marcius, and entreating her with tears to have compassion on their children and their country,

---

[26] On these names, especially of the women, see D. A. Russell, "Plutarch's Life of Coriolanus," *JRS* 53 (1963) 21–28, at p. 22, and *Plutarcho vite parallele: Coriolano e Alcibiade* (ed. Maria Cesa, Lucia Maria Raffaelli, Luisa Prandi, and John Denton; Milan: Biblioteca Universale Rizzoli, 1992). Dionysius compares these women to those who "by their own intercession put an end to the war that had arisen between Romulus and the Sabines and by bringing together both the commanders and the nations made this city great from a small beginning" (40.4; cf. 2.38–40 and 45–46). For another Greco-Roman historian who stresses the noble acts of women, see Kenneth S. Sacks, *Diodorus Siculus and the First Century* (Princeton: Princeton University Press, 1990) 30, 76.

to become the suppliant of her son and ask him not to harm his country (39.4–5). They go to the house of Veturia and of Volumnia, Marcius' wife, who asks why they are so distressed and humble. Veturia replies asking her, if there remains in her a gentle and humane spirit (ψυχῆς ... φιλανθρώπου) to have mercy (ἐλέησον) on women who shared the same sacrifices and rites and, taking Volumnia and her children, to go to Marcius, "asking of him this one favour in return for many (μίαν ἀντὶ πολλῶν χάριν)," to make peace and return to his country (40.3). Veturia thinks that there is little hope, for Marcius "has hated his whole family together with his country" (41.2). She reports that after his banishment, despite being a lover of his country as he claimed, he had returned home and said:

> No longer shall Marcius be your son henceforth, mother, but our country has deprived you of the support of your old age; nor shall he be your husband, Volumnia, from this day, but may you be happy with another husband more fortunate than I; nor shall he be your father, dearest children (ὦ τέκνα φίλτατα, πατήρ), but orphans and forsaken, you will be reared by these women till you come to manhood (41.4).

She continues, asking:

> Tell me and instruct me. Shall I exhort (παρακαλῶ) him to spare his fellow citizens, by whom he was exiled ...? To be merciful and compassionate to the plebeians, from whom he received neither mercy nor compassion (οὔτ' ἐλέου μετέσχεν οὔτε συμπαθείας)? Or perhaps to abandon and betray those who received him when an exile, and notwithstanding the many calamities he had previously inflicted on them, showed to him, not the hatred of enemies, but the affection of friends and relations? What courage can I pluck up to ask my son to love those who have ruined him (τὰ μὲν ἀπολέσαντα φιλεῖν) and to injure those who have preserved him? ... nor ought you either, women, to compel us to ask of him things that are neither just in the sight of men nor right in the eyes of the gods, but permit us miserable women to lie abased (ταπεινάς) as we have been cast down by Fortune, committing no further unseemly act (42.1–2).

However, she does go to Marcius, all the women connected by friendship or kinship accompanying her, and he lays aside the symbols of his office, so great is his reverence and veneration for the ties of kinship (44.4). Seeing his mother's rent garments of mourning, tears, and pitiable condition, his hard-hearted sternness is melted by his emotions into human kindness (ὑπὸ τῶν παθῶν ἐπὶ τὸ ἀνθρώπινον), so he weeps, embraces his mother, wife, and children, asking her why she has come (45.2).[27] She explains, and he at first rejects her request, asking her to look "upon my friends and enemies as your own" (47.4).

Then she gives a remarkable speech (48–53) to her "dear and only son" (τὸν ἀγαπητὸν καὶ μόνον υἱόν; 48.1). She employs several maxims (παιδεύματα ... λόγων), one of which is that "it is the part of wise men, when they seem to be prosperous, to husband their good fortune, but when their fortunes become low [humble] and paltry, to submit to nothing that is ignoble" (48.4). She asks him whether by his many fine returns to the Volscians he has not by the nearly limitless favors (χαρίτων) he has bestowed surpassed the kindnesses (εὐεργεσίας) he received from them (49.2)?[28] She appeals to the example (παράδειγμα) of Tarquinius, who freed his fellow citizens from tyrants, but was later accused and banished; he did not resent this, but continued loyal to his country and its friend (49.6).[29]

> Conceding the point nevertheless, and granting the right to all who have suffered grievously not to distinguish whether those who have injured them are friends or aliens (εἴτε φίλιον ... εἴτε ἀλλότριον), but to direct their anger against all impartially, even so have you not taken a sufficient revenge on such as abused you, now that you have turned their best land into a sheep-walk.... But you carry your wild and mad resentment even to the point of enslaving them and razing their city; and you showed no regard even for the envoys sent to you by the senate, men of worth and your friends.... For my part, I cannot commend these harsh and overbearing claims, which overstep the bounds of human nature, when I observe that a refuge for all men and the means of securing forgiveness for their offenses one against another (παραιτήσεις ὧν ἂν ἐξαμαρτάνωσι περὶ ἀλλήλους) have been devised in the form of suppliant boughs and prayers, by which all

---

[27] Cf. Judith P. Hallett, *Fathers and Daughters in Roman Society: Women and the Elite Family* (Princeton: Princeton University Press, 1984) 41 n. 8, who accepts the (ironic) interpretation of Coriolanus as the Roman archetype of the perpetual momma's boy.

[28] On giving more in return than one was originally given, see A. R. Hands, *Charities and Social Aid in Greece and Rome* (Ithaca: Cornell University Press, 1968) chap. 4.

[29] Cf. the similar value in Cic. *Amic.* 12.42.

anger is softened and instead of hating one's enemy one pities him (ἀντὶ τοῦ μισεῖν τὸν ἐχθρὸν ἐλεεῖ)....[30] For the gods themselves, who in the first place instituted and delivered to us these customs, are disposed to forgive the offenses (συγγνώμονες ... ἁμαρτήμασι) of men and are easily reconciled (εὐδιάλλακτοι); and many have there been ere now who, though greatly sinning against them (μεγάλα εἰς αὐτοὺς ἐξαμαρτάνοντες), have appeased their anger by prayers and sacrifices. Unless you think it fitting, Marcius, that the anger of the gods should be mortal, but that of men immortal! You will be doing, then, what is just and becoming both to yourself and to your country if you forgive (ἀφείς) her her offences, seeing that she is repentant (μετανοούσῃ) and ready to be reconciled (διαλλαττομένη) and to restore to you now everything that she took away from you before (50).[31]

She recalls that he owes her his body and soul, gratitude for his life, that when she was a widow, she was not only his mother but his father, nurse, sister and everything that is dearest (πάντα τὰ φίλτατά σοι; 51.3). She asks one favor, that he will be reconciled to his fellow citizens and cease his implacable anger against his country (52.2). But if he turns away his mother with indignity, unhonored, she will kill herself before the eyes of friends and enemies, leaving him cursed, and she prays, "may there be no occasion for this, O gods who guard the empire of the Romans" (53.1–3). She will submit to any humiliation to save her country (53.4).[32]

Marcius replies, "though you have saved your country, you have ruined me, your dutiful and affectionate son" (τὸν εὐσεβῆ καὶ φιλόστοργον υἱὸν ἀπολώλεκας; 54.1). He agrees with his mother to ask the Volscians to admit their enemies into friendship and to make a just treaty with them (54.2). Dionysius then by narrating their epiphanies reproves the readers who think that the gods have no power over man's [human] reason (56.1).

---

[30] Cf. *Ant. Rom.* 8.32.5; 34.1.

[31] Breytenbach, *Versöhnung*, 57 n. 37, cites *Ant. Rom.* 8.51.5, probably a mistake for 8.50.4.

[32] Contrast Antigone in Sophocles' trajedy; for her the claims of kinship have priority beyond those of the *polis*. Cf. Mary Whitlock Blundell, *Helping Friends and Harming Enemies: A Study in Sophocles and Greek Ethics* (Cambridge: Cambridge University Press, 1989) 106–48. Cf. nn. 9 and 34.

The result of Marcius' change is that the Volscian Tullus jealously whets the anger of fellow citizens against him and summons him to trial for treason (57), where there are calls to "stone him," which occurs, although some want to apprehend the murderers for the lawless deed (59.1-2). After his death they show fitting gratitude and honor a brave man.

> Such was the end of Marcius, ... the greatest general of his age, ... who was most ready to relieve the wants of his friends as soon as he was informed of them .... But it was impossible that all the virtues should be found together in a human being's nature (60).

> In any case the divinity who bestowed these virtues upon him added to them unfortunate blemishes and fatal flaws .... In the case of Marcius, ... it was nothing else but his passion for exact and extreme justice[33] that drove him from his country .... For when he ought to have made reasonable concessions to the plebeians, ... he would not do so, but by opposing them in everything that was not just (πρὸς ἄπαντα τὰ μὴ δίκαια ἀντιλέγων) he incurred their hatred and was banished by them .... He received a sorry reward for his extreme justice (61.1, 3).

However, as observed at the beginning of this retelling of the story, for a year both the Volscians and the Romans mourned his death.

Dionysius' sequel to his story of the first sedition is a textbook case of conflicting views of friendship. Coriolanus becomes the vengeful, successful enemy of his former friends, resulting in Minucius' accusation that he violates the laws of nature and the duties of religion. But Coriolanus finds it absurd not to hate those who hate him and to love those who love him. Friends are determined by their services and deeds. "We all love those who do us good and hate those who do us harm," and "renounce our friends when they injure us," which is just, honorable, and holy (34.1-3).

Veturia verbalizes a different view: to the other women she wonders whether she can ask him to be merciful and compassionate to the plebeians, to exhort him to love those who have ruined him (42.1-2). To her son she argues, however, that all men need forgiveness for their offenses against one another; when an enemy becomes a suppliant, instead of hating, one pities him

---

[33] Cf. Cic. Amic. 12.42.

(50.3). The gods are easily reconciled and forgive those who sin greatly against them; therefore she asks Marcius to forgive and be reconciled to a repentant Rome (50.4). This mother will submit to any humiliation to save her country (53.4).[34] In this story, the mother and the son, the female and the male, have very different views of love.

Love of country remains the highest value in this story of Coriolanus' hatred of the plebeians, and his subsequent humiliation and death, a love of country better exemplified by the mother than by her son, who did not continue to love and forgive Rome even when it injured him. Love of country means making reasonable, even if not precisely just, concessions to the poor plebeians (61.2–3). Coriolanus' claim to be a "lover of his country" is falsified.[35] Because he was unwilling to make reasonable concessions to the plebeians, he was banished. By his aristocratic hatred of the Roman poor, he tried to destroy the community, a harmony and friendship restored by his mother. Rome's mourning for Coriolanus honored Veturia.

Conclusions

I have narrated four stories, then at the end of each section drawn conclusions about Graeco-Roman forms of friendship. To summarize, the first story in *Ant. Rom.* 3 is of friendship between enemies, whom the Romans are willing to make equal citizens as long as the defeated enemies accept Roman hierarchical order. In this case Romans forgive their former enemies everything. The same story insists on love of country more than of any family member, narrating a brother's murder of his sister, a murder approved by their father, because she loved one of Rome's enemies, her cousin and fiancée. Deutschland über alles; love your country or leave it.

---

[34] Compare the mother in 4 Maccabees (2:11–13; 13:23–14:1; 14:13, 20; 15:4–17:10; 18:6–19) who loves (not her country but) the law. She "encouraged and persuaded her sons to die [opposing the tyrant Antiochus] rather than violate God's commandment" (16.24).

[35] The story has a happy ending: Coriolanus is mourned by the Romans, but in the narrative, he is banished, humbled, and finally stoned. He loves his mother, never the poor Roman plebeians.

The second story in *Ant. Rom.* 6 narrates internal civic conflict in which patricians and plebeians, rich and poor, hate each other. The poor want their debts forgiven and to have land, which when there is a political crisis, the rich promise, but rarely deliver. Dionysius emphases the contrast with earlier Greek states, whose murderous internal conflicts contributed to their defeat. In Rome these two classes successfully persuade each other with words (compare Cicero on friendship), remaining "one body" until the Gracchi.

The third story in *Ant. Rom.* 7 values harmony between rich and poor in the city more than the honor of its most successful general, amazing in a country oriented toward imperialistic conquest. The plebeians gain the power to banish a haughty hater of the poor, an act accepted by wealthy patricians for the sake of the commonwealth (again compare Cicero on friendship).

The fourth story in *Ant. Rom.* 8 contrasts two views of friendship, both of which assume that love of country is paramount. The general hates those citizens who hate him and loves those—including former enemies—who love him, hating those who harm him. His mother, in contrast, insists that all humans need forgiveness; the gods are easily reconciled, and humans too should forgive and have mercy on repentant enemies, in this case a repentant Rome. If the general refuses, the mother threatens to commit suicide, a curse of her son who fails to love their country. Reconciliation between rich and poor is more important than justice, understood from the viewpoint of the patricians. The general responds to his mother, not to the poor; his death and humiliation follow. The mother's acts and words based on her view of friendship restore harmony to the state.

An Extraordinary Friend in Chariton's *Callirhoe*: The Importance of Friendship in the Greek Romances

Ronald F. Hock

The Greek romances are a neglected resource for the study of Greco-Roman friendship. Of the five complete romances, Chariton's *Callirhoe* is especially detailed in its portrayal of friendship, presenting a pair of friends as well as examples of groups of friends, political friendships, utilitarian friendships, and perhaps a new form of friendship–that between husband and wife.

Several texts that have not received due attention in studies of friendship are the Greek romances. Five complete romances are extant as well as small fragments or summaries of several others,[1] but for the purposes of this essay I will limit myself to those romances that are roughly contemporary with the New Testament. In fact, most attention will be devoted to Chariton's *Callirhoe*–written as early as the mid-first century and certainly by the end of the first or early years of the second[2]–because it has the most

---

[1] The Greek romances are now easily accessible in English translation in *Collected Ancient Greek Novels* (ed. B. P. Reardon; Berkeley: University of California Press, 1989). Editions of the Greek texts and very basic bibliography are cited in the introductions to each romance in this volume. The best single volume discussion of the romances as a whole is T. Hägg, *The Novel in Antiquity* (Berkeley: University of California Press, 1983). For short studies see also B. P. Reardon, "The Greek Novel," *Phoenix* 23 (1969) 291–301, and E. L. Bowie and S. J. Harrison, "The Romance of the Novel," *JRS* 83 (1993) 159–78. Detailed bibliographical updates are available in each issue of *The Petronian Newsletter*, edited by G. Schmeling.

[2] The dating of Chariton's romance has varied widely. E. Rohde's dating to the fifth or even early sixth century (cf. *Der griechische Roman und seine Vorläufer* [4th ed.; Hildesheim: Georg Olms, 1960] 489) became untenable with the discovery of papyrus fragments of this romance from the second century. But the range is still considerable, as dates extend from the first century BCE to the early second CE—although recent scholarship has tended to fix Chariton's date to the first century CE.

detailed descriptions of friendship. Besides Chariton, two mid-second century romances–Xenophon's *Ephesian Tale* and Achilles Tatius' *Leucippe and Clitophon*–will receive some attention, as they have a number of words often found in discussions of friendship. In contrast, a third second century romance, Longus' *Daphnis and Chloe*, has little on the subject of friendship and so will be omitted here. Finally, Heliodorus' *Ethiopian Story*, whether it is dated to the third century or, as is more likely, to the fourth, is too late for consideration.[3]

The romances as a whole have received little attention from scholars,[4] and hence it is not surprising that they have not been the subjects of studies of friendship. Scholars interested in friendship will not find analytical discussions of friendship in the manner of

---

For details on the various datings, see the introduction to *Chariton von Aphrodisias Kallirhoe: Eingeleitet, übersetzt und erläutert von Karl Plepelits* (Bibliothek der griechischen Literatur 6; Stuttgart: Anton Hiersemann, 1976) 4–9. Plepelits himself favors a mid-first century dating, a view accepted by B. P. Reardon (*The Form of Greek Romance* [Princeton: Princeton University Press, 1991] 17 n. 3). For a late first or early second century dating, see C. Ruiz-Montero, "Aspects of the Vocabulary of Chariton of Aphrodisias," *CQ* 41 (1991) 484–89. For an insightful literary analysis of this romance, see Reardon, "Theme, Structure and Narrative in Chariton," *YCS* 27 (1982) 1–27. For a review of all the issues surrounding this romance, see Ruiz-Montero, "Chariton von Aphrodisias: Ein Überblick," *ANRW* 2.34.2 (1994) 1006–54.

[3] Xenophon's romance has long been dated to the mid-second century (see H. Gärtner, "Xenophon von Ephesos," *PW* 9A.2 [1967] 2055–89, esp. 2086–87). The romance by Achilles Tatius, once dated to the late second century, has, on the basis of recently discovered papyrus fragments of this romance, been pushed back "to a date no later than the middle of the second century" (see W. H. Willis, "The Robinson-Cologne Papyrus of Achilles Tatius," *GRBS* 31 [1990] 73–102, esp. 76). Longus' date is more difficult to establish, but the late second or even early third century is likely (see R. L. Hunter, *A Study of Daphnis and Chloe* [New York: Cambridge University Press, 1983] 3–15). The difficulty of pinning down specific dates for these romances only shows how apt they for the entire period under consideration.

[4] This lack of attention, prompted by a disdain for literature so late and seemingly so frivolous, is less and less true today, however, as the romances are enjoying something like a renaissance, both as the subject of literary analysis and as sources for the social life of the early Roman Empire. Indeed, Bowie and Harrison ("Romance," 159) say: "The ancient novel has become one of the hottest properties in town." For a broader look at the reasons for the shift in attitudes toward this literature, see D. Konstan, "What's New About New Approaches to the Classics," *Classics: A Discipline and Profession in Crisis?* (ed. P. Culham and L. Edmunds; Lanham, MD: University Press of America, 1989) 45–49.

Aristotle's *Nicomachean Ethics*, nor will they find narratives focused specifically on friendships in the manner of Lucian's *Toxaris*.[5]

To be sure, the romances are obviously and principally love stories, but they are also, given their length, breadth of coverage, and amount of detail, important sources for many other social and intellectual institutions in the Greco-Roman world, an importance which is increasingly recognized today.[6] Friendship, however, has not been one of the institutions studied.

Accordingly, what follows will be an initial attempt to present what the romances, in particular Chariton's *Callirhoe*, have to say about friendship. The presentation will cover three subjects: first, the traditional, if also extraordinary, friendship between Chaereas, the story's hero, and Polycharmus; second, the various other kinds of friendships that are portrayed in this romance; and third, a modest proposal regarding the centrality of friendship for understanding love in the romances.

Polycharmus - An Extraordinary Friend

Discussions of φιλία, or friendship, ordinarily focus on the so-called φιλία ἑταιρική, a form of friendship which assumes "a reciprocal bond of obligation and affection offering security to those involved and demanding actions as proofs of affection and trust."[7] Such friendships usually involve a pair of young men, and various pairs of friends, beginning with Achilles and Patroclus,

---

[5] It is striking how often the same sources are cited in studies of Greco-Roman friendhip, from the pioneering survey of G. Bohnenblust, *Beiträge zum Topos ΠΕΡΙ ΦΙΛΙΑΣ* (Inaug. Diss., Univ. Bern; Berlin: Gustav Schade [Otto Francke] 1905) 26–44, to the recent survey by C. White, *Christian Friendship in the Fourth Century* (New York: Cambridge University Press, 1992) 13–44. The romances have been consistently ignored in these studies, even though the romances come from the relevant centuries and much more obscure sources are cited instead.

[6] For a survey of the social world as it is depicted in Chariton's *Callirhoe*, see Ruiz-Montero, "Cariton de Afrodisias y el Mundo Real," in *Piccolo Mondo Antico: Appunti sulle Donne, gli Amori, i Costumi, il Mondo Reale nel Romanzo Antico* (ed. P. Liviabella Furiani and A. M. Scarcella; Napoli: Edizioni Scientifiche Italiane, 1989) 107–49. For an incisive analysis of one institution in this romance, namely marriage, see B. Egger, "Women and Marriage in the Greek Novels: The Boundaries of Romance," *The Search for the Ancient Novel* (ed. J. Tatum; Baltimore: Johns Hopkins University Press, 1994) 260–80.

[7] White, *Friendship*, 14.

became traditional.⁸ Lucian's *Toxaris* extends the tradition forward to include exemplary pairs from the early empire, that is, to the time contemporary with the Greek romances. Belonging to this tradition of φιλία έταιρική are two of Chariton's characters, the hero Chaereas and his "extraordinary friend" (φίλος έξαίρετος) Polycharmus (1.5.2).⁹ Their inclusion in this tradition is made explicit by Chariton himself when he compares them with Achilles and Patroclus (1.5.2). Moreover, throughout the story Polycharmus is consistently characterized by the word φίλος (4.2.2; 3.1, 4; 4.4.7; 5.1.1; 2.4; 10.10; 6.2.8; 7.1.2; 2.3; 8.8.12), and at the end Chaereas persuades the Syracusan assembly to proclaim Polycharmus a "trusted friend" (φίλος πιστός) (8.8.12).

We have in Chariton's romance, then, yet another pair of friends to set alongside, say, Lucian's Agathocles and Deinias (*Tox.* 12–18) or Demetrius and Antiphilus (27–34). This new pair, whose relationship is narrated in detail by Chariton, can, therefore, further clarify what was meant in the mid to late first century by φιλία έταιρική.

Unfortunately, Polycharmus and hence his friendship with Chaereas have been ignored by scholars, in part because B. Perry dismisses him as a "colorless satellite" of Chaereas¹⁰ and in part because B. Reardon renders him invisible by his insistence that the heroes of the romances are isolated individuals and that Chaereas

---

⁸ Achilles and Patroclus, Orestes and Pylades, and Theseus and Perithoüs are termed "friends of old" (παλαιοί φίλοι) by Lucian (*Tox.* 10). See further n. 14 below.

⁹ The text used will be *Charitonis Aphrodisiensis de Chaerea et Callirhoe Amatorium Narrationum libri octo* (ed. W. E. Blake; Oxford: Clarendon Press, 1938). All translations are my own. This text is long out of print, but Reardon has a forthcoming Teubner text, and a Loeb edition has recently appeared: *Chariton, Callirhoe* (ed. and trans. G. P. Goold; LCL 481; Cambridge: Harvard University Press, 1995).

¹⁰ See B. E. Perry, "Chariton and his Romance from a Literary-Historical Point of View," *AJP* 51 (1930) 93–134, esp. 103. Perry dismisses Polycharmus from his analysis because he finds most other minor characters—Theron, Dionysius, Leonas, Plangon, Artaxates *et al.*—to have been better drawn by Chariton. See also his *The Ancient Romances: A Literary-Historical Account of their Origins* (Berkeley: University of California Press, 1967) 96–147, esp. 126, 137. Polycharmus is omitted even by J. Helms, whose *Character Portrayal in the Romance of Chariton* (The Hague: Mouton & Co., 1966) esp. 66–106, 127–46, concentrates instead on other minor characters: Dionysius, Artaxerxes, Statira, Theron, Plangon, Leonas, and Artaxates.

Greek Romances (Chariton, *Callirhoe*)   149

in particular "is alone; deprived alike of the support of his friends and of the presence of his beloved, he is left to find . . . his own salvation."[11]

Colorless? Possibly. But invisible? Certainly not! For, as a matter of fact, Chaereas is never alone[12] and, once fortune turns against him, he always has the support of his friend Polycharmus and forms a number of new friendships along the way. A review of Polycharmus' role as φίλος in this romance, therefore, will underscore his visibility and importance in the story and demonstrate that his importance derives from his role as the φίλος ἐξαίρετος, the one who, to use Lucian's definition of a φίλος, "obligates himself to share his friend's every blow of fortune" (χρὴ τοῖς φίλοις ἁπάσης τύχης κοινωνεῖν) (*Tox.* 6).[13]

---

[11] Reardon, "Greek Novel," 296, an opinion he repeats later (for the romances as a whole) in his *Greek Romance*, 28–29, 79, 138, 172, and esp. 30 n. 12: "The element of isolation in hero and heroine . . . seems to me central in the shape of such stories."

[12] When the story opens Chaereas is surrounded by family and his fellow youths at the gymnasium. When he leaves Syracuse in search of his wife, he goes with five picked ambassadors and his friend Polycharmus, not to mention the prayers and tears of the entire city. Even when captured he is sold with Polycharmus to a single master. When his identity becomes known to his master Mithridates, he and Polycharmus are quickly included in Mithridates' group of friends and later accompany him as part of a large entourage of friends and relatives to the trial in Babylon. When Chaereas leaves Babylon, he and Polycharmus quickly join forces with the Egyptian rebels and are soon placed over a contingent of Greek mercenaries who regard Chaereas as their friend. With several victories under his belt, he then finds Callirhoe and sails back to Syracuse to be reunited with his family and adoring city. Isolation, then, is hardly the term to use when analyzing the romance. Similar doubts are expressed in G. Anderson, "The *pepaideumenos* in Action: Sophists and their Outlook in the Early Empire," *ANRW* 2.36.4 (1990) 79–208, esp. 134.

[13] The visibility and importance of friends are also true of Xenophon's and Achilles Tatius' romances. The respective protagonists, Habrocomes and Clitophon, have friends and are aided by them at important points in the stories. For example, the runaway Habrocomes befriends the brigand Hippothoos (Xen. Eph. 2.14.2) and the two travel together for a while in search of Habrocomes' wife, Anthia (3.3.6). Later, Hippothoos purchases a slave from a brothel (5.9.9), but when he learns that she is Anthia he treats her with utmost respect because of his friendship for Habrocomes (5.9.13). At the end Hippothoos returns with Habrocomes and Anthia to Ephesus, where they are lifelong friends (5.15.3–4). Similarly, Achilles Tatius tells of the friendships of Clitophon. For example, Clitophon meets a young man named Menelaos on board ship (2.33.2). The latter soon becomes Clitophon's dearest friend (3.18.5) and aids him in a variety of ways, including offering comfort to Clitophon at the supposed death of his beloved Leucippe (5.8.1).

Polycharmus first appears in the story shortly after Chaereas, the subject of a plot by Callirhoe's suitors, suspects his young wife of adultery and in a jealous rage has struck her a seemingly fatal blow. Chaereas soon learns the truth from Callirhoe's closest slave and then wants nothing other than to kill himself. It is at this point that we first meet Polycharmus, introduced, in the language used above, as a φίλος ἐξαίρετος. He has heard of the incident, as indeed all the city has, but he goes directly to Chaereas' house, where he prevents the distraught Chaereas from committing suicide (1.5.2).

On the following day Chaereas is tried for murder and, despite his efforts at self-denunciation, is acquitted of the charge (1.5.2–6.1). Frustrated by the outcome, Chaereas begins again to seek for a means to kill himself. And once again, Polycharmus intervenes, this time with a speech: "You traitor of the dead girl, are you not even going to remain around long enough to bury Callirhoe? Are you going to entrust her body to strangers? Now is the time for you to be concerned about lavish offerings for the dead and to make preparations for a royal burial" (1.6.1). This speech, Chariton notes, persuaded him (1.6.2).

Callirhoe's death, however, is only a *Scheintod*, as her tomb robbers quickly discover. She is taken, along with the riches that had been buried with her, to Ionia, and her experiences there of being sold as a slave and later of being married to Dionysius of Miletus (in order to provide a father for Chaereas' and her unborn child) shift the story away from Syracuse (1.7–3.2). When the narrative returns to Syracuse Chaereas, after finding her tomb empty and her body stolen, heads a search party and at least captures the leader of the tomb robbers, Theron. The latter under interrogation mentions Miletus (3.4.14), and the Syracusans immediately authorize an embassy to negotiate Callirhoe's return (3.4.16–18).

Chaereas, of course, volunteers for the embassy, and then Chariton narrates in some detail "another, not ignoble, act of friendship" (ἄλλο φιλίας ἔργον οὐκ ἀγεννές) on the part of Polycharmus, the first presumably being his earlier act of having dissuaded Chaereas from suicide. In any case, Polycharmus says to his parents that Chaereas is his φίλος, but adds that friendship does not extend to "sharing danger with him" (αὐτῷ συγκινδυνεύειν). Consequently, he is nowhere to be seen while the embassy was getting ready, but when the ship sets sail, Polycharmus is on board and so beyond the reach of parental authority (3.5.7). Presumably, the litotes οὐκ ἀγεννές makes allowance for Polycharmus' lying to his parents, if such an action is on behalf of his friend.

In any case, Chaereas and Polycharmus, from now on, are an inseparable pair as they go in search of Callirhoe. Therefore, Polycharmus is vitally linked to the central task of the story: to get Callirhoe back (3.4.16). They soon reach Miletus and in fact land at the very estate where Callirhoe had been sold. The two explore the surroundings and come upon a country shrine to Aphrodite which contains a golden statue of Callirhoe, the costly ἀνάθημα of her new husband Dionysius. Chaereas recognizes the likeness, learns of her new status from a temple attendant, and understandably becomes distraught. Polycharmus, however, keeps his senses and prevents Chaereas from divulging his identity to the temple attendant. After leading him out of the temple and allowing him to express his feelings in an ἠθοποιία, Polycharmus tries to comfort (παραμυθεῖν) him (3.6.2–8).

From this point on the situation only worsens. Chaereas and Polycharmus, along with the others on the embassy, are attacked. Some are killed, others captured and then sold as slaves. Among the latter are Chaereas and Polycharmus who plead with their captors to be sold to a single master and in fact are sold together to a Mithridates of Caria to work on his estate (3.7.3). Chaereas, however, is unable to do his share of the labor and is beaten as a result. Polycharmus therefore asks the foreman to separate the two of them out from the rest. The foreman agrees, and Polycharmus then does the work of two, since he was "virile by nature and not enslaved to Eros" (ἀνδρικὸς τὴν φύσιν καὶ μὴ δουλεύων Ἔρωτι). He does this work, Chariton says, "in order that he might save his friend" (ἵνα περισώσῃ τὸν φίλον) from further blows (4.2.1–2).

Shortly afterward, Chaereas and Polycharmus become innocent victims of a plot by the other slaves when they murder the guard and attempt to run away. They fail, and all, including Chaereas and Polycharmus, are ordered to be crucified. But Polycharmus, as he was being led to the cross, mutters the name of Callirhoe as the cause of all his woes; a guard hears the name and thinks that she was part of the plot and thus takes him to Mithridates for further questioning. Mithridates wants the full story, but Polycharmus hesitates, saying that it would take so long to tell that his φίλος will have been crucified and he wanted "to die with him" (αὐτῷ συναποθανεῖν) (4.2.14). Still, Polycharmus does identify himself and Chaereas, noting that he was Chaereas' companion (συμφοιτητής) and friend (φίλος) and briefly rehearses their plight before begging Mithridates to order the executioner not to separate (διαζεῦξαι) their crosses (4.3.5).

Mithridates' questioning, however, does elicit enough information so that the truth becomes known and both are saved from crucifixion. Mithridates recognizes in particular Callirhoe's name, since he had seen her in Miletus at what was ostensibly Chaereas' funeral since Dionysius and Callirhoe had been led to believe that Chaereas had died in the attack on the ship. Chaereas' instinct is to dash off to Miletus to reclaim his wife, but Mithridates, claiming now to be his φίλος, persuades him from acting so rashly and suggests instead that Chaereas write a letter to Callirhoe. In the letter Chaereas says that he is alive and briefly tells of his circumstances, including the fact that he is with his φίλος Polycharmus (4.4.7). But Chaereas is frustrated by having to wait, and Polycharmus must again comfort (παραμυθεῖν) him (4.4.1).

The letter, by another turn of events, does not reach Callirhoe but falls instead into the hands of Dionysius who, convinced that Chaereas is dead, assumes some plot on his wife by Mithridates. Dionysius accuses him of adultery to the Great King, and soon all parties, including Chaereas and Polycharmus as part of Mithridates' entourage of φίλοι and relatives, are en route to Babylon (see 5.4.7). Once in Babylon Chaereas stays with his φίλος Polycharmus (5.2.4), but becomes despondent at being unable to see his wife, so that once again Polycharmus must comfort (παραμυθεῖν) him (5.2.6).

The subsequent trial is dramatic. Dionysius' speech clearly puts Mithridates on the defensive, but Mithridates is able to gain an acquittal by in effect raising the dead, as Chaereas is brought out at the appropriate moment to confute Dionysius' charges. When

Mithridates, now free, is ready to return to Caria, Chaereas feigns illness and sends Polycharmus to thank their benefactor. Once he is alone, however, Chaereas prepares to hang himself, but the preparations take so much time that his φίλος Polycharmus can return and restrain him (5.10.6–10).

Still unresolved after the trial, however, is the issue of whether Chaereas or Dionysius is Callirhoe's rightful husband. The King promises to resolve the issue, but his own infatuation with Callirhoe prompts him to delay his decision for thirty days. This delay once again depresses Chaereas, so that he stops eating and wishes to die. But his φίλος Polycharmus once again tries to prevent his suicide, but now Chaereas lashes out, saying that Polycharmus has "the appearance of a friend" (σχῆμα φίλου) but is really his worst enemy (πολεμιώτατος). If he were a true φίλος, he would not keep him from escaping from his persecuting δαίμων. After this tirade Chaereas reaches for his sword, so that Polycharmus has to bind him and keep watch over him (6.2.8–11).

At this point, events take yet another turn. A revolt in Egypt leads to the mobilization of the Babylonian army and to a king too busy to decide between Dionysius and Chaereas. After the army has left, Chaereas and his φίλος Polycharmus search Babylon for Callirhoe (7.1.2). When they are told that the women, including Callirhoe, have left with the king and that Callirhoe has been given to Dionysius to insure his faithful service, Chaereas once again threatens suicide, this time in front of the palace (7.1.2–6). In this instance, however, Polycharmus realizes that Chaereas was justifiably beyond comforting and thus advises him as follows:

> For a long time I've been comforting (παρεμυθούμην) you, my dearest friend (φίλτατε), and frequently I've prevented your death. But now your deliberations seem to be correct. Indeed, I'm so far from preventing you at this point that even I'm ready to die with you (συναποθανεῖν). But let's consider which way of dying would be better. For the one way I have in mind does bring some reproach to the king as well as shame to him in the future, but it does not effect sufficient punishment for what we've suffered. It seems to me that the death we've once decided on for the purpose of vengeance should destroy this tyrant. For it's a noble thing that we cause him grief and bring about his repentance by a deed, and it's also a glorious thing that we leave behind for future generations a story in which two Greeks, after

being unjustly treated, paid back the Great King and then died like men. (7.1.7-8)

Chaereas objects, citing their being poor, alone, and foreigners, but Polycharmus retorts:

> What you've said would be correct, if there were not a war. But as it is, we hear that Egypt has revolted, Phoenicia has fallen, and Syria is being overrun. The King will encounter fighting even before he crosses the Euphrates. Therefore, the two of us are not alone. We have as many allies, as many weapons, as many resources, as many ships as the Egyptian commands. Let's use another's might for our own vengeance. (7.1.10-11)

Chaereas is persuaded, and the two leave Babylon and soon reach the rebel camp where they offer their services to the leader of the Egyptians. Soon thereafter Chaereas is put in charge of a contingent of Greek mercenaries and leads them to several military victories, including the capture of the city of Tyre and the island of Aradus, where the Great King had put the Persian women for safekeeping. Polycharmus hears of an especially proud woman among those captured and thinks he could interest Chaereas in a new love so as to comfort (παραμυθεῖν) him for his loss of Callirhoe (8.1.6-9). This proud woman is of course Callirhoe herself, so that Polycharmus has in fact brought about their reunion.

After a brief embrace Callirhoe is led out of her quarters, flanked on either side by Chaereas and Polycharmus as δορυφοροῦντες, and presented to Chaereas' soldiers (8.1.12). Polycharmus then reminds Chaereas that they are still in the midst of a war. He, however, wants to be with his wife and so turns everything over to Polycharmus (Πολυχάρμῳ πάντα ἐπιτρέφειν) (8.1.13).

Events now turn out well. Chaereas and Callirhoe, after a brief stop at Cyprus to honor Aphrodite, sail victoriously into the harbor of Syracuse to the delight of her father Hermocrates and all the city. Polycharmus, who had been entrusted with the rest of the fleet (ἦν πεπιστευμένος τὸν ἄλλον στόλον) and instructed to follow Chaereas' ship into the harbor (8.6.9), is, however, not forgotten as the story draws to a conclusion. All go to the theatre to hear how Chaereas has regained Callirhoe. Hermocrates brings the crowd up to date by recalling *inter alia* that Polycharmus, Chaereas' φίλος, had willingly sailed out with him (ἑκούσιος συνεξέπλευσε) for Ionia (8.7.8). Then Chaereas carries the story forward recounting his journey, saying at one point that he had often contemplated suicide because of his separation from Callirhoe, but that Polycharmus, who alone among all his friends proved loyal (ὁ μόνος ἐν πᾶσι φίλος πιστός), had saved him (8.8.7). Chaereas goes on to thank his φίλος Polycharmus publicly for his good will (εὔνοια) and exceptional loyalty (πίστις ἀληθεστάτη). He also gives Polycharmus his sister for a wife as well as a part of the spoils from their campaigns. The people approve these gifts and publicly proclaim him "a loyal friend" (φίλος πιστός) (8.8.12).

With this summary of Polycharmus' actions toward his friend Chaereas, it should now be clear that Chaereas was not alone, bereft of friends, and thus required to seek his own salvation, as Reardon supposes. Throughout the story—from Syracuse to Miletus to Caria to Babylon to Tyre to Aradus to Cyprus and back to Syracuse—Chaereas' search for Callirhoe is done with the extraordinary companionship and assistance of his φίλος Polycharmus. In fact, without Polycharmus it is unlikely that Chaereas, who is otherwise prone to suicide, rash in his actions, and generally incapacitated by Eros, would have long survived, much less regained Callirhoe and attained his own salvation.

Rather, like the friends of Lucian's *Toxaris*, Polycharmus shared every blow of fortune, every τύχη, of his friend Chaereas—his grief, his travels, his enslavement, his toil, his dangers, even his death, had that been necessary, but also his triumphs, his responsibilities, his return to Syracuse, his spoils, and the public acknowledgement of his loyalty. Indeed, Polycharmus and Chaereas could easily be added as a sixth pair of Greek friends to the five presented in Lucian's *Toxaris*.

To say that Polycharmus and Chaereas form a sixth pair of exemplary friends is to acknowledge that there is much in their portrayal that reflects the conventions of friendship long familiar from other sources. Chariton, in other words, is familiar with the traditions of friendship. For example, his comparison of Chaereas and Polycharmus with Achilles and Patroclus (1.5.2) points to his knowledge of the παλαιοὶ φίλοι.[14] He also knows that a proof of friendship is a willingness to share a friend's adverse fortune.[15] Hermocrates notes Polycharmus' willingness to share each turn of events (8.7.8), and Chariton indicates their sense of sharing linguistically by using words for Polycharmus that have the prefix σύν-, such as "to share danger with" (συγκινδυνεύειν) (3.5.7), "to sail with" (συμπλεῖν) (8.7.8), and especially "to die with" (συναποθανεῖν) (4.2.14; 7.1.7); such σύν-compounds are common in discussions of friendship.[16] In addition, this sharing of each other's fate is also clear in their mutual desire to be sold to one master (3.7.3) as well as in Polycharmus' plea not to have his cross separated (διαζεύγειν) from that of his φίλος (4.3.5). That only Polycharmus among Chaereas' friends shared his many reversals in fortune (8.8.7) underscores the rarity of true friendship, another familiar convention.[17]

Other friendship conventions are especially prominent in Chariton's depiction of Polycharmus. For example, Polycharmus repeatedly provides comfort (παραμυθεῖν) to Chaereas, often when the latter is suicidal (3.6.8; 4.4.1; 5.2.6; 8.1.6). Such repetition bothered Perry,[18] but providing comfort is once again an obligation of friendship.[19] Other conventions are used with a slightly different purpose, such as Polycharmus' readiness not so much to die for his friend as to die with him (συναποθανεῖν)

---

[14] Patroclus and Achilles are often cited among pairs of παλαιοὶ φίλοι. See, e.g., Plutarch, *De amic. mult.* 93E; Lucian, *Tox.* 10; and Libanius, *Progymn.* 3 (8.73, 1–6 Förster). Other evidence in Bohnenblust, *ΠΕΡΙ ΦΙΛΙΑΣ*, 41; G. Stählin, "φίλος," *TDNT* 9 (1974) 151–54, esp. 153; and White, *Friendship,* 15, 20, 38, 40. That Chariton should cite this Homeric pair is consistent with his use of Homeric quotations and allusions throughout the romance.

[15] On this *topos* of friendship, see, e.g., Cicero, *Amic.* 25.92. Further evidence in Bohnenblust, *ΠΕΡΙ ΦΙΛΙΑΣ,* 32–34.

[16] For σύν-compounds, see, e.g., Aristotle, *EE* 1245b 3–5; Plutarch, *De amic. mult.* 95C; 96F; Epictetus, *Diss.* 2.22.37; *Ench.* 32.3; and Lucian, *Tox.* 7, 18. Among the romances: Achilles Tatius, 2.27.2; 5.14.2; 7.10.1.

[17] See, e.g., Aristotle, *EN* 1156b 25, and Bohnenblust, *ΠΕΡΙ ΦΙΛΙΑΣ,* 37–38.

[18] Perry, *Ancient Romances,* 126.

[19] For such comforting on the part of friends—the verbs are either παραμυθεῖν or παρηγορεῖν—see, e.g., Aristotle, *EN* 1171b 3, and Lucian, *Tox.* 58, 60. This aspect of friendship is especially emphasized in Achilles Tatius (see, e.g., 4.10.1; 5.8.1; 7.6.1, 6; 7.14.4).

(4.2.14; 7.1.7).[20] And, finally, the friendship of Polycharmus and Chaereas helps us to identify conventions of friendship not noticed elsewhere. For example, Chaereas' decision to marry his sister to Polycharmus, an action that so befuddled Perry,[21] seemingly follows convention, too. At any rate, such marriages show up in discussions of friendship: Orestes' marriage of his sister to his friend Pylades, Sostratos' marriage of his sister to his friend Gorgias, and Toxaris' marriage of his sister to his friend Sisinnes.[22]

In sum, Chariton's portrayal of Chaereas and his φίλος ἐξαίρετος Polycharmus is fully within the tradition of describing such pairs of friends, but the detail used to narrate their friendship is fuller than it is for the other pairs. Consequently, Chariton's portrayal of this pair provides an especially valuable source for studying φιλία ἑταιρική.

Other Friendships in Chariton's *Callirhoe*

Thus far we have focused on the principal friendship in Chariton's *Callirhoe*, that between Chaereas and Polycharmus. But friendship language in Chariton is not restricted to this pair. In fact, the types of friends in this romance are surprisingly varied. For example, several characters belong to social groups which are termed "friends" (φίλοι). Thus Hermocrates has φίλοι who provide gifts for the funeral offerings for his daughter Callirhoe (1.6.4). Dionysius also has φίλοι who travel with him when he visits his estate (2.2.3). While there they accompany him to the rural shrine of Aphrodite when he first meets Callirhoe (2.5.1) and these friends are involved, along with relatives, when marriage to Callirhoe is discussed (3.1.7). Back in Miletus he also dines with

---

[20] Dying for a friend is often noted: Seneca, *Ep.* 6.2; Plutarch, *De amic. mult* 93E; Lucian, *Tox.* 10, 58–60. Cf. Bohnenblust, ΠΕΡΙ ΦΙΛΙΑΣ, 41. Among the romances, see Achilles Tatius, 3.22.1; 7.14.4.

[21] Perry, *Ancient Romances*, 137.

[22] For Orestes and Pylades, see Euripides, *Elec.* 1249; *Orest.* 1658; Apollodorus, *Epit.* 6.28; for Sostratos and Gorgias, see Menander, *Dysk.* 233–392 and 748–83; for Toxaris and Sisinnes, see Lucian, *Tox.* 60. D. Konstan (*Sexual Symmetry: Love in the Ancient Novel and Related Genres* [Princeton: Princeton University Press, 1994] 79) refers to the marriage of Chaereas' sister as a conventional gesture of comic closure, but the evidence cited here suggests something broader.

these φίλοι (2.4.1). They seem to form a local group, although Pharnaces of Lydia and Mithridates of Caria seem to be included, at least when they are in Miletus (4.6.1; 5.6.2; cf. 5.7.7). Mithridates likewise has a circle of φίλοι who urge him to investigate the murder of his slave-guard (4.2.11). Later he includes Chaereas in this circle (4.3.6; cf. 8.8.4), and all go with him to Babylon to stand by him during the trial (5.4.7). Finally, King Artaxerxes has his φίλοι who act as entourage and advisors on a number of occasions (4.6.5; 5.4.12-13; 5.8.6-7). Companionship, advice, support—these seem to be the functions of groups of φίλοι.[23]

Another type of friendship is less social, more political. For example, Dionysius is introduced in the story as a "friend of the Great King" (φίλος τοῦ μεγάλου βασιλέως) (1.12.6), and the relationship, if not the terminology, is also applied to Hermocrates because of his victory over the Athenians (2.6.3). The term φίλος thus verges on "ally," and it is so used in other, clearly military, contexts for allies of the king (6.8.5; 8.4.3; 8.10). Here perhaps belongs the use of φίλοι for Chaereas' Greek allies (7.3.2), though the relationship with these "fellow soldiers" (συστρατιῶται) (8.2.10) may be more,[24] as other friendship terms are used which suggest a special bond. Thus the soldiers love (φιλεῖν) Chaereas (7.5.10), and he in turn calls them "partners" (κοινωνοί) in his victories, credits their being of one mind (ὁμονοεῖν) as the reason they had gained control of the sea (8.2.10), and thanks them for their "good will and trust" (εὔνοια τε καὶ πίστις) (8.2.13).[25]

Thus far the friendships have tended to involve aristocratic men, and those friendships do predominate in Chariton, but that

---

[23] For similar groups of friends (φίλοι) in other romances, see Achilles Tatius, 7.9.4; 10.1; Xenophon of Ephesus, 3.6.4.

[24] Aristotle (EN 1159b 27-28) notes that fellow soldiers call each other friends. Here is the one place where friendship impinges on Ruiz-Montero's analysis (see "Mundo Real," 136).

[25] For these terms in friendship contexts, see the following: for partnership, see, e.g., Aristotle, EN 1171b 33, and Lucian, Tox. 7, 20, 28, 32, and among the romances, see Achilles Tatius, 2.4.2; 27.2; 33.1; 3.21.6; 7.7.4. See further Bohnenblust, ΠΕΡΙ ΦΙΛΙΑΣ, 11. For being of one mind, see, e.g., Aristotle, EN 1168b 8; Dio Chrys., Orat. 4.42; Plutarch, De amic. mult. 96F; and Bohnenblust, ΠΕΡΙ ΦΙΛΙΑΣ, 27. For good will and trust, see, e.g., Lucian, Tox. 7; Plutarch, De amic. mult. 93F; and Bohnenblust, ΠΕΡΙ ΦΙΛΙΑΣ, 36, 43.

is not the whole story. For Chariton also speaks of friendships among other groups. For example, friendships among aristocratic women would naturally be rarer, given their confinement within the women's quarters, but Chariton mentions friendships that Callirhoe formed during her stay in Babylon, and specifically while she stayed in the women's quarters of the royal palace (5.8.9), and later as she traveled with the other aristocratic women of Babylon during the war against the Egyptian rebels (6.9.5–7). When Chaereas is about to send the women back to Babylon, Callirhoe reports this decision and addresses Rhodogyne as her "first friend among the Persians" (πρώτη μοι φίλη Περσίδων) and Statira, the Queen, as her "dearest friend" (φιλτάτη) (8.3.8). An explicit gesture of friendship happens shortly after when Callirhoe asks the departing Statira to write letters to her often (8.4.8).

Friendships among those of non-aristocratic status are also described. There are passing references to making friends of slaves for one reason or another. Thus the parasite charged with gaining access into Chaereas' house in order to make Chaereas believe that Callirhoe was being unfaithful makes a friend (φίλην ποιεῖν) of Callirhoe's closest slave (1.4.1). The same language is used by Dionysius in instructions to the slave Plangon. She is instructed to make Callirhoe, who at this point in the story is a slave of Dionysius, her friend (2.6.5), in order that he might gain his desire. The relationship between Callirhoe and Plangon does become close, but the language suggests a relationship more like that of parent and child (2.7.5: "She loves [φιλεῖ] me as a daughter;" cf. 2.10.2, 3; 11.6). In any case, these relationships are friendships that Aristotle would have classified as based solely on utility.

This form of friendship is especially well presented in the relationship that arises between Leonas, the slave-manager of Dionysius, and Theron, the brigand who had kidnapped Callirhoe but who now is passing himself off as a slave-merchant. They meet outside a workshop (1.12.6), and Theron learns that Leonas' master is recently widowed and has put him in charge of his master's baby girl. Theron sees in Leonas' domestic responsibility an opportunity to sell Callirhoe, who, he assures Leonas, would make a good nurse. Leonas is grateful and invites Theron to his house as his guest and "friend" (φίλος) (1.12.10). Theron accepts the invitation and by "offering toasts to Leonas in a friendly manner" (φιλοφρονεῖσθαι ταῖς προπόσεσι τὸν Λεωνᾶς) he forges a partnership (κοινωνία) (1.13.2) in which they agree to handle the transaction the following day out in the country. The next day Theron hands over the girl with the comment that Leonas can pay him when he gets a bill of sale in the city. After all, he says, Leonas is his "friend" (φίλος) (1.14.3). Leonas likewise affirms that he "trusts" (πιστεύειν) Theron and gives him the money (1.14.4). Aristotle notes that friendships based on utility are not likely to last, which is precisely what happens here. Theron does not even stay for a meal after the sale but rushes back with his money to his pirate ship and sails away (1.14.6).[26]

Husband and Wife as Friends

There is one final relationship in the romances that may deserve attention in terms of friendship, and that is the central relationship itself—in the case of Chariton's romance, the love between Chaereas and Callirhoe. I draw attention to this relationship more as a proposal for further study than as a hypothesis complete with supporting data. In fact, to do so would greatly extend the scope of this essay. Nevertheless, two scholarly treatments, one on friendship and the other on the romances, have prompted my proposal. In her study of friendship in Aristotle, M. Nussbaum[27] notes that Aristotle included among various friendships that between husband and wife but adds that this relationship was clearly not the highest form of friendship. That friendship was between two males, whose mutual feelings, virtuous character, and daily association in the activities of the polis and other shared interests allowed friendship to flourish. Then Nussbaum adds: "If he [Aristotle] had not had his views about female inferiority, he would very likely have preferred this sharing to extend into the sphere of the household as well: thus an even more perfect *philia* would be a good marriage, in which the full

---

[26] On utilitarian frienships being shortlived, see Aristotle, *EN* 1157a 14–15.
[27] See M. Nussbaum, *The Fragility of Goodness: Luck and Ethics in Greek Tragedy and Philosophy* (New York: Cambridge University Press, 1986) 354–72.

range of the aspirations and concerns that make up a human life might be accommodated."[28]

In his study of the romances, D. Konstan[29] argues that it is precisely the equality between husband and wife that distinguishes the romances from all other amatory genres of antiquity. He uses the term "sexual symmetry" to emphasize the equality of age and status, the mutuality of passion, and the same commitment to fidelity that characterize all the protagonists in the romances. In the case of Chariton's *Callirhoe*, it is clear that Chaereas and Callirhoe share these characteristics. They come from the leading families of Syracuse and are of marriageable age; they both fall deeply in love on their first encounter; and they never falter in their commitment to one another.

But the equality extends even further than Konstan imagines. For example, throughout the romance Callirhoe is portrayed as an intelligent and educated young woman. She is not so naive as to be taken in by Theron's hypocrisy (1.13.7–11). Chariton in fact calls her a πεπαιδευμένη, or an educated woman (7.6.5), which is demonstrated by her writing a letter to Dionysius (8.4.4–6) and by her ability to express herself according to the rhetorical conventions of ἠθοποιία, as when, for example, she speaks just before fording the Euphrates en route to Babylon (5.1.4–7).[30] More generally, as a result of their adventures Chaereas and Callirhoe have a wealth of shared experiences—separation, enslavement, capture, grief, etc. Such would not have been the case if he had remained active at the gymnasium and in political affairs and she had remained confined to the women's quarters.

---

[28] Nussbaum, *Goodness*, 358.

[29] For a summary of his thesis, see Konstan, *Sexual Symmetry*, 7–12.

[30] I single out this genre of speech, the ἠθοποιία, which is an advanced progymnasma, since it suggests that Chariton, if not Callirhoe herself, is making playful use of an educational convention. One of the standard topics for students to treat when composing an ἠθοποιία is: "What words would a dweller on the mainland say on first seeing the sea?" (Aphthonius, *Progymn.* 11 [p. 35, 4–6 Rabe]). Readers familiar with this standard topic would sense that Callirhoe has inverted it: "What words would a woman from the coast say on heading into the Asian interior?" Such inversions would underscore her designation as a πεπαιδευμένη (7.6.5) and hence identify her as an intellectual equal of Dionysius and Chaereas.

Given this relative equality of education and experience, paired with their symmetry in age, status, passion, and commitment, the relationship between Chaereas and Callirhoe begins to look a lot like φιλία. In other words, I propose that what was inconceivable to Aristotle is now held out as a possiblity in the romances: a husband and wife living out the highest form of friendship.

Conclusion

It should now be clear that the Greek romances, long neglected in studies of friendship, are an important source for observing the conventions not only of the classic pair of friends but also of various other kinds as well—the social groups of male friends, political friendships, friendships between aristocratic women, and utilitarian friendships between master and slave or between slaves and those with whom they came in contact. And perhaps, during the early Roman empire the husband-wife relationship was beginning to be viewed as yet another, indeed the highest, form of friendship. Such then is the consequence of turning to documents whose length, amount of detail, and comprehensiveness permit an almost anthropological study of friendship within the complex of institutions that made up the social and intellectual world of the early Roman Empire. Others, I hope, will not overlook a Polycharmus and the many other friends who fill the pages of the Greek romances, but rather will include them in their fuller and more sophisticated studies of friendship in the Greco-Roman world.[31]

---

[31] I wish to thank my good friend and colleague Edward N. O'Neil for his many and helpful comments on earlier drafts of this paper.

WITH LUCIAN: WHO NEEDS FRIENDS? FRIENDSHIP IN THE *TOXARIS*

Richard I. Pervo

The *Toxaris* of Lucian treats many of the venerable themes of friendship in narrative form. This essay proposes that Lucian may be mocking sentimental concepts of friendship, such as those found in ideal novels.

Although it appears straightforward enough, Lucian's *Toxaris*[1] has some perplexing qualities.[2] *Toxaris* is a dialogue in form; its contents are a collection of stories.[3] Symposia and dialogues provided means for dressing such collections in culturally respectable clothing.[4] Its formal transparency is a problem. Would Lucian write a serious exposition of friendship illustrated by sentimental and fabulous stories?

---

[1] The full title is Τόξαρις ἤ Φιλία. One ms. (Φ, Codex Laurentianus, tenth century) presents the title Τόξαρις ἤ περὶ Φιλίας at the conclusion. The latter associates the work with a large number of treatises entitled "On Friendship." The text cited is that of M. D. MacLeod, *Luciani Opera III* (Oxford: University Press, 1980). Translations, unless otherwise noted, are those of A. M. Harmon, *Lucian* (LCL; 8 vols.; Cambridge: Harvard University Press, 1936) 5.103–207.

[2] G. Anderson (*Studies in Lucian's Comic Fiction* [Mnemosyne Suppl., 43; Leiden: E. J. Brill, 1976]) finds that it "has been almost wholly neglected" (12). His study (pp. 12–23) includes many valuable reflections, especially upon matters of source and structure.

[3] E. Rohde's appendix, "Über griechische Novellendichtung und ihren Zusammenhang mit dem Orient," *Der griechische Roman und seine Vorläufer* (3d ed.; Leipzig: Breitkopf und Hartel, 1914; repr., Darmstadt: Georg Olms, 1960) 578–601, remains a valuable discussion of ancient story collections. For the Greek novella, see O. Weinreich, *Fabel, Aretalogie, Novelle* (Heidelberg: C. Winter, 1931), and S. Trenkner, *The Greek Novella* (Cambridge: The University Press, 1958).

[4] Kindred dialogues in the Lucianic corpus include *The Lover of Lies* and *The Ship*. G. Anderson observes that, whereas *The True Story* relates marvelous adventures in narrative form, *Tox.* and *Philopseudes* use "mock-serious dialogue," the one devoted to adventure, the other to marvels (*Comic Fiction*, 12).

On the surface *Toxaris* is a rhetorical ἀγών, a σύγκρισις in which a Greek, Mnesippos by name, and Toxaris, a Scythian, each relate five stories, all sworn to be true and of recent vintage, to demonstrate the superiority of their respective national groups in the quality of friendship. The penalty for defeat is grave (10–11). In the event there is no penalty, for the two neglected to appoint a judge. They swear friendship instead (62–63). The contest thus concludes with a perfectly happy ending, like an epic encounter in which the antagonists exchange armor and leave in peace. This framework constitutes a sort of story outside of the stories, bringing a safe resolution to the dilemma that should have been keeping readers in suspense. Yet it is unlikely that this dilemma *does* keep readers in suspense, and the failure of the dreadful penalty in store to arouse any concern constitutes part of the reader's dilemma. The frame is not to be taken seriously.

The question remains: how is *Toxaris* to be read? As a comic fantasy,[5] a typically lucianic parody, or as pleasant, sentimental fictions? C. P. Jones characterizes *Toxaris* as quite unusual, wrestles with several options, and concludes that it is better to view the work as exceptional, since "the tone does not favor" reading it as a piece of parody.[6] Jones states that Lucian did not despise well-crafted and attractive fiction. This is doubtless true, but it does not resolve the issue. Ben Perry states that the themes of the stories are "ideal or tragic adventure," each of which "is a miniature romance in itself, and their value as romantic stories far outweighs the author's pretense that they are told only as illustrations of what friendship amounts to among Greeks and Scythians respectively."[7] Both Perry and Jones emphasize links

---

[5] So J. Bompaire, *Lucien ecrivain: imitation et creation* (Paris: E. de Boccard, 1958) 682–87.

[6] *Culture and Society in Lucian* (Cambridge, Mass.: Harvard University Press, 1986) 56–58. Jones regards *Tox.* as a mixture of two genres. As an example of the first he notes Plutarch's work *Mulierum Virtutes*. The other is Greek romance, "which often employs the theme of male comradeship."

[7] B. E. Perry, *The Ancient Romances: A Literary-Historical Account of Their Origin* (Berkeley: University of California Press, 1967) 234. He had earlier (p. 91) described *Tox.* as "*Rahmenerzaehlung* in the true Greek style," with its simple framework and coordinated stories rather than some artificial means of connection.

with popular fiction. In a recent survey Simon Swain denies that *Toxaris* is comic and dissociates it from romance:

> And so Lucian's piece should perhaps be placed alongside collections exemplifying virtue rather than being viewed primarily as entertainment. The moral message is uppermost, something unusual but not implausible in this author.[8]

Graham Anderson, against the general trend, forthrightly assumes that *Toxaris* is amusing and that the stories are preposterous or absurd. I rather incline to agree with Anderson. Moreover, I believe that a leading element of its relation to Greek romance is an often subtle parody[9] of the kinds of sentimental views of Greek male friendship depicted in romantic novels,[10] as well as popular myth, legend, and saga. Lucian may, in addition, be making some typical hits at the philosophical tradition, glorifying friendship and stories employed as *exempla* in this tradition. This proposal does not deny the value of *Toxaris* for comparisons with early Christian literature, since its parodies, if parodies they are, directly relate to the encomiastic tradition. One could construct a substantial commentary on the *Toxaris* by listing the parallels to the surviving treatises on friendship by Aristotle, Cicero, and Plutarch, among others.[11]

A Reading of the Text

The treatise opens as Mnesippos, an Athenian, questions the Scythian Toxaris about his people's practice of sacrificing to

---

[8] "Dio and Lucian," *Greek Fiction* (ed. J. R. Morgan and R. Stoneman; London: Routledge, 1994) 166–80. Pp. 174–76 treat *Tox*. The quotation is from 175–76.

[9] An example of subtle parody in Lucian is *The Syrian Goddess*, which has often been viewed as a serious and therefore unusual work. For its parodic features see Anderson, *Comic Fiction*, 68–82, and, in particular, R. Oden *Studies in Lucian's Dea Syria* (HSM 15; Missoula, Montana: Scholars Press, 1977).

[10] G. Anderson (*ComicFiction*, 83–89) agrees with Jones (*Culture and Society*, 58) that Lucian was probably familiar with romantic novels.

[11] Examples of these traditional views about friendship may be found in the other essays in this collection, as well as references in the following notes. Relationship to the tradition is patent in the classic definition of friendship offered by the Scythian Toxaris, χρὴ τοῖς φίλοις ἁπάσης τύχης κοινωνεῖν (5). G. Stählin ("φιλέω, κ.τ.λ.," *TDNT* 9 [1974] 113–71, 152) says that in Greek discussions of friendship, "The motif of κοινωνία especially recurs with considerable monotony."

Orestes and Pylades.[12] One imagines that Lucian is once more going to ridicule the worship of human beings, but Toxaris gives a utilitarian, ethical explanation of the cult: to encourage virtuous actions. Presently the dialogue leads to a Scythian encomium of the friendship represented by that famous pair of Greeks.[13] After Mnesippos shares some negative stereotypes about the Scythians, Toxaris states his thesis: Greeks utter many fine words about friendship but fail to live up to them in practice (9).[14] One irony of this work is the "barbarian"[15] Toxaris's manifest rhetorical skill, upon which Mnesippos more than once remarks.[16]

The Scythian proposes the duel and its rules. Each identifies an apposite penalty: loss of right hand for the action-bent Scythian, loss of tongue for the Greek wordsmith. Apposite but steep, and steeped in irony. The challenger yields first innings to Mnesippos, who leads with the tale of Agathocles and Deinias (12–18).[17] The two were friends from boyhood, but drifted apart in adult life because Deinias became wealthy.[18] This brings him a flock of drinking and carousing buddies, but no friends. Agathocles had little money and less interest in the dissolute life, but went along

---

[12] Orestes and Pylades, one of the classic pairs of friends (for the "canonical" list of these pairs, found, for example, in Plutarch, *De amic. mult.* 2.93E; Cicero, *Amic.* 15, *Fin.* 1.65; and Valerius Maximus 4.7, as well as *Toxaris* 10, see the essay of E. O'Neil in chapter five of this volume), rescued Iphigenia from the Taurians. Note also Trenkner, *Novella*, 72, who observes that Orestes and Pylades are the friends most often discussed and provides references to earlier studies of the subject.

[13] The worship of Hellenic heroes by "barbarian" Scyths suggests a certain irony.

[14] The opposition between words and deeds is, of course, a commonplace in Greek philosophical texts. For references to this subject in Lucian, see H. D. Betz, *Lukian von Samosata und das Neue Testament* (TU 76. Berlin: Akademie-Verlag, 1961) 104–6.

[15] G. W. Bowersock (*Fiction as History. Nero to Julian* [Berkeley: University of California Press, 1994] 44–46) finds *Tox.* unlike the tradition of romantic novels in that it does not derogate non-Greeks. Perhaps this assumption of Hellenic pride in literary works he regarded as inferior irritated the Syrian atticist Lucian.

[16] 8, 35, 63. Toxaris's examples are no less illustrative of Greek conventions than are his opponent's. Toxaris promises to avoid rhetorical embellishment, which does not conform to Scythian *mores* (35), but the preamble to his contributions continues until 38!

[17] Deinias is the name of a major character is Antonius Diogenes' novel *The Marvels beyond Thule.*

[18] Cicero discusses the problem of presuming that childhood friends should remain friends for life (*Amic.* 74).

for the ride until his reprimands put him into disfavor. He is a genuine friend rather than a mere flatterer, and a text-book illustration thus far.[19]

Meanwhile, enter the boon companions of Deinias, who engage in collusion with an experienced *femme fatale*, one Charicleia,[20] who induces him to perform an economic strip-tease. Once he has dropped the last vestige of one of the leading fortunes of Ionia,[21] she dropped him. At that point of low ebb, he bethought himself of his old boyhood friend, Agathocles, who hastened to sell all that he had and give it to Deinias.

The latter set out to pour these modest three talents down the drain, but soon ran afoul of Charicleia's husband, whom he slew, together with his wife, in a grisly bedroom encounter. Deinias was exiled for life; Agathocles chose to share his fate[22] and, when their funds ran out, supported them by engaging in manual labor,[23] and nursed Deinias during a long illness. Following the eventual demise of his friend, Agathocles elected to remain on the island of their exile.

This is a sad little melodrama, with sentimental coloring, suitable for a sub-plot in a novel.[24] As a tale of friendship it bespeaks great loyalty, but no reciprocity.[25] Agathocles did not help his friend with his generous gift, an act that none of the

---

[19] The need for frank reproof is another emphasis of Cicero (*Amic.* 44). See also Aristotle, *Nich. Eth.* 9.3.3–5.

[20] Charicleia resembles the "bad women" rivals to the heroines of the romantic novels. She shares her name with the heroine of Helidorus's *An Ethiopian Story* (which probably appeared long after Lucian's time). With *Tox.* 15 compare Ach. Tat. *Leucippe and Clitophon* 5.23; Hel. 1.9.

[21] Deinias' gifts to Charicleia included συνοικίαι ὅλαι καὶ ἀγροὶ καὶ θεράπαιναι καὶ ἐσθῆτες εὐανθεῖς καὶ χρυσὸν ὁπόσον ἐθελήσει (15). For the catalogue compare Mark 10:29–30.

[22] Seneca defines a friend as *"Quem in exilium sequar"* (*Ep.* 9.10).

[23] The work involves diving for shells (18), arduous and shocking toil for one of gentle birth. Manual labor is one of the ordeals romantic heroes may have to undergo, as in *An Ephesian Tale* 5.8. In *Callirhoe* 4.2 Polycharmus performs much of the labor assigned to his friend Chaireas.

[24] For examples of male friendship in ancient novels, see the contribution of R. Hock in chapter seven of this volume.

[25] This is a case of friendship between unequals, a subject discussed by the ancient authorities. Reciprocity is the basis of friendship according to Aristotle, *Nich. Eth.* 8.

writers on the topic would recommend,[26] and his loyalty beyond the grave is wretched excess. Perhaps one should understand it as unrequited homosexual passion.[27] I doubt that readers are meant to approve.

The second episode (19–21) introduces an old favorite: storm at sea.[28] Euthydicos, hale and hearty, follows his frail friend Damon into the deep when the latter went overboard while attending to his *mal de mer*. Crew and passengers could provide no aid beyond heaving wood and cork,[29] and the two were left to their fate.

Retardation caused by a rhetorical apostrophe requires ardent intervention by Toxaris to learn how the tale ended: in mutual death, or ἐκ παραλόγου σωτηρία? (21) The latter, it transpires, in the form of the ship's boarding ladder, which they found, mounted, and drifted ashore. At the time of the telling both were pursuing philosophical studies at Athens.

Here is a fine romantic story with an unexpected happy ending. The tale is more appropriate for lovers than for friends.[30] Dying to save a friend is not quite the same as hastening to join him in death.[31] κοινὰ τῶν φίλων is being taken beyond the limits of μηδὲν ἄγαν. Lucian may be sneering here at the "new kind of

---

[26] Present day theory would view this donation as a form of "enabling" behavior in circumstances that require intervention rather than support. It is like giving an addict money knowing that it will be used to purchase drugs.

[27] The friends in *Tox.* are, of course, men. It is possible that their undying devotion to one another mocks the romantic loyalty of the heterosexual pairs in the romantic novels, as may be the case also in Petronius's *Satyrica*. For stories of homosexual pairs, see Trenkner, *Novella*, 27, 28, 57, 111.

[28] Mnesippos need do no more than enter by title the motifs of this *topos*, 19. *Satyrica* 114.10 already parodies the theme (as does Lucian in his comic *True Story* 1.6).

[29] Lucian is fascinated by the properties of cork: *True Story* 2.4, *Lover of Lies* 13.

[30] Mnesippos (20) refers to this act as a superlative demonstration of εὔνοια. That common noun from the vocabulary of friendship seems a bit tame for the context.

[31] On laying down one's life for one's friends, see Plato, *Symp.* 179b, 208d, Seneca, *Ep.* 9.10, Epictetus, *Diss.* 2.7.3, and Aristotle, *Nich. Eth.*9.8, 1169a18–1169b2, as well as John 10:11; 15:13. An example from novels is Ach. Tat. 3.22.1 ὑπὲρ φίλου, κἂν ἀποθανεῖν δεήσῃ, καλὸς ὁ κίνδυνος, γλυκὺς ὁ θάνατος. The last imbues the theme with highly romantic colors.

hero" found in romantic novels, the individual who prefers death to separation from one's true love.

Story three involves three persons: Eudamidas, Aretaios, and Charixenos (22–23).[32] This is a tale of unequal friends. Eudamidas, quite poor, left the obligation of supporting his mother[33] and providing a dowry for his daughter as a bequest to his wealthy friends. A mocking crowd, comprising those who knew of Eudamidas's poverty but not of his friendships, provides an interesting foil.[34] When Charixenos died within five days after his friend's demise, the undaunted Aretaios carried on the project alone. Mnesippos elicits the point by questioning Toxaris, who gives the correct answer (23).[35]

If there is anything unusual in this vignette, it is the romanticization of social convention. What could have been described as a far from unusual example of reciprocity within a social network has received a dramatic and sentimental coloration. The wealthy are not simply doing their duty; they are engaging in extraordinary generosity. Sentimental perception of this quality doubtless comes from those closer to Eudamidas on the social scale. It witnesses to a romantic view of life, the kind of view Lucian seems elsewhere to scorn.

The fourth item in the hellenic package (24–26) also deals with marriage of the moneyless. Menecrates has suffered political disgrace, falling from honor and wealth into poverty and shame. His daughter, Cydimache, was disfigured and given to seizures.[36] Menecrates did nothing to improve her chances for marriage. Never mind. Zenothemis forced the issue and consummated the marriage, even flaunting his wife in public to demonstrate his disdain for wealth and beauty.

---

[32] 22–23. Toxaris's third tale (44–55) also features three. The stories thus stay within the conventions favoring one or two genuine friends.

[33] Cf. John 19:25–27.

[34] Such mocking crowds may also appear in *novelle* describing the miraculous, as in Mark 5:38–40, for example.

[35] For the technique, see Matt. 21:31, 40, etc.

[36] Feigned epilepsy disqualifies Anthia from compulsory service in a Sicilian brothel: *An Ephesian Tale* 5.7.

Virtue was rewarded.[37] The ill-favored Cydimache produced a beautiful baby boy, the very sight of whom moved the Massiliotes to rescind the penalty against his grandfather. Once again there is a very sentimental story, based upon an extravagant and impulsive exhibition of friendship. Rather than applaud Zenothemis for helping to restore the fortunes of his friend's family by uniting himself with it, this *novella* singles out the contrast between the handsome young principal and his repellent wife. I suspect that cultivated aristocrats would have found this story in poor taste.[38] From the perspective of Greek romance, it is a nearly perfect foil. Instead of a beautiful couple struck by mutual *coups de foudre*, there is a handsome young man who claims a hideously unattractive young woman by rape. Rather than experiencing separation, they are constantly together. In this tale friendship between men overrides the possibility of a marriage based upon mutual erotic attraction.

The well-known adventures of Demetrios of Sunium and Antiphilos of Alopece constitute Mnesippos's final and longest tale (27–34).[39] Like Agathocles and Deinias (the first pair),[40] these two have been friends from boyhood. They went together to Egypt (presumably Alexandria) to school. Antiphilos was a medical student;[41] Demetrios pursued Cynic philosophy. Motivated by a desire to see the shadowless pyramids and to hear Memnon hail the rising sun, Demetrios set off on a tourist voyage. This common device[42] removed him from the scene. The plot thickened.

---

[37] αὐτὸν ἠμείψατο ἡ τύχη (26).

[38] Modern readers are likely to squirm at Zenothemis's flaunting of his disfigured spouse. She is a mere object. This would be less likely to offend ancient men, but it does set up a dissonance with the romanticism of the plot.

[39] Demetrios gets top billing. L. M. White ("Morality between Two Worlds: A Paradigm of Friendship in Philippians," *Greeks, Romans, and Christians. Essays in Honor of Abraham J. Malherbe* [ed. D. Balch, E. Ferguson, W. A. Meeks; Minneapolis: Fortress Press, 1990] 201–15) makes a number of useful comments about *Tox.*, but incorrectly characterizes Antiphilos as the slave of Demetrios.

[40] This is one example of the symmetry within and between the two sets of five stories.

[41] This career choice does not suggest a person of high social status.

[42] Ach. Tat. 3.9–4.5 is one example. Demetrios's credulity is somewhat surprising in a Cynic. For an historical parallel to this tour, see P Tebt. 33 (= *Select Papyri* [ed. A. S. Hunt and G. C. Edgar; LCL 266 and 282; 2 vols.; Cambridge: Harvard University

Antiphilos's slave, Syros, participated in a robbery of the temple of Anubis. His owner was implicated by circumstantial evidence and arrested while in class. The odium attached to this crime of sacrilege brought disgrace and brutal treatment by the jailer; other acquaintances (who were thereby exposed as less than true friends) shunned him. Antiphilos, a delicate creature, began to waste away and decided to hasten the process by starvation.[43]

In the very nick of time Demetrios, quite unaware of what had happened, returned and attempted to visit his friend. The recognition, impeded by Antiphilos's deterioration and the dreadful conditions, caused both to swoon.[44] Demetrios came sooner to his senses, revived Antiphilos, and began to care for him, beginning by splitting, like St. Martin, his cloak in two. From that time forth they shared all. Demetrios engaged himself as a longshoreman to support the two[45] (and bribe the jailer). He slept on a bed of leaves just outside the prison door. When a mysterious death led to tightened security, Demetrios went to the governor, implicated himself in the crime,[46] and thus joined his friend in bonds, even winning the privilege of sharing his chains. They bore the burdens of confinement together.[47]

At this point fate takes a hand. The other prisoners engineered an escape and fled, killing the guards. Our couple, however, not only refused to take flight;[48] they also seized the guilty slave Syros.

Press, 1932–34] 2.416 [112 BCE]).

[43] Threatened suicide is quite common in ancient novels. In Chariton's *Callirhoe* the principal function of Chaireas' friend, Polycharmus, is to dissuade the hero from taking his own life.

[44] Swooning is common in the romantic novels. When Chaireas and Callirhoe are reunited (*Callirhoe* 8.1), both swoon, as in *Tox.* 30.

[45] Cf. the willingness to resort to manual labor in the opening story (18), another instance of symmetry.

[46] On the motif of self-accusation to share the fate of another, see Trenkner, *Novella*, 75.

[47] ὥστε ῥᾷον ἔφερον μετ' ἀλλήλων κακοπαθοῦντες (32). An obvious parallel is Gal. 6:2a Ἀλλήλων τὰ βάρη βαστάζετε, on which see Betz, *Galatians* (Hermeneia; Philadelphia: Fortress Press, 1973) 298–99, who cites texts from the friendship tradition.

[48] One discussion of the numerous parallels with Acts 16:19–40, with references, is R. Pervo, *Profit with Delight* (Philadelphia: Fortress Press, 1987) 23–24. For a different approach to the material, see B. Rapske, *The Book of Acts and Paul in Roman Custody*

Their meritorious conduct ignited the process that would eventuate in their ultimate release.

Demetrios rejected clemency on these grounds and demanded a full investigation. In due course this took place. Full vindication was its result, together with reparations in the amount of 10,000 drachmas for Antiphilos and 20,000 to his faithful friend.[49] Mnesippos noted that in his courtroom speech (omitted lest it contribute to the stereotype of Greek fondness for words) Demetrios cast all blame upon himself,[50] but was saved when Syros confessed under torture.

Able to manage with meager resources,[51] Demetrios left his money to Antiphilos and went off to India and the Brahmans, reasoning that 30,000 drachmas would substitute for the presence of a friend. Assuring his opponent that he has simply pulled out of a potentially vast repertory[52] the first five stories that came to mind, Mnesippos challenges Toxaris to match his examples.

This final friendship *novella* belongs to the realm of Greek romance, as the parallels in Chariton indicate.[53] What is the implied reader to conclude? Demetrios does exemplify Cynic self-sufficiency. He can be happy even in prison—so long as he is with his friend. On the other hand, classical Cynicism would seem to have viewed the conventions of friendship, with its entanglements and dependencies, as suspect, and Demetrios's voyages of exploration in Egypt as well as his expedition to the

---

(Grand Rapids: William B. Eerdmans, 1994) 115–34 *et passim*.

[49] For a similar reward, see Xenophon of Ephesos, 4.4.1.

[50] Romantic heroes (such as Chaireas, *Callirhoe* 1.5) seem to revel in assuming full share of the blame.

[51] For self-sufficiency, see 2 Cor 6:10, Phil 4:11–12, etc., as well as Crates, *Epistle* 7 (ed. Malherbe, 58), and Teles (ed. O'Neil), 38, 54, 84–85. Cicero associates self-sufficiency with friendship in *Amic.* 30.

[52] 35. Cf. John 20:30–31, 21:25.

[53] On friendship in Chariton, see the contribution of R. Hock in chapter seven of this volume. In romantic novels the change of circumstances would probably be referred to a benevolent Τυχή or to Providence.

Brahmans[54] place him in potential proximity to Peregrinus, who was not for Lucian the model Cynic.[55]

Had both friends been in prison and Demetrios bolstered his more delicate colleague (as Polycharmus did for Chaireas in Chariton 4.2), the story would exhibit greater probability. As it stands, the suddenly penniless Demetrios (who had, after all, possessed the resources to study in Egypt and travel there) devoted all of his energy to sustaining Antiphilos and none of it to seeking legal vindication. Rather than pursue release for his wronged friend, he perjured himself to join him in prison. Only after their release did Demetrios begin to demand an investigation. Even then he preferred false self-incrimination to a genuine inquiry after the facts. Syros could, after all, have been tortured at any time. Only τι προσπεσόν[56] prevented a tawdry ending.

Demetrios's ultimate desertion of Antiphilos, with its implication that wealth relieves one of the necessity for friends, is equally strange. The last time he left Antiphilos alone, disaster struck, and there is little reason to believe that the latter is now more capable of taking care of himself. I strongly suspect that Lucian is poking fun at the kind of sentimental friendship relations described in Greek romances. The holes in the story suggest that Antiphilos, however passionate in his devotion, was something less than the best kind of friend.

All five of these tales treat subjects at home in the popular tradition: voyage at sea, domestic intrigue, charges of murder, a will, trial in court. If read as serious moralizing, they are in conflict with the values and attitudes normally espoused by Lucian. *Pace* C. P. Jones, they exude a sentimentality so effectively demolished by Lucian that his ridicule of it has made a substantial contribution to his literary immortality.

---

[54] "Brahmans" might include the Gymnosophists much admired by Cynics. Cf. Plutarch, *Alex.* 64, *Alexander Romance* 3.6.

[55] Cf. Lucian's *The Death of Peregrinus*.

[56] 33. "An accident," in Harmon's translation (*Lucian*, 5.157).

Here endeth the first lesson, retailing the affairs of Greeks condemned by the *Pax Romana* to deal with minor matters. What will the uncouth Scythians have to offer?

A great deal. Toxaris, for his part, begins with a reiteration of the "deeds speak louder than words" theme.[57] His opening remarks underscore a basic piece of irony: Greeks live in secure peace, whereas conflict reveals true friendship. One irony is that the traditional icons of Greek friendship are pairs of heroes whose exploits were essentially military.[58] Lucian may be questioning the relevance of these models. In any case, those seeking modern examples of traditional friends must go beyond the limits of the empire.

Such exploits Toxaris can supply, for he will speak of deeds of derring-do, masculine acts of bravery and might: not of ugly wives but φόνους πολλοὺς καὶ πολέμους καὶ θανάτους ὑπὲρ τῶν φίλων (36). Scythian friendship is an indispensable instrument of war. Paragraph 37 describes a solemn ceremony of blood brotherhood. Scythians may engage in no more than three such covenants.[59] More would be comparable to female promiscuity (38–41).[60] Scythian friendship is, then, a matter of choice among adult males and thus conforms to classical Greek norms and ideals.

The first Scythian story concerns Dandamis and Amizoces (38–41), sworn friends of three days' vintage. A surprise raid by Sauromatians sweeps all before it: prisoners taken, goods plundered, women assaulted, and all before the *eyes* of the hapless victims. Amizoces, who had been taken prisoner, reminds Dandamis of their pact. The latter plunges into the Don, swims

---

[57] τὰ ἔργα ὑπερφθέγγηται τοὺς λόγους (35). He builds suspense by two full (Oxford text) pages of preliminary material before words give way to narrative about deeds. Irony should not be ruled out.

[58] Piling irony upon irony, Toxaris uses the image of a storm as the best test of a sea-captain's skill (36). One of Mnesippos's stories had been set in a storm at sea (19–21), although its principal characters were not in charge of the ship.

[59] This conforms to the Greco-Roman norm: *quod ex omnibus saeculis vix tria aut quattuor nominantur paria amicorum* (Cicero, *Amic.* 15).

[60] Such promiscuity marked the first Greek story. 37 includes another hit at the romantic tradition, where Toxaris states that Scythians court friends as Greeks pursue potential wives.

across, is nearly slain, but is finally accepted as an emissary seeking to redeem a captive. Unfortunately all of Dandamis's property had been seized. The ransom demanded was his eyes. These he freely gave, and returned with his friend, now his guide.

The obvious relevance of this incident to Gal 4:14–15: "Though my condition put you to the test, you did not scorn or despise me, but welcomed me as an angel of God, as Christ Jesus. What has become of the good will you felt? For I testify that, had it been possible, you would have torn out your eyes and given them to me" (NRSV) has been duly noted.[61] The sacrifice of Dandamis was extraordinary.

Scarcely less noteworthy were its effects: the incident roused[62] the Scythians to reflect that friendship, the greatest of all their possessions,[63] had not been plundered. They rallied, counter-attacked, and routed the enemy. Amizoces, offended by his eyes, plucked them out, and the two now live happily at public expense, like Olympic victors. This may be a bit too much of a good thing, a gruesome ending to a tale about the power of friendship. The parallel with the first Greek story, in which one friend shared the other's exile, is apparent, as is the comparable excess of devotion.

After a bit of *praeteritio*, in which Toxaris ironically notes what could have been embellished but was not,[64] he launches into the brief story of Belitta and Basthes. While they were hunting the latter was attacked by a lion. Belitta, with considerable effort, induced the lion to attack him, managing to stab it before he died. Basthes, too, died, and all three (lion included) were buried in adjoining tombs. Mnesippos's second story featured a friend

---

[61] Betz (*Galatians*, 220–27) provides a valuable commentary. See also A. Mitchell's remarks on Betz's observations in his contribution to this collection (chapter eleven). In *A True Story* 1.25 Lucian speaks of eyes stored in a bank. For the motif see also fable 22 of Avianus (= Perry 580 [B. E. Perry, *Babrius and Phaedrus* (LCL; Cambridge: Harvard University Press, 1965) 532–33]), and Athenaeus, *Deipn.* 248E, 249A. Finally, Petronius ridicules the convention: *Hunc oculum pro vobis impendi* (*Sat.* 1.1).

[62] παρεμυθήσατο, 41.

[63] This is another *topos*. Cf. Cicero, *Amic.* 55.

[64] One of his examples is an omitted speech (42), precisely what Mnesippos had also omitted (34), and for the same reason.

who was willing to join the other in death. Toxaris's corresponding entry exhibits someone who laid down his life *with* his friend. This is clearly fictitious.[65]

The next tale, which celebrates Macentes, Lonchates, Arsacomas (44–55), is Toxaris's showpiece. This is a long story, with enough travel and incident for a full novel, an example of which it may draw upon and abridge.[66] While on a diplomatic mission Arsacomas falls in love at first sight with Mazaea, a highly sought-after daughter of a king. The various suitors boast of their wealth. Arsacomas, for his part, points to his two friends as his riches. The audience laughs.[67] The irony is that he will win Mazaea with the help of these very friends. Deceit, chicanery, assassination, and war are employed toward the desired end. This novella, which could be "Exhibit A" in a demonstration of the principle that "All's fair in love and war," is as exotic and bloody a story as any fond soul might crave.

These splendid fellows appear to be bound by no law or scruples other than loyalty to one another and their people. The story is utterly (and appropriately) "barbaric." The friendship it displays is a socially destructive force. The friends are quite willing

---

[65] See the note of Harmon, *Lucian* 5.173. Perry (*Babrius and Phaedrus*, 479) records a fable (no. 284) featuring a monument of a man strangling a lion. Cf. also *Select Papyri* 2.109. In the novel of Iamblichus (*A Babylonian Story* 3) there is a "leonine stele."

[66] This tale was first linked with a novel by Rostovtzeff. The fragment in question is called *Calligone* by modern editors. The text includes PSI 981 (= Pack 2.2628) and PCair. 47992. For a translation, see B. Reardon (ed.), *Collected Ancient Greek Novels* (Berkeley: University of California Press, 1989) 826–27. F. Zimmermann ("Lukians Toxaris und das Kairener Romanfragment," *PhilWoch* 55 [1935]:1211–16) was skeptical about the relation of these fragments to *Tox.* Swain ("Dio and Lucian," 175) is equally dubious. G. Anderson (*Comic Fiction*, 15–19) does not rule out dependence. The commentary of R. M. Rattenbury ("Romance: The Greek Novel," *New Chapters in the History of Greek Literature* [ed. J. Powell; Oxford: The University Press, 1933] 240–44) remains valuable. See now S. A. Stephens and J. J. Winkler (eds.), *Ancient Greek Novels: The Fragments* (Princeton: Princeton University Press, 1995) 267–76. The possibility of a novelistic source for this story does not depend upon the *Calligone* fragment alone. Lucian might have had access to another "Scythian" novel.

[67] Note the parallel in the Greek marriage tale, 22–23, also treating an impoverished candidate for marriage and a scoffing crowd.

to die for or with one another and to kill anyone who stands between a friend and the satisfaction of his desires.

Decorating this intricate tale of intrigue and adventure are many of the typical themes associated with Greek friendship. The three friends constitute εἷς ἄνθρωπος (46) and are εἰς ἕνα (53).[68] Macentes's oration on the theme that friends constitute one body deserves extensive citation:[69]

> Stop making me a different person from yourself! To express gratitude to me for what I have done in this is just as if my left hand should be grateful to my right for ministering to it when it had been wounded and taking care of it fondly while it was weak. So with us—it would be ridiculous if, after having fused ourselves together long ago and united, as far as we could, into a single person, we should continue to think it a great thing if this or that part of us has done something useful in behalf of the whole body; for it was working in its own behalf as a part of the whole organism[70] to which the good was being done.[71]

The resultant dissonance raises questions about this ethic of friendship. If one can use hellenic themes to illustrate barbaric action, what are the implications for the ethic? At the very least, friendship without a ground in public morality can be a questionable virtue. The contrast with Mnesippos's tale of poor Eudamidas whose friends cared for his mother and daughter

---

[68] For references to the friend as one's other self, see Stählin, "φιλέω," 152. μία ψυχή, is, of course, used in Acts 4:32 in conjunction with commonalty of possessions. The language brings to mind Mark 10:8 and Plato, *Symp.* 192E.

[69] 53, trans. Harmon, *Lucian* 5.189–91.

[70] Cf. 1 Cor 12:26–27: "If one member suffers, all suffer together with it; if one member is honored, all rejoice together with it. Now you are the body of Christ and individually members of it" and Eph 4:15–16: "But speaking the truth in love, we must grow up in every way into him who is the head, into Christ, from whom the whole body, joined and knit together by every ligament with which it is equipped, as each part is working properly, promotes the body's growth in building itself up in love." (NRSV)

[71] Παῦε . . . ἄλλον με ποιῶν σεαυτοῦ· τὸ γὰρ χάριν ἐμοὶ ὁμολογεῖν ἐφ' οἷς ἔπραξα τούτοις τοιόνδε ἐστιν ὥσπερ ἂν ⟨εἰ⟩ ἡ ἀριστερά μου χάριν εἰδείη τῇ δεξιᾷ διότι τρωθεῖσάν ποτε αὐτὴν ἐθεράπευσε καὶ φιλοφρόνως ἐπεμελήθη καμνούσουης. γελοῖα τοίνυν καὶ ἡμεῖς ἂν ποιοῖμεν εἰ πάλαι ἀναμιχθέντες καὶ ὡς οἷόν τε ἦν εἰς ἕνα συνελθόντες ἔτι μέγα νομίζομεν εἶναι εἰ τὸ μέρος ἡμῶν ἔπραξέ τι χρηστὸν ὑπὲρ ὅλου τοῦ σώματος· ὑπὲρ αὐτοῦ γὰρ ἔπραττεν, μέρος ὂν τοῦ ὅλου εὖ πάσχοντος (MacLeod, *Luciani Opera III*, 254–55).

could scarcely be greater. Toxaris's story is very complex and quite long; Mnesippos's is brief and poignant. Deeds speak louder than words.

This adventure has been a bit much for Mnesippos, who finds these stories πάνυ τραγικά and μῦθοις ὅμοια (56).[72] The Scythian has sworn to tell the truth, but the Scythians in his stories are quite willing to lie.[73] Toxaris quickly shifts gears. His fourth story is a personal account of how Sisinnes was of assistance to him. This takes place in the Greek world. While returning from their studies of Greek *paideia*, the pair were robbed in Amastris. Toxaris, like the hero of a novel, opts for suicide, But Sisinnes, like the friend of a romantic hero, dissuaded him from this course, engaged in menial labor to sustain the two, and finally made their fortune by risking his life in mortal combat. Toxaris thereafter cared for his wounds and married him to his sister. This corresponds advantageously to the Greek story of Demetrios and Antiphilos, a friendship marked by reciprocity, with one of the pair (Sisinnes here) who was both resourceful and intelligent. Manual labor is indignity enough. Enrolling oneself as a gladiator[74] was the equivalent of selling oneself into slavery, and may well exceed the limits of propriety. Becoming a gladiator is rather uncivilized conduct, although, it must be conceded, so is the robbery of tourists.

Toxaris's final contribution is quite brief (61). Gyndanes was wounded while fighting off robbers who had attacked a party that included his friend Abauchas, and the latter's family. When a fire broke out in their residence, Abauchas carried out his injured friend and, shrugging off his wife and children, left them to fend for themselves. Wives and children can be replaced, but not proven friends.[75] Comparison with the Greek story of Zenothemis,

---

[72] See the comments of C. P. Jones, *Culture and Society*, 57.

[73] On the use of oaths here, see M. Caster, *Lucien et la pensée religieuse de son temps* (Paris: Belles Lettres, 1937) 322, and Anderson, *Comic Fiction*, 15, n. 17, who points to Lucian's interest in absurd oaths.

[74] On this fascinating topic see Carlin A. Barton, *The Sorrows of the Ancient Romans* (Princeton: Princeton University Press, 1993) esp. 12–16, 22–27, 34–36, and 46.

[75] For such sacrifices in tragic stories, see Trenkner, *Novella*, 75 n. 7. One may reflect upon Gospel traditions that prefer following Jesus to family membership.

who married the ugly daughter of Menecrates (22–24), is appropriate. Rather than promote domestic and civic life, Scythian friendship appears to subvert it. How would Greeks of the Imperial age have regarded this story? With ambivalence, at best.

Toxaris finishes with the observation that, like his opponent, he has culled these selections from many. He then raises the question of a judge. Mnesippos finds this request a bit tardy, for none has been appointed. He suggests a properly adjudicated re-match only to reject it, then advances an alternative proposal: "Let's be friends!" Friends are the greatest of possessions. By vowing friendship they will each gain another set of limbs and organs, rather than each suffer a vital loss of the same. Mnesippos closes with the image of two or three friends as one body.[76] His partner happily agrees. Mnesippos has the last word: Toxaris has convinced him ἀπὸ τῶν λόγων! This is the final, but not the least telling, example of irony.

Conclusion

Toxaris is an amusing dialogue because the two contestants engage in a dire duel without a judge and tell fictitious stories sworn to be true. It is difficult to believe that Lucian would choose this often ludicrous context as a frame for serious views about friendship. The contestants are unreliable narrators. Although many of the traditional *topoi* about friendship emerge in the narrations, the settings used to illustrate them often fail to redound to their advantage. They are grotesque. Lucian seems to view the tradition of male friendship as rather out-dated, linked as it is to the heroic past (and to homosexuality, of which he does not seem to approve). For present day examples of homeric proportions one must look to "barbaric" cultures, where friendship often produces grim results potentially destructive of civic responsibilities and loyalties.

One of his targets may well be the sentimental friendships (and romantic relationships) celebrated in romantic novels, where

---

[76] The notion of friends forming one body is also stated in *Tox.* 53, discussed above.

heroes and friends are often more prepared to die for friends and lovers than to live without them. Given Lucian's rather unsentimental literary *persona*, this interpretation deserves consideration. Whatever its specific target, *Toxaris* abounds in paradox, irony, and excess. Rather than having produced an entertaining work extolling traditional friendship, Lucian appears to be up to his normal mischief. In so far as the ancient ideals of friendship no longer accorded with such social realities as civic duty and the status of women, this mischief may have been useful as well as usual.

Friendship in Greek Documentary Papyri and Inscriptions: A Survey

Katherine G. Evans

A sampling of 18,000 papyri and inscriptions has revealed the use of friendship terminology in 203 texts including letters, epitaphs, dedications and devotions. The extant evidence is mainly representative of adult property holding males and demonstrates a utilitarian view where friends are relied upon to help with business and family matters.

A comprehensive study of friendship in the papyri is beyond the scope of a single article. The reasons for this become manifest when one considers that the evidence spans nearly ten centuries (3rd c. BCE–7th c. CE), is written in Greek, Latin, Demotic, and Coptic, consists of diverse form and genre types, and covers a variety of ethnic and religious groups including Egyptian, Greek, Roman, Jewish, Christian and various combinations within these groups. Up to this point, no secondary study has been done on friendship in Greek and Roman Egypt although some work has been done on the "friendly" letter in the papyri. These studies, however, tend to focus on the formulaic aspects of the letters rather than on an assessment of the meaning of friendship. Because of the complexity of the topic, what this study proposes to accomplish is threefold: 1) to discuss the special methods, issues, and problems for studying friendship in Greek and Roman Egypt; 2) to provide the results of a survey of the use of the terms φίλος and φιλία in a random sampling of 18,000 papyri and inscriptions; and 3) to indicate areas which may be fruitful for further study. As we shall see, the documentary evidence for friendship is difficult to isolate, relatively scanty in quantity, and generally presents a practical, even utilitarian, view of friendship where a friend is someone who does favors for you.

Methodological Issues

One of the first considerations for researching friendship in Greek and Roman Egypt is understanding the limitations of the extant sources. Although literally tens of thousands of papyri have survived, they are not accurately representative of the population of Egypt in any sense: chronological, geographical, or other demographic, including ethnicity, gender, age, and socio-economic status. There are far more extant papyri from the Roman period than the previous Ptolemaic. Geographically, the papyri mainly represent the rural areas and a very large, if serendipitous, discovery at Oxyrhynchus. In contrast, very little has survived from the northern delta areas and the four Greek cities (Alexandria, Naukratis, Ptolemais, and later Antinoopolis), which were the centers for education, commerce, government, and the elite of society. Many diverse groups are clearly under-represented in the papyri, including Egyptians, women and children, and servants. Persons with wealth, especially property owners, are the primary subjects of the documentary papyri whereas the poor are notably absent and slaves are usually mentioned only in their capacity as moveable property.

A second consideration regarding the limitations of the extant evidence is the fact that most documents lack a situational context. With some exceptions, most papyri describe an event and personages for whom no other evidence is available. We can determine nothing about the relationships of the people involved except for what is given in the brief document itself. This becomes particularly problematic when one is trying to determine on the basis of a few written words if two people were friends, relatives, business associates, master and servant, or other. It is also difficult if not impossible to reconstruct what friendship may have meant to two people when we can only pinpoint one isolated exchange between them. This is a major limitation that one does not encounter in literature, which usually provides discourse between its main characters as well as descriptions of their family and status.

Given these limitations of the papyri as source material, the methods for determining the existence of friendship in the papyri can be investigated. One obvious criterion would be the use of vocabulary that explicitly means friend or friendship. A subsection of the papyri surveyed for this study was examined for relevant terminology. After surveying a number of papyri, it became evident that the only vocabulary used to describe friend and friendship was φίλος and φιλία respectively. A search was made using Preisigke's *Wörterbuch der griechischen Papyrusurkunden* for other possible terms associated with Greek ritualized friendship such as ἑταῖρος and ἐπιτήδειος, and it was found that these appeared only in literary texts.[1] A search of φίλος and φιλία through the random sample of 18,000 papyri surveyed here yielded only 203 documents which utilized one of these terms. Φίλος was occasionally attached to a name as a type of identifier. In private letters, φίλος appears often on the address on the verso such as X- to Y- his friend. Elsewhere φίλος appears incidental to the message of the text. Φιλία only occurred in private letters and was usually used with παρά when persons were requested to do a favor "on account of friendship."

Since specific friendship terminology appeared to be in little evidence, an in-depth look was taken at the one genre type that we know was specifically used in the ancient world to maintain friendship, the private letter. Evidence of the importance of the letter for friendship maintenance is replete in classical literature, including references in Aristotle, Seneca, and the extant letters of Apollonius of Tyana, Cicero and Pliny.[2] There also existed in Egypt during the Greek and Roman periods handbooks on epistolary style which included guidelines for writing a "friendly" letter.[3] At least in theory, letters between friends should have been easily identified.

---

[1] Friedrich Preisigke, *Wörterbuch der griechischen Papyrusurkunden* (Berlin: Selbstverlag, 1925–1971); for ritualized friendship terminology, see Gabriel Herman, *Ritualised Friendship and the Greek City* (Cambridge: Cambridge University Press, 1987) esp. p. 10–11.

[2] See Klaus Thraede, *Grundzüge griechisch-römischer Brieftopik* (Monographien zur klassischen Altertumswissenschaft 48; Munich: Beck, 1970).

[3] The most complete examples are Pseudo-Demetrius *Epistolary Types* (dated between the 3rd c. BCE and the 3rd c. CE) and *Epistolary Styles*, attributed to both Libanius and Proclus (dated between the 4th and 6th centuries CE). These and others have been excerpted and translated in Abraham J. Malherbe, *Ancient*

Letters in the papyri were highly formulaic, especially in their openings and closings. Since approximately the same form was used for private letters, business correspondence, and petitions to officials, it is necessary to distinguish among these types based on their content. F. Exler has done a detailed study of the opening formulae used in the different types of letters.⁴ The basic opening address is: A- (addresser) to B- (addressee) greetings. Letters were often personalized by the addition of words to the basic greetings. For example, private letters often modify "greetings" to read "many greetings" or even "very many greetings." In addition, a term of familiarity may be added following the addressee's name. The most common examples of these in men's letters are: A- to B- his dearest (τῷ φιλτάτῳ), his most esteemed (τῷ τιμιωτάτῳ), his sweetest (τῷ γλυκυτάτῳ), and his own (τῷ ἰδίῳ). With the exception of ὁ φίλτατος, these terms of familiarity were also used in the opening formulae of letters from women. H. Koskenniemi has noted that men used ὁ φίλτατος in the opening address of letters to men and not to women. He concluded that this was a term of familiarity used exclusively between men.⁵

On the surface these embellishments to the standard opening formula might appear to be indications of friendship. In fact, Julius Victor writing on epistolary style in the fourth century CE said, "The openings and conclusions of letters should conform with the degree of friendship (you share with the recipient) or with his rank, and should be written according to customary practice."⁶ A detailed study of phraseology in papyrus letters done by Koskenniemi, however, has revealed that the terminology was

---

Epistolary Theorists (SBLSBS 19; Atlanta: Scholars Press, 1988).

⁴ Francis Xavier J. Exler, *The Form of the Ancient Greek Letter of the Epistolary Papyri (3rd c. B.C. – 3rd c. A.D.): A Study of Greek Epistolography* (Washington: Catholic University of America, 1923; repr. Chicago: Ares, 1976) 23–68.

⁵ Heikki Koskenniemi, *Studien zur Idee und Phraseologie des griechischen Briefes bis 400 n. Chr.* (Helsinki: Suomalaisen Kirjallisuuden Kirjapaino Oy, 1956) 97–98. Katherine G. Evans, "Women's Greek Papyrus Letters: a Description of the Letters and a Study of the Opening Formula" (M.A. thesis, Claremont Graduate School, 1985) 45, found only one instance in which a woman addressed a man as her "dearest" and no cases where a woman used the term to another woman.

⁶ The translation is that of J. Neyrey in Malherbe, *Ancient Epistolary Theorists*, 65, who cites Julius Victor, *The Art of Rhetoric* 27.

used too indiscriminately to indicate the relationship of the persons involved.[7] He found that the recipient of such letters may be a family member, a business associate, a government official, or even a tax collector. These findings confirm the report of Pseudo-Demetrius in his manual on epistolary styles who wrote:[8]

> The friendly type, then, is one that seems to be written by a friend to a friend. But it is by no means (only) friends who write (in this manner). For frequently those in prominent positions are expected by some to write in a friendly manner to their inferiors and to others who are their equals ... There are times, indeed, when they write to them without knowing them (personally). They do so, not because they are close friends and have (only) one choice (of how to write), but because they think that nobody will refuse them when they write in a friendly manner ....

The difficulty of interpreting an opening formula is complicated by the tendency in the papyri to use familial terms for persons who were not blood relations. Koskenniemi studied numerous occurrences of these familial terms and found that not only were they used for blood relatives but also for unrelated persons to show respect or affection.[9]

Because of the many difficulties described above, no obvious criteria could be established for determining friends and friendship in the papyri except for the actual use of the terms φίλος and φιλία. Therefore the results of the survey which will be discussed next are based exclusively on the use of one of these terms in a document.

A Survey of Papyri and Inscriptions

Since it would have been unwieldy for the scope of this project to survey all published papyri, a random sampling was chosen.[10]

---

[7] Koskenniemi, *Studien*, 88–127.

[8] Malherbe, *Ancient Epistolary Theorists*, 33; extract of Pseudo-Demetrius, *Epistolary Types* 1.

[9] Koskenniemi, *Studien*, 105.

[10] Abbreviations of papyri will follow the standard as given in John Oates, *et al.*, *Checklist of Editions of Greek Papyri and Ostraca* (3d ed.; Chico, California: Scholars Press, 1985). Translations quoted are those in the published editions unless otherwise specified.

An attempt was made to ensure that the random sample was representative of the population by choosing published collections known to emanate from different geographical areas as well as both the Ptolemaic and Roman periods.[11] The original intention of the study was to look exclusively at documentary papyri. While examining the *Sammelbuch griechischer Urkunden aus Aegypten* which collects both papyri and inscriptions published in journals, however, it was discovered that there was some very relevant evidence to be found in inscriptions. This included the main evidence for the friendship of women, children, and Jews as well as the unofficial use of φίλος during the Ptolemaic period. Therefore, in addition to the Greek papyri, several collections of inscriptions were consulted in order to give a more complete overview of the evidence of different form and genre types.[12]

On the Meaning of Friendship

The ideal evidence for friendship in Egypt would be if persons in the papyri commented on the meaning of friendship, and, in fact, two of the papyri do just that. In P. Mert. I.12 (dated 58 CE) a man who was possibly a doctor and certainly well educated wrote a letter to his physician friend:[13]

> P. Mert. I.12. Chairas to his dearest Dionysius, many greetings and continual health. I was much delighted at receiving a letter from you as if I had indeed been in my native place; for apart from that we have nothing. I may dispense with writing to you with great

---

[11] Collections surveyed include: P. Amh., P. Ant., P. Col., P. Fay., P. Freib., P. Giss., P. Harris, P. Heid., P. Hib., P. Leid.Inst., P. Lond., P. Mert., P. Mich. v. 9–15, P. Michael., P. Oslo, P. Oxy., P. Petrie, P. Princ., P. Ryl., P. Strassb., P. Tebt., P. Wash. Univ., and SB (a compilation of papyri and inscriptions published in journals and unindexed catalogs).

[12] Besides those found in SB, use has been made of Jean-Baptiste Frey, *Corpus of Jewish Inscriptions: Jewish Inscriptions From the Third Century B.C. to the Seventh Century A.D.* (New York: Ktav, 1975) = CIJ; Etienne Bernand, *Recueil des Inscriptions Grecques du Fayoum* (Cairo: Institut Français d'Archéologie Orientale du Caire, 1981); and André Bernand, *Les Portes du Désert: Recueil des Inscriptions Grecques d'Antinooupolis, Tentyris, Koptis, Apollonopolis Parva et Apollonopolis Magna* (Paris: Editions du Centre National de la Recherche Scientifique, 1984).

[13] P. Mert. I.12, translated by John L. White, *Light From Ancient Letters* (Philadelphia: Fortress Press, 1986) 145.

gratitude, for it is (only) required that one express thankfulness with words to those who are not friends.

The second document, a Christian letter from the fourth century, P. Oxy. XXXI.2603, is more philosophical in nature. It describes how a man who is enlightened can look in a mirror and see himself for how he really is as well as see the true sincerity of the friendship which others may show him.

> P. Oxy. XXXI.2603. To my lord brother S[erapio]n Paul (wishes) well-doing. A man who has acquired a mirror, or holds in his hand something else of that sort, in which faces are seen represented, has no need of one to tell him, or testify about the character that lies upon him, and his complexion, and his appearance, how it is. For he himself has become a witness by himself, and can speak about his own likeness. And when someone speaks to him, or explains about the beauty and comeliness about him, he does not then believe. For he is not like the rest who are in ignorance, and standing far from the mirror that displays the likeness of all. And it is the same with you my good friend. For as through a mirror you have seen my implanted affection and love for you ever fresh. Now concerning the acquaintances of ours who are bringing down the letter to you, there is no need for me to write (knowing as I do) your friendship and affection to all, especially towards our brethren. Receive them therefore in love, as friends, for they are not catechumens but belong to the company of Ision and Nikolaos, and if you do anything for them, you have done it for me.

These two examples are noteworthy for their rhetorical devices similar to those used in epistolary manuals. Their use here is probably indicative of a high level of education since epistolary style appears to have been taught towards the end of secondary education.[14] As has often been noted, however, the papyri tend to be practical in nature and generally bereft of philosophical comment which makes these two examples unique.

Besides these examples of the meaning of friendship in its abstract sense is evidence for the development of φίλος as terminology associated with official and quasi-official titles. This is most evident in its use as an administrative rank by Ptolemaic

---

[14] Malherbe, *Ancient Epistolary Theorists*, 7.

officials in the third through first centuries BCE and contrasts to its use by Christians in the sixth and seventh centuries. In the Ptolemaic period, φίλος was added to the political title of several ranks of advisors to the king. These ranks included τῶν πρώτων φίλων or those "of the first friends" of the king and its lower forms of "equivalent to a first friend" and simply "of the friends."[15] The "first friends" and "friends" of the king were not only his personal advisors but also served in many administrative capacities (including judicial) throughout the kingdom. This use of φίλος as an administrative rank is common in Ptolemaic papyri where the use of φίλος in a non-official sense appears only rarely.[16] An examination of inscriptions, however, proved that in that medium φίλος was still being used in a non-official sense all through the Ptolemaic period.

Only three of the documents surveyed here mention the friends of the Roman prefect. These are of interest to compare with the evidence for the "first friends" of the Ptolemaic king. In 98 CE the Emperor Trajan wrote a letter to the Alexandrians (P. Oxy. XLII.3022) reporting that he had commended their welfare to his friend the prefect Pompeius Planta. That Egypt's prefect would be a friend of the Roman emperor is hardly surprising given the strategic importance of Egypt for Rome. Another document, P. Oxy. IV.706, dated in 115 CE, has the prefect M. Rutilius Lupus taking counsel with his friends before deciding the outcome of some legal proceedings. Here the prefect's friends appear to be formally his advisors. The third document, P. Oxy. XXXVI.2754 of 111 CE, consists of several injunctions regarding legal procedure. The relevant passage reads: "Let those who have obtained friends of the prefect on previous occasion as judges and who have not yet had their cases settled petition Julius Maximus, archistrator and friend." This suggests that in the early second century CE the prefect had a system very like that of the Ptolemaic

---

[15] A complete discussion of Ptolemaic ranks is in Kathleen Chrimes Atkinson, "Some Observations on Ptolemaic Ranks and Titles," *Aegyptus* 32, fasc. 1 (gennaio-giugno, 1952) 204–14.

[16] Just a few examples include P. Oxy. XIV.1635 and SB V.8230, 8874, 8892; X.10664.

kings where a group of advisors known probably quasi-officially as "friends" heard judicial cases.

Moving from the Roman to the late Byzantine period reveals evidence for the two ways that forms of φίλος were being used for Christian officials of the sixth and seventh centuries. In the first way, Christian officials were referred to in the opening formula of letters with some variation of "your most magnificent friendliness." Examples include P. Oxy. XVI.1843: "The letter written by your magnificent and all-wise friendliness" and P. Oxy. XVI.1863: "Before all things I salute and greet your most honourable friendliness many times." In P. Amh. II.154 the letter is addressed to two Christian officials who are called "your eminent sincere friendlinesses." In its other form φίλος appears as the address on the verso of the letter in some variation of that used in P. Oxy. XVI.1845: "To my master the most illustrious and honourable true friend and brother George."[17]

Aside from the above examples, φίλος is generally used in a more mundane capacity descriptive of daily life activities. Therefore for the remainder of the discussion it is necessary to survey the documentary papyri and inscriptions to determine how terms like φίλος and φιλία were used in real life situations and then extrapolate from these a larger picture regarding the meaning of friendship. In doing so, an additional attempt will be made to represent the use of friendship language by different demographic groups such as Romans, Greeks, Egyptians, Jews, Christians, men, women, and children.

Genre Types in the Papyri and Inscriptions

In addition to the texts where forms of φίλος or φιλία are used as official titles, there are 203 where it is used in some type of daily life setting. Of the 203, six are official in nature, six are legal, eight are business related, four are religious, five are wills, twenty-five are devotions or προσκύνημα, forty-nine are epitaphs, nine are dedications and ninety-one are private letters.

One characteristic that is shared by both official and business documents is the incidence of a friend acting as a sort of proxy for

---

[17] See also P. Oxy. XVI.1841.

a man in his absence. No evidence was found of a friend acting as a proxy for a woman but in a society where most women's business was handled by male guardians, one would not expect to find such evidence. One use of a proxy was for the formal application that was made in behalf of 14 year-old boys of special social status requesting that they be made exempt from the personal poll tax or only have to pay at a reduced rate. Such an application requires a sworn statement as to the boy's legal status, and according to the Gnomon of the Idios Logos, persons who lied about their or another's status were subject to confiscation of a quarter of their property.[18] There are two cases where a friend made the application and sworn statement which made him legally liable: one dated in 160/1 CE (P. Oxy. VIII.1109) where the father of the boy apparently was absent on business and one dated 291 CE (P. Oxy. XXXVIII.2855) where the boy's father was deceased.

Friends also acted as proxies in business matters. Many people in Egypt owned units of lands which were miles apart, owned land in the country and lived in the city, or otherwise were engaged in matters which caused them to be absent. In these cases a friend or a family member was relied upon to act as a proxy in his stead. The standard formula for this was: X- to Y- through Z- his friend. The document then proceeds in the first person as if the originator of the document were writing it and not the friend. An example of this is P. Oxy. IV.724 dated 155 CE:[19]

> P. Oxy. IV.724. Panechotes also called Panares, ex-cosmetes of Oxyrhynchus, through his friend Gemellus, to Apollonius, writer of short hand, greetings.

Two documents which were addressed to deities display different sides of friendship: business and pleasure. One dated in the late third century or early fourth century (P. Oxy. XII.1477) is a form list of possible questions to a deity (or oracle) with a number preceding each one, which may have been a cross-listing to the appropriate magical spells. Some of the questions include

---

[18] Naphatali Lewis, *Egypt Under Roman Rule* (Oxford: Clarendon Press, 1983) 33.
[19] Cf. also P. Oxy. XII.1427 and XXXVIII.2869.

"If I am to profit by the transaction?," "If I have been poisoned?," and "If I will receive assistance from my friend?"[20]

The other example, the top portion of a fragmented papyrus (P. Oxy XLI.2976), is considered an anomaly by its editor since it appears in the form of a letter to the Egyptian deity Thoeris regarding a dream but is unlike other dream texts.[21] It reads: "To Thoeris most great goddess, I was dining yesterday with my friends in your most fortunate precinct. Overcome by sleep . . ." and here the remainder of the document is lost. This incident of someone falling asleep while dining with friends, however, does point to another indirect type of testimony for friendship. That is the large number of invitations which have survived including invitations to dine, to attend weddings, and to help celebrate festivals.[22]

Inscriptions have yielded two genre types which provide some interesting insights on friendship, the epitaph and the προσκύνημα or act of devotion. Friends appear in a variety of ways in epitaphs, one of which is a semi-formulaic expression where the deceased is called χρηστὴ πασιφίλη or "excellent one and friend to all." An example of this in its simplest form is SB V.7883 from 28 BCE: "Tatis, excellent woman, friend to all, about 28 years old. In the second year, Phamenoth 28."[23] This "friend to all" expression is used for men, women, and children over several centuries and is particularly prevalent in Jewish epitaphs.[24] Other epitaphs are more free form expressions of how the deceased has been deprived of friendship or how their friends have been deprived of him or her, as in CIJ 1490 (117 BCE): "Weep for the man who has left the most dignified . . . and his city, and the haunts and friendship of humanity."

---

[20] P. Oxy. XII.1477, edited by B. P. Grenfell and A. S. Hunt.

[21] P. Oxy. XLI.2976, edited by J. C. Shelton.

[22] A few examples of invitations include P. Oxy. I.110, 111, 112; III.523, 524; IV.747; VI.926; IX.1214; XII.1484, 1485, 1486, 1487. Various papyri give some information on these social events, such as contracts to hire dancers and musicians. See also P. Oxy. III.472, where a man believed he was poisoned while dining out.

[23] SB V.7883 (translation mine).

[24] CIJ 1452, 1453, 1456, 1460, 1464, 1466, 1468, 1470, 1471, 1473, 1474, 1475, 1483, 1488, 1490, 1493, 1494, 1495, 1497, 1498, 1500, 1501, 1502, 1504, 1513, 1514, 1518, 1519, 1521, 1523, 1526, 1528; cf. also SB III.6230.

There are several instances of epitaphs which appear to have been dedicated by friends which suggest that either the person died without family in the area, or, as in this next case, the friends wished to commemorate the person separately. The following epitaph, SB I.4456 dated in the second century BCE, was found in Alexandria but says that the deceased, Nikolaos, died in Libya. Nikolaos may have been a soldier.[25]

> SB I.4456. The sacred earth of Libya has (claimed) Nikolaos a noble son of his native city Miletus, who was the admiration of his friends and now gone. For he came to this common lot by fate. Nikolaos, excellent one, farewell.

The προσκύνημα was a statement of devotion to a god inscribed usually in the locale of a temple. There are twenty-five examples in this survey where the act of devotion is said to be made either with or in behalf of one or more friends. One example from the Roman period, SB III.6041 reads: "The act of devotion of Naeouios son of Hilarion for the gods in Abudos also of his children Tapiomis and Heliopoleites and of his friends."[26] Another example is SB V.8664 from the 2nd century CE:[27]

> SB V.8664. Kronios son of Harpochration and Harchemis son of Petemeineos came and worshipped the lady Isis with the friends of Kronios and Didumos together with Truphon, and Harpochration son of Sarapion and we made the act of devotion for Harpochration son of Eponichos and for all the others.

Interestingly, although people were remembering their friends in their devotions to the gods, they apparently were not remembering them in their wills. Of four wills which mention friends, in one, SB X.10500 from 134 CE, the friend is only a witness to the will. In a will dated in 224 CE (P. Oxy. XXII.2348), the friend is requested to oversee the testator's funeral dress and the erection of his tomb but is not left anything. Another will, P. Ryl. II.153 dated in the mid second century CE, mentions friends twice. One is given permission to continue living in the testator's house after his death and the other is requested to become the

---

[25] SB I.4456 (translation mine).
[26] SB III.6041 (translation mine).
[27] SB V.8664 (translation mine).

guardian of the testator's minor son. In the fourth will, P. Oxy. VI.907 from 276 CE, which divides a considerable estate, a friend is left an annual gift of 30 jars of wine and an unknown portion of wheat. This brief evidence suggests that people were more likely to bequeath friends responsibilities than material goods. One other will is worth mentioning here, P. Oxy. III.490. A woman in 124 CE left her entire estate to a minor boy, the son of a freedman, clearly of no relation to her and she did it κατὰ φιλοστοργίαν, on account of his affection for her. Whether she would have considered the youth to be a φίλος cannot be determined, but this does seem to be a type of friendship between an adult and a child.

There are many extant wills in the Greek papyri and all give generously not only to family members but to freed men, women, and children. It is curious that friends are generally not included, at least not in the wills considered in this survey. An explanation would require a separate study, but it may have been indicative of a philosophy that material assets should be kept in the family. Freed persons remained legally liable to their former masters in certain situations and therefore were considered part of the extended household unit. It may also be indicative of an ancient understanding of friendship; friends were expected to perform services for each other but did not share in each other's financial assets.

It is not surprising that the majority of the references to friends appear in private letters since, as has been noted, this was the customary means for maintaining remote friendships. In a number of letters friends only appear in the greetings at the end. It was customary at the end of private letters to ask the recipient to greet various persons by name. Some letters also request the recipient to greet his or her friends without giving specific names.[28] The majority of the letters, however, either reveal a person performing a service for a friend, or, making a request that a friend perform a service. For example, friends were relied upon to deliver goods including letters (P. Mert. I.24, P. Leid.Inst. 31)

---

[28] P. Mert. I.28 (3rd c. CE); P. Oxy VIII.1155 (104 CE), XIV.1676 (3rd c. CE); SB V.8089 (date unknown), XII.10803 (4th c. CE), 11016 (13 CE), 11127 (88 CE); P. Tebt. II.412 (2nd c. CE).

and supplies (P. Lond. II.356; P. Oxy. I.115, IV.742, VIII.1158, XIV.1657). Friends may be asked to help with business affairs at home as is the case in P. Fay. 131, where the writer in the context of discussing irrigation problems adds, "but by all means water the vegetables of our friend Decasius."

Friends are also often asked to look after the writer's family especially a man's wife and children. A letter from the late second century (P. Oxy. VI.933) is from a man who had been watching over his friend's home and young daughter. He tells his friend, "Have no more anxiety about your household than you would if you were present." Also in a papyrus from Antinoopolis (P. Ant. I.44) from the 4th or 5th century a man requests his friend to help his younger brother acquire suitable clothing.

The majority of services rendered by friends, however, have to do with the borrowing, lending, collecting, and transporting of money. Banks in Egypt were for official business and not personal transactions. People relied on private persons to handle their financial matters.[29] Informal loans, ones without a contract, were very common as individuals were often expected to supply money for an absent friend's personal or business affairs and then be reimbursed upon the other's return. For example, P. Oxy. XXXIV.2726 from the second century CE, is a letter from one man to another whose relationship to him is unclear requesting that the latter have two documents registered and filed. He assures him: "So whatever you spend you shall report. And if anything is wanting for the scribe's fee my friend will give it to you and I shall give it back to him." P. Tebt. II.418 dated in the 3rd century CE illustrates the loaning of money for personal affairs. Sotericus writes to his friend Origenes whom he calls both friend (in the address) and brother (in the text). The relevant section reads: "You will do well, brother, to come up and bring my wife with you, for I have written to her to come with you; and give her any money she may need until you arrive and receive it back from me in good faith, as I have trusted no one to take it to her."[30] Formal

---

[29] Alan K. Bowman, *Egypt after the Pharaohs, 332 BC–AD 642: From Alexander to the Arab Conquest* (Berkeley: University of California Press, 1989) 113.

[30] P. Tebt. II.418. Other examples of friends forwarding money on another's behalf include P. Amh. II.131; P. Leid.Inst. 31; P. Mert. I.24; P. Oxy. III.530,

or contractual loans were probably less common between friends since presumably friends were likely to be financial equals.

Human nature in antiquity was perhaps much as it is today, and we find in private letters many instances where a friend is reminded of an unfulfilled obligation. This was sometimes handled in a civil manner as was done in P. Oxy. IV.745 from 1 CE: "I ask you therefore not to do otherwise; but I know that you will do everything well. I do not want to have any dispute with you, as you are my friend."[31] Civility between friends apparently was not always productive and occasionally they resorted to stronger measures. In P. Oxy. XII.1483 from the late 2nd or early 3rd century CE a man threatens his friend: "Know that, unless you pay all quickly and discharge the claims made against you, I shall seize your surety, until you pay me the value of the claims." There is also the case of P. Oxy. LI.3644 from the third century CE, where a man writes his father that his friend had apparently literally beaten him up when he did not make good with some letters of credit. What is surprising in this last case is not that his friend beat him up, as physical violence is common in the papyri, but rather that he still refers to him in the letter as his friend!

Private letters generally show more instances though of people deriving benefit and support from their friends. Letters of recommendation were a common epistolary form and there were three in the present survey. P. Oxy. XXXI.2603, a Christian letter, has already been quoted in full above. The second, P. Oxy. LI.3643, is written on behalf of the nephew of a very close friend of the writer and is very fragmented. The third letter of recommendation, P. Oxy. I.32, is in Latin but I have included it because it is an important witness to both the genre and to Roman friendship.

> P. Oxy. I.32. To Julius Domitius, military tribune of the legion, from Aurelius Archelaus, his beneficiarius, greeting. I have previously recommended to you my friend Theon, and now I beg once more, sir, that you will regard him as if he were myself. He is indeed a man worthy of your affection. He left friends, property and

---

VII.1062, VIII.1158, XXXIV.2726, XXXIV.2732, XXXVIII.2861, XLI.2975, XLI.2983, XLI.2996.

[31] Cf. also P. Lond. II.2448.

business, and followed me, and has throughout secured my comfort. I ask you therefore to grant him admittance to your house; he will be able to relate to you all that we have done. Whatever he tells you about me you may take as a fact....

The final example of letters to be given here is one which was written for almost the sole purpose of moral exhortation. P. Oxy. XLII.3069 from the 3rd or 4th century CE was delivered to "Sarapion the philosopher from his friend Aquila," and in it Aquila congratulates the other on his ascetic lifestyle and encourages him to stay with it:[32]

> P. Oxy. XLII.3069. Aquila to Sarapion, greetings. I was overjoyed to receive your letter. Our friend Callinicus was testifying to the utmost about the way of life you follow even under such conditions—especially in your not abandoning your austerities. Yes, we may deservedly congratulate ourselves, not because we do these things, but because we are not diverted from them by ourselves. Courage! Carry through what remains like a man! Let not wealth distract you, nor beauty, nor anything else of the same kind: for there is no good in them, if virtue does not join her presence, no, they are vanishing and worthless. Under divine protection, I expect you in Antinoopolis. Send Soteris the puppy, since she now spends her time by herself in the country. Good health to you and yours! Good health!

Friendship Among Different Demographic Groups

Besides the evidence of the various genre types in the papyri and inscriptions, this study also examined the evidence for friendship in the different demographic groups, including ethnic, gender, age, and religious groups. Native Egyptians were often a disenfranchised ethnic group during Greek then Roman rule, but they were able to avail themselves of the benefit of friends. In the second century CE (P. Tebt. II.314) a man who was most likely an Egyptian priest wrote another that his friends had assisted him in getting approval for the circumcision of a boy from the High Priest, who apparently had been delaying the matter. Boys becoming Egyptian priests were required to be circumcised, but

---

[32] P. Oxy. XLII.3069, edited by P. J. Parsons, who suggests that the ascetic philosophy is reminiscent of Philostratus or Plotinus.

each circumcision had to be approved by the High Priest, a Roman administrative appointee.[33] Here the Egyptian's friends clearly had some influence and were willing to exert it.

An example of friendship between Roman citizens was given in the letter of recommendation quoted above (P. Oxy. I.32). Roman citizens were a rather vague category, however, since Roman citizens could have been either originally from Rome or persons from Egypt who were granted citizenship. This latter group is not easily identified since they may have used Greek or Egyptian names rather than the Roman *tri nomina*. After the passing of the Constitutio Antoniniana by the Emperor Caracalla in 212 CE, most of the people in the Roman Empire became Roman citizens, making this an even more nebulous category in Egypt. Likewise "Greek" was an unclear category since many Greeks intermarried with Egyptians. Egyptians often used Greek names and vice-versa. Given the diversity of ethnic groups, it is only natural to inquire how the various groups interrelated. Unfortunately, this is exceedingly difficult to answer from the documentary evidence on friendship (or from any source for that matter) because of the difficulties in distinguishing between the groups in Egypt, which was both an ethnic and a prosopographical melting pot.[34] The only real way to distinguish a Roman citizen from a Greek citizen (of one of the four Greek cities) or from a Greco-Egyptian is if there is some other evidence in the document regarding the person's legal status. In short, although the subject of the friendship of and between these ethnic groups is an important one, the scanty information available here is insufficient for any real discussion.

---

[33] Bowman, *Egypt after the Pharaohs*, 180.

[34] Roman citizens in Egypt, unlike other provinces, do not appear to have felt the need to use their full names. Even in quasi-formal documents they frequently used only one or two parts of the *tri nomina*. Since the cognomen portion of the *tri nomina* was often Greek for provincials, such as Gaius Julius Apolinarius, the sole use of the cognomen would mean that the evidence for Roman citizenship was lost. Some of the most curious evidence, though, has been cited in an article by John Oates, where he notes a man who is a third generation Roman citizen named Gaius Gemellus Horigenes who prefers to be known by the Egyptian name Horion. Cf. John F. Oates, "The Romanization of the Greek East: The Evidence of Egypt," *BASP* 2.2 (February, 1965) 57–64.

Information regarding friendship between men is plentiful and constitutes the bulk of the documents in this survey, which is not surprising since the papyri in general are more representative of men than they are of women and children. In spite of the over-representation of men in friendship documents, there is insufficient evidence to make finer distinctions based on socio-economic status or to determine whether unequal groups such as patron/client or master/slave could have been friends.

Evidence for friendship between men and women is sparse. In the documents surveyed, there was no instance of a man referring to a woman as his friend. There are three instances where a woman calls a man her friend. An undated letter (SB VI.9017, no. 20) has as its opening formula "Thermouthis to Horion her brother and friend very many greetings."[35] Another document of the late third century CE, P. Oxy. XIV.1657, is a list of utensils which a woman is sending to her friend Theon. P. Tebt. II.413 of the second or third century CE is from a woman to her mistress and says at the end that all of her friends in the feminine, αἱ φίλαι, send greetings to her friends in the masculine, τοὺς φιλοῦντες. This evidence is very slight but at least does indicate that women knew men whom they regarded as their φίλοι and presumably men had women friends, too. It is possible that the practice of men and women referring to each other affectionately as brother and sister generally took the place of the use of the word friend and so tends to mask the evidence for male-female friendships.

P. Tebt. II.413 also provides the only direct evidence for women referring to their friends with a form of ἡ φίλη. One possible piece of additional evidence may be the epitaph SB I.5629 from the 3rd century BCE and dedicated by a friend. It is unknown whether the friend is male or female but the general tone of the epitaph suggests a woman.[36]

> SB I.5629. The tomb and not the place of sleep, the rock to point out the deceased, who and of whom is the departed Aida? But lost to me through death O friend, set to rest in the ground. Gaze upon

---

[35] SB VI.9017, no. 20 (translation mine).
[36] SB I.5629 (translation mine).

these chiseled words twice young girls. Her father was Eirenaios, her home Memphis. Proclaim the names of her unborn children
. . . .

The woman's will mentioned above (P. Oxy. III.490) suggested that an adult might consider a child as a φίλος. There is also one piece of evidence that children could be φίλοι to each other. This is an epitaph for a five year old boy of unknown date from the collection of Jewish inscriptions (CIJ 1512). It is written in the first person and in it the little boy reports, "My friends miss their companion and playfellow."

The only evidence encountered here for Jewish friendships was the use of the word φίλος in epitaphs and this was in no way unique from the common usage. There is some evidence for Christians making much wider usage of the terms φίλος and φιλία. This is evident in the two ways φίλος and φιλία were used as titles for Christian officials of the sixth and seventh centuries as described above. A broadening of the meaning of friend can also be seen in the latter portion of the Christian letter of recommendation P. Oxy. XXXI.2603 quoted above, where the persons being recommended are referred to as mutual acquaintances, γνώριμοι, but the recipient is asked to receive them as friends, φίλοι. In general, however, Christian letters are like the Greco-Roman ones, displaying little knowledge of the tension between Christian love (ἡ ἀγάπη) and friendship which characterized monastic and other medieval Christian theology.[37]

Recommendations for Further Research

A disadvantage of doing an overview survey of papyri and inscriptions is that many questions are raised that due to time constraints must remain unanswered. The advantage is that it allows for a broad picture of friendship in the daily life of

---

[37] See Brian Patrick McGuire, *Friendship & Community: the Monastic Experience, 350–1250* (Cistercian Studies Series 95; Kalamazoo, Michigan: Cistercian Publications, 1988); Adele M. Fiske, *Friends and Friendship in the Monastic Tradition* (CIDOC Cuaderno 51; Cuernavaca, Mexico: Centro Intercultural de Documentacion, 1970); Paul J. Wadell, *Friendship and the Moral Life* (Notre Dame, Indiana: University of Notre Dame Press, 1989); for more Christian letters see, for example, P. Oxy. XVI.1872, XXXIV.2732; SB X.10463, XII.10841.

antiquity. Another advantage is that a survey of a random sampling can point to potentially fruitful directions for further study.

One obvious direction would be to expand the survey size to include all published papyri. This would be facilitated by the availability of computer searching since most published papyri are available in electronic form[38] but hindered by the fact that many papyri lack translations. This latter adds a lengthy intermediate step in the analysis of documents on friendship. Another possibility would be to expand the investigation of inscriptionary evidence since only a small sample of these was added here as an afterthought.

On the other hand, it may also be fruitful to narrow the focus of the study to one genre type such as wills, epitaphs, or especially private letters. Each of these genres has its own corpus of secondary literature which could fill in many of the gaps created when a sample document is examined in isolation. For example, more work could be done on the terms of affection used in the opening formula of private letters. Their use in papyri could be compared to their use in literature. In particular, a study of literary letters could yield information on friendship terminology or special themes and topics that could be compared to papyrus letters. Another possibility would be a comparison of friend and friendship language in Christian private letters with the writings of early Church fathers.[39] Overall, it would seem that a comparative approach using literary letters and papyrus letters could yield the most immediate results even if they turn out to be largely negative.

Summary and Conclusions

The most perplexing aspects of this study were the many limitations caused by the nature of the sources, the quantity of sources, and then the confusing ethnography of the Egyptian

---

[38] Packard Humanities Institute, *Greek Documentary CD-ROM #6* (Los Altos, Ca: P.H.I., 1992); updated at regular intervals.

[39] See the preliminary work that has been done on this by Thraede, *Grundzüge*, 109–124.

society itself. As noted, the extant papyri are predominantly from rural areas and so are typically more representative of those with little education. If more papyri had survived from Alexandria or the other Greek cities, one might expect to find greater use of rhetorical devices as a reflection of both the friendship concerns and the educational attainment of the cultural elite. This may be particularly true of private letters between friends, but, as demonstrated, it is practically impossible to distinguish a letter between friends from one between family members or even strangers.

Although there was little evidence for what persons in the papyri thought of friendship, it was at least learned from P. Mert. I.12 that a friend is a reminder of home and that friends have no need to thank each other for favors. Another letter, P. Oxy. XXXI.2603, described how friends can see each other for who they really are and thus have no need to doubt each other's sincerity.

This study has also shown that "friend" was not just an intimate acquaintance but also could be an official rank. In the Ptolemaic period the "first friends" were administrative advisors to the king. There is some indication that similar advisors to the Roman prefect were also known at least quasi-officially as "friends." In Christian letters of the sixth and seventh centuries "your magnificent friendliness" seems to be a distinct title for Christian officials but more work needs to be done to situate its meaning in its Christian context.

The survey of a random sampling of papyri and inscriptions revealed that friends were mentioned in a variety of genre types. Friends were mentioned in the papyri in official, legal, business, and religious documents, in wills, and above all in private letters. Friends are mentioned most often in inscriptions in the epitaphs and προσκύνημα, and in an occasional dedication. In official and business texts, friends are found acting as official proxies in the other's absence. Epitaphs may mention how a person will miss or be missed by his or her friends. More commonly, though, the deceased is referred to with the formulaic phrase "friend to all." The προσκύνημα was an act of devotion made to a deity and according to inscriptions this devotion was frequently done either with or in behalf of one's friends. Friends were rarely mentioned in wills and then it was usually in the form of a request for some service to be performed after the testator's death.

As noted, friends are mentioned most often in private letters and here it is usually in the context of performing services for each other. This may include watching over each other's families or property and delivering or receiving goods. Friends were very often relied upon in money matters, especially taking care of debts in the other's absence which would be reimbursed upon the other's return. Money matters brought out the universality of human nature in the papyri as we saw persons having to threaten their friends to pay up their debts. Besides the basically free form references to friends in private letters, other friendship letters were found which conformed to known epistolary types, including letters of recommendation and a letter of exhortation.

The study yielded little evidence for describing the friendship of different demographic groups. This was partially due to the nature of the extant materials where many groups were under-represented, including Egyptians, Jews, women, children, slaves, and the poor. It was also due to the nature of the ethnic mix of ancient Egypt and their use of names which made it difficult to differentiate one group from another. At least limited evidence was found for friendship in most groups except for slaves and the poor. Although most of the evidence represented men, and probably men who were property owners, it was difficult to determine beyond that their ethnic and socio-economic status.

While the survey did not point to an obvious area which may be fruitful for further study, it is recommended that a study be done of friendship in literary letters to isolate specific terminology, topics, or themes that may be developed as criteria for reexamining friendship in the papyri, especially private letters. The overall result of the evidence here is to accentuate the extent to which people relied on their friends to perform services in their behalf. It would be interesting to see if this was a characteristic similarly demonstrated in the literary letters.

THE BOND OF HUMANITY: FRIENDSHIP IN PHILO OF ALEXANDRIA

Gregory E. Sterling

Among Jewish writers indebted to Hellenistic philosophy, Philo of Alexandria has the most extensive comments on friendship. Although his observations are brief and bound up with his exegetical enterprise, he appears to have made use of the Stoic understanding of friendship as a means of universalizing the particularism of his native Judaism.

> "It seems clear to me that we were born in such a state that there is a certain partnership among all...."
>
> Cicero, *Amic.* 19[1]

In his discussion of the *Aqedah*, Philo listed several reasons why we should praise Abraham, including the recognition that his paternal love for Isaac surpassed both the temperate forms of love and "the forms of friendship, as many as have become famous (τὰς φιλίας, ὅσαι δι' ὀνόματος γεγόνασι)."[2] What celebrated forms of friendship does the Torah exegete have in mind? We can dismiss the LXX as a potential source since it lacks any classification of types. In the Greek translations of the books which eventually formed the Hebrew Bible the term φιλία appears only in Proverbs.[3] In the larger corpus of the LXX the tempo of frequency does pick up, yet the the scattered and limited nature of the references does not commend any of these works as a suitable background.[4] We might attribute this reticence to the

---

[1] I have used LCL editions for the major authors cited in this work unless otherwise noted. All translations are my own.

[2] *Abr.* 194.

[3] Prov 5:19 (*bis*); 7:18; 10:12; 15:17; 17:9; 19:7; 25:10a; 27:5.

[4] Wis 7:14; 8:18; Sir 6:17; 9:8; 22:20; 25:1; 27:18; 1 Macc 8:1, 11, 17; 10:20, 23, 26, 54; 12:1, 3, 8, 10, 16; 14:18, 22; 15:17; 2 Macc 4:11; 6:22.

Hebrew aversion to abstract nouns except for the fact that the same pattern holds true for φίλος. There are more references, yet they are more numerous in the later literature and still fail to provide a schema of the types of friendship.[5] If we turn to non-canonical Hellenistic Jewish literature which is openly indebted to Hellenistic philosophical discussions, we again find some material but nothing suitable for the reference here.[6] There can be no doubt that Philo was thinking of the classifications of friendship in the Greek philosophical tradition which began with Aristotle and were common in Stoicism and Middle Platonism.[7]

The nature of this reference is indicative of the presentation of friendship in Philo. Like his Jewish predecessors, Philo does not offer readers a sustained treatment of φιλία. The closest he comes

---

[5] Φίλος appears 159 times in the LXX: 62t. as a translation of a Hebrew original, 6t. as an addition to the biblical text, and 91t. in the apocryphal/deutero-canonical works where it is most frequent in Sir (47t.) and 1 Macc (35t.). It renders a number of Hebrew words for companion: רֵעַ (33t.: Exod 33:11; Deut 13:7; 1 Chr 27:33; Esth 9:22; Job 2:11; 6:27; 19:21; 32:3; 35:4; 36:33; 42:7, 10; Ps 138:17 [139:17 MT]; Prov 3:29; 6:1, 3 (bis); 14:20; 16:29; 17:17, 18; 19:4 (bis); 25:8, 17, 18; 26:19; 27:10 (bis), 14; 29:5; Mic 7:5; Jer 9:4), אֹהֵב (8t.: Esth 5:10, 14; 6:13; Prov 14:20; 27:6; Jer 20:4, 6; 37:14), מֵרֵעַ (4t.: Judg 14:20; 15:2, 6; Prov 12:26), אַלּוּף (2t.: Prov 16:28; 17:9), and the Aramaic חַדָּבָר (Dan 3:91 [3:24 MT], 94 [3:27 MT]; cf. also Θ at 2:13, 17, 18). The word also renders nouns denoting royal offices (שַׂר [Esth 1:3; 2:18; 3:1; 6:9], חָכָם [Esth 1:13; 6:13], and אִישׁ [Prov 25:1; cf. also Job 32:1]), שָׁלוֹם (Jer 20:10), and various verbal forms (שָׁלַם [Prov 15:28a {16:7 MT}], שָׁמַע [Prov 25:10], שָׁכֵן [Prov 27:10]; cf. also יָדַע [Job 19:13]). Additions in the LXX include Judg 5:30 (where there may be some confusion between רַחְמָה and רַחֲמִים); Prov 14:20; 18:1; 22:24; Dan 5:23; 6:14. The most extensive discussions of friendship in the LXX are Sir 6:5-17; 22:19-26; 37:1-6. Cf. also 11:29–12:18. For a careful summary of the evidence see Gustav Stählin, "φιλέω, καταφιλέω, φίλημα, φίλος, φίλη, φιλία," *TDNT* 9 (1974) 113-71, esp. 154-59.

[6] See *Ep. Arist.* 225, 228, 231; Pseudo-Phocylides 91-94, 195-97, 219; and 4 Macc 2:9-14; 8:5; 12:5; 13:19–14:1; 14:13–15:23. On Pseudo-Phocylides see Pieter van der Horst, *The Sentences of Pseudo-Phocyclides: With Introduction and Commentary* (SVTP 4; Leiden: E. J. Brill, 1978), esp. 176-77 and Pascale Derron, *Pseudo-Phocylide Sentences* (Collection des Universités de France; Paris: Les Belles Lettres, 1986) esp. 44. On 4 Macc see Hans-Josef Klauck, "Brotherly Love in Plutarch and in 4 Maccabees," *Greeks, Romans, and Christians: Essays in Honor of Abraham J. Malherbe* (ed. David L. Balch, Everett Ferguson, and Wayne A. Meeks; Minneapolis: Fortress, 1990) 144-56.

[7] Aristotle *EE* 7; *EN* 8-9. For Stoic classifications see H. F. A. von Arnim, *Stoicorum veterum fragmenta* (4 vols.; Leipzig: Teubner, 1905-24; reprint ed., Dubuque, IA: Wm. C. Brown) 3.26-27 (§112). Hereafter this is abbreviated *SVF*. The Middle Platonists are represented by Alcinous, *Didaskalikos* 33.3; Apuleius, *De Platone et eius dogmate* 13-14; and Clement of Alexandria, *Strom.* 2 (= *SVF* 3.181, §723).

to an extended discussion is his presentation of "philanthropy" (φιλανθρωπία) in *De virtutibus*.⁸ What we find instead are scattered references made *en passant*. Unlike his predecessors, however, these references are extensive enough to permit us to reconstruct a general understanding of φιλία in Philo. I have attempted to do this by examining all of the references to φιλία, φίλος, and the vocabulary which is associated with them in the Philonic corpus.⁹ In spite of the *ad hoc* nature of this material, I will argue that Philo does have a coherent theory of friendship, a theory which is heavily indebted to Stoicism. This thesis is made doubly difficult because the extant Stoic material is itself fragmentary.¹⁰ As we will see, however, there is enough agreement at the critical points to substantiate the identification. If I am correct, Philo is one of our most important extant witnesses to the Stoic view of friendship.

What is Friendship?

I would like to begin where Plato left off his aporetic discussion of friendship in the *Lysis*: what is a friend or, as the question is recast in light of subsequent discussions, what is friendship?¹¹ Philo's fullest discussion comes in the midst of his allegory on the progress of the soul through the presentation of Noah's work as a planter. Philo exhorts his readers who are still in the middle stages

---

⁸ *Virt.* 51–174. On φιλανθρωπία see David Winston, "Philo's Ethical Theory," *ANRW* 2.21.1 (1984) 391–400.

⁹ As is true in other texts, Philo moves back and forth between an adjectival use of φίλος as "dear" (passive sense, φιλούμενος) and a substantival use of "friend." In the footnotes I have set adjectival uses after the substantival and introduced them with cf. I have not listed every use of the terms but have included all those which have a direct bearing on Philo's understanding of friendship.

¹⁰ Stoics who we know wrote tractates περὶ φιλίας are Cleanthes (Diogenes Laertius 7.174 [=*SVF* 1.107, §481]) and Chrysippus (Plutarch, *de Stoic. repugn.* 1039b [=*SVF* 3.182, §724]).

¹¹ *Ly.* 223b. D. B. Robinson, "Plato's *Lysis*: The Structural Problem," *ICS* 11 (1986) 63–83, has a very helpful analysis of the dialogue. The aporetic nature of the dialogue is underscored in the final line: οὔπω δὲ ὅ τι ἔστιν ὁ φίλος οἷοί τε ἐγενόμεθα ἐξευρεῖν. Aristotle provided his answer in *EE* 1236a (7.2.8): φίλος δὲ γίνεται ὅταν φιλούμενος ἀντιφιλῇ καὶ τοῦτο μὴ λανθάνῃ πως αὐτούς. Cf. also 1236b (7.2.16); *EN* 1156a (8.2.4); 1166a (9.4.1); *Rh.* 1380b–1381a (2.4.1–2), where he defines φιλία along similar lines.

of the "appropriate acts" (καθήκοντα) to take the task of planting seriously.[12] As a biblical warrant he cites Lev 19:23–25 which gives instructions for the planting and care of trees in the promised land.[13] One of his examples is the tree of φιλία.[14] Philo follows the order of the biblical text by opening his exposition with instructions for pruning. The first outgrowth to receive the knife is prostitution. You can see "call-girls" (ἑταῖραι) clinging to their clients "as if they were madly in love–yet they do not love them but themselves and are greedy for their daily earnings."[15] Their meretricious character thus subverts any interest other than self-interest and excludes them from the ranks of friends. We ought to remember that Lucian later used this same contrast in *Toxaris*. The first example of friendship Mnesippus offered to Toxaris was that of Deinias and Agathocles. In the story, Charicleia, who was as skillful as any ἑταίρα in the powers of seduction, woed the gullible Deinias until she completely stripped him of all his wealth. Agathocles remained loyal to Deinias to the point of selling all his possessions and giving Deinias the proceeds. He even went so far as to accompany Deinias into exile after his friend killed Charicleia and her husband, Demonax.[16] Philo's use of call-girls as counterfeit friends may, therefore, reflect a common *topos*.

The second pruned outgrowth certainly does. "It is possible to see flatterers nourishing indescribable hatred for those whom they court as they relish fine dishes and gluttony."[17] In no fewer than six texts Philo contrasts flatterers with friends.[18] In *Leg.* 3.182 he unequivocally declares: "flattery is a disease to friendship

---

[12] *Plant.* 94. I understand this to be a reference to "appropriate acts" as defined in Stoicism. For a discussion of the concept in Stoicism, see J. M. Rist, *Stoic Philosophy* (Cambridge: Cambridge University Press, 1969) 97–111.

[13] *Plant.* 95.

[14] *Plant.* 104–06.

[15] *Plant.* 104–05. Cf. also *Leg.* 3.182.

[16] *Tox.* 12–18. Cf. also 37 where Lucian suggests that someone who has many friends is like a promiscuous woman. For details see the essay by Richard Pervo in chapter eight of this volume.

[17] *Plant.* 105.

[18] *Leg.* 2.10; 3.182; *Agr.* 164; *Plant.* 104–05; *Conf.* 48; and *Migr.* 111–12. He gives an example of the process in *Flacc.* 19.

(νόσος γὰρ φιλίας ἡ κολακεία)."[19] Aristotle thought that flattery was a form of compensation in unequal relationships.[20] Subsequent treatments did not, however, follow this lead; instead they condemned it as feigned friendship. The *topos* is ubiquitous: Theophrastus, Philodemus, Plutarch and Maximus of Tyre all wrote treatises on it; Cicero dealt with it at length; and Stobaeus has a chapter of collected quotes on the topic.[21] The other side of the coin is "frank criticism" (παρρησία) which characterizes a true friend. In *Her.* 21 Philo openly states, "frank criticism is related to friendship (παρρησία δὲ φιλίας συγγενές)."[22] He is once again following the philosophical discussion. The same authors who warned against κολακεία also encouraged παρρησία: Philodemus wrote a tractate Περὶ παρρησίας; Plutarch's *How to Tell a Flatterer from a Friend* first deals with κολακεία (48e–59a) and then with παρρησία (59a–74e); Stobaeus reverses the order and has a chapter περὶ παρρησίας before his περὶ κολακείας.[23] There were, however, limits to openness. In common with others, Philo warns against divulging the secrets of a friend.[24] In *Her.* Philo proceeds to extend the contrast between true and false forms of

---

[19] Cf. *Conf.* 48: κολακείας νόθης ἑταῖρος ὤν, φιλίας γνησίου πολέμιος.

[20] Aristotle, *EE* 1239a (7.4.7); *EN* 1159a (8.8.1).

[21] Theophrastus, Περὶ κολακείας (cf. William W. Fortenbaugh *et al.*, *Theophrastus of Eresus: Sources for his Life, Writings, Thought and Influence* [PhilAnt 54.1–2; 2 vols.; Leiden: E. J. Brill, 1992] 2.373 [frgs. 547–48]); Philodemus, Περὶ κολακείας (3 vols. = PHerc 222, 223, 1082, 1089, 1457, 1675); Plutarch, *Quomodo adulator ab amico internoscatur* 48e–74e; Maximus of Tyre, Τίσι χωριστέον τὸν κόλακα τοῦ φίλου 18 (= *Or* 14.18 Hobein); Cicero, *Amic.* 26, 88–100; Stobaeus, *Ecl.* 3.14 (C. Wachsmuth and O. Hense, *Ioannis Stobaei: Anthologium* [5 vols.; 1884–1912, 1958²; reprint ed., Berlin: Weidmann, 1974] 3.468–76. All references to Stobaeus are to this edition). Cf. also Pseudo-Phocylides 91. For further references see van der Horst, *The Sentences of Pseudo-Phocylides*, 176.

[22] *Her.* 19–21. Cf. also *Migr.* 115–17; *Fug.* 6; *Ios.* 74; *Spec.* 2.19; and *Flacc.* 43, for the same thought in different terms.

[23] Philodemus Περὶ παρρησίας (=PHerc 1471. The text was edited by Alexander Olivieri, *Philodemi* ΠΕΡΙ ΠΑΡΡΗΣΙΑΣ [Leipzig: B. G. Teubner, 1914]); Stobaeus, *Ecl.* 3.13 (Wachsmuth and Hense 3.453–68). Cf. also *Ep. Arist.* 125 and Cicero, *Amic.* 44, 88–100.

[24] *Hypoth.* 8.7.8. This is part of a common ethic among Hellenistic Jews. Josephus also includes the prohibition in *CA* 2.207. Contrast *Somn.* 1.191 which refers to the privileges of friendship. Others who warn against divulging secrets include: Isocrates, *To Demonicus* 22, 24; Plutarch, *How to tell a flatterer from a friend* 53f–54b; Stobaeus, *Ecl.* 3.41 (Wachsmuth and Hense 3.757–59).

friendship to include the distinction between "friendship/to love" (φιλία/τὸ φιλεῖν) on the one hand, and " kiss/to kiss" (φίλημα/καταφιλεῖν) on the other.[25]

What fruit will the tree of friendship bear after pruning? Philo answers: "impartiality" (τὸ ἀδέκαστον).[26] He explains: "For goodwill (εὔνοια) is a desire that good things come to your neighbor for his own sake."[27] This response can only be understood within the context of the philosophical tradition. The question whether friendship is altruistically or egoistically motivated surfaced as early as Plato and became an important issue in Aristotle.[28] It was, however, the inter-school rivalry between the Epicureans and Stoics that set the stage for this statement. While the position of Epicurus on friendship is arguable,[29] the ancient perception that the Epicureans held an

---

[25] *Her.* 42, 44, 51.

[26] This answer may reflect the common proverb attributed to Pythagoras in Diogenes Laertius 8.10: "friendship is equality" (φιλία ἰσότης).

[27] *Plant.* 106.

[28] For Plato's presentation in the *Lysis*, see Gregory Vlastos, "The Individual as Object of Love in Plato," *Platonic Studies* (Princeton: Princeton Univeristy Press, 1981²) 3–42, who accuses Plato of egocentrism; and A. W. Price, *Love and Friendship in Plato and Aristotle* (Oxford: Clarendon, 1989) 1–14, who argues against him. Important recent treatments on Aristotle's position are John M. Cooper, "Aristotle on Friendship," *Essays on Aristotle's Ethics* (ed. Amélie Oksenberg Rorty; Major Thinkers Series 2; Berkeley/Los Angeles/London: University of California Press, 1980) 301–40, who argues for an altruistic view for all three forms of friendship; Price, *Love and Friendship in Plato and Aristotle*, 131–61, who modifies Cooper's analysis by arguing that well-wishing rather than goodwill lies behind Aristotle's analyses of different forms of friendship; David K. O'Connor, "Two Ideals of Friendship," *History of Philosophy Quarterly* 7 (1990) 109–22, who makes a distinction between goodness-friends and utility-friends; and the essay by Frederic M. Schroeder in chapter two of this volume.

[29] Some of the more important works in the recent debate about Epicurus' views are: John M. Rist, "Epicurus on Friendship," *CP* 75 (1980) 121–29, who maintains that Epicurus was not altruistic; Phillip Mitsis, "Epicurus on Friendship and Altruism," *Oxford Studies in Ancient Philosophy* 5 (ed. J. Annas; Oxford, 1987) 127–53, which is reprinted in Phillip Mitsis, *Epicurus' Ethical Theory: The Pleasures of Invulnerability* (Cornell Studies in Classical Philology 48; Ithaca/London: Cornell University Press, 1988) 98–128, who contends that Epicurus was altruistic; and David K. O'Connor, "The Invulnerable Pleasures of Epicurean Friendship," *GRBS* 30 (1989) 165–86, who affirms that while friendship was thoroughly hedonistic for Epicurus the demands of tranquility did not allow it to be egoistic in expression.

egoistic view of friendship based on *utilitas* is not.³⁰ Cicero tells us that the Stoics emphatically rejected justice or friendship *propter utilitates*; on the contrary, they insisted that both are impossible "unless they are desired *per se*."³¹ Philo joins the fray by citing *verbum pro verbo* the Stoic definition of εὔνοια. Andronicus preserves the Stoic view: Εὔνοια μὲν οὖν ἐστι βούλησις ἀγαθῶν ⟨ἑτέρῳ⟩ αὐτοῦ ἕνεκεν ἐκείνου.³² Philo writes: εὔνοια γάρ ἐστι βούλησις τοῦ τῷ πλησίον εἶναι τὰ ἀγαθὰ αὐτοῦ χάριν ἐκείνου.³³ Friendship must therefore spring from altruistic motives.

How does φιλία relate to εὔνοια? Philo repeatedly uses the terms as virtual synonyms.³⁴ In this he differs from Aristotle who distinguished between the two. The Stagirite contended that εὔνοια could exist without φιλία, but φιλία could not apart from εὔνοια. Εὔνοια is the beginning of φιλία which develops through association.³⁵ He calls it "idle friendship" (ἀργὴ φιλία).³⁶ In later traditions, most notably the Middle Stoa and Middle Platonic, εὔνοια and φιλία became interchangeable.³⁷ Once again, it is evident that Philo has co-opted an Hellenistic position.

Philo also knows the standard definitions of a friend. He writes: "In the works of Moses a friend is so near that he does not differ from a person's own soul. For he says: 'the friend, the equal of your soul.'"³⁸ This is very similar to the famous aphorism that a

---

³⁰ See Cicero, *Fin.* 2.78–85a.

³¹ Cicero, *Fin.* 3.70. Cf. also *Leg.* 1.49 (=*SVF* 3.12, §43).

³² Andronicus, Περὶ παθῶν 6 (=*SVF* 3.105, §432). Cf. also Diogenes Laertius 7.116 (=*SVF* 3.105, §431, which incorrectly cites this as Diogenes Laertius 7.115).

³³ *Plant.* 106.

³⁴ *Plant.* 90, 106; *Conf.* 48; *Fug.* 40; *Somn.* 2.108; *Abr.* 194; *Ios.* 74; *Spec.* 1.52, 317; 2.239–40; 3.155. Cf. also *Leg.* 3.182 and *Spec.* 1.316–17, where he uses φιλία in association with εὔνους; *Migr.* 116; *Fug.* 6; *Abr.* 153; *Spec.* 3.155; 4.70, where φίλος and εὔνοια are connected (cf. also *Spec.* 1.250); and *Ios.* 79; *Flacc.* 18, where Philo brings φίλος and εὔνους together.

³⁵ Aristotle, *EE* 1241a1–15 (7.7.1–3); *EN* 1155b–1156a (8.2.3–4); 1167a (9.5.1–4).

³⁶ Aristotle, *EN* 1167a (9.5.3).

³⁷ Cicero, *Amic.* 19–20, 22; Plutarch, *De amicorum multitudine* 93f; *De fraterno amore* 478b, 481c, 482b; Alcinous, *Didaskalikos* 33.1; Apuleius, *De Platone et eius dogmate* 13. See also Lucian, *Tox.* 32, 37.

³⁸ *Her.* 83 citing Deut 13:7. He expresses the same thought in *Det.* 33: συμμάχους οὖν καὶ φίλους οὐκ ἐν ἴσῳ τιμητέον ἑαυτοῖς; and *Virt.* 103, where the nation is to

friend is another "I". For example, Aristotle said that a friend is an alter ego: "he feels about his friend just as he does about himself; for a friend is another self."³⁹

Beyond these standard descriptions, Philo associates φιλία and φίλος with the same vocabulary we find in philosophical discussions. So he makes the connection between φιλία and φιλεῖν which weaves its way through the discussions like an unbroken thread.⁴⁰ He also connects φιλία to "oneness of mind" (ὁμόνοια),⁴¹ "harmony" (συμφωνία),⁴² "partnership" (κοινωνία),⁴³ "companionship" (ἑταιρία),⁴⁴ and "close association" (συνήθεια).⁴⁵ Similarly, he uses "friend" (φίλος) and "companion" (ἑταῖρος) as synonyms⁴⁶ and regularly juxtaposes φίλος with "enemy" (ἔχθρος),⁴⁷ "hostile" (δυσμενής),⁴⁸ and "enemy" (πολέμιος).⁴⁹

---

love proselytes μὴ μόνον ὡς φίλους καὶ συγγενεῖς ἀλλὰ καὶ ὡς ἑαυτούς. Cf. also *Spec.* 1.68.

³⁹ Aristotle, *EN* 1166a (9.4.5). The same formulation appears in *EN* 1170b (9.9.10); *EE* 1245a (7.12.13); Pseudo-Aristotle, *MM* 1213a (2.15.5). Cf. also Cicero, *Off.* 1.56: "the result is what Pythagoras desires in friendship, that one comes from many (*ut unus fiat ex pluribus*)."

⁴⁰ *Her.* 42, 44; *Spec.* 3.155. Cf. also *Plant.* 104–06. For the tradition see e.g., Plato, *Ly.* 212a-b; Aristotle, *EN* 1159a-b (8.8.4); Cicero, *Amic.* 26, 100; *Fin.* 2.78; Stobaeus *Ecl.* 2.7.11m (=Wachsmuth and Hense 2.108 and *SVF* 3.160–61. §630). Philo can also associate φιλία and ἔρως (but never ἐράω): *Post.* 157; *Congr.* 166; *Fug.* 58; *Abr.* 194; *Spec.* 4.161; *Virt.* 55.

⁴¹ *Spec.* 1.70; *Virt.* 35; *Praem.* 154. For Philo it is a given that friends concur, *Her.* 246. Cf. Aristotle, *EE* 1241a16–34 (7.7.3–8); *EN* 1167a-b (9.6.1–4); Zeno according to Athenaeus 13.561C (=*SVF* 1.61, §263); Stobaeus, *Ecl.* 2.7.11m (=Wachsmuth and Hense 2.108 and *SVF* 3.160–61, §630); Stobaeus 2.7.11k (=Wachsmuth and Hense 2.106 and *SVF* 3.166, §661).

⁴² *Sacr.* 36; *Virt.* 35. Cf. Stobaeus, *Ecl.* 2. 7.51 (=Wachsmuth and Hense 2.73–74 and *SVF* 3.26–27, §112); 2.7.11k (=Wachsmuth and Hense 2.106 and *SVF* 3.166, §661).

⁴³ *Spec.* 2.119. Cf. Stobaeus, *Ecl.* 2.7.51 (=Wachsmuth and Hense 2.74 and *SVF* 3.26–27, §112); Diogenes Laertius 7.124 (=*SVF* 3.161, §631).

⁴⁴ *Det.* 15. Cf. Stobaeus, *Ecl.* 2.7.51 (=Wachsmuth and Hense 2.74 and *SVF* 3.26–27, §112).

⁴⁵ *Spec.* 4.161. Cf. Stobaeus, *Ecl.* 2.7.51 (=Wachsmuth and Hense 2.74 and *SVF* 3.26–27, §112). Philo also associates φίλος with συνήθης in *Spec.* 1.68; *Contempl.* 41; *Legat.* 268. Cf. also *Abr.* 65; *Flacc.* 18.

⁴⁶ *Post.* 91; *Deus* 55; *Fug.* 3; *Somn.* 1.111; *Prob.* 42, 44; *Contempl.* 13; *Flacc.* 32. Cf. also *Leg.* 3.182; *Spec.* 2.132; *Legat.* 327–28.

⁴⁷ *Leg.* 3.1, 182; *Cher.* 20; *Det.* 37, 166; *Post.* 25, 172; *Gig.* 43, 66; *Deus* 27, 98; *Agr.* 155; *Ebr.* 159; *Migr.* 112, 116; *Her.* 48, 203; *Somn.* 2.104; *Abr.* 153; *Ios.* 79; *Mos.* 1.45, 307,

To summarize, we may say that Philo knows the standard themes and vocabulary of the philosophical discussions of φιλία. He clearly stands within the Hellenistic tradition and appears to share the Stoic concept of φιλία as goodwill for others on their behalf. The citation of the Stoic definition of εὔνοια does not, however, prove his allegiance to the Stoic understanding of friendship: Philo is fully capable of citing a definition of a *terminus technicus* or of using technical vocabulary without accepting the larger discussion in which it is embedded.[50] We need more evidence.

The Practice of Friendship

On at least four different occasions Philo alludes to or comments on well known *topoi* on the practice of friendship. The first and least significant is the allusion to "the table and salt which humans have devised as the signs of genuine friendship."[51] This is a common trope for friendship attested in a range of sources including Aristotle, Cicero, and Plutarch.[52] Philo chooses not to

---

310; *Spec.* 1.313, 316, 340; 4.70; *Virt.* 46, 125; *Praem.* 127; *Contempl.* 41, 44; *Flacc.* 18; *Legat.* 40. Cf. also *Deus* 167; *Ebr.* 165; *Her.* 243; *Virt.* 195.

[48] *Leg.* 3.1, 71; *Det.* 37, 165; *Agr.* 88; *Flacc.* 62; *Praem.* 118. Cf. also *Agr.* 159; *Ebr.* 69, 176; *Virt.* 195.

[49] *Mos.* 1.280; *Spec.* 1.313. Cf. also *Her.* 243; *Congr.* 91. The three terms are largely used as synonyms. The grammarian Ammonius, Περὶ ὁμοίων καὶ διαφόρων λέξεων 208 (Klaus Nickau, *Ammonii, Qui dicitur liber de adfinium vocabulorum differentia* [Bibliotheca scriptorum Graecorum et Romanorum Teubneriana; Leipzig: B. G. Teubner, 1966] 55), distinguished them as follows: ἐχθρὸς μὲν γάρ ἐστιν ὁ πρότερον φίλος, πολέμιος δὲ ὁ μεθ' ὅπλων χωρῶν πέλας, δυσμενὴς δὲ ὁ χρόνιον πρὸς τόν ποτε φίλον τὴν ἔχθραν διατηρῶν καὶ δυσδιαλλάκτως ἔχων. Edward O'Neil has a very helpful collection of the common *topoi* in Plutarch which are very similar to those listed here. See his essay in chapter five of this volume.

[50] Philo cites the Stoic definition of φιλοσοφία in *Congr.* 79 (cf. Sextus, *M.* 9.13 [=*SVF* 2.15, §36]; Cicero, *Off.* 2.5; Seneca, *Ep.* 89.5) and yet no one considers him a Stoic. An example of his use of Stoic language without accepting the conceptual framework in which the language originally occurred is *Opif.* 8–9, where he cites the standard Stoic description of an active Cause and passive object as an explanation of the origin of the cosmos (cf. Sextus, *M.* 9.75 [=*SVF* 2.112, §311]) while maintaining a Middle Platonic cosmology. For details see David T. Runia, *Philo of Alexandria and the Timaeus of Plato* (PhilAnt 44; Leiden: E. J. Brill, 1986) 143–44.

[51] *Ios.* 210; *Contempl.* 41.

[52] Aristotle, *EE* 1238a2 (7.2.46); *EN* 1156b (8.3.8); Cicero, *Amic.* 67; Plutarch, *De amicorum multitudine* 94a; *De fraterno amore* 482b.

expand the reference, but is willing to let it stand as a *recherché* allusion.

The second occasion occurs during Philo's recital of the Deuteronomic code of war for a besieged city. Deut 20:10–13 specified a code of behavior for the Israelites when they laid siege to a city. Philo recounts this text twice; in both instances he refuses to cast the Israelites as aggressors. In *De specialibus legibus* he presents the Israelites as the besiegers, but states that the besieged were rebellious members of the Israelite alliance.[53] He was apparently concerned that this still did not go far enough, so in the appendices to his earlier exposition which we know as *De virtutibus*, he reversed the roles and made the Israelites the besieged rather than the besiegers. When a foreign army began to lay siege they were to send out an embassy to negotiate for "the greatest good" (τὸ μέγιστον ἀγαθόν), namely φιλία. While the biblical text mentions negotiations, the reference to φιλία is Philo's own contribution. Is this merely rhetorical or is something more afoot? In isolation the present context does not permit us to answer.[54]

Philo apparently forgot the role reversal he had introduced. Later in *Virt.* he interpreted the prohibition against felling fruit-bearing trees in Deut 20:19.[55] Sounding like an environmentalist, Philo explains that the prohibition included not only trees within the homeland, but the trees of an enemy's land. The reason for the latter is that the enemies may sue for peace and become friends. Not only individuals but states should follow the ancient maxim: "one must form friendships without forgetting the possibility of animosity and one must conduct hostilities with the possibility of future friendship in mind."[56] While Philo's application of this maxim to matters of foreign policy appears to

---

[53] *Spec.* 4.219–23.

[54] *Virt.* 109. Simon Légasse, "Morale hellénistique et morale chrétienne primitive: Les rapports interhumaines illustrés par deux exemples," *Études sur le Judaïsme Hellénistique (Congrès de Strasbourg [1983])* (ed. R. Kuntzmann, J. Schlosser; LD 119; Paris: Cerf, 1984) 330–31, argues that *Virt.* 110–15 reflects the Stoic "idée de nature commune à tous les hommes."

[55] *Virt.* 149–154. Cf. also *Spec.* 4.226–29.

[56] *Virt.* 152. Cf. *Flacc.* 62.

be unique, the aphorism is common.⁵⁷ Philo's repeated insistence on the humanity of Israelite warfare is in keeping with the views of someone like the Stoic Panaetius, but need not be dependent on them.⁵⁸

The third application of friendship to a specific situation is the issue of the limits of friendship: can a person do something wrong for a friend? Philo responds to this issue with an unequivocal no. In his comments on the prohibition of taking God's name in vain (Exod 20:7), the exegete formulates an *a minore ad majus* argument. He wonders how a person could approach a friend (φίλος) and plead with him to testify falsely: "For the sake of our companionship (ἑταιρία) do wrong, transgress, act impiously with me." Philo responds decisively: "For it is evident that, if he hears such words, he will bid good riddance to a supposed companionship (ἑταιρία) and reproach himself for having ever formed the beginning of a friendship (φιλία) with such a person," then, "he will flee as if [he were fleeing] from a wild and raging beast." He completes the argument by observing that if it is inappropriate to ask a friend to testify falsely, how much less appropriate is it to expect God to do so?⁵⁹

While such a view could come from Judaism, the formulation of the question suggests Philo has the Greek philosophical tradition in mind. The discussion appears to have begun with Aristotle who matter of factly affirms that friends "neither ask for what is morally worthless nor supply such things [to one another]."⁶⁰ His successor, Theophrastus, was not, however, content with such a broad judgment. He provided a more nuanced answer: "A small and insignificant disgrace or defamation should be endured if by that means a great benefit

---

⁵⁷ Sophocles, *Aj.* 679–83; Demosthenes, *Ag. Arist.* 122; Aristotle, *Rh.* 1389b (2.13.4); 1395a (2.21.13–14); Cicero, *Amic.* 59; Diogenes Laertius 1.87; 8.23.

⁵⁸ See Cicero, *Off.* 1.34–35. Panaetius is Cicero's main source for books one and two.

⁵⁹ *Dec.* 89–90. Cf. also *Spec.* 2.26 (commenting on Lev 5:1); 3.155 (commenting on Deut 24:16). Philo presumes that friends act on behalf of friends (*Det.* 37, 165; *Agr.* 88; *Her.* 203; *Somn.* 1.110; *Spec.* 1.97; *Virt.* 173) or even the friends of friends (*Spec.* 2.132). Friends should not be hurt (*Gig.* 43, 66).

⁶⁰ Aristotle, *EN* 1159b (8.8.5).

can be provided for a friend."⁶¹ Cicero, according to Gellius, followed Theophrastus' lead when writing *De amicitia*, but not carefully.⁶² This perhaps explains the ambiguity in the former. On the one hand he could say: "Therefore let this law be ratified in friendship that we neither ask for any dishonorable thing nor do anything dishonorable for one who asks."⁶³ On the other hand, he later equivocates. He explains the specific limits of friendship as follows: "even if it happens by some chance that the desires of friends which are less than right should be accepted in situations which involve their life or reputation, it is necessary to depart from the path only provided that no great disgrace follows." He summarizes: "There are limits to the goodwill of friendship."⁶⁴ How should we explain this inconsistency? I suggest that in the former Cicero articulates the standard Stoic position and in the latter adds a qualification which he drew from Theophrastus. Why he chose to add the qualification is open to dispute.⁶⁵ The vehemence and length of his early exposition, however, suggest that it rather than the latter represents his own view. Why were Cicero or the Stoics and Philo so dogmatic? We may attribute their insistence to an inter-school debate. Epicurus reluctantly–apparently–argued that he could do something unjust if there were no complications.⁶⁶ Based upon this John Rist maintains that in situations where fear of detection was not an issue, Epicurus would support the unjust actions of his friends.⁶⁷ If he is correct, this could serve as an impetus for Philo's vehemence. It appears that equivocation was possible in a non-polemical context, but

---

⁶¹ Περὶ φιλίας 1 preserved in Gellius, *Noctes Atticae* 1.3.23. I have used the OCT edition reproduced in Fortenbaugh, *Theophrastus of Eresus*, 2.358 (frg. 534). Cf. 2.353–73 (frgs. 532–46) for his work *On Friendship*.

⁶² Gellius, *Noctes Atticae* 1.3.10–13 (Fortenbaugh, *Theophrastus of Eresus*, 2.356, frg. 534), says: "*strictim atque cursim transgressus est.*"

⁶³ Cicero, *Amic.* 40. See also 44 where it is repeated and called the *prima lex*. See 34–44 for his full treatment along with 76, 82.

⁶⁴ Cicero, *Amic.* 61.

⁶⁵ For an historical interpretation, see J. G. F. Powell, *Cicero: Laelius, On Friendship & The Dream of Scipio* (Warminster, England: Aris & Phillips, 1990) 107–08.

⁶⁶ See Cicero, *Fin.* 2.28–30; Plutarch, *Adversus Colotem* 1127d.

⁶⁷ Rist, "Epicurus on Friendship," 128–9.

that the polemics of the Stoic-Epicurean debate moved the participants to positions of extremes.[68]

The issue of the limits of friendship leads to a fourth example of a common *topos*: the Alexandrian's use of the famous proverb κοινὰ τὰ φίλων. Philo employs this in two different types of contexts. First, in keeping with the literary tradition of presenting elite groups among the people of the East in the garb of Western philosophy, Philo tells us that the Essenes and Therapeutae had their possessions in common.[69] This appears to be an apologetic device claiming that these groups practiced the highest ideals of the Greek philosophical tradition.[70] Second, as Philo retells the lives of Abraham and Moses he cites the proverb but gives it a different twist. When Abraham returned from recovering Lot, Melchizedek threw a feast considering Abraham's success his own. Philo explains that it was in fact just as the proverb says: "The possessions of friends are held in common." He then adds: "This is even truer of the possessions of the good for whom there is one aim, to be well-pleasing to God."[71] The same understanding surfaces in a panegyric on Moses.[72] In return for abandoning the wealth of Egypt, God shared his possessions with Moses. Philo argues this by means of syllogistic reasoning: major premise, "the possessions of friends are common"; minor premise, Moses is God's friend (Exod 33:11); conclusion, therefore Moses shares God's possessions. He buttresses his argument with the explanation that it is a natural consequence if we take seriously the Stoic notion of a κοσμοπολίτης: he is a citizen of the world,

---

[68] It should be noted that Chrysippus did not require the termination of friendships for all wrongs (Plutarch, *De Stoicorum repugnantiis* 1039b = *SVF* 3.182, §724).

[69] Essenes: *Prob.* 85-87; *Hypoth.* 8.11.4-13; Therapeutae: *Contempl.* 13-17, which presents the divestiture of their property.

[70] Philo makes the apologetic nature of his presentation of these groups explicit in *Prob.* 74-75, 88-91; *Hypoth.* 8.11.18; *Contempl.* 2-9, 40-89. Philo does not present this as a practice of all Jews; he can speak of the assistance of friends, e.g., *Fug.* 29; *Mut.* 40. On the literary tradition and the apologetic nature of the presentations, see my "'Athletes of Virtue': An Analysis of the Summaries in Acts (2:41-47; 4:32-35; 5:12-16)," *JBL* 113 (1994) 679-96.

[71] *Abr.* 235.

[72] *Mos.* 1.147-62.

not a single city.⁷³ Since the aphorism, κοινὰ τὰ φίλων, may go back to Pythagoras and is ubiquitous in ancient literature, it is not surprising to find it in Philo.⁷⁴ What is interesting is that he connects the proverb to human-divine relationships.

These four examples illustrate Philo's awareness of popular themes associated with friendship. While it would be impossible to argue responsibly for an identification of Philo's understanding of friendship from these alone, they again point in the direction of Stoicism. This is particularly true of the third example where Philo takes the Stoic line in a polemical situation.

The Extent of Friendship

The possibility of thinking of God as a friend brings us to the final area of consideration: what were the boundaries of friendship? Or, if I may paraphrase a famous question in the Gospel of Luke: Who is my friend?⁷⁵ In a warning against the destructive powers of "desire" (ἐπιθυμία), Philo notes that when ἐπιθυμία is directed to glory, individuals "form friendships and hostilities without any forethought, with the result that they easily substitute one for the other."⁷⁶ The implication is that the formulation of friendships is far too important for cavalier treatment. This view is in agreement with the philosophical tradition.⁷⁷ Plato began the discussion by considering whether only the good can be friends.⁷⁸ His most celebrated student advised individuals to form only a few friendships.⁷⁹ The Stoics

---

⁷³ *Mos.* 1.156–57. Diogenes is reported to have coined the term. When he was asked where he came from, he replied: κοσμοπολίτης (Diogenes Laertius 6.63). For Philo's use of the term see *Opif.* 3, 142, 143; *Gig.* 61; *Conf.* 106; *Migr.* 59; *Mos.* 1.157; *Spec.* 2.45.

⁷⁴ The claim that it goes back to Pythagoras is in Diogenes Laertius 8.10. Plato, *Ly.* 207c and Aristotle, *EN* 1168b (9.8), note its proverbial nature in their day.

⁷⁵ Luke 10:29, Καὶ τίς ἐστίν μου πλησίον;

⁷⁶ *Spec.* 4.88.

⁷⁷ Cf. also Sir 6:5–17; 11:29–12:18, where great care in the selection of friends is encouraged.

⁷⁸ Plato, *Ly.* 214d–16e.

⁷⁹ Aristotle, *EE* 1237b–1238a (7.2.45–48); *EN* 1156b (8.3.8); 1158a (8.6.2–3); 1170b–1171a (9.10.1–6).

maintained that only the "wise" (σοφοί) can be friends.⁸⁰ Not surprisingly Plutarch composed a tractate on the subject.⁸¹

The issues we must address are: how far did Philo extend this relationship and on what basis? For Philo it is axiomatic that φιλία should extend to fellow Israelites. On two occasions he speaks of the Jewish practices which have served as either the bonds of φιλία or have fostered φιλία among the Israelites.⁸² In *De vita Mosis* it is common for him to refer to Hebrews as "relatives and friends" (συγγενεῖς καὶ φίλοι).⁸³ Such usage may be no more significant than a predilection for connecting φίλος and συγγενής.⁸⁴ The issue is the basis for the tie. This becomes transparent in his comments on proselytes: "It is necessary to regard everyone who has resolved to honor the Creator and Father of the all–even if they did not at first but later embraced a belief in one sovereign rather than many–as the dearest friends and relatives." The reason is that "they have demonstrated a disposition at friendship with God (θεοφιλὲς ἦθος) which above all leads "to friendship and affinity (εἰς φιλίαν καὶ οἰκειότητα)."⁸⁵

The reference to friendship with God was fairly widespread in antiquity and is not particularly surprising in Philo.⁸⁶ He can speak of God's friends in general; or more specifically of Abraham,

---

⁸⁰ Zeno *apud* Diogenes Laertius 7.32-33 (=*SVF* 1.54, §222); the school *apud* Diogenes Laertius 7.124 (=*SVF* 3.161, §631); Stobaeus, *Ecl.* 2.7.11m (=Wachsmuth and Hense 2.108 and *SVF* 3.160-61, §630).

⁸¹ Plutarch, *De amicorum multitudine* 93a-97b. For a similar sentiment from the second century CE, see Lucian, *Toxaris* 37.

⁸² *Spec.* 1.69-70; *Praem.* 154.

⁸³ *Mos.* 1.39, 303, 307, 322; 2.42, 171, 273.

⁸⁴ *Leg.* 2.85; 3.71, 205; *Post.* 172; *Gig.* 33; *Deus* 79; *Agr.* 155; *Abr.* 65; *Mos.* 1.39, 303, 307, 322; 2.171; *Spec.* 1.52, 68, 247; 2.19; 3.85, 90, 155; 4.141; *Virt.* 179; *Praem.* 17; *Prob.* 9, 35; *Contempl.* 14; *Flacc.* 60, 64, 72. Cf. also *Virt.* 173; *Contempl.* 13, 41.

⁸⁵ *Virt.* 179. See also *Spec.* 1.51-52.

⁸⁶ He uses φιλία in reference to human-divine relationships in *Plant.* 90; *Her.* 21; *Fug.* 58; *Contempl.* 90. The most important treatment of the topic in Philo is H. Neumark, "Die Verwendung griechischer und jüdischer Motive in den Gedanken Philons über die Stellung Gottes zu seinen Freunden" (Dissertation, Würzburg, 1937). Neumark is also known as Y. Amir. Josephine Massyngbaerde Ford, *Redemption as Friendship* (forthcoming) has a brief treatment as well. For references to the literature in antiquity, see David Winston, *The Wisdom of Solomon* (AB 43; Garden City, New York: Doubleday, 1979) 188-89. We should point out that Aristotle did not think that friendship with gods was possible, *EN* 1159a (8.7.5-6).

Jacob, Moses, and the wise as God's friends.[87] Nor is it particularly surprising to think of friendship with God as a basis for the common bond among Jews and proselytes. What is surprising is Philo's extension of this principle. We can see the extension in two different formulations.

The first is a redefinition of friendship and kinship. In no fewer than six texts Philo affirms that the worship of the one God is the basis for φιλία.[88] In three of these he connects friendship and kinship (συγγένεια) on the basis of commitment to God and elevates these bonds over the ties of blood and marriage.[89] So, for example, when Moses instructs the Levites to slay those who had cast the golden calf, Philo places a definition of friendship and kinship in Moses' mouth: "Let each slay relatives and friends with the conviction that among good men only piety constitutes friendship and kinship (φιλία καὶ συγγένεια)."[90] Correspondingly, only the friends of God share in the divine attributes.[91] Philo has thus redefined the boundaries of friendship and kinship along religious lines. His procedure is similar to the claims of Isocrates who defined Greeks in cultural rather than ethnic categories or of Plutarch who proferred an ethical definition.[92] Where Philo

---

[87] Generally: *Somn.* 1.193 (those whom God addresses by name, i.e., Moses, Abraham, Jacob [193–96]); 2.219; *Prob.* 42; Abraham: *Sobr.* 55–57; *Migr.* 44–45; *Somn.* 1.193–95; *Abr.* 273; Jacob: *Somn.* 1.193–200 (by implication); Moses: *Sacr.* 130; *Ebr.* 94; *Migr.* 45; *Her.* 21; *Somn.* 1.193–94; *Mos.* 1.155–57; *Prob.* 44; Wise: *Leg.* 3.1; *Her.* 21.

[88] *Mos.* 2.171; *Spec.* 1.52, 317; 3.155; *Virt.* 35, 179.

[89] *Mos.* 2.171; *Spec.* 1.317; 3.155. Cf. also *Prob.* 79 for the connection between φιλία and συγγένεια.

[90] *Mos.* 2.171. This is an expansion of Exod 32:27. Philo's paraphrase is based on καὶ ἀποκτείνατε ἕκαστος τὸν ἀδελφὸν αὐτοῦ καὶ ἕκαστος τὸν πλησίον αὐτοῦ καὶ ἕκαστος τὸν ἔγγιστα αὐτοῦ.

[91] *Leg.* 3.204; *Somn.* 1.232; 2.219, 297. This plays into the allegory of the soul where Philo contrasts what is φίλος to God or the soul with what is φίλος to the body. See *Leg.* 3.20, 71, 152; *Post.* 91; *Gig.* 33, 35; *Agr.* 25, 168; *Plant.* 25; *Ebr.* 58; *Her.* 186, 243; *Somn.* 1.111.

[92] Isocrates, *Paneg.* 50: καὶ τὸ τῶν Ἑλλήνων ὄνομα πεποίηκε μηκέτι τοῦ γένους ἀλλὰ τῆς διανοίας δοκεῖν εἶναι, καὶ μᾶλλον "Ἕλληνας καλεῖσθαι τοὺς τῆς παιδεύσεως τῆς ἡμετέρας ἢ τοὺς τῆς κοινῆς φύσεως μετέχοντας. For Plutarch see *De Alex. fort.* 329c-d, esp. d: ἀλλὰ τὸ μὲν Ἑλληνικὸν ἀρετῇ τὸ δὲ βαρβαρικὸν κακίᾳ τεκμαίρεσθαι. Cf. also Dionysius of Halicarnassus, *AR* 14.5.5–6 and Strabo 1.4.9 (following Eratosthenes). NT authors use fictive kinship language to describe community relations, e.g., Matt 12:46–50//Mark 3:31–35//Luke 8:19–21.

differs is in the specific content which stems directly from his Jewish background.

The second basis for friendship is squarely in line with the Middle Stoic and Middle Platonic traditions. The term which Philo juxtaposes with φιλία in *Virt.* 179 is "affinity" (οἰκειότης). This is not the only time he joins these terms: they appear together four times.[93] In some texts he offers his redefinition. For example, he urges: "Let there be one bond of affinity (μία οἰκειότης) and one symbol of φιλία, namely full devotion to God and that everything that we say or do promotes piety." He follows with the comparison: "As for those so-called relationships (συγγένειαι) which have come down from our ancestors and are based on blood or those οἰκειότητες which are based on intermarriage or any other similar cause, let them all be rejected," he exhorts, "if they do not urgently press on to the same goal, the honor of God which is the indissoluble bond of the εὔνοια that completely unites."[94]

On two other occasions Philo speaks of the bond of friendship which nature implants within the heart of human beings. The first is his exposition of Lev 19:3 where he argues that God enjoins fear rather than love for parents because "φιλία for parents is self-learned and self-taught (αὐτομαθὴς καὶ αὐτοδίδακτος) and has no need of a command."[95] The second helps to explicate what Philo has in mind here. In one of his descriptions of the Essene community he observes that the Essenes did not have any slaves. They criticised those who did for violating not only the law of equality but "for destroying the precept of nature (φύσις) which, like a mother who has given birth to and nurtured all in the same way, has made them genuine brothers—not in name only but in fact." The reason this is unrecognized is that "the flourishing of treacherous greed has thrown συγγένεια into a state of confusion:

---

[93] *Leg.* 3.182; *Spec.* 1.317; *Virt.* 179; *Prob.* 79. He also joins φίλος and οἰκεῖος in *Leg.* 3.205; *Det.* 165; *Mos.* 1.31; 2.42; *Spec.* 1.52, 97, 340; 3.11; 4.70; *Virt.* 96, 125, 218. See also *Mos.* 2.273. For the adjectival uses, see *Ebr.* 69, 176; and the phrase "nearest and dearest" in *Opif.* 77; *Cher.* 20; *Sacr.* 20, 129; *Ebr.* 66; *Fug.* 89; *Spec.* 1.313; 3.126; *Praem.* 134. Cf. also *Spec.* 1.250; *Virt.* 195.

[94] *Spec.* 1.317.

[95] *Spec.* 2.240. Compare the treatment in Seneca, *Ben.* 4.17.2.

it has produced alienation in the place of affinity (οἰκειότης) and hostility in the place of φιλία."⁹⁶

This text is a condensed statement of the view which was worked out in the Middle Stoa.⁹⁷ The Stoics held that φύσις implanted φιλία in every child.⁹⁸ From the parent-child relationship they extended φιλία to other relationships.⁹⁹ The most important statement of this view is that of Antiochus of Ascalon who argued that the bond which holds families together should be extended concentrically through blood relationships, in-laws, friends, neighbors, fellow-citizens, until it embraced the entire human race.¹⁰⁰ The result for the Stoics was that the human race should be held together through a bond of friendship.¹⁰¹

Can we square Philo's two formulations? How does the principle of the unity of the human race based upon nature relate to the unity of those who serve the one God? For Philo there is no tension between God and nature nor should there be between Jews and humanity as a whole.¹⁰² For Philo, Judaism does not turn inward, but outward. It is the vanguard to lead humanity to God.¹⁰³ In one of the few texts where Philo allows himself to break into a Messianic vision he writes: "This is what the most sacred prophet wishes to create through the entirety of his legislation: oneness of mind, partnership, unanimity, blending of feelings (ὁμόνοια, κοινωνία, ὁμοφροσύνη, κρᾶσις ἠθῶν) from which

---

⁹⁶ *Prob.* 79. On nature as the source of human equality cf. *Decal.* 41, 132–34; *Spec.* 4.14; *Praem.* 92; and *QG* 2.60.

⁹⁷ I am following the analysis of H. C. Baldry, *The Unity of Mankind in Greek Thought* (Cambridge: Cambridge University Press, 1965) 173–203.

⁹⁸ Cicero, *Amic.* 27; Plutarch, *De fraterno amore* 478e.

⁹⁹ On φύσις as the source see e.g., Cicero, *Fin.* 3.62–63; Plutarch, *De fraterno amore* 479c-d.

¹⁰⁰ Cicero, *Fin.* 5.65; 2.45; Augustine, *De civ. D.* 19.3.

¹⁰¹ Cicero, *Leg.* 1.34.

¹⁰² It is worth remembering that Philo affirmed humanity's relationship to God in his exposition of the first creation account, *Opif.* 77.

¹⁰³ For specific examples see Winston, "Philo's Ethical Theory," 398–400. He writes: "At every possible opportunity, Philo emphasizes the universal aspects of Jewish particularism."

families, cities, nations, countries, and the entire human race may progress to the supreme state of happiness."[104]

Conclusions

Was Philo a σπερμολόγος who collected and dropped ideas in a haphazard fashion in the course of his exegesis or did he have a comprehensive understanding which assumed different forms on different occasions? In this specific case I would contend for the latter. In particular I have argued that Philo knew and used the Stoic concept of friendship. The identification of his understanding with that of the Stoa is evident in a number of crucial aspects of friendship: he knows the Stoic concept of εὔνοια, sides with them against the Epicureans on the limits of friendship, and most important, draws from the Middle Stoa for his vision of the unity of the human race.

Why did Philo accept the Stoic view? We should remember that he lived in cosmopolitan Alexandria, an environment which demanded the acceptance of Hellenism. The demand was formulated in a number of ways: negatively, through the omnipresent charge of "Jewish separatism";[105] positively, by the realization that the only avenue to advancement was assimilation. These social forces help us to understand why an Alexandrian Jew might be open to the larger world; they do not, however, explain Philo's specific choice. I think that he was attracted to the Stoic understanding of friendship for several reasons. First, he found the ethnic and covenantal nomistic views of Judaism problematic: both had a tendency toward exclusivity. Consequently, he redefined the ethnic understanding—as we have seen—and

---

[104] *Virt.* 119. There are several important recent treatments of Philo's universal perspective: Peder Borgen, "'There Shall Come Forth a Man:' Reflections on Messianic Ideas in Philo," *The Messiah: Developments in Earliest Judaism and Christianity* (ed. James H. Charlesworth; Minneapolis: Fortress, 1992) 341–61, who speaks of "particularistic universalism"; Ellen Birnbaum "The Place of Judaism in Philo's Thought: Israel, Jews, and Proselytes" (Ph.D. Dissertation, Columbia University, 1992) esp. 4–9, 391–96, where she she calls Philo an "inclusive particularist"; and her article with the same title in *SBLSP* 32 (1993) 54–69.

[105] On Jewish strangeness see J. N. Sevenster, *The Roots of Pagan Anti-Semitism in the Ancient World* (NovTSup 41; Leiden: E. J. Brill, 1975) 89–144.

diplomatically side-stepped the biblical concept of the covenant.[106] Second, his commitment to philosophical thought naturally led him to look for a philosophical construct which would permit him to present his universal perspective. The Stoic understanding of friendship provided such a construct.[107] It is, therefore, more than coincidental that at key points where Philo's thought becomes universal he uses the language of friendship.

At the same time, Philo did not accept the Stoic perspective *tout à fait*. His intellectual and social commitment to Judaism and the Jewish community led him to modify it in a major way: he wed it to his particular understanding of monotheism. Viewed from the perspective of the Jewish community, friendship meant the enlargement of Judaism to all who shared the same Friend. Viewed from the outside, it meant that Jews were not a closed group. In this way friendship became the vehicle for a Jewish universal understanding of the human race.[108]

---

[106] Philo wrote two books Περὶ διαθηκῶν (*Mut.* 53; cf. also *QE* 2.34) which are unfortunately lost. The references which we have in his corpus ignore the significance of the historical covenant with Israel and stress the symbolic meaning which is most frequently God's grace (*Sacr.* 57 [διαθήκη δ' ἐστὶ θεοῦ συμβολικῶς αἱ χάριτες αὐτοῦ]; *Mut.* 51–53 [52: ὥστε σύμβολον εἶναι διαθήκην χάριτος], 57–60; *Somn.* 2.223–25; *QG* 2.10; 3.40). Cf. also *Leg.* 3.85; *Det.* 67–68; *Her.* 313; *Mut.* 263; *Somn.* 2.237; *QG* 3.42; *QE* 2.106). He uses it to refer to a will in *Spec.* 2.16 (the only occurrence in the Exposition) and *QG* 2.60. The most important studies are Annie Jaubert, *La notion d'alliance dans le Judaïsme aux abords de l'ère chrétienne* (Patristica Sorbonensia 6; Paris: Du Seuil, 1963) 375–42, who overemphasizes Philo's continuity with the biblical presentation; E. P. Sanders, "The Covenant as a Soteriological Category and the Nature of Salvation in Paletinian and Hellenistic Judaism," *Jews, Greeks and Christians: Religious Cultures in Late Antiquity (Essays in Honor of William David Davies)* (ed. Robert Hamerton-Kelly and Robin Scroggs; SJLA 21; Leiden: E. J. Brill, 1976) 11–44, esp. 22–39, who rightly calls attention to the tension between Philo's universalism and particularism. Birnbaum, "The Place of Judaism in Philo's Thought," 234–36, has a brief but judicious treatment.

[107] The Neopythagoreans also used friendship to express a universal outlook. According to Iamblichus, *VP* 229: "Pythagoras handed down in the clearest possible way: 'Friendship of all with all.'" See 229–30. I have used John Dillon and Jackson Hershbell, *Iamblichus, On the Pythagorean Way of Life: Text, Translation, and Notes* (SBLTT 29; Atlanta: Scholars Press, 1991). For details see the essay by Johan C. Thom in chapter four of this volume.

[108] I want to thank the members of two groups who made numerous suggestions to presentations of this material in various stages: the Hellenistic and Moral Philosophy and Early Christianity Consultation of the Society of Biblical Literature (November 1991) and the Christianity and Judaism in Antiquity Seminar of the University of

Notre Dame (November 1993). In particular I would like to thank Professors Frederic M. Schroeder of Queen's University and Blake Leyerle of the University of Notre Dame for their formal responses.

"GREET THE FRIENDS BY NAME": NEW TESTAMENT EVIDENCE FOR THE GRECO-ROMAN *TOPOS* ON FRIENDSHIP[*]

Alan C. Mitchell

New Testament authors, particularly Paul, Luke, and John, show familiarity with the Greco-Roman *topos* on friendship and adapt it to the needs of their communities. These writers use friendship traditions to build and maintain relationships with their communities and to foster better relationships among the members of those communities. In these ways they contribute to the friendship tradition.

One remarkable thing about the use of the friendship *topos* among New Testament authors is the conspicuous scarcity of the words φιλία and φίλος.[1] Their reluctance to use the terms, however, has not deterred them from invoking friendship conventions associated with the normal sense of those words.[2] It is, nevertheless, striking that, while employing terms and appealing to conventions associated with the friendship *topos*, these writers have not more plainly shown their hand. Impressive, too, is the variety of ways that friendship is interpreted in the New Testament. On the one hand, there is evidence for Peter Marshall's claim that NT authors do not attempt to ignore the institution of friendship, but on the other, one has to wonder

---

[*] I am grateful to Gregory E. Sterling, who carefully read an earlier version of this manuscript and offered suggestions for improving it. Unless otherwise noted, all translations of Greek and Latin authors are taken from the Loeb Classical Library.

[1] Φιλία occurs only at James 4:4 and φίλος at Matt 11:19; Luke 7:6, 34; 11:5 (*bis*), 6, 8; 12:4; 14:10, 12; 15:6, 9, 29; 16:9; 21:16; 23:12; John 3:29; 11:11; 15:13, 14, 15; 19:12; Acts 10:24; 19:31; 27:3; James 2:23; 4:4; 3 John 15. See G. Stählin, "Φιλέω, κτλ.," *TDNT* 9 (1974) 113–71.

[2] Cf. P. Marshall, *Enmity in Corinth: Social Conventions in Paul's Relations with the Corinthians* (WUNT 2.23; Tübingen: J. C. B. Mohr [Paul Siebeck], 1987) 132–33.

about how it is being used.³ My purpose in this essay is to look at the places where evidence for the friendship *topos* has been discovered and to raise some questions about the peculiarity of its use. For the most part, my intention is to survey work already done on the topic and then to make some observations about that. I hope this will stimulate discussion on the issue of how friendship has undergone transformation in the New Testament. I would like to suggest that this modification is not necessarily an aberration from the friendship tradition but is, rather, a positive contribution to it.

Friendship in Paul

The use of the *topos* on friendship has been identified in 1 Thessalonians, Galatians, 1 and 2 Corinthians, Romans, and Philippians. Paul's avoidance of the words φίλος and φιλία, while still appealing to conventions associated with friendship, is striking.⁴ The picture is complicated further by the way friendship itself symbolizes the different relationships he had with the communities to which he wrote. Paul uses the friendship *topos* as a barometer. He invokes the language and conventions of friendship in order to indicate the quality of his relationship with the communities he addresses. Curiously, he does this without using the words φίλος and φιλία.

1 Thessalonians

Paul's paraenetic style in 1 Thessalonians betrays his familiarity with friendship traditions. But an effort to distance himself from them is evident, too.⁵ To the characteristics of the friendly letter at 2:17 and 3:6–10 should be added elements from the *topoi* on love and quietism in 4:9–10. But in relation to this, Paul's preference for φιλαδελφία over φιλία should be noticed. According to Malherbe, Paul's coinage of θεοδίδακτοι not only provides a clear

---

³ Ibid., 132.

⁴ A. J. Malherbe, *Paul and the Thessalonians: The Philosophical Tradition of Pastoral Care* (Philadelphia: Fortress, 1987) 104.

⁵ See A. J. Malherbe, *Paul and the Popular Philosophers* (Minneapolis: Fortress, 1989) 63; idem, *Paul and the Thessalonians*, 68–71.

motive for Christian love, but may also align him with Stoic and Platonic criticism of the Epicurean notion of friendship.[6] If such subtleties were evident to the Thessalonians, then the φιλία they were familiar with outside of Christian fellowship was likely to be seen as different from the φιλαδελφία to which Paul exhorted them within it.[7]

Galatians

H. D. Betz's rhetorical analysis of Gal 4:12-20 identifies how dependent Paul is on the friendship *topos* in this personal appeal to the letter's recipients.[8] The particular focus of Paul's use of elements of this *topos* has to do with the distinction between a true and a false friend. Betz has mined the philosophical literature on the issues of equality, harmony, and likeness, which contribute to the sentiment that the sharing of everything in life by friends reaches a high point in the idea that friendship is best demonstrated by becoming as much as is possible like one's friend.[9] I shall simply list the elements he identifies: 1) an appeal for true friendship marked by reciprocity (v. 12);[10] 2) the epistolary cliché in the expression, "You did me no wrong" (v. 12), indicating the quality of the Galatians' friendship towards Paul; true friends are unable to wrong one another;[11] 3) the example of the way they responded to Paul's illness (vv. 13-14);[12] 4) the theme of enmity

---

[6] Malherbe, *Paul and the Popular Philosophers*, 63.

[7] By the same token it must be added that Paul's interpretation of φιλαδελφία in this context meant something different from its normal usage: what usually described a natural kinship relationship now refers to a fictive one (cf. Malherbe, *Paul and the Popular Philosophers*, 63; idem, *Paul and the Thessalonians*, 48-51; H.-J. Klauck, "Kirche als Freundesgemeinschaft? Auf Spurensuche im Neuen Testament," *MTZ* 42 (1991) 10-13).

[8] H. D. Betz, *Galatians: A Commentary on Paul's Letter to the Churches in Galatia* (Hermeneia; Philadelphia: Fortress, 1979) 220-37.

[9] Lucian, *Toxaris*, with its interest in how friends share all their fortunes and misfortunes, is particularly useful on this point (Betz, *Galatians*, 222).

[10] A stock element of the *topos* was to see the friend as another self (cf. Cicero, *Amic.* 7.23; cf. G. Bohnenblust, *Beiträge zum Topos ΠΕΡΙ ΦΙΛΙΑΣ* [Berlin: Universitäts-Buchdruckerei von Gustav Schade (Otto Francke), 1905] 39-42).

[11] Betz, *Galatians*, 223. See Plato, *Lysis* 208E; Aristotle, *EN* 8.4.3 (1157a).

[12] Ibid., 228. Betz appeals to the example of Dandamis who gave his eyes as a ransom for his friend Amizoces, who was so distressed by the sight of his blind friend

which helps to distinguish true friends from false (v. 16);[13] 5) the portrayal of his opponents in Galatia as flatterers, as well as the accompanying theme of exclusion, which prevents true friendship (v. 17);[14] 6) the themes of constancy and loyalty even when friends are absent from each other (v. 18);[15] 7) the metaphor of the loving mother (v. 19).[16]

The number of themes from the friendship *topos* which Betz has identified here is striking. His analysis does not, however, evaluate how these elements are appropriated by Paul. Rather he claims that "[t]he argumentative force lies in the topic itself, the marks of 'true' and 'false' friendship."[17] Is it simply the case that in alluding to them, Paul is able to convince the Galatians of his friendship with them as well as remind them of the quality of theirs with him? Or, by selecting the elements he has, does Paul wish to address himself to a particular situation, giving rise to his sentiments, prompted by the opposition he faced in Galatia? If the latter is true, then Paul must have carefully selected from the *topos* in order to shape the argument he makes about the reciprocity of his relationship with the Galatians and how they ought to honor that by being more loyal to him.

Peter Marshall refines our understanding of Paul's use of the friendship *topos* in Gal 4:12–20 by highlighting the theme of enmity, which he sees dominating the text.[18] The question of Paul's illness, which points to his weak status in the eyes of the Galatians and their acceptance of him, despite it, involves putting aside the usual conventions of friendship. On the basis of Paul's remarks in 1:6–10, Marshall sees the problem as one of criticism made against Paul by his opponents. They charged him with being inconstant and untrustworthy, two things which go directly against the friendship tradition. They used this as an occasion to set forth their own gospel, and, in persuading the Galatians away from

---

that he put out his own eyes too.

[13] Ibid., 228–29.
[14] Ibid., 230.
[15] Ibid., 231–32.
[16] Ibid., 233.
[17] Ibid., 221.
[18] Marshall, *Enmity in Corinth*, 152.

Paul, they drew them into friendship with themselves. The transfer of allegiance does not necessarily make Paul the Galatians' enemy, in Marshall's estimation. But it does involve them in the enmities between Paul and his opponents. In Gal 4:12-20, then, Paul rehearses the history of his friendship with the Galatians and invokes the conventions of friendship, not merely to describe his relationship with them. Paul's opponents exploited friendship conventions against him in Galatia. His response is to address this directly, by exposing their strategy.[19] He appeals to some of the same friendship conventions to accomplish this.

H.-J. Klauck has recently concurred with Betz and Marshall on the use of the friendship *topos* in Gal 4:12-20.[20] But he would rather identify Paul's source for this in hellenistic diaspora Judaism. He refers to Philo, the book of Wisdom and Sirach, but only really focuses on Sir 6:5-17. Certainly, this text should be added to the ones supplied by Betz and Marshall, especially for its mention of πειρασμός (v. 7), ἐχθρός (vv. 9, 13) and μετατιθεῖναι (v. 9),[21] but beyond these things it seems likely that Paul knew the *topos* from other sources as well.

Gal 6:2 and 6 offer yet other examples of friendship language within the letter.[22] In 6:2 the notion of sharing burdens recalls examples from Xenophon and Menander, which speak specifically of friends sharing one another's burdens.[23] In 6:6 the sharing expresses either that the student will supply the teacher with some material benefit, or, more broadly, a benefit that includes the spiritual as well. Betz believes the saying is related in some way to the Pythagorean notion of πάντα κοινὰ τῶν φίλων.[24] Given the communal setting of some philosophical schools, Betz conjectures that this saying may point to an

---

[19] Ibid., 152-56.
[20] Klauck, "Kirche als Freundesgemeinschaft," 8-9.
[21] Although μετατιθεῖναι does not occur in Galatians 4:12-20, the notion of friends changing into enemies does in vv. 15-16.
[22] See Betz, *Galatians*, 298-301; 304-6; Klauck, "Kirche als Freundesgemeinschaft," 7-8.
[23] See Betz, *Galatians*, 299, nn. 58-59.
[24] Ibid., 304.

educational institution among the Galatian churches, although he concedes it may simply refer to the support of teachers.[25]

The Corinthian Correspondence

Peter Marshall has proposed a setting for Paul's use of the themes of friendship and enmity in his letters to the Corinthians that is similar to the one he suggested for Galatians. In general, he finds five aspects of friendship in Paul's letters: hospitality, patronal relations, recommendation, enmity, and reciprocity exemplified by giving and receiving. Paul conducts his relationships with his churches according to these conventions of friendship, but reserves the right to assert his autonomy from them when he comes in conflict with the churches over status-related issues.[26]

This is what happened at Corinth, where friendship was the norm until a conflict arose over Paul's refusal of Corinthian financial help. This particular conflict is featured throughout these two letters, but certain texts are important for Marshall's analysis: 1 Cor 9:1–23; 2 Cor 1:13–24; 10–12. The scenario he extracts from them runs thus. By means of the convention of self-commendation Paul initiated friendship with the Corinthians. But when he refused to commend himself a second time, they interpreted that as a cessation of friendship. Paul's enemies in Corinth, and rival apostles there, became friends by means of mutual recommendation. This made them enemies of Paul, too. At issue is Paul's refusal to accept aid from the Corinthians, which they intended as an offer of friendship in the form of a gift. This refusal became especially problematic in light of his acceptance of aid from the Philippians. Paul may have had very good reasons for turning down Corinthian aid. Among them was his wish not to be further obligated to them. Since acceptance, rather than refusal was the norm, Paul's action was construed as an act of enmity. The enmity escalated when his opponents employed invective against him by likening him to a flatterer and used the rhetorical device of comparison against him. Thus Marshall believes his study of

---

[25] Ibid., 305–6.
[26] Marshall, *Enmity in Corinth*, 136–64.

friendship and enmity in the Corinthian correspondence leads to a more accurate picture of the struggle between Paul and his rivals. Their judgment against him was basically a socio-cultural one, and the conflict represented in the letters is one between social equals. The outcome of the rivalry is a "profound socio-theological statement of Paul's apostleship."[27]

Romans

Some scholars have called attention to the use of the friendship *topos* in Rom 5:6–8.[28] They find here an idea similar to one expressed in John 15:13, μείζονα ταύτης ἀγάπην οὐδεὶς ἔχει, ἵνα τις τὴν ψυχὴν αὐτοῦ θῇ ὑπὲρ τῶν φίλων αὐτοῦ. The sentiment of dying for one's friend is widely represented in the philosophical literature.[29] What is unusual about Paul's appropriation of this idea is the transformation he gives it by claiming that Christ died for sinners and enemies of God.[30]

Ben Fiore identifies language and rhetorical devices, usually associated with ancient descriptions of friendship, in Rom 12:1–15:33.[31] The concluding exhortation in 15:14–33 captures the overall development of the paraenesis begun in 12:1. Friendship language is prominent in this final section. In addition to the projected visit mentioned in 15:23–24, an element of a friendly letter, Fiore notes Paul's expectation of hospitality and support for his further travel (v. 24), two friendship motifs. When Paul names

---

[27] Ibid., passim and especially 396–404.

[28] A. Deissmann, *Light from the Ancient East: The New Testament Illustrated by Recently Discovered Texts from the Greco-Roman World* (London: Hodder and Stoughton, 1927) 118; O. Michel, *Der Brief an die Römer* (MeyerK 4; 13th ed.; Göttingen: Vandenhoeck & Ruprecht, 1966) 134, n. 1; C. E. B. Cranfield, *A Critical and Exegetical Commentary on the Epistle to the Romans* (ICC; 2 vols.; Edinburgh: T. & T. Clark, 1975) 1.265; U. Wilckens, *Der Brief an die Römer* (EKKNT 6.1; Zürich: Benziger; Neukirchen-Vluyn: Neukirchener, 1978) 296; M. Wolter, *Rechtfertigung und zukünftiges Heil: Untersuchungen zu Röm 5, 1–11* (BZNW 43; Berlin, New York: de Gruyter, 1978) 171–72; D. Zeller, *Der Brief an die Römer* (RNT; Regensburg: Friedrich Pustet, 1985) 111; Klauck, "Kirche als Freundesgemeinschaft," 9–10.

[29] Plato, *Symp.* 179B, 208D; Seneca, *Ep.* 9.10; Lucian, *Toxaris* 36; Epictetus, *Diss.* 2.7.3. See Wolter, *Rechtfertigung*, 171, nn. 619–22.

[30] See Klauck, "Kirche als Freundesgemeinschaft," 10.

[31] B. Fiore, "Friendship in the Exhortation of Romans 15:14–33," *Proceedings of the Eastern Great Lakes and Midwest Biblical Societies* 7 (1987) 95–103.

the collection κοινωνία in v. 26 and refers to the mutual sharing (κοινωνέω) and obligation (ὀφείλω) which motivated the gift from Macedonia and Achaea to Jerusalem (v. 27), he shows familiarity with that aspect of the friendship tradition that stressed how much friends have in common. Even the paraenesis reflects the friendship tradition when Paul praises the recipients for their goodness, knowledge, and ability to instruct others (15:14) and reminds them of how bold he had to be with them elsewhere in the letter (v. 15). This affectionate feeling makes correction more easily accepted among friends.[32]

Going back over the entire exhortation from 12:1, Fiore isolates motifs of the friendship tradition. The stress on virtue as the basis of their mutuality (12:9), the unity of their affection for one another (12:10), contributing to the needs of the saints and showing hospitality to strangers (12:13), showing sympathy for the other's joys and sorrows (12:15), as well as holding one another in equal esteem (12:16), are all recognizable elements in the tradition of Greco-Roman friendship.[33] Paul's insistence on neighbor love as the basis for the fulfillment of the law (13:8–10) is not unlike the call for reciprocity found in the friendship ideal. When that is extended to the struggle between the weak and the strong (14:1–15:13), Paul's emphasis on mutual esteem and benevolence, the pragmatic end of community and equality, looks a lot like the object of friendship in the Classical tradition.[34]

Quite practically, then, Fiore understands this hortatory section of the letter to be strongly under the influence of friendship language and motifs. Paul's object, of course, is to resolve tensions which had arisen over the obligation of law and the divisions which had occurred in the community. In the end, if Paul can persuade the Romans to this kind of friendship, he, too, may avail himself of their hospitality and generosity; he, too, can become their friend.[35]

---

[32] Ibid., 97.
[33] Ibid., 98.
[34] Ibid., 99.
[35] Ibid., 100.

J. N. Sevenster finds it odd that Paul does not call those he greets in Rom 16:3–16 friends. He connects this with the lack of the terms φίλος and φιλία in Paul. Comparing Paul to Seneca on this point, he finds it striking that Paul avoided using these terms in a context where it would be most natural for him to attest to friendship. Sevenster believes Paul's preferred designation, fellow workers, tells why he avoids using the words "friends" or "friendship." The bonds of fellow workers who have labored together, perhaps even suffered together for the sake of the gospel, cannot be expressed in terms of friendship.[36]

Philippians

Perhaps the richest Pauline treasure of friendship is his letter to the Philippians. In it he not only employs the conventions of the friendly letter, but he also utilizes the conventions of friendship in expressing his relation to a community that was apparently quite beloved to him. Scholars have noticed in Philippians the elements of the friendly letter in Paul's warmly expressed feelings for the recipients.[37] The *topos* itself is appealed

---

[36] J. N. Sevenster, *Paul and Seneca* (NovTSup 4; Leiden, E.J. Brill, 1961) 174–80; idem, "Waarom spreekt Paulus nooit van vrienden en vriendenshap? (ad Rom 16:1-16)," *NedTTs* 9 (1954) 359–63. One final note on the use of friendship terminology in Romans comes from A. J. Wedderburn's observation that the παρακαλῶ constructions in 12:1-2, 15:30, and 16:17 take the form of a request used by friends and is also used in communications between friends and equals. He places greater weight, however, on its diplomatic or ambassadorial usage in Romans (*The Reasons for Romans* [Minneapolis: Fortress, 1991] 67–68).

[37] L. T. Johnson identifies Philippians as a letter of friendship, marked by the language of κοινωνία (1:5; 2:1; 3:10 and 4:15) with its heavy use of the *syn-* prefix (1:5, 27; 2:2, 17, 18, 25; 3:10, 17, 21; 4:3, 14) and its stress on likeness and equality (1:6, 27, 30; 2:2, 6, 18, 20; 4:3). Its parenetic function counters the impulse to self-assertion (*The Writings of the New Testament: An Interpretation* [Philadelphia: Fortress, 1986] 341–42). See also S. K. Stowers, *Letter Writing in Greco-Roman Antiquity* (LEC 5; Philadelphia: Westminster, 1986) 58–78, esp. 60; L. Michael White, "Morality Between Two Worlds: A Paradigm of Friendship in Philippians," *Greeks, Romans, and Christians: Essays in Honor of Abraham J. Malherbe* (ed. D. L. Balch, E. Ferguson, and W. A. Meeks; Minneapolis: Fortress, 1990) 206. Also, see A. J. Malherbe, "Ancient Epistolary Theorists," *OJRS* 5 (1977) 31, 65, 71; J. T. Fitzgerald, "The Epistle to the Philippians," *ABD* 5.320; J. L. Jaquette, "A Not-So-Noble Death: Figured Speech, Friendship and Suicide in Philippians 1:21-26," *Neot* 28 (1994) 177–92; and J. T. Fitzgerald (ed.), *Friendship, Flattery, and Frankness of Speech: Studies on Friendship in the New Testament World* (NovTSup 82; Leiden: E. J. Brill, 1996), which contains essays

to throughout the letter, especially at 1:27; 2:2; 2:6–11; 2:30; 4:10–11, and 4:12–20.³⁸

L. Michael White sees friendship in Philippians both as a social convention and an ideal of virtue. Terms like κοινωνία, τὸ αὐτὸ φρονεῖν, and ἀγάπη show up in the legal/contractual, hospitality/recommendation, and patronage/benefaction complexes. Within those complexes these terms each have a particular function, but they are all grounded in a common semantic field, that of φιλία. Since friendship can have ethical implications, White identifies it as the basis for a moral paradigm. When Paul employs the language of friendship and appeals to its conventions in Philippians, then, he presupposes a paradigm of virtue. As expressed in the Christ hymn, friendship exemplifies the altruism, reciprocity, and willingness to sacrifice one's self, which are marks of a true friend.³⁹

P. Marshall has zeroed in on the expression κοινωνεῖν εἰς λόγον δόσεως καὶ λήμψεως in 4:15 as an expression of friendship. He believes further that, instead of simply addressing his embarrassment over their gift, Paul is actually qualifying his relationship to the Philippians as "warm and lasting."⁴⁰

Martin Ebner goes even further in examining the language complexes associated in this section of the letter (4:10–20).⁴¹ He observes how commercial and banking language are integral to the philosophical discussions of friendship. There are two language complexes operating in this section of the letter. One draws on the language of accounting, the other money-lending.

---

on friendship language in Philippians by John Reumann, "Philippians, Especially Chapter 4, as a 'Letter of Friendship': Observations on a Checkered History of Scholarship," 83–106; Ken L. Berry, "The Function of Friendship Language in Philippians 4:10–20," 107–24; Abraham J. Malherbe, "Paul's Self-Sufficiency (Philippians 4:11)," 125–39; and J. T. Fitzgerald, "Philippians in the Light of Some Ancient Discussions of Friendship," 141–60.

³⁸ See A. J. Malherbe, *Moral Exhortation, A Greco-Roman Sourcebook* (LEC 4; Philadelphia: Westminster, 1986) 144, 154; White, "Morality Between Two Worlds," 211; Marshall, *Enmity in Corinth*, 133, 151, 157–64.

³⁹ White, "Morality Between Two Worlds," 210–15.

⁴⁰ Marshall, *Enmity in Corinth*, 157–64.

⁴¹ M. Ebner, *Leidenslisten und Apostelbrief: Untersuchungen zu Form, Motivik und Funktion der Peristasenkataloge bei Paulus* (FB; Würzburg: Echter, 1991) 331–64. I am grateful to A. J. Malherbe for bringing this work to my attention.

The accounting terminology in 4:15 represents the reciprocal, as it speaks of giving and receiving. The money-lending language in 4:17–18, however, represents the agonistic, as it deals with credit and debt. These language complexes address the interest in equality/mutuality and obligation, respectively. The common point of departure for both is need, so the friendship involved here is one of utility.[42]

According to Ebner, Paul's understands friendship to consist in likeness and sharing (κοινὰ τὰ φίλων), which create κοινωνία. Such community is based on mutuality, but it is also marked by need. The additional language Paul employs helps bring this to light. When the fundamental definition of friendship as likeness or equality is joined to commercial/money-lending language, friendship is qualified by three inter-related components: a financial component (money), a local component (place), and an ethical component (morale). Since the necessity of the second is debatable, he finds the first and third to be essential to friendship. These he finds in Philippians at 4:15 (financial) and 4:14 (ethical). Thus 4:14–20 embodies the ideal of a community of friends. So both commerical language and community language dominate the text in giving expression to friendship.[43]

As the κοινωνία language and commercial language are overlaid, however, a problem results from the tension between the two: Paul is required to shift roles from a fellow community member to a banker. The problem is heightened by what Paul says in 4:11–13, where he asserts his self-sufficiency. The autonomy he voices there calls his friendship with the Philippians into question. Paul solves the problem by invoking the two different kinds of language, κοινωνία and commercial. In 4:14–16 he looks to the past and he acknowledges the help they gave him. This recalls the basis of their friendship. In 4:17–19, however, he looks to the future and takes on the role of a banker, crediting their profit (v. 17), as well as the role of a priest, offering their sacrifice (v. 18). The relationships he enters into in each of these roles are forms of friendship, and each, in its own way, contributes to the

---

[42] Ibid., 345–53.
[43] Ibid., 352–58.

establishment of κοινωνία with fellow humans and with God. The relationship between humans, marked by the sharing of material goods, is expressed in 4:14–17. The relationship between God and humans, marked by the offering of a sacrifice, is expressed in 4:18. Ebner believes Paul's ultimate purpose here is to facilitate friendship between the Philippians and God. And this is how Ebner understands 4:19, where Paul mentions that God will fulfill all their needs, which is an essential function of a friend. God takes Paul's place in the community of friends, but on a grander scale. Where friends may only partially fulfill other friends' needs, God will fulfill all of theirs. Since Paul knows what God can do in this matter (4:13), his self-sufficiency becomes the occasion of his ability to mediate friendship between God and the Philippians. In the end, when its needs are filled by God rather than by Paul, the community, too, becomes self-sufficient.[44]

Ebner sketches out a development of the idea of friendship between Paul and his communities. In Gal 6:6 the relationship is described as a community of goods between teacher and student. At Philippi, his first community, it was represented as a community of friends. At Corinth, however, he refrained from accepting similar support. When he wrote Philippians, then, he might have been affected by what happened in Corinth, and preferred to stress his self-sufficiency. In the end, he modified his enthusiasm for friendship at Philippi. The aim of the whole process is to work for a κοινωνία between the community and God. This is the object of his preaching.[45]

Friendship in Luke-Acts

Like Paul, Luke shows familiarity with the friendship *topos* and, at times, appeals to it directly. But unlike Paul, Luke does not hesitate to use the term φίλος, perhaps even as a title for Christians.[46] Luke alone has the Parable of the Persistent Friend

---

[44] Ibid., 358–63.

[45] Ibid., 363–64.

[46] Luke 7:6, 34; 11:5 (*bis*), 6, 8; 12:4; 14:10, 12; 15:6, 9, 29; 16:9; 21:16; 23:12; Acts 10:24; 19:31; 27:3. See Stählin, "Φιλέω, κτλ.," 159–64. Although 12:4 is the only place where Christians are explicitly called friends, the title may be implicit in 11:5; 14:12; 21:16 and Acts 27:3. Perhaps the address to Θεόφιλος in Luke 1:3 and Acts

(11:5-8) and uses φίλος more than any other NT author, adding it in some places in the Gospel where it is lacking in synoptic parallels (Luke 7:6; 12:4; 15:6; 21:16). As Marshall points out, many of the occurrences of φίλος in Luke-Acts are standard, indicating a polite form of address (Luke 12:4; 14:10), or a particular level of friendship (Luke 7:6; 15:6, 9; 16:9; 23:12; Acts 10:24; 19:31).[47] Sometimes it alludes to the idea of reciprocity and obligation (Luke 11:5-8; 14:12-14; 21:16; Acts 10:24).[48]

It is especially in relation to reciprocity and obligation that Luke's particular interest in the friendship traditions emerges.[49] Notably in Acts, one detects Luke's special perspective on friendship. My own interest in this topic has centered on the social function of friendship in Luke-Acts. I believe Luke intended to challenge his community to extend friendship to one another across status divisions.[50] My point of departure is the description of the early Jerusalem community in Acts (2:44-47; 4:32-37). But I believe what is summarized there points to sentiments expressed in the Gospel and in other sections of Acts.

These two summaries in the beginning of Acts have been studied from a variety of vantage points, and frequently authors have noted Luke's appeal to friendship maxims in them.[51] Some

---

1:1 ought also to be viewed as a possible use of φίλος as an identifying term for Lukan Christians.

[47] Marshall, *Enmity in Corinth*, 130-31.

[48] Ibid., 131.

[49] Related issues of hospitality and table fellowship should be included here (cf. Stählin, "Φιλέω, κτλ.", 160-61).

[50] Here follows an abridgment, with modifications, of my article, "The Social Function of Friendship in Acts 2:44-47 and 4:32-37," *JBL* 111 (1992) 255-72.

[51] J. J. Wettstein, *Novum Testamentum Graecum* (2 vols.; Amsterdam: Dommerian, 1751-52) 2.470-71; L. Cerfaux, "La composition de la première partie du Livre des Actes," *ETL* 13 (1936) 667-91; idem, "La première communauté chrétienne à Jérusalem (Actes 2, 41-5,42)," *ETL* 16 (1939) 5-31; H. Conzelmann, *Acts of the Apostles: A Commentary on the Acts of the Apostles* (Hermeneia; Philadelphia: Fortress, 1987) 23-24, 36; J. Dupont, "La communauté des biens aux premiers jours de l'Eglise (Actes 2,42.44-45; 4,32.34-35)," *Etudes sur les Actes des Apôtres* (Paris: Cerf, 1967) 503-19; idem, "L'union entre les premiers chrétiens dans les Actes des Apôtres," *Nouvelles Etudes sur les Actes des Apôtres* (LD 118; Paris: Cerf, 1984) 296-318; L. T. Johnson, *Sharing Possessions: Mandate and Symbol of Faith* (OBT 9; Philadelphia: Fortress, 1973) 120; idem, *The Literary Function of Possessions in Acts* (SBLDS 39; Missoula, Montana: Scholars Press, 1977) 1-5; H.-J. Klauck "Gütergemeinschaft in der klassischen Anti-

studies have focused on the highly idealized depiction of the early Jerusalem community. These view the summaries as Lukan retrospectives to a time when union of hearts and souls translated directly into sharing of possessions. Often the question of a primitive communism or an early Christian social welfare program has come up.[52] Sometimes comparisons with ancient non-Christian authors on the topic of utopia have sought to represent Luke as a hellenistic writer conversant with the secular traditions of his day.[53]

A problem emerges when one tries to identify the source of the maxims ἅπαντα κοινά (2:44, 4:32) and ψυχὴ μία (4:32). They appear in a variety of different writers,[54] and even as early as Aristotle's day they were already considered proverbial (*EN* 9.8.2 [1168b]). Perhaps because of their gnomic quality their meaning was not univocal.[55] Another problem relates to the debate over the definition of common and private property. The variety of expressions similar to οὐδὲ εἷς τι τῶν ὑπαρχόντων αὐτῷ ἔλεγεν ἴδιον εἶναι (4:32b) witnesses to this debate.[56] Whereas the multiple

---

ke, im Qumran, und im Neuen Testament," *RevQ* 11 (1982) 47–79; D. P. Seccombe, *Possessions and the Poor in Luke-Acts* (SNTU B.6; Linz: A. Fuchs, 1982) 200–9.

[52] See E. Haenchen, *The Acts of the Apostles: A Commentary* (Oxford: Blackwell, 1971) 233–35; M. Hengel, *Property and Riches in the Early Church: Aspects of a Social History of Early Christianity* (Philadelphia: Fortress, 1974) 31–34; F. J. Foakes-Jackson and K. Lake, *The Beginnings of Christianity: The Acts of the Apostles* (London: Macmillan, 1920–1933; repr. Grand Rapids: Baker, 1979) 5.140–51. Klauck provides additional bibliography ("Gütergemeinschaft," 48, n. 6).

[53] See E. Plümacher, *Lukas als hellenistischer Schriftsteller: Studien zur Apostelgeschichte* (Göttingen: Vandenhoeck & Ruprecht, 1972) 17–18; D. L. Mealand, "Community of Goods and Utopian Allusions in Acts II-IV," *JTS* 28 (1977) 97.

[54] "Ἅπαντα κοινά: Plato, *Critias* 110C; κοινὰ πάντα: Plutarch, *Coniug. Praec.* 143A, Iamblichus, *De Vita Pythagorica* 168 and Lucian, *De Merc. Cond.* 19–20; μία ψυχή Aristotle, *EN* 9.8.2 (1168b), *EE* 7.6.6 (1240b), Plutarch, *De amic. mult.* 96F and Iamblichus, *De Vita Pythagorica* 168. For a complete list of ancient authors using these aphorisms, see Dupont, "La communauté des biens," 505–9, 513–14; Cerfaux, "La première communauté," 26–27; Plümacher, *Lukas als hellenistischer Schriftsteller*, 17–18 and Klauck, "Gütergemeinschaft," 48–52.

[55] Plutarch, *Coniug. Praec.* 143A, applies the maxim πάντα κοινά to the mutuality of husband and wife, and Lucian, *De Merc. Cond.* 19–20, uses it satirically to describe Timocles' hopes for gain in the house of a wealthy Roman.

[56] Plato, *Resp.* 5.462C; Seneca, *Ep.* 90, cf. 9.14–15, and Iamblichus, *De Vita Pythagorica* 167–69. See Mealand, "Community of Goods and Utopian Allusions," 97–98; Plümacher, *Lukas als hellenistischer Schriftsteller*, 17; Cerfaux, "La première com-

attestation of these maxims and ideas shows the vitality of the friendship tradition, their extensive use leads one to wonder exactly what Luke was thinking when he quoted them, and the question of meaning is only one part of the problem.[57] For this reason, making formal comparisons between Luke and other ancient authors on the notion of friendship falls short. A look at the function of this material in the two summaries in Acts helps to clarify Luke's thought. My point is that due to their social and ethical implications, friendship traditions became a vehicle Luke used to encourage upper status people in the community to benefit those beneath them. This is done specifically by showing how some of the benefits they took for granted, ones facilitated by friendship in the society of their day, could be shared with community members who came from lower status. Luke's ultimate purpose, then, in using the friendship tradition is to encourage greater unity in the community across status lines.

In his investigation of the *Sitz im Leben* of the Lukan community, Robert J. Karris discusses Luke's interest in the tradition of friendship.[58] By confining his study to the Gospel, Karris does not fully investigate the function of the friendship *topos* in Luke-Acts and its social function. While he looks at Luke's view of the Roman cultural tradition of reciprocal giving in the Gospel, he does not examine Luke's additional thoughts on the matter in Acts.[59] Moreover, he claims Luke does not argue against the reciprocity ethic, giving for a return, in Acts 2 and 4.[60] Karris' understanding of Luke's view of friendship is a beginning, but

---

munauté," 27; Dupont, "La communauté des biens," 506.

[57] Plümacher notes the difficulty of identifying Luke's sources for these traditions (*Lukas als hellenisticher Schriftsteller*, 17–18).

[58] R. J. Karris, "Poor and Rich: The Lukan Sitz im Leben," *Perspectives on Luke-Acts* (Perspectives in Religious Studies, Special Studies Series 5; Danville, VA: Association of Baptist Professors of Religion; Edinburgh: Clark, 1978) 112–25.

[59] Karris, however, does allude to several texts from Acts (ibid., 117 n. 24).

[60] Karris, "Poor and Rich," 117, n. 23. Karris, however, acknowledges H. J. Degenhardt's insight into Luke's attempt to counter a cultural tendency, among his Gentile constituents, against helping the poor (ibid., 115). Degenhardt focuses primarily on the lack of concern for the poor among non-Jews in the Greco-Roman world (*Lukas Evangelist der Armen: Besitz und Besitzverzicht in den lukanischen Schriften: Eine traditions- und redaktionsgeschichtliche Untersuchung* [Stuttgart: Katholisches Bibelwerk, 1965] 180–81, 221–22).

one must go further to see how Luke uses friendship to question the cultural expectation of reciprocity as practiced in his day. I see Luke challenging the reciprocity ethic in both the Gospel and Acts, especially in Acts 2 and 4, by showing how Christians can become friends regardless of culturally promoted and accepted status divisions and without the need to give with an eye to a return. This necessarily involves a suspension of some of the normal conventions of friendship in his day.[61]

The matter is obscured somewhat when the question of utopia enters the picture. Golden Age myths function in several different ways. By highlighting what all humans have in common and by examining a past era which knew no strife or division, they serve to comment on social division in the present.[62] They lead us to think that prior to the advent of private property social life was irenic and harmonious. Having all things in common insured that everyone was friends. Texts usually taken from Plato, where friendship maxims are invoked in relation to the utopian ideal, support the notion of a perfect society. But zeroing in on such

---

[61] Considering the Greco-Roman friendship ideal this way situates Luke's use of it in a familiar setting, since it was commonly associated with a particular political philosophy (see H. Hutter, *Politics as Friendship: The Origins of Classical Notions of Politics in the Theory and Practice of Friendship* [Waterloo, Ontario: Wilfred Laurier Press, 1978] 25–55. Friendship was an important element of life in the πόλις. It was normally sought by political equals, people of the same status, as the stress on likeness and equality in the discussion of who can be friends shows (See, for example, Aristotle, *EN* 8.5.5 [1158a]; 8.8.5 [1159b]; 8.11.5 [1161a]; 8.13.1 [1162b]; 9.8.2 [1168b]; Cicero, *Amic.* 4.15; 6.20; Plutarch, *Quomodo adulator* 51C; *De amic. mult.* 96D-F; Diogenes Laertius, 8.10; Dio Chrysostom, *Or.* 17.9–10. Cf. Bohnenblust, *Beiträge Zum Topos ΠΕΡΙ ΦΙΛΙΑΣ*, 27, 39). Equality, however, was not absolute. Proportional or distributive justice was normative for determining appropriate exchanges between individuals: to each one his or her due (Aristotle, *Pol.* 2.1.5 [1261a], EN 5.3.7–17 [1130a–1131b], 5.5.6 [1133a], 8.8.5 [1159b], 8.9.1[1159b]). For Aristotle, even equality under political justice could be proportional (*EN* 5.6.4 [1134a]). See N. Wood, *Cicero's Social and Political Thought* (Berkeley: The University of California Press, 1988) 92. When questions of honor, benefit, and reciprocity enter the picture, friendship's capacity as both a bond and a barrier becomes evident. Its social implications are inescapable.

[62] For the ways ancient authors, like Plato and Plutarch, use the myth of the Golden Age to comment on the deplorable state of society and to suggest how communities might better organize themselves, see H. C. Baldry, *The Unity of Mankind in Greek Thought* (Cambridge: Cambridge University Press, 1963) 77, 162. See also Seneca, *Ep.* 90.2–6.

perfection in society can miss the fact that the myth was not accepted uncritically.[63]

Focusing on the early Jerusalem community as a utopia obscures Luke's purpose in the summaries under discussion. To begin with, the Platonic version of the myth does not easily apply to the early Jerusalem community. If, as some have proposed, it influenced Luke's thinking, then the apostles would be like Plato's Guardians, who did not need to own property, since the other classes of citizens in the state supported them.[64] In the Platonic myth, it is the Guardians who hold all things in common, not the citizenry as a whole. Luke's picture of the Jerusalem community in Acts 2:44-45 and 4:32 differs, of course, since it depicts all the believers as holding everything in common, for the good of the entire community.

This brings us to a second reason against viewing these summaries as Lukan descriptions of an early Christian utopia. Non-Platonic versions of the Golden Age myth symbolize total harmony among people by excluding the right of private property.[65] Luke's stress on the harmony of the Jerusalem

---

[63] Seccombe mentions this in his criticism of Mealand, but does not go far enough (*Possessions and the Poor*, 201); cf. Johnson, *Sharing Possessions*, 124-25. While Plato, for example, invoked idyllic descriptions of primitive society, his ideal state represented the perfect and harmonious community of goods only among the Guardians (*Resp.* 3.413C-417B; 5.462E-464B; 8.543A-C). On Plato and primitivism, see A. O. Lovejoy and G. Boas, *Primitivism and Related Ideas in Antiquity* (New York: Octagon Books, 1965) 155-68. Regarding human moral development, Plato is critical of the primitive ideal. He asked in *Laws* 678b, "How can we possibly suppose that those who knew nothing of all the good and evil of cities could have attained their full development, whether of virtue or vice?" (Ibid., 164). Aristotle opposed the common ownership of property because he doubted that it would result in harmony, or that such property would be cared for properly (*Pol.* 2.1.8-10 [1261b-1262a]). For him, common ownership is more likely to create division and strife than overcome it (*Pol.* 2.1.15 [1262b] - 2.2.6 [1263b]). Epictetus shares this view when he notes how greed and gluttony result from the common ownership of property (2.4.8-11. Cf. Seneca, *Ep.* 90.38).

[64] *Tim.* 18B; *Critias* 110D; *Resp.* 3.416D-417B. Cf. Plümacher, *Lukas als hellenistischer Schriftsteller*, 17-18; Mealand, "Community of Goods and Utopian Allusions," 97-98; Hengel, *Property and Riches in the Early Church*, 8-9; Seccombe, *Possessions and the Poor*, 201-2.

[65] M. Hengel correctly mentions only those verses of the summaries (2:44 and 4:32) which do not deal with private property when he compares the picture of the primitive community to the myth of the Golden Age (*Property and Riches in the Early*

community, however, does not preclude the right of private property. The stories of Barnabas and of Ananias and Sapphira show that people owned property until there was need in the community. Selling it was voluntary, as was the donation of the proceeds to the apostles for the welfare of all. Therefore, appealing to primitivistic or utopian models for the Jerusalem community does not describe Luke's view of it accurately, nor does it resolve the fundamental tension in the texts.[66] How can the Jerusalem community represent a utopian ideal, when, on the question of the possession of goods, it differed from Platonic and non-Platonic versions of the myth? The allowance of private property in Jerusalem not only challenges the picture of the community there as a utopia, it also serves as the basis for declaring it non-utopian. Judas, Ananias, and Sapphira hardly embody a utopian ideal. Furthermore, the tension between the Hellenists and the Hebrews over the distribution of food in chapter 6 seems not to testify to a Golden Age of Christianity in Jerusalem.

Some scholars have tried to resolve that tension by an appeal to source criticism, whereas others see the tension arising from Luke's view of the primitive community.[67] Thus, he can present a general ideal, while showing how it breaks down in the daily life of the Jerusalem community: sometimes they hit the mark, but at others they missed.[68]

Church, 8).

[66] Likewise, comparisons with the Qumran sectarians do not help. Community of goods at Qumran was sufficiently different from Luke's description of the Jerusalem community to discount it as a model (see Johnson, *Sharing Possessions*, 126–27; idem, *Literary Function of Possessions*, 4; Degenhardt, *Lukas Evangelist der Armen*, 202–7). D. L. Mealand gives a good summary of the state of the question regarding the community of goods at Qumran ("Community of Goods at Qumran," *TZ* 31 [1975] 126–39). For a detailed comparison between Qumran and Acts 2 and 4, see H. Braun, "Qumran und das Neue Testament: Ein Bericht über 10 Jahre Forschung, 1950–1959," *TRu* 29 (1963) 149–59; J. A. Fitzmyer, "Jewish Christianity in Acts in Light of the Qumran Scrolls," *Studies in Luke-Acts* (eds. L. Keck and J. L. Martyn; Philadelphia: Fortress, 1980) 241–44; Klauck, "Gütergemeinschaft," 52–79.

[67] Source theories abound; see Dupont, *The Sources of Acts: The Present Position* (London: Darton, Longmann and Todd, 1964) 32–61, 67–91; Foakes-Jackson and Lake, *The Beginnings of Christianity*, 5.141–47; Haenchen, *Acts*, 193–96.

[68] Cf. M. Del Verme, "La Communione dei beni nella communitá primitiva di

Hans Conzelmann, for one, sees Luke describing an ideal without intending to influence charitable sharing of goods in the community of his day.[69] This introduces into the picture a dichotomy between the theoretical and the practical. The utopian ideal represents a desired end which is nearly impossible to realize in practice. If one stresses the formal similarities between the description of a mythical Golden Age and Luke's description of the early Jerusalem community, this is deceptively appealing. But when the emphasis shifts to the social function of friendship in these texts, the tension has less to do with perfect society vs. imperfect society than with the use of property: common (κοινός) vs. private (ἴδιος). Thus Luke appears not to oppose theory to practice, but rather to be concerned with a very practical matter of community organization: how property will be held.

The ancient discussion of the place of property and ownership in a well ordered state supports the view that Luke is being very practical about the use of possessions in his community. Especially helpful are authors who share anti-utopian views and uphold the right of private ownership, while still advocating common or public use of property.[70]

Gerusalemme," *RivB* 23 (1970) 377–82. Dupont resolves the tension by emphasizing that the expression "they held everything in common" implies no legal transfer of goods. Christians, he says, place their possessions at the disposal of others because of affection, which allows a needful person to ask something of another as if it belonged to him ("La communauté des biens," 508). This makes the owner more an administrator of common goods than a donor. But does that interpretation not go beyond the text itself? In my opinion, Luke wants property owners to participate actively in the life of the community. Johnson sees the community of goods restricted to the early days of the Church since it follows the outpouring of the Spirit at Pentecost, but is not evident in subsequent outpourings (*Sharing Possessions*, 128).

[69] Conzelmann, *Acts*, 24; cf. Johnson, *Literary Function of Possessions*, 5.

[70] Aristotle raises the question of function in the *Politics:* "But is it better for a city that is to be well ordered to have community in everything which can possibly be made common property, or is it better to have some things in common and others not?" (2.1.2 [1261a]). And again: "In connexion with this we have to consider the due regulation of property in a community that is to have the best political institutions: Should property be owned in common or privately?" (2.2.1 [1262b]). The appearance of a high ideal in the image of a well ordered city and the best political institutions does not belie Aristotle's practical concern about how property will be held. He lists three options: private ownership, common ownership, or a mix of both. Attempting to overcome the disadvantages of common ownership, he shows how property can be both common and private. The interpretation of κοινὰ τὰ

Cicero addresses this concern from a middle Stoic point of view. The text is from *De Officiis:*

> This, then, is the most comprehensive bond that unites together men as men and all to all; and under it the common right to all things that nature has produced for the common use of man is to be maintained, with the understanding that, while everything assigned as private property by the statutes and by civil law shall be held as prescribed by those same laws, everything else shall be regarded in the light indicated by the Greek proverb: 'Amongst friends all things in common.'[71]

Although he uses the language of a high ideal for all humans joined by nature, Cicero addresses a quite practical matter. He states further that having all things in common properly refers to benefiting others freely but in a much less radical way than the maxim κοινὰ τὰ φίλων would seem to suggest, as when it is associated with the utopian ideal. The ultimate norm for charitable giving in Cicero is "... that we may continue to have the means for being generous to our friends" (*Off.* 1.51–52).[72] For him "having all things in common" does not affect one's private property. Indeed, there is a rationalization for retaining one's wealth in his caution against being overly generous.[73] His use of

---

φίλων from the standpoint of function (πρὸς τὸ χρῆσθαι) is decisive: "... for individuals while owning their property privately put their own possessions at the service of their friends and make use of their friends' possessions as common property" (2.2.4–5 [1263a]). He concludes, "It is clear therefore that it is better for possessions to be privately owned, but to make them common property in use ..." (2.2.5 [1263a]; see A. R. Hands *Charities and Social Aid in Greece and Rome* [Ithaca, NY: Cornell University Press, 1968] 39).

[71] 1.51. See Isocrates, *Areopagiticus* 35 where, in a description of the old Athenian constitution, not a mythic Golden Age, he claims that people owned property privately, but commonly enjoyed its use. Later, in that work (83) Isocrates states that "no one had any need." He exhorts his listeners to imitation of their ancestors in order to cure society's present ills (84).

[72] He cites Ennius, "No less shines his," referring to the person who lights a wayfarer's lamp without diminishing his own.

[73] *Off.* 2.54: "We must often distribute from our purse to the worthy poor, but we must do so with discretion and moderation. For many have squandered their patrimony by indiscriminate giving. But what is worse folly than to do the thing you like in such a way that you can no longer do it at all? Then, too, lavish giving leads to robbery; for when over-giving men begin to be impoverished, they are constrained to lay their hands on the property of others. And so, when men aim to be kind for the sake of winning good-will, the affection they gain from the objects of their gifts is

the friendship maxim, then, supports the *status quo* of upper status society.[74] According to Cicero, the state exists to secure the right of individuals to accumulate private property, and having all things in common cannot compromise that.[75] One finds similar thinking in Seneca and Plutarch.[76]

This kind of evidence points to a discussion about what the maxim κοινὰ τὰ φίλων meant in the practical order. It also provides an important clue to Luke's use of that tradition. Authors like Aristotle, Cicero, Seneca, and Plutarch appealed to the maxim κοινὰ τὰ φίλων to uphold conventional status

---

not so great as the hatred they incur from those whom they despoil." Also, 2.55–56: "There are, in general, two classes of those who give largely: the one class is the lavish, the other the generous. The lavish are those who squander their money on public banquets, doles of meat among the people, gladiatorial shows, magnificent games, and wild-beast fights — vanities of which but a brief recollection will remain, or none at all. The generous on the other hand, are those who employ their own means to ransom captives from brigands, or who assume their friends' debts or help in providing dowries for their daughters, or assist them in acquiring property or increasing what they have."

[74] Baldry, *The Unity of Mankind*, 199, 201.

[75] For a good treatment of Cicero's views on private property and how the right to it upholds the social order, see Wood, *Cicero's Social and Political Thought*, 105–19. W. Den Boer claims: "There is, then, no question of a universal love of all mankind in the writings of Cicero, who, as an ex-consul and senator would not have known what this concept meant" (*Private Morality in Greece and Rome*, [Leiden: E. J. Brill, 1979] 80).

[76] Seneca (*Ben.* 7.4.2) uses the example of the king, who rightfully owns everything, but assigns individual ownership to others. As for the relationship of common ownership to private ownership of property, he concludes: "It is not necessarily true that what I have is not mine if what is mine is also yours; for it is possible that the same thing may be both mine and yours" (7.4.7). His discussion about kings, masters, and slaves indicates that he does not advocate a change in the social order. Further on (7.12.3–5) he says, "there are many ways of owning things in common.... Whatever our friend possesses is common to us, but it is the property of the one who holds it; I cannot use things against his will." Here he distinguishes ownership from use. See also *Ep.* 81. Plutarch's criticism of Plato's ideal of common property shows that the maxim κοινὰ τὰ φίλων was not absolute (*Amat.* 767E). In *Quaest. Conv.* 2.10.644C-D, the proverb's meaning is determined by the context of a banquet: "Private possession in such matters does not disturb the general fellowship (κοινωνίαν) and this is due to the fact that the most important characteristics of a gathering and those worth most serious attention are in fact common, namely, conversation, toasts, and good fellowship . . . ." For the use of the maxim in other contexts, see *Coniug. praec.* 140D; *Quaest. Rom.* 266A; *Quaest. Conv.* 743E; *Non posse suaviter* 1102F.

divisions within society.⁷⁷ They did not invoke it to advocate reform and social levelling. Luke, however, places the maxim, and others with it, in a context that shows him questioning the social order of his day.

Philip Esler's study of Luke's theology of the poor supports this point.⁷⁸ He concludes that Luke challenged prevailing social arrangements, but sought not to overturn them. Rather, he asked the higher status members of his community to eschew the benefits of those arrangements for themselves. I would add that Luke wanted the upper status members of his community to extend the benefits of their status associations to lower status community members. The vehicle for this is the institution of friendship, which normally would have kept the two separate. In other words, Luke appeals to an institution very familiar to people of means, friendship, in order to get them to share their possessions with the poor of the community. By stressing a friendship between non-equals, Luke challenged these upper status individuals to use their normal "power-brokering" technique to care for the poor in their midst. Seen in this light the implications of what Luke asks show the extent of his social objective.

Treatments of the reciprocity ethic, giving for a return, show that largess was frequently kept within social boundaries: like to like. Friendship between non-equals was possible, but it could resemble a patron-client relationship with different expectations.⁷⁹

---

⁷⁷ See Den Boer, *Private Morality in Greece and Rome*, 62–92.

⁷⁸ Whereas Esler briefly mentions these summaries in Acts and calls attention to Luke's expectation of giving without receiving, he does not discuss Luke's use of the friendship ideal in making the point (*Community and Gospel*, 169).

⁷⁹ The institution of *clientela*, which brought together people of differing statuses, differed from friendship and had its own rules and conventions (see G. Alföldy, *The Social History of Rome* [Totowa, New Jersey: Barnes and Noble, 1985] 101). Patrons, who protected their clients, expected the latter to return loyalty, votes at election time, military support, and honor (see J. E. Stambaugh and D. L. Balch, *The New Testament in Its Social Environment* [LEC 2; Philadelphia: Westminster, 1986] 63–67; White, "Morality Between Two Worlds," 211). H. Moxnes argues for Luke's interest in a radically transformed patronage system as the basis for social relations in his community ("Patron-Client Relations and the New Community in Luke-Acts," *The Social World of Luke-Acts* [ed. J. H. Neyrey; Peabody, Massachusetts: Hendrickson, 1991] 241–68). Especially problematic in his analysis is the lack of attention to

New Testament Evidence 247

Still, *mutatis mutandis*, friendship in both contexts (between equals and non-equals) was governed by the reciprocity ethic.[80] The practice of giving for a return was fairly standard, then, in Luke's day.[81] That Luke wished to encourage his community to share

friendship language and the absence of exegetical data showing precisely where the language of patronage is present in the texts he cites from Luke-Acts. Moxnes oversimplifies when he reduces all social relations in Luke's community to the "patron-broker-client type" or the "patron-client type" (ibid., 265). He does not distinguish among patronage, benefaction, and friendship, so it is difficult to assess how these relate to sharing possessions in Luke-Acts. Peter Garnsey and Greg Woolf caution against overrating the significance of patronage in the ancient world and look to a cluster of dependency relationships including philanthropy, benefaction, and kinship for a more accurate picture of society ("Patronage and the Rural Poor in the Roman World," *Patronage in Ancient Society* [ed. A. Wallace-Hadrill; London and New York: Routledge, 1989] 153–70). Even if there is some sharing of ideas among these institutions, or overlap in language used to describe them, the question of function must be addressed. All friendship is not patronage (see R. P. Saller, *Patronage Under the Early Empire* [Cambridge: Cambridge University, 1982] 3, 7–39; idem, "Patronage and Friendship in Early Imperial Rome: Drawing the Distinction," in Wallace-Hadrill, *Patronage*, 49–62). Furthermore, Moxnes' study raises questions about why Luke would appeal to an institution that was often viewed negatively for its exploitation of clients as a model, even one transformed along the lines he suggests, for early Christians to emulate (see P. Millett, "Patronage and its Avoidance in Classical Athens," in ibid., 16; P. Garnsey and G. Woolf, "Patronage and the Rural Poor," in ibid., 157–8; J. Drinkwater, "Patronage in Roman Gaul and the Problem of the Bagaudae," in ibid., 189–93). Thus, it is more likely that Luke sought an extension of friendship across social lines in his community than the creation of a new kind of patronage.

[80] Hands discusses the self-regarding nature of gift-giving. The failure to return a gift for one received is tantamount to declaring enmity (*Charities and Social Aid*, 26). Thus there is an "agonistic" element in friendship, a competition between giver and receiver (see M. Mauss, *The Gift* [Glencoe: Free Press 1954] 3, 51, 118; Marshall, *Enmity on Corinth*, 2; P. Veyne, *Bread and Circuses: Historical Sociology and Political Pluralism* [London: Allen Lane, The Penguin Press, 1990] 78–80).

[81] Hands, *Charities and Social Aid*, 30. Hands cites Democritus, Aristotle, Terence, and Seneca, who represent the belief that anonymous giving, or giving without expected return, is a higher form of gift, and that reciprocal giving was the norm among social equals. Maintaining such relationships required some means (ibid., 32). See also Marshall, *Enmity in Corinth*, 8 and Degenhardt, *Lukas Evangelist der Armen*, 181. Aristotle saw gift-giving as a way of making friends (*EN* 4.3.24–25 [1124b]). Ritualized or guest friendship facilitated the crossing of social and ethnic lines. Although the mutual benefits in guest friendship may have been externally quite similar to friendship between equals, the social bonding was quite different. Gabriel Herman's fascinating study of ritualized friendship, ξενία, in Classical and Hellenistic Greek cities, shows how it divided a small minority of aristocrats at the top of the social pyramid from οἱ πολλοί (*Ritualised Friendship and the Greek City* [Cambridge: Cambridge University Press, 1987]). Herman defines ritualized

possessions easily across status divisions, and thus challenge the reciprocity ethic, is supported by the following evidence.

First, Luke's view of possessions and benefactions expects that higher status Christians will freely and naturally help those of lower status, but without expecting a return. This is confirmed by redacted material in his Gospel:

> And if you lend to those from whom you hope to receive, what credit is that to you? Even sinners lend to sinners, to receive as much again. But love your enemies, and do good, and lend expecting nothing in return . . . (Luke 6:34–35a RSV).[82]

---

friendship simply as, ". . . a bond of solidarity manifesting itself in an exchange of goods and services between individuals originating from separate social units" (ibid., 10). Unlike φιλία, ξενία normally crossed social boundaries and was found among people of differing statuses. Synonyms for ξένος can refer to people of the same or of different social units (ibid., 11–12). The ritual aspect in this kind of friendship came from a gesture, and an exchange of goods and services. Frequently, the gesture was the δέξιος, the right hand of fellowship, but it had other forms. Additional study is needed before it can be determined whether Luke saw ritualized friendship playing a role in early Christianity. At the least, it should be noted that the story of Barnabas in Acts 4 fits the context of ritualized friendship, because of the ethnic and status differences between the parties and the ritualized gesture involved in the exchange between them.

[82] The origin of these verses is uncertain. Although much of the material surrounding them derives from Q, they are unparalleled in Matthew. R. A. Edwards notes that "the editorial activity of Matthew and/or Luke is quite extensive in this section," but fails to identify the source of Luke 6:34–35a (*A Theology of Q: Eschatology, Prophecy, and Wisdom* [Philadelphia: Fortress, 1976] 86). In his Q concordance he lists only πλὴν ἀγαπᾶτε τοὺς ἐχθρούς in 6:35a (idem, *A Concordance to Q* [Missoula, Montana: Scholars Press, 1975] 100). J. S. Kloppenborg shows no parallel in Matthew 5 and puts Luke 6:34–35a in parentheses, indicating an unclear origin (*Q Parallels: Synopsis, Critical Notes and Concordance* [Sonoma, California: Polebridge, 1988] 28, 31). He cites a saying from *Gos. Thom.* 95: "If you have money, do not lend it at interest. Rather, give [it] to someone from whom you will not get it back," something quite different from Luke (ibid., 29). In another work he expresses doubt over the Q origin of Luke 6:34–35a (idem, *The Formation of Q: Trajectories in Ancient Wisdom Collections* [Philadelphia: Fortress, 1987] 175–176). Neither are these verses part of A. Polag's reconstruction of Q (see I. Havener, *Q: The Sayings of Jesus* [Good News Studies 19; Wilmington, DE: Michael Glazier, 1987] 70, 126). It is not unreasonable, then, to consider them as Lukan redaction (cf. J. A. Fitzmyer, *The Gospel according to Luke I–IX* [AB 28; Garden City, New York: Doubleday, 1985] 627, 640; R. Tannehill *The Narrative Unity of Luke-Acts* [Philadelphia: Fortress, 1986] 129; S. Schulz, *Q: Die Spruchquelle der Evangelisten* [Zürich: Theologisher Verlag, 1972] 130–31; R. Bultmann, *The History of the Synoptic Tradition* [New York: Harper and Row, 1963] 96).

When you give a dinner or a banquet, do not invite your friends or your brothers or your kinsmen or rich neighbors, lest they also invite you in return and you be repaid. But when you give a feast, invite the poor, the maimed, the lame, the blind, and you will be blessed, because they cannot repay you. You will be repaid at the resurrection of the just (Luke 14:12-14 RSV).[83]

The thought re-appears in Acts 20:35, "It is more blessed to give than to receive" (RSV).[84] Here we see how different Luke's expectations are from those prevailing in the culture of his day.[85]

---

[83] These verses may be from L, but as Fitzmyer notes, that does not preclude free Lukan composition (*The Gospel according to Luke I-IX*, 83–84). See also G. Schneider, *Das Evangelium nach Lukas* (2 vols.; OTNT 3.1-2; Gütersloh: G. Mohn; Würzburg: Echter, 1984) 1.27; D. P. Moessner, *Lord of the Banquet: The Literary and Theological Significance of the Lukan Travel Narrative* (Minneapolis: Fortress, 1989) 247 n. 274. For the prevailing cultural attitude, see Juvenal, *Satires* 5.12-23, 167-73.

[84] Haenchen (*Acts*, 594-95 n. 5) and Conzelmann (*Acts*, 176) note that Luke has Christianized a Greek proverb here by changing ἥδιον to μακάριον. Curiously, however, only one example they cite is a closely-worded parallel to Acts 20:35 in reverse (λαμβάνειν μᾶλλον ἢ διδόναι, Thucydides 2.97.4), and none of the examples they provide involves disinterested giving. The reference to the lavish giving customs of the Persian kings in Thucydides really comes in a discussion of the Odrysian kings who, in taking rather than giving, were their opposites. Xenophon's discussion of this custom (*Cyr.* 8.2.7, 14) shows how Cyrus used it to win the loyalty of his friends and subjects (ibid., 8.2.1-22). The citation from Plutarch, *Reg. et imperat. apoph.* 173D, recalling a saying of Artaxerxes, and another reference to Plutarch, *Reg. et imperat. apoph.* 181-82, reproducing a saying of Ptolemy, son of Lagus, speak respectively of giving rather than taking away, and enriching rather than becoming rich, as more kingly things to do. But these are hardly disinterested sentiments since the king is strengthened as a result. The relevance of the saying of Ptolemy is unclear, since it occurs in a context where he uses his friends' houses, dishes, linens, and tables to give a banquet. The example from Seneca, *Ep.* 81.17 has to do with repaying benefits, where the purpose is so that one may receive future benefits. Perhaps the closest parallel comes from a saying attributed to Epicurus in Plutarch, *Max. cum Princip. Phil.* 778C, τοῦ εὖ πάσχειν τὸ εὖ ποιεῖν οὐ μόνον κάλλιον ἀλλὰ καὶ ἥδιον. Even that, however, has a measure of interest attached to it, since it is invoked as a justification for why a philosopher should associate with powerful people. The reason is not that the philosopher will benefit as much as the powerful people will learn how to become good from that association, and then all of society will be better off as a result. Whatever the background of this proverb, Luke's placing it in the context of an exhortation to help the weak shows how differently he understood it from the authors cited by Haenchen and Conzelmann.

[85] Cf. Degenhardt, *Lukas Evangelist der Armen*, 180-81, 221-22; Karris, "Poor and Rich," 115.

These texts establish an important context for appreciating the message of Acts 2 and 4.

Second, the language of the summaries stresses unity and harmony, and to achieve this Luke selects from the friendship traditions elements that highlight equality.[86] The purpose here goes against the cultural tradition of reinforcing friendship within rank only. Egalitarian language in the summaries challenges the normal expectation of friendship by showing how people of unequal statuses could join together as friends who hold "all things in common." Equality results from their willingness to cross social lines.

We see the real power of this language of equality in the way its message reaches into the narratives surrounding the summaries in Acts 2 and 4. More than once there is mention of the community's "togetherness" (ὁμοθυμαδόν in 1:14; 2:46; 4:24; 5:12 or ἐπὶ τὸ αὐτό in 1:15; 2:1, 44, 47).[87] For Luke, these concepts are synonymous with being of one heart and mind (καρδία καὶ ψυχὴ μία) and having all things in common (ἅπαντα κοινά).[88] The negative examples of Judas and of Ananias and Sapphira, who violated the principle of κοινωνία, help the reader to understand how Luke sees the importance of this unity. Instead of joining the others (ἐπὶ τὸ αὐτό), Judas sought a place of his own τὸν τόπον τὸν ἴδιον (1:25). The believers claim that nothing is their own, and some demonstrate this with the sale of fields and homes in order to benefit those in need. Judas, however, buys his own field

---

[86] For Seccombe the absence of ἰσότης in these summaries indicates Luke's lack of concern for equality or social levelling among members of his community (*Possessions and the Poor*, 209). Luke, however, does appeal to the ideal of equality in the language of these summaries much the way he includes friendship maxims without actually using the word φιλία. Seccombe grants the latter (ibid., 203). Cf. Dupont, "La communauté des biens," 516–18.

[87] On the importance of these words in Luke, see J. Dupont, "L'union," 305–309; R. Rasco, "Beauté et exigences de la communion ecclésiale (Ac 2; 4; 5)," *Assemblées du Seigneur* n.s. 23 (1970) 122.

[88] Johnson understands the two expressions to mean more than just being together; they imply a deeper unity transforming the notion of "friends" in the Greco-Roman ideal into the idea of "believers" (*Literary Function of Possessions*, 187). See Cerfaux ("La première communauté chrétienne," 27–28) for the parallels to ἐπὶ τὸ αὐτό in the Greco-Roman friendship tradition.

(1:18).⁸⁹ It was purchased with a reward, a μισθὸς τῆς ἀδικίας which contrasts with τὰς τιμὰς τῶν πιπρασκομένων of the believers in 4:34. A similar pattern is uncovered in the case of Ananias and Sapphira, who, rather than contribute to the common holdings, held something back (ἐνοσφίσατο ἀπὸ τῆς τιμῆς, 5:2). Here we see, especially, the contrast between common and private property. By stressing "togetherness," on the one hand, and presenting the negative examples of unbridled individualism, on the other, Luke suggests that the distinction "mine" and "yours" should be adjusted.⁹⁰ Since that distinction was especially evident in status separation, Luke challenges his hearers to relax social boundaries in their community.

Third, LXX traditions help Luke to distinguish his objective from the Greco-Roman cultural understanding of friendship in his day.⁹¹ The Deuteronomic ideal of an Israel where the needs of all were met (ὅτι οὐκ ἔσται ἐν σοὶ ἐνδεής [Deut 15:4]) brings the practice of sharing property in Jerusalem in line with the Jewish ideal.⁹² Additional religious motivation comes from Deut 4:29, where ἐξ ὅλης τῆς καρδίας σου καὶ ἐξ ὅλης τῆς ψυχῆς σου epitomizes Israel's seeking for God. Akin to this are the traditions of Deut 6:5, 10:12, 11:13 and 18, 13:3, 26:16 and 30:2, 6, 10, where

---

⁸⁹ See Johnson, *Literary Function of Possessions*, 180–82.

⁹⁰ Seccombe discounts the story of Ananias and Sapphira as primarily "a negative aspect of the sharing of goods" (*Possessions and the Poor*, 211). Rather, it functions chiefly "to give illustration and content to the idea that fear surrounded the primitive community" (ibid., 211) and "to demonstrate the holiness of the primitive community" (ibid., 213). In the end, however, he assigns the story a role in relation to possessions: "It provides another clear example of the destructive power of greed" (ibid., 214). Curiously, he does not discuss Barnabas' generosity as a sign of the community's holiness, which one might expect if this were part of Luke's purpose in contrasting him with Ananias and Sapphira. The story of Ananias and Sapphira deals with the problem of possessions more than Seccombe will grant. Johnson is correct to see their story as "a negative contrast to the picture of community life in 4:32–37" (*Literary Function of Possessions*, 205).

⁹¹ On the LXX background of καρδία καὶ ψυχὴ μία and οὐδὲ εἷς τι τῶν ὑπαρχόντων αὐτῷ ἔλεγεν ἴδιον εἶναι in Acts 4:32 and οὐδὲ γὰρ ἐνδεής τις ἦν ἐν αὐτοῖς in 4:34, see Dupont, "La communauté des biens," 509–10, 512–13; idem, "L'union," 303; Johnson, *Literary Function of Possessions*, 199; idem, *Sharing Possessions*, 128; Degenhardt, *Lukas Evangelist der Armen*, 170–72; Del Verme, "La communione dei beni," 367–68, 381.

⁹² See Degenhardt, *Lukas Evangelist der Armen*, 177–80, 183–87.

Israel's total response to God is expressed as the devotion of one's heart and soul.[93] In the LXX, ψυχὴ μία can simply refer to a person (Lev 4:27; Num 15:27; 31:28), but in 1 Chr 12:39, where it connotes Israel's unanimity in the choice of David as king, it echoes the Greek friendship ideal.[94] If upper status members of Luke's community needed additional encouragement to cross social boundaries in order to benefit the poorer members of their community, Luke found it in these LXX allusions. They help Luke put the Greco-Roman friendship ideal in a new light, by interpreting the equality of the friendship ideal in terms of religious obligation. The union of hearts and souls captures both the vertical and horizontal aspects of Israel's covenant with God. In that context, alleviating need in the community gives new meaning to the idea of friends benefiting friends, by making more inclusive the sphere of individuals who have all things in common. By appealing to the LXX, Luke shows upper status members of his community how the advantages of friendship may be applied effectively within the community to help the poor.

Fourth, Luke butresses this stress on unity with an important image in chap. 4. The example of Barnabas is as powerful as anything Luke might say on the subject. As a landowner, he must have been a person of some means and fairly high status.[95] When he sells his field, he shows how generous he is. But he does more, in a gesture of humility, when he places the proceeds of the sale at the apostles' feet.[96] The image is one of a landowner bowed before Galilean fishermen, someone who owns property before those

---

[93] Dupont correctly sees the joining of heart and soul as more biblical than Greek, perhaps allowing Luke to recast the friendship maxim μία ψυχή in LXX language ("La communauté des biens," 513).

[94] Deut 13:7, ἢ ὁ φίλος ὁ ἴσος τῆς ψυχῆς σου, knows the tradition of a friend as another self, which is similar to ψυχὴ μία.

[95] On the meaning of status in the first century CE and how to measure it, see Alföldy, *Social History*, 94–156; B. Holmberg, *Sociology and the New Testament: An Appraisal* (Minneapolis: Fortress, 1990) 21–28; R. MacMullen, *Roman Social Relations: 50 B.C. to A.D. 284* (New Haven: Yale University Press, 1974) 88–120; W. A. Meeks, *The First Urban Christians: The Social World of the Apostle Paul* (New Haven, Yale University Press, 1983) 20–22, 53–55.

[96] The gesture actually appears to be one of supplication, an element of the guest-friendship tradition. See J. Goold. "Hiketeia," *JHS* 93 (1973) 74–103; V. Pedrick, "Supplication in the *Iliad* and the *Odyssey*," *TAPA* 112 (1982) 125–40.

who, in Luke 18:28, proclaim that they left their possessions (τὰ ἴδια) and, in 5:11, πάντα to follow Jesus.[97] Normal societal conventions would have dictated the opposite scene, since Barnabas is the superior in this relationship.[98] Judging by those standards he ought not to have been at the apostles' feet.[99] What a striking reversal Luke presents!

It is true that there is more to this scene than meets the eye. Luke Johnson sees it in terms of authority. Barnabas is an important figure in the Gentile mission, who now brings himself under the authority of the apostles.[100] Johnson is on firm ground when he cites the LXX evidence where the gesture of being at another's feet symbolizes submission. But must this subordination express proper lines of authority alone? If, customarily, benefactors wielded power by accumulating honor and prestige through their benefactions, what else might this submissive gesture communicate?[101] The exchange of status roles in this scene implies that more is going on than a clarification of authority. There is a powerful example here of how social

---

[97] Luke's redaction is instructive: at 19:28 he substitutes τὰ ἴδια for πάντα in Mark 10:28. In place of τὰ δίκτυα in Mark 1:18 and τὸν πατέρα αὐτῶν in Mark 1:20, the things Simon, Andrew, and Zebedee's sons left behind, he has πάντα. At 5:28 Luke adds that Levi, getting up, καταλιπὼν πάντα to follow Jesus to Mark's simple notice that he got up and followed Jesus (2:14). Esler contests Mealand's reading of τὰ ἴδια as compromising the total renunciation made by the apostles (*Community and Gospel*, 167). I agree it should be interpreted in terms of the earlier reference to "everything" but note that it does specify what were their own possessions according to 18:29. See Karris, "Poor and Rich," 123.

[98] Cicero gives us an insight into the status gulf between Barnabas and the apostles when, in ranking occupations, he puts fishermen at the very bottom and agriculturalists at the top of the list (*Off.* 1.150–51). The latter refers to landowners, whose property was the basis of their wealth (cf. M. I. Finley, *The Ancient Economy* [Berkeley and Los Angeles: The University of California Press, 1974] 56–61). Esler estimates that some of Luke's community were possibly from the *ordo decurionum* (*Community and Gospel*, 184).

[99] They may have exchanged the δέξιος, the right hand of fellowship, or some other gesture that would not have been quite as demeaning.

[100] Johnson, *Literary Function of Possessions*, 201–4.

[101] On the connection between wealth and prestige in relation to the Pharisees in Luke 16:14–15 and elsewhere in Luke's Gospel, see R. Tannehill, *Narrative Unity*, 181. Whether or not the image of the Pharisees has actual relevance for Luke's community, it is likely that the link between wealth and prestige does (cf. Degenhardt, *Lukas Evangelist der Armen*, 132; Karris, "Poor and Rich," 122).

lowering, within the community, might work. Barnabas can hardly expect a return from those who have no property. His submission before the apostles does not even provide the honor and prestige he might have derived from a benefaction that could not be reciprocated in kind. Giving without receiving, then, implies foregoing the social benefit of public honor to which upper status benefactors were accustomed. Here Luke sets a quite different example for the well-off in his community.

Fifth, another example in the story of Ananias and Sapphira shows the opposite approach to the use of possessions. Karris conjectured, in light of the teaching in Luke 16:14–15, that some of Luke's community may have believed Jesus abrogated the Jewish teaching about almsgiving, or they may have sought theological justification for their cultural bias against it.[102] Still, he wavers when, in a note, he expresses reservation over whether Luke attacks this idea.[103] But a link can be made between Luke and Acts on this very point.

In the Gospel we read: "The Pharisees, who were lovers of money (φιλάργυροι), heard all this and they scoffed at him. But he said to them, 'You are those who justify yourselves before men, but God knows your hearts; for what is exalted among men is an abomination in the sight of God'" (Luke 16:14 RSV). At issue is Jesus' claim that one cannot serve God and mammon. Whether it is a sign of divine favor or not, the Pharisees reject Jesus' claim, implying that they think there is a way of serving God and mammon. The contrast between their justification before humans and God's knowledge about them points to deception on their part. They try to deceive others and may be fooling themselves, too.

Ananias and Sapphira are portrayed as deceptive individuals. Witholding some of what they had promised to the community illustrates an attempt to have it both ways, to serve God and

---

[102] Karris, "Poor and Rich," 122–23. See also E. Klostermann, *Das Lukasevangelium* (HNT 5; 3d ed.; Tübingen: J. C. B. Mohr [Paul Siebeck] 1975) 166; J. A. Fitzmyer, *The Gospel According to Luke X-XXIV* (AB 28A; Garden City, New York: Doubleday, 1985) 1112.

[103] Karris, "Poor and Rich," 123, n. 48.

mammon.¹⁰⁴ Perhaps this is why Luke uses language reminiscent of the Gospel when Peter confronts them. Acts 5:4 asks τί ὅτι ἔθου ἐν τῇ καρδίᾳ σου τὸ πρᾶγμα τοῦτο; and declares οὐκ ἐψεύσω ἀνθρώποις ἀλλὰ τῷ θεῷ. Luke 16:15 provides the context for understanding this language: ὑμεῖς ἐστε οἱ δικαιοῦντες ἑαυτοὺς ἐνώπιον τῶν ἀνθρώπων, ὁ δὲ θεὸς γινώσκει τὰς καρδίας ὑμῶν ὅτι τὸ ἐν ἀνθρώποις ὑψηλὸν βδέλυγμα ἐνώπιον τοῦ θεοῦ. Both stories address a tension between human perception and divine knowledge, and both locate the problem in the hearts of the deceivers. Like the Pharisees, Ananias and Sapphira contrived the deed in their hearts. Their attempt to cover their deception is not unlike the way the Pharisees disguised their self-righteousness. But God, who knows their hearts, cannot be fooled.

As Luke portrays, in this wily couple, an opposite example to Barnabas, and one related to the Pharisees' attitude towards money in the Gospel, it is not unreasonable to think that he is addressing rationalization for not sharing possessions. Karris may be correct that some in Luke's community sought theological legitimation for not giving alms. It is possible, too, that this story represents the Greco-Roman cultural attitude we saw in Cicero, where he justifies restricted giving under the rationalization of being able to benefit his close circle of friends. Both attitudes give justifications for not sharing possessions across social boundaries, something Luke tries to overcome in his community.

Sixth, the example of Peter's benefaction towards the lame man at the Temple in 3:1–10 points to a different attitude in giving. In 4:9 Peter refers to this act as εὐεργεσία, a technical term for a benefaction. As such acts normally were done to enhance the status of the benefactor, who expected and received a return for the work, Peter's attitude in bestowing the favor is not usual.¹⁰⁵ He does not give silver or gold, and expects nothing in return. He seems to exemplify the mandate of Luke's gospel which distinguishes community members from those outside: "'The kings of the Gentiles exercise lordship over them; and those in

---

[104] Tannehill connects making friends, being faithful, and serving God rather than mammon as ways of talking about disposing one's wealth for those in need (*Narrative Unity*, 131). Cf. Seccombe, *Possessions and the Poor*, 220.

[105] See Veyne, *Bread and Circuses*, 5–69.

authority over them are called benefactors (εὐεργέται). But not so with you; rather let the greatest among you become as the youngest, and the leader as one who serves'" (Luke 22:25-26 RSV).[106] It should also be noted in relation to this that Bohnenblust, in his study of the friendship *topos*, found that friendship is sometimes portrayed as better than riches.[107]

Seventh, even though, as Johnson has observed, the mention of the community of goods is not found in the subsequent chapters of Acts, the crossing of social boundaries is.[108] Luke shows people of differing statuses sharing in the community as the book proceeds. Karris points to the stories of Simon Magus, the Ethiopian Eunuch, Cornelius, and Sergius Paulus.[109] Other examples may be added. The mention of everyone contributing to the collection at Antioch according to ability to pay implies a variety of status levels (11:29). The mother of John Mark hosts a number of people in her house in 12:12, giving another example of a woman of means (she has a servant girl, Rhoda) supporting the mission.[110] At 13:1 we are told that Manaen, an intimate friend (σύντροφος) of Herod the Tetrarch, is part of the community at Antioch. Lydia invites Paul, Silas, and Timothy to her house to stay in 16:15, and when they get out of prison they return there (16:40). At Beroea many Greek men and women of standing become believers (17:12). Paul seems to exemplify the proper attitude towards property and giving in his speech to the Ephesian elders at Miletus in Acts 20:33-35. There we are told he coveted no one's silver or gold or apparel, he provided for his own needs and the needs of his companions by working, and he set the example that giving was indeed better than receiving. We could add the women of means who aided the mission in the Gospel, Mary Magdalene, Johanna, Susanna, as well as many others (8:3).

---

[106] Cf. F. W. Danker, *Benefactor: Epigraphic Study of a Greco-Roman and New Testament Semantic Field* (St. Louis: Clayton Publishing House, 1982) 404, 324.

[107] Bohnenblust, *Beiträge Zum Topos ΠΕΡΙ ΦΙΛΙΑΣ*, 15, 29. See Dio Chrysostom, *Or.* 44.2.

[108] Johnson, *Sharing Possessions*, 128.

[109] Karris, "Poor and Rich," 125.

[110] Dupont also considers her house as evidence that people still held private property ("L'union," 301).

The picture is one of people from differing statuses joining together, and, often, those of a higher status aiding those of a lower one.

This evidence supports the view that Luke had more in mind than alluding to a primitive Christian utopia when he incorporated elements of the Greco-Roman friendship ideal in his summary descriptions of the early Jerusalem community. The context of the maxims, ἅπαντα κοινά and καρδία καὶ ψυχὴ μία, directs their function towards the practical problem of how property will be held in his community and how those who have it will benefit those who do not by adopting a new view of friendship.

Friendship in John

In his discussion of friendship in the New Testament, F. Hauck notes that it is in John's Gospel that the word-group φιλία, φίλος, and φιλεῖν gains greater significance than it has elsewhere in the New Testament.[111] In light of the evidence already presented on the topic, that assertion may no longer be maintained, but still one has to recognize the peculiar use of the word group in the Johannine literature. In the Gospel φίλος usually connotes a special relationship between Jesus and other humans (3:29; 11:11; 15:14–15). Once, however, it is used to invoke the theme of enmity (19:12). The implication is that if Pilate releases Jesus, he is Jesus' friend rather than Caesar's.[112] Φιλεῖν expresses Jesus' friendship with humans and with God (5:20; 11:3, 36; 20:2; 21:15, 16, 17 [*bis*]). It also expresses the reciprocity of friendship between God and humans, when they have befriended Jesus (16:27 cf. 15:23). The use of φιλεῖν invokes the theme of enmity in 15:19 where the love of the world is contrasted with its hatred of those who belong to Jesus (cf. 7:7; 17:14). In 3 John 15, φίλος

---

[111] F. Hauck, "Die Freundschaft bei den Griechen und im Neuen Testament," *Festgabe für Theodor Zahn* (Leipzig: A. Diechertsche, 1928) 219.

[112] Marshall (*Enmity in Corinth*, 131–32) follows E. A. Judge ("Paul as Radical Critic of Society," *Interchange* 16 [1974] 196) in claiming that this notion of *amicus Caesaris*, reflected in John's interest in patronal friendship, informs the definition of φίλοι in John. See also W. Grundmann, "Das Wort von Jesus Freunden (Joh. XV, 13–16) und das Herrenmahl," *NovT* (1959) 67–68; Stählin, "Φιλέω, κτλ.," 166–67.

seems primarily to refer to a group of Christians allied with Gaius, although it may have wider reference to other Johannine Christians.[113]

Quite specifically, the tradition of dying for a friend lies behind John 15:13, μείζονα ταύτης ἀγάπαν οὐδεὶς ἔχει, ἵνα τις τὴν ψυχὴν αὐτοῦ θῇ ὑπὲρ τῶν φίλων αὐτοῦ.[114] The idea of self-sacrifice for one's friends, placed here in the context of love for one another, contributes to the thinking that φίλοι was used to identify Johannine Christians, perhaps as a synonym for ἀδελφοί. The same kind of sacrifice is predicated of the Good Shepherd, who lays down his life for the sheep (10:11, 15, 17–18). At 1 John 3:16, a similar sentiment is voiced with specific reference to how Jesus laid his life down and how community members should do that for their brothers and sisters (ἀδελφοί).[115]

Compared to how other NT authors use the love command, it is striking that love of enemies is not part of the Johannine author's concerns. Rather, love of friends, symbolized by the willingness to die for another, has a more prominent place.[116] This

---

[113] See A. J. Malherbe, "The Inhospitality of Diotrophes," *God's Christ and His People: Studies in Honor of Nils Alstrup Dahl* (ed. Jacob Jervell and Wayne A. Meeks; Oslo: Universitetsforlaget, 1977) 226–27; Klauck, "Kirche als Freundesgemeinschaft," 1–2; A. von Harnack, *Über den dritten Johannesbrief* (TU 15; Leipzig: J. C. Hinrichs'sche, 1897) 13; R. E. Brown, *The Epistles of John* (AB 30; Garden City, New York: Doubleday, 1982) 726–27; G. Strecker, *Die Johannesbriefe* (MeyerK 14; Göttingen: Vandenhoeck & Ruprecht, 1969) 373–74; R. Alan Culpepper, *The Johannine School* (SBLDS 26; Missoula, Montana: Scholars Press, 1975) 272; F. Segovia, *Love Relationships in the Johannine Tradition* (SBLDS 58; Chico, California: Scholars Press, 1982) 190; A. von Dobbeler, *Glaube als Teilhabe* (WUNT 2.22; Tübingen: J. C. B. Mohr [Paul Siebeck], 1987, 262, n. 63.

[114] See R. E. Brown, *The Gospel According to John XIII–XXI* (AB 29A; Garden City, New York: Doubleday, 1977) 664; R. Schnackenburg, *Das Johannesevangelium* (HTKNT 4.3; Freiburg: Herder, 1975) 124–25; Klauck, "Kirche als Freundesgemeinschaft," 5; M. Dibelius, "Joh 15:13, Eine Studie zum Traditionsproblem des Johannes-Evangeliums," *Zu den "Syrischen Göttern": Festgabe für Adolf Deissmann* (Tübingen: J. C. B. Mohr [Paul Siebeck], 1927) 168–86. On the philosophical background, see above n. 29.

[115] Schnackenburg (*Johannesevangelium*, 125) sees in these passages a joining of Jewish brother/sister language with Greek friendship language, even though Jesus is specifically preaching about the love of friends. On the change from φίλοι to ἀδελφοί and the inclusion of sisters in the latter, see Klauck, "Kirche als Freundesgemeinschaft," 5, 10–11.

[116] CF. R. Bultmann, *The Gospel of John: A Commentary* (Philadelphia: Westminster,

may arise from special sectarian nature of the Johannine community, and the possibility of real persecution, which could call for self-sacrifice.[117]

Klauck finds an additional element of the friendship *topos* alluded to in 15:15. The servant does not share information with the master, but friends have no secrets from one another.[118] He does not supply an example, but perhaps he refers to the sentiment expressed by Cicero in *De Amicitia* 6.22, "*Quid dulcius quam habere quicum omnia audeas sic loqui ut tecum?*" ("What is sweeter than to have someone with whom you may dare discuss anything as if you were communing with yourself?").[119]

Observations and Conclusions

Of all the material surveyed, perhaps the most enigmatic use of friendship traditions comes from Paul. While he does not hesitate to invoke the conventions of friendship, he avoids φιλία/φίλος. Some have attributed this to his feeling that the ideas are too anthropocentric, and his belief that all derives from God prevents him from using the actual terms.[120] E. A. Judge, on the other hand, sees the reason in Paul's desire to avoid the status implications of patronal friendship.[121] If Ebner is correct that Paul learned a lesson about patronal friendship in the conflict between himself and the Corinthians, Judge's sentiment makes sense as a development of Paul's attitude towards the terms φιλία/φίλος. But since Paul avoids the terms from the time of his first letter, it would seem that he had trouble with them even before he learned

---

1971) 542, n. 4. H.-J. Klauck, "Brudermord und Bruderliebe: Ethische Paradigmen in 1 Joh 3, 11–17," *Neues Testament und Ethik: Für Rudolf Schnackenburg* (Freiburg, Basel, Wein: Herder, 1989) 151–69.

[117] See R. E. Brown, *The Community of the Beloved Disciple: The Life, Loves, and Hates of an Individual Church in New Testament Times* (New York: Paulist, 1979) 42, 43, 65; J. L. Martyn, *History and Theology in the Fourth Gospel* (Nashville: Abingdon, 1979) 47; D. Rensberger, *Johannine Faith and Liberating Community* (Philadelphia: Westminster, 1988) 79, 128.

[118] Klauck, "Kirche als Freundesgemeinschaft," 5.

[119] Cf. Aristotle, *EN* 8.11.6(1161a).

[120] See J. N. Sevenster, *Paul and Seneca*, 178–80; Malherbe, *Paul and the Thessalonians*, 104; idem, *Paul and the Popular Philosophers*, 62–63.

[121] Judge, "Paul as Radical Critic," 196; Marshall, *Enmity in Corinth*, 134.

the pitfalls friendship could bring. Perhaps Klauck is correct about the preference for brother/sister terminology over friendship terminology in early Christian communities. The ethics of brother/sister relationships and the ethics of friendship relationships converge in the New Testament, while the language of fictive kinship is preferred.[122]

Beyond the terminology, a troubling factor emerges from the use of the friendship *topos* in the Corinthian correspondence and in Philippians. If White is correct that Paul articulates a moral paradigm, based on friendship, in this letter, and Martin Ebner is also right about the Paul's need to assert his self-sufficiency in order to correct the Philippians' idea of friendship, how can both positions be reconciled? Generally speaking, friendship and self-sufficiency are incompatible, so Paul's example in asserting his autonomy goes against the ethics of the self-emptying friendship articulated in Philippians and especially supported by the Christ hymn. Does this in any way affect White's thinking that the unity of friendship in Philippians argues in favor of the letter's literary integrity?[123] Is the conflict due to anything more than the harsh lesson Paul learned at Corinth?

Marshall's and Ebner's analyses not only show Paul's dependence on friendship traditions in forming communities, but the perils he faced in maintaining relationships with them. Most striking is the level of social obligation friendship imposed, and the problems it created for Pauline churches, composed of people of differing social statuses. It seems that as easily as he could create friendship with the Corinthians, so also could his opponents. Given the rules for friendship and enmity, factions could result all too easily. In addressing the needs of these communities Paul's self-sufficiency emerges as a critical issue. Will he be bound by the conventions of friendship or can he stand free of them in order to preach the gospel as he feels himself obligated to do? Thus if Paul relied on some of the conventions of friendship in order to create communities, he seems also to adjust those conventions in maintaining them. Paul, then, wanted to

---

[122] Klauck, "Kirche als Freundesgemeinschaft," 10–11.
[123] White, "Morality Between Two Worlds," 214, n. 59.

guide the use of friendship for his purpose, rather than to be guided by the conventions of friendship themselves.

Luke is is not as shy as Paul is about using the term φίλος, and in some instances Luke seems to use it as a technical term for Christians.[124] Still, if the above analysis is correct, Luke understands it differently than many of his non-Christian contemporaries did. What I wonder about is how dramatic a transformation his interpretation of friendship for Lukan Christians is. In light of Luke's re-direction of the social expectations of friendship among Christians, why not drop φίλος altogether? Is this a deliberate attempt to augment the friendship tradition by logically extending its own teaching on equality? Or, is it a way of directing Christians to understand their obligations towards one another by co-opting a social convention quite familiar to them? Whatever the reason may be, it remains clear that Luke sees friendship within the Christian community differently than outside of it.

John, too, does not hesitate to use the word φίλος, and appears to use it even more technically than Luke. The context of friendship and enmity provides John with the vocabulary and associated ideas not only to describe the relationships between Jesus and his followers, but also their relationship with the world. The duality suggests an attempt at self-definition. The expectations of friendship in this context point to the quality of relationships among those within the Johannine circle. The fact that John shows special interest in the aspects of the *topos* on friendship that stress self-sacrifice, even to the point of death, may be due to the sectarian situation of the Johannine church.

The meaning of these variations among New Testament authors who have borrowed from the friendship tradition will become even clearer when more is known about that tradition in non-New Testament authors. Certainly, it would be premature to conjecture where the investigation of the topic might lead. At the very least one might say that the significance of the appropriation of friendship language and conventions by NT authors will very

---

[124] See Stählin, "Φιλέω, κτλ.," 162–63; Klauck, "Kirche als Freundesgemeinschaft," 7.

likely be grasped in examination of function more than mere form. To that extent these authors may have subordinated friendship to other concerns. Still the way they use friendship and related ideas should be seen in a positive more than a negative light. The vitality of the *topos* on friendship and the tradition that grounds it indicate that it was seen as something more than a matrix of stock ideas, maxims, and illustrations. The development of friendship over time argues for growth and adaptation to the circumstances of the various groups who appropriated it. Thus, the New Testament authors who invoke friendship language and traditions might be seen to contribute to a conversation. Their works should take a place alongside those authors who are usually seen as sources for New Testament views on the topic.

INDEX OF NAMES AND PLACES

For the names of ancient authors, see the Index of Ancient Authors and Texts.

Abauchas 178
Abraham 203, 215, 218
Abudos 192
Achaea/Achaeans 25–26, 232
Achilles 5, 19–20, 22, 25–26, 28, 121, 147–48, 155, 156n
Aemilius Paullus 72n
Agamemnon 21–23, 25–26, 28
Agathocles 148, 166–67, 170, 206
Agesilaus 27n
Aida 198
Ajax (son of Telamon) 19, 26n, 28n
Alba/Alban 123–26
Alcibiades 105n
Alexandria/Alexandrians 79, 112, 170, 182, 188, 192, 201, 203, 215, 221
Amastris 178
Amizoces 174–75, 227n
Ananias 242, 250–51, 254–55
Anaxilaus of Larissa 79
Andrew 253n
Anthia 149n, 169n
Antigone 36n, 141n
Antilochus 19n
Antinoopolis 182, 194, 196
Antioch 256
Antiochus IV Epiphanes 143n
Antiphilos (Antiphilus) 148, 170–73, 178
Antium 135
Anubis 171
Apamea 79

Aphrodite 151, 154, 157
Apollonius 190
Aquila 196
Aradus 154–55
Archias 74n
Archimedes 40
Aretaios 169
Argives 23, 26
Arpinum 70n
Arsacomas 176
Artaxates 148n
Artaxerxes 148n, 158, 249n
Asia 161n
Athens/Athenian 14n, 105n, 121n, 122, 158, 165, 168, 244n
Attius, Tullus 135, 142
Augustus 79
Aurelius Archelaus 195
Automedon 19n
Axylus 21n
Babylon/Babylonian 149n, 152–55, 158–59, 161
Barnabas 242, 248n, 251n, 252–55
Basthes 175
Belitta 175
Beroea 256
Brahmans 172–73
Briseis 28
Caelius 74n
Calix 71n
Callinicus 196
Callirhoe 5, 149n, 150–55, 157, 159–62, 171n
Caracalla 197

Caria   151, 153, 155
Carthage   124n
Castor   32
Chaereas (Chaireas)   5, 147–62, 167n, 171n, 173
Chairas   186
Chalcis   80
Charicleia   167, 206
Charixenos   169
Claudius Sabinus, Appius   127, 129–30, 132–33
Cleinias of Tarentum   91, 101
Clitophon   149n
Clodius   62n
Cluentius   70n
Cluilius   124
Corinth/Corinthians   230–31, 236, 259–60
Coriolanus, Gaius [Gnaeus] Marcius   4, 123, 128n, 131–44
Cornelius   256
Crassus   69n
Critias   7n
Croton   96
Curiatii   126
Curiatius (father of the Curiatii)   126
Curio, C. Scribonius   72n
Cydimache   169–70
Cylon   96
Cynics   (see the subject index)
Cyprus   154–55
Cyrene   91
Cyrnus (Kurnos)   30n, 33
Cyrus   249n
Damon   91–92, 94, 101, 121, 168
Dandamis   174–75, 227n
Daphnaeus   137n
David (King)   126, 252
Decasius   192
Decius, Marcus   133–34
Deinias   148, 166–67, 170, 206
Demetrios (Demetrius)   148, 170–73, 178
Demonax   206
Didumos   192
Diogenes the Cynic   120n, 216n
Diomedes   21n
Dionysius   186
Dionysius of Miletus   148n, 150–53, 157–59, 161
Dionysius of Syracuse   91–92, 94
Egypt/Egyptian   6, 149n, 153–54, 159, 170, 172–73, 181–83, 186, 188–89, 190–91, 194, 196–97, 200, 202, 215
Eirenaios   199
Electra   121
Epameinondas   121
Ephesus/Ephesian   146, 149n, 256
Epicureans   (see the subject index)
Eponichos   192
Essenes   (see the subject index)
Ethiopian   146
Eudamidas   169, 177
Euphrates (river)   154, 161
Euphrates the Philosopher   86
Eurotas   32
Euryphamus   100n
Euthydicos   168
Fabius Pictor, Quintus   124n
Fidenae/Fidenates   124–26
Fufetius, Mettius   124–26
Gades   79
Gaius   258
Gaius Gemellus Horigenes   197n
Gaius Julius Apolinarius   197n

Index of Names and Places 265

Galatia/Galatian 227–30
Galilee 252
Gaul 72n
Gemellus 190
George 189
Gerasa 82
Glaucus 19n, 21n
Goliath 126
Gorgias 157
Gracchi 144
Gracchus, Gaius 132n
Greece/Greek/Hellenic/Hellenistic
  1, 3–6, 8n, 11, 13–15, 18, 21, 23–
  24, 26–27, 30, 32–36, 41, 43, 51,
  53, 56–57, 65, 77–80, 82, 88–89,
  105–7, 109n, 120n, 122, 126,
  127n, 129n, 131, 137n, 138n,
  143–45, 147, 149, 153–54, 158,
  162, 163n, 164–66, 169–70, 172–
  75, 176n, 177–79, 181–83, 186,
  189, 193, 196–97, 199, 201, 203–
  4, 209, 211, 213, 215, 218, 221,
  225, 232, 239n, 240n, 244, 247n
  249, 250n, 251–52, 255–57, 258n
Gymnosophists 173n
Gyndanes 178
Habrocomes 149n
Harchemis 192
Harpochration 192
Hebrews 242
Hector 22–23, 26n
Helen 24
Heliopoleites 192
Hellenists 242
Hermocrates 154, 156–58
Herod the Tetrarch 256
Hilarion 192
Hippobotus 94

Hippocoon 19n
Hippothoos 149n
Horatii 126
Horatius (father of the Horatii) 126
Horion 197n, 198
India 172
Ionia 150, 155, 167
Iphigenia 166n
Isaac 203
Ision 187
Isis 192
Italy 70n, 71, 78, 91
Jacob 218
Jerusalem 232, 237–38, 241–43,
  251, 257
Jesus Christ (see the subject index)
Johanna 256
Judas Iscariot 242, 250
Julius Caesar 62n, 69n, 72n, 76
Julius Domitius 195
Julius Maximus 188
Junius Brutus, Lucius 130, 132
Kronios 192
Kurnos (see Cyrnus)
Lacedaemon 32
Laelius 66
Lamprias 111n
Laodamas 24–25
Larissa 79
Leucippe 149n
Leonas 148n, 159–60
Levi/Levites 218, 253n
Libya 192
Lonchates 176
Lot 215
Luca 62n
Lucullus 74n
Lycurgus 116

Lydia 158, 256
Lysis 100n
M. Rutilius Lupus 188
Macedonia 232
Macentes 176–77
Manaen 256
Marcus Antonius 74n
Martin (St) 171
Mary Magdalene 256
Massiliotes 170
Mazaea 176
Mediterranean 11
Melchizedek 215
Memnon 170
Memphis 199
Menecrates 169, 179
Menelaos 149n
Menelaus 23–25
Menenius Lanatus, Agrippa 128–30
Miletus 150–52, 155, 157–58, 192, 256
Milo 74n
Minucius Augurinus, Marcus 132, 134, 136–38, 142
Mithridates of Caria 149n, 151–53, 158
Mnesippos 5, 164–66, 168n, 169, 172, 174n, 175, 177–79, 206
Moderatus of Gades 79
Moses 209, 215, 218
Myllias 94, 95n
Naeouios 192
Naukratis 182
Neanthes 94
Neopythagoreans (see the subject index)
Nestor 22–23

Nicostrate 85
Nigidius Figulus 79
Nikolaos 187, 192
Noah 205
Odrysia 249n
Odysseus 19, 21–25
Olympia 175
Orestes 121, 148n, 157, 166
Origenes 194
Oxyrhynchus 182, 190
Panares 190
Pandarus 24
Panechotes 190
Paris 24
Patroclus 5, 19, 25, 28, 121, 147–48, 155, 156n
Peirithoüs 121–22, 148n
Peisistratus 22
Pelagon 19n
Pelopidas 121
Peregrinus 173
Peripatetics (see the subject index)
Perses 30
Persia/Persian 154, 159, 249n
Petemeineos 192
Peter (Simon) 253n, 255
Pharisees (see the subject index)
Pharnaces 158
Philinus of Acragas 124n
Philippi/Philippians 230, 233–36, 260
Phintias 91–92, 94, 101, 121
Phocian 122
Phoenicia 154
Phoenix 19
Plancius 74n
Plangon 148n, 159
Platonists (see the subject index)

Index of Names and Places 267

Podes 23–24
Pollux 32
Polycharmus 5, 147–57, 162, 167n, 171n, 173
Polyneices 36n
Pompeius Planta 188
Pompey 60n, 62n, 68n, 69n
Pomponius Atticus 70n
Pontius Pilate 257
Prorus of Cyrene 91, 101
Protogenes 137n
Ptolemaic/Ptolemies 182, 186–88
Ptolemais 182
Ptolemy, son of Lagus 249n
Publius Vatinius 79
Pylades 121, 148n, 157, 166
Pythagoreans (see the subject index)
Quintus Scaevola 70n
Quintus Sextius 79
Qumran 242n
Rhesus 19n
Rhodogyne 159
Rome/Roman 1, 3–6, 8n, 9, 11, 14n, 23–24, 33–34, 48, 60, 65, 68–71, 75–76, 79, 89, 105–6, 108n, 109, 120, 122–45, 146n, 147, 162, 174, 181–83, 186, 188–89, 192, 195–97, 199, 201, 225, 232, 239, 240n, 250n, 251–52, 257
Romulus 123n, 138n
Sabines 123–24, 126, 138n
Samos 78
Sapphira 242, 250–51, 254–55
Sarapion 192
Sarapion the philosopher 196
Sarpedon 19n
Sauromatians 174

Scepsis 24
Scipio Africanus 48, 66
Scythian 5, 164–66, 174–75, 176n, 178–79
Serapion 187
Sergius Paulus 256
Sestius 74n
Sicily/Sicilian 82, 85, 91, 94, 169n
Sicinius Bellutus 129–30
Silas 256
Simon Magus 256
Sisinnes 157, 178
Socrates/Socratic 3, 7n, 36n, 65n
Sostratos 157
Sotericus 194
Soteris 196
Sotion the Younger 79
Sparta/Spartan 24, 111
Statira 148n, 159
Stoics (see the subject index)
Sulpicius Rufus 70n
Susanna 256
Syracuse/Syracusan 91, 148, 149n, 150, 154–55, 161
Syria/Syrian 154, 166n
Syros 171–73
Tapiomis 192
Tarentum 78, 91
Tarquinius Collatinus 140
Tatis 191
Taurian 166n
Tauromenium 92, 96
Telemachus 22, 25
Theano 85, 86n
Theon 195, 198
Theramenes 7n
Therapeutae (see the subject index)

Thermouthis 198
Theron 148n, 150, 159–61
Theseus 121–22, 148n
Thessalonica/Thessalonians 227
Thestor of Posidonia 101
Thoeris 191
Thymaridas of Parus 101
Tiberias Caesar 257
Timocles 238n
Timothy 256
Timycha 94, 95n
Toxaris 5, 157, 164–66, 168–69, 172, 174–76, 178–79, 206
Trajan 188
Troy/Trojan 23–24, 26
Truphon 192
Tullus Hostilius 124–25
Tullus the Volscian (see Attius, Tullus)
Tyana 79–82, 86, 96
Tyre 154–55
Valeria 138
Valerius, Manius 128–29, 133
Valerius Publicola, P. 138
Veientes 124
Veturia 123, 138–43
Volscians 127, 130–32, 135–36, 138, 140–42
Volumnia 139
Zebedee 253n
Zenothemis 169–70, 178

INDEX OF SUBJECTS

absence/separation 62, 75, 161, 169–70, 190, 194, 201–2, 228
abuse/slander 100
accord 65n, 66
acting so as not to preclude future friendships 85, 92–93, 95–96, 212–13 (see also enmity)
activity/actions 21, 35, 39–41, 43, 57, 61n, 62n, 63, 68, 88–89, 99–100, 106, 113, 124n, 129, 132, 138, 142, 144, 147, 150–53, 155, 157, 160, 166–67, 168n, 174, 177–78, 206, 213n, 214 (see also deeds)
admiration 49, 66
admonition/correction/criticism 64–65, 72, 88–89, 100, 108, 116, 124, 134, 167, 213, 232
adult-child friendship 6, 193 (see also children and parents)
adultery/infidelity 85, 150, 152
advancement 60, 64, 73, 76
advantage/advantageous 23, 33, 42–44, 49, 59, 62, 64n, 66, 68, 73, 84, 125, 138 (see also utility)
adversity/adverse circumstances/ calamities/woes, etc. 9n, 30, 33, 63, 87, 91, 100, 114, 118, 135, 139, 152, 155
advice/counsel 23, 32, 64, 66n, 74–75, 85, 88, 89n, 128, 158
affection 116
affection/affectionate/liking 13, 15n, 17–21, 26n, 34, 36n, 37, 42, 47, 51, 55, 59, 64, 66n, 70, 71n, 73–75, 107, 116, 138–39, 141, 147, 185, 187, 193, 195, 198, 200, 232, 243n, 244n
affinity 217, 219–20
alienation between friends/family 25, 31, 220
allegory 81, 205, 218n
ally/alliance 20, 36, 67n, 136, 154, 158, 212
almsgiving 254–55
altruism 3, 37–41, 56–57, 61n, 66, 208–9, 234
ambassador/embassy/envoy 124, 130, 136, 140, 149n, 150–51, 175, 212, 233n
analogy 42, 43n, 51
— analogy of the arts 39
anger/rage/wrath 22, 25–26, 32, 46, 84, 88, 89n, 100, 110n, 121n, 128–29, 132, 136, 140–42, 150
apology/defend 64, 72, 97n, 132, 215
apostle 230, 241–42, 252–54
"appearance" of a friend 153
appropriation 61
Aqedah 203
aristocracy/aristocratic 5, 24, 30–31, 68, 70, 107n, 128, 130, 132, 134, 143, 158–59, 162, 170, 247n
artisans 128
aunt 127
autonomy 62n, 230, 235, 260
avarice 129
bandits/brigands 125, 149n, 159 (see also robbery)
barbarians/barbarism 166, 176–77, 179

beasts (wild)   22, 53, 85, 96, 97n, 126, 128, 130, 213, 245n
beauty   49, 169, 187, 196
benefaction   62n, 66–67, 234, 247n, 248, 253–55
benefactor   66–67, 71n, 89n, 99, 153, 253–56
beneficence   39, 45, 49, 65n, 68
beneficiary   66–67, 74n
benefit/beneficial   62n, 68, 73, 88–89, 120, 132–34, 138, 195–96, 213, 229, 239, 240n, 244, 246, 247n, 249n, 250, 252, 254–55, 257
benevolence/benevolent   47, 60, 62, 64–65, 68, 74n, 96, 172n, 232
betrayal/treason   29, 31, 100, 139, 142, 150
blame   113, 125, 127, 172
blood brotherhood   174
body   18, 129–31, 134, 141, 144, 150, 177, 218n
brother   19n, 23, 30, 32, 59, 96, 98, 105, 107n, 126–27, 143, 187, 194, 198, 219, 249, 258, 260
burial   126, 150, 175
business/commerce/finances   6, 33, 59, 68, 73, 75, 160, 181–82, 184–85, 189–90, 193–94, 196, 201 (see also debts)
— commercial language   234–35
— loans between friends   194–95
canon of traditional pairs of friends   107, 121–22, 147–48, 155, 156n, 162, 166n
caring for
— a banished friend's family   137
— a dead/absent friend's family or property   87, 169, 177, 192–94, 202
— a dead friend's funeral/tomb   192
— a sick/injured friend   94, 171, 178
censure   113, 119, 213
cessation of friendship   25, 100, 166, 230 (see also dissolving friendships)
character friendship   3, 37, 42–45
child/children   98, 127n, 134, 137–40, 150, 159, 178, 182, 186, 189, 191–94, 196, 198–99, 202, 220
— child-adult friendship   6, 193
— child-child friendship   199
— childhood friends   166
— children and friendship   186, 191
chreia   120n
Christians/Christian friendship   6, 10, 181, 187–89, 195, 199–201, 225–62 (see also monastic friendship)
client   45, 66, 70n, 71, 74n, 107–8, 123n, 128–29, 132–33, 135, 198, 246, 247n (see also patron)
comedy/comic   8n, 164–65
— Middle Comedy   78
— New Comedy   7–8, 57
comfort   138, 149n, 151–54, 156, 196
commitment   161–62, 218
common, friends hold all things and friends in   46, 64, 65n, 77, 87, 92, 94, 95n, 120, 167–68, 171, 177n, 215–16, 229, 232, 236, 238,

Index of Subjects

240–42, 243n, 244–45, 250, 252 (see also sharing)
commonwealth   132–33, 135, 138, 144
community/communal   17n, 71n, 76n, 78, 85, 98, 128, 130, 143, 218n, 222, 225–26, 229, 232–33, 235–39, 240n, 241–43, 246–47, 250–52, 253n, 254–61
compassion   133, 138–39, 142
comrade(ship)/companion(ship)   19–20, 23, 25, 28, 31n, 49, 62n, 84, 91, 152, 155, 158, 164n, 173, 199, 204n, 209–11, 213, 256
confidence   61n, 68
conflict/strife/discord   4, 18n, 23, 26–27, 31, 69n, 76, 85, 98n, 99–100, 123–24, 126–28, 130, 144, 174, 230–31, 240, 241n, 259–60
constancy/steadfastness   62n, 63, 65, 91–92, 137n, 228
constitution   40, 53, 123n, 244n
Constituto Antoniniana   197
conventions of friendship   5–6, 155–57, 172, 225–26, 228–30, 233–34, 240, 259–61
converging narrative   124
cosmic friendship   97, 99
cosmopolitanism   35, 47, 52–53, 56–57, 215
country   4, 48, 123–24, 126, 128n, 129, 131–32, 135, 138–44, 221
courage/bravery/valor   26, 95, 124n, 126–27, 139, 142, 174, 196
cousin   126–27, 143
covenant   174, 221–22, 252
cross/crucifixion   151–52, 156
cult   166

cuttlefish   115
Cynics   170, 172–73
daily association   52, 71n, 91, 94, 160
daughter   126, 159, 169, 176–77, 179, 194, 245n
death/killing   20n, 26, 41, 56, 62n, 76, 91, 111, 124, 126–28, 133, 137, 142–44, 151–55, 167–69, 171, 174–77, 191–92, 198, 202, 206, 218, 261 (see also dying, *Scheintod*, and suicide)
— death of a friend   25, 62, 87, 167, 169, 191–92, 198, 202
debts   72, 127–30, 144, 202
— assume a friend's debts   245n
— cancellation/abolition of debts   129–30
deceit/deception/duplicity   29, 31, 136
dedications   6, 181, 189, 201
deeds speak louder than words   166, 174, 178
definitions of friendship   205–9, 211
degrees of friendship   61n
delight   114–15, 117
democracy   129
desertion by a friend   173
desire/longing/appetite   9n, 38, 63n, 115, 118, 121, 156, 159, 177, 208–9, 210n, 214, 216
despondent/distraught   151–52
devotions   6, 189, 191–92, 201–2
dialogue   5, 163, 166, 179
dining with friends   157–58, 191
disgrace/shame   63, 72–73, 111–12, 126, 153, 169, 171, 213–14

disloyalty   27–28, 31
disposition   32, 38, 47, 55, 116, 217
dispute   125, 195
dissolving/renouncing/abandoning friendships   7n, 67n, 73n, 90, 100, 125, 138, 142, 215n (see also cessation of friendship)
dissuade   150, 171n, 178
distrust   125
documentary papyri   3, 5–6, 181–202
dowry
— provide a dowry for a friend's daughter   169, 245n
duties/obligations/responsibilities   21, 24, 27, 32, 36, 42, 45, 47, 56, 59, 66–68, 70n, 71n, 72–76, 99, 108, 110n, 132, 136, 138, 141–42, 147, 149, 155–56, 159, 169, 179–80, 193, 195, 230, 232, 235–36, 252, 260–61
dying/suffering
— for an enemy   231
— for a friend   20n, 41, 65, 156, 157n, 167–68, 174, 179–80, 231, 234, 258
— with a friend   152–53, 156, 168, 176–77
egoism (selfishness)   18, 37–40, 50, 56, 61n, 208–9
electioneering   69–73
eminent/eminence   128, 131, 136
emotion, friendship as an   47
enmity/enemy/hatred   26n, 62n, 73n, 84–85, 87–90, 92–93, 95–96, 100, 105–6, 113, 116, 118n, 123–44, 153, 175, 206, 210, 212, 216, 220, 227–31, 245n, 247n, 257–58, 260–61
— former enemies as friends   60n, 73n, 85n, 92, 95–96, 135, 137–39 (see also acting so as not to preclude future friendships)
— former friends as enemies   85n, 92, 96, 123, 135, 137, 139, 142, 229n
— love of enemies   248, 258
entertainment   124, 165, 180
envy   46, 118, 124–26
Epicureans   3, 57, 60, 63, 66n, 67n, 68, 116n, 208, 215, 221, 227
epiphanies   141
epitaph   6, 181, 189, 191–92, 198–201
equity/equality/equals   44–46, 64, 66n, 71n, 75, 77, 90, 93, 95n, 107, 121–22, 125–26, 133, 138, 143, 161–62, 185, 195, 208n, 219, 220n, 227, 231–32, 233n, 235, 240n, 247, 250, 252, 261
erotic friendship   49, 107, 179
error/sin/transgression/offense   32, 89n, 90, 124n, 133, 140–42
Essenes   215, 219
ethnic friendship   52, 55–56, 71n, 163–80, 197–98, 202
etymology of φίλος   15–18
example/model/paradigm   20n, 38, 40, 44, 46n, 48, 50, 56, 62n, 66, 75, 94, 105, 107, 117, 120n, 133–34, 140, 143, 164–66, 169, 174, 179, 227, 229, 245n, 247n, 251n, 254, 256, 260, 262
exchange of goods/services   62, 248n

Index of Subjects

exclusion from friendship 46, 86, 94–97, 100n, 102, 228

exhortation/encouragement/paraenesis 6, 9n, 74–75, 94, 101, 134, 138–39, 142, 143n, 166, 196, 202, 219, 226–27, 231–32, 233n, 249n, 252

exile/banishment 69n, 131, 134–35, 137–40, 142–44, 167, 175, 206

false testimony 213

familial and natural friendship 31, 36, 40n, 45–46, 49–51, 54–56, 70–71, 98–99, 106–7, 137n

family/relatives/kinship 4, 6, 17, 18n, 30, 36n, 40, 46, 49–50, 61n, 62n, 66n, 70n, 73, 74n, 76n, 84, 87–88, 91, 96, 98, 123, 125–27, 135, 137, 139, 140n, 141n, 143, 149n, 152, 157, 161, 170, 178n, 181–82, 185, 190, 192–94, 201–2, 217–21, 227n, 247n, 249, 260 (see also aunt, brother, child/children, cousin, daughter, father, grandfather, husband, kin/kinship, mother, nephew, parents, sister, son, uncle, and wife)

— friends as family 84

— friends as superior to family 178

farmers/agriculturalists 128n, 253n

father 14n, 84, 96, 100, 108, 126–27, 139, 140n, 141, 143, 150, 154, 190, 195, 199

faultfinding 46, 88

favor 67–68, 70n, 114n, 129, 134, 139, 141

feigned friendship 23, 33, 63, 207

fellowship 227, 237n, 245n, 248, 253n

fiction/fictitious 164–65, 176, 179

fidelity 161

flattery/flatterer 11, 23–24, 32–33, 62, 65, 88, 105, 109–10, 113–16, 118–21, 167, 206–7, 228, 230

focal meaning 41–42, 54–55

foreign affairs 4, 123, 212 (see also treaties)

forgiveness/pardon 89n, 125, 127, 133, 140–44

fortune 9n, 63–64, 118, 136, 139–40, 149, 155–56, 165n, 170n, 172n

frankness of speech 11, 23, 65, 113, 116–17, 119, 121, 124n, 167n, 207

freedman 71, 193

freedom/liberty 87, 100, 133

friend(ship), false/unfaithful 27–33, 206–7, 213, 227–28

friend, genuine/true/faithful/firm/etc. 11, 19n, 23, 28, 30–33, 63, 116, 125, 132, 148, 153, 167, 169n, 171–72, 189, 207, 227–28, 234 (see also true friendship)

friend as a polite form of address 237

friend as an official rank or title 187–89, 201, 204n (see also king and prefect)

friend to all 191, 201

friendliness 189, 201

friendship among the sciences 98

friendship as a way of life 93

friendship between those who have never met   101
friendship maintenance   183 (see also persistence/preservation of friendship)
friendship of animals   98n
friendship with animals   83, 98–99
function   6, 37–38, 42, 43n, 70n, 74, 83, 158, 237, 239, 243, 244n, 247n, 257, 262
generic predication   41
generosity/generous/liberality   21, 25, 62n, 74n, 167, 169, 193, 232, 244, 245n, 251n, 252
gift   20n, 22, 155, 167, 193, 230, 232, 234, 244n, 247n
giving   91, 155, 244, 245n, 255
— giving and receiving   140n, 230, 234–35, 239, 246–47
— giving as better/more pleasurable than receiving   62n, 249, 256
— giving without receiving   68, 246n, 247n, 248–49, 254
gnomes   90
Gnomon of the Idios Logos   190
God/gods/*daimones*/divine   10, 22, 33, 47, 65, 67, 88, 93, 96, 101, 126–27, 133, 135–36, 138–39, 141–44, 153, 175, 190–92, 196, 201, 213, 215–20, 231, 236, 251–52, 254–55, 259
— friend of   10, 83, 86–87, 98–99, 102–3, 215–18, 222, 236, 257
— union with   101–2
Golden Age myth   240–43, 244n
good, the   39, 41–43, 50, 61n, 84, 92, 215–16, 218

good faith   129, 194
goodwill   38, 46–47, 54, 63n, 69n, 70, 72, 86, 92, 96, 106, 113–14, 119, 155, 158, 175, 208–9, 211, 214, 219, 221, 244n
graciousness   118–20
grandfather   170
gratitude/grateful   33n, 45, 49, 66–68, 74n, 129, 133, 141–42, 159, 177, 187
Great King   152–54
greed   31, 206, 219, 241n, 251n
grief/sorrow   vii, 38, 62n, 63n, 153, 155, 161
groups of friends   145, 149n, 157–59, 162
guardians (Platonic)   241
guest friendship   17, 20–21, 24–25, 27, 49, 247n, 252n
guide/guidance   74, 89, 175
happiness/happy   39–41, 61n, 63n, 109, 139, 168, 172, 221
harm/hurt/wrong   32, 33n, 132, 139, 142, 144, 213n, 227
harmony/concord   4, 22, 47, 66, 77, 93, 96, 98, 99n, 102, 106, 125, 128, 131, 134–35, 143–44, 210, 227, 241, 250
haughty/arrogant   128–29, 132, 134–36, 144
Haustafeln (household or domestic code)   53, 80
help/assist/do favors for   28, 33, 65, 69n, 74, 88, 101, 167, 176, 178, 181, 183, 191, 194, 196, 201, 215n, 248, 249n, 255

helping friends and harming enemies   22n, 135, 137–38, 141n, 142, 144
history of friendship   10n, 14n
homonymy (equivocation)   41–42, 45
homosexuality   168, 179
honor/honorable/esteem/prestige   20, 41, 64, 66–67, 71n, 73, 88, 108, 124n, 125–27, 130, 134, 142–44, 154, 169, 219, 228, 232, 240n, 246n, 253–54
hope   139
hospitality   20–21, 49, 230–32, 234, 237n (see also guest friendship)
household   14n, 17, 36n, 43, 53, 71, 84, 126, 160, 193–94
humanity/humane   6, 21n, 39–40, 52–53, 63, 67, 71n, 76n, 129, 132–33, 139, 191, 203, 213, 220
humble/humbled   128–31, 133–35, 137, 139–40, 143n, 252
humiliation   141, 143–44
husband   5, 139–40, 151, 153, 167, 206 (see also wife)
— husband-wife as friends   5, 45, 85, 137n, 145, 160–62 (see also male-female friendships)
hypocrisy   161
ill-will   46
illness/sickness/disease   100–1, 153, 167, 206, 227–28
immanence   35, 56
imitation   115–16
immoderate   54
impartiality   208
inconstant   228
indispensability of friendship   118

individualism   52–53, 89
inequity/inequality   64, 66n, 70, 71n (see also unequal)
ingratitude   67
injure/injury   32, 124–25, 136, 138–40, 142–43, 178
injustice   45, 47n, 48, 154, 214
— doing injustice for the sake of friendship   45–46, 48, 213–15, 221
inscriptions   5–6, 181–202
intimacy/intimate/close   19n, 26n, 49, 57, 68, 69n, 71n, 85, 91, 107n, 108, 113–14, 117–18, 195, 201, 210, 256
intrapersonal friendship   18, 98–99
invective   230
irony   5, 129, 140n, 166, 174–76, 179–80
jealousy/jealous   130, 142, 150
Jesus/Christ   10n, 53n, 108, 127n, 175, 177, 178n, 231, 234, 253–54, 257–58, 260–61
— disciples as friends of Jesus   257
— Jesus as God's friend   257
Jews/Israelites/Judaism/Jewish   6, 129n, 181, 186, 189, 191, 199, 202–4, 207n, 212–13, 215n, 217–21, 229, 251–52, 254, 258n (see also Essenes, Pharisees, and Therapeutae)
joy/rejoice   19n, 38, 63
judgment within friendship   100–2
justice/just   28n, 40, 44, 68, 83n, 95, 98–99, 124, 127–29, 131–32, 138–39, 141–44, 209, 240n

kind/kindness 73, 113, 129, 137, 140, 244n
king/emperor/ruler/Caesar, friend of (the) 10, 108n, 110, 158, 188–89, 201, 257 (see also prefect)
kiss/kissing 20n, 208
knowledge 42, 83, 232, 255
labor/laborer/toil 128, 151, 155, 167n, 178, 233 (see also manual labor)
Lamprias Catalogue 111n
land 136–37, 140, 144, 190, 212
landowner 253n
Latin/Latin League 3n, 136, 181, 195
law/legal/lawyer 44–46, 67, 70, 74n, 84, 89n, 93, 98, 100, 125, 136, 142, 143n, 176, 188–90, 197, 201, 214, 219, 221, 232, 234, 243
letter 4, 6, 60n, 74n, 75–77, 80, 85–86, 106, 152, 159, 161, 181, 183–89, 193–202, 226–27, 229–34, 259–60
— epistolary clichés 227
— friend's letter of recommendation 75–76, 195–97, 199, 202
— friendly letter 74, 75, 181, 183–85, 202, 226, 231, 233
— letter closings 184, 193
— letter openings 184–85, 189, 198, 200
— letters as means to maintain friendships 183, 193
likeness 61n, 63n, 75, 101, 107n, 115–16, 187, 227, 233n, 235, 240n

limited number of friends 29–31, 46, 52, 56, 61n, 169n, 174, 216 (see also numerous friends)
love/lover/beloved 4, 7n, 15, 18, 20, 37–39, 41, 43–45, 49–50, 55–57, 61n, 62–63, 64n, 66n, 71n, 94, 117–18, 123–24, 126–27, 129, 131–32, 135, 137n, 138–39, 142–44, 147, 149, 151, 154–55, 158–61, 168–69, 176, 180, 187, 203, 206, 208, 210n, 219, 226–28, 232–33, 245n, 248, 254, 257–58
loyalty/loyal 28, 31, 62n, 69n, 92, 100–1, 140, 155, 167–68, 176, 179, 206, 228, 246n, 249n
lying 151, 178
male-female friendships 5–6, 137n, 198 (see also women and husband-wife friendships)
manual labor 167, 171n, 178
marriage 22n, 76n, 147n, 150, 157, 160, 169–70, 176n, 178–79, 218–19
— marry a friend's sister 155, 157, 178
materialism 63n
maxims/clichés/platitudes/proverbs/*topoi*/etc. vii, 4, 6, 10, 20, 22n, 64–65, 77, 81–83, 85n, 86–87, 89, 90n, 97n, 106, 110, 112–20, 140, 162, 166n, 168n, 175n, 179, 206–7, 208n, 211–13, 215–16, 225–29, 231, 233, 236–40, 244–46, 249n, 250n, 252n, 256–57, 259–62
mercy/clemency 139, 142, 144, 172
metaphors/similes 120–21, 228

Index of Subjects

miserliness 50
mockery/ridicule/scorn 5, 86, 163, 166, 168n, 169, 173, 175n, 176n
moderation 25, 54, 136
modern ethics/philosophy, friendship in 2n, 36, 42, 56
modesty 128
monastic friendship 10n, 199
morality/morals/ethics 5, 27, 32, 42, 49, 52, 54, 61n, 63n, 65–66, 68, 74–75, 83, 86–87, 97, 99–100, 106, 127, 137n, 165–66, 177, 196, 218, 234–35, 239, 260
mother 123, 127, 132, 134, 137–44, 169, 177, 219, 228
murder 150–51, 158, 173–74
mutual/mutuality 18, 19n, 63, 66, 68, 69n, 74, 83, 125, 132, 156, 160–61, 168, 170, 199, 230, 232, 235, 238n, 247n
— mutual affection 18n, 21–22, 51
— mutual erotic attraction 170
— mutual esteem 232
— mutual hatred 125, 132
— mutual obligation 45, 76
— mutual reconciliation 125
— mutual sharing 232
— mutual support 83–84, 89
— mutual trust 19n
nature/natural 40, 49–50, 54–55, 60, 61n, 62, 63n, 67n, 73, 84n, 98–99, 102, 107, 119, 120n, 127n, 136, 137n, 138, 140, 142, 151, 212n, 218n, 219–20, 244
necessities of life 133, 135
necessity/necessary 60, 61n, 63n, 66, 88, 108, 128, 134, 173

need 37, 44, 49, 52, 63, 65n, 66n, 75, 91, 108–9, 118–19, 129, 137, 144, 167n, 201, 232, 235–36, 242, 243n, 244n, 252, 255–56, 260
neighbor 53, 71, 208, 216n, 220, 232, 249n
Neopythagoreans (see Pythagoreans)
nephew 195
notebooks 105, 110–12
novel/novella/romance, Greek 5, 145–65, 166n, 167, 168n, 169–70, 171n, 172–73, 174n, 176, 178–79
numerous/many friends 61n, 70–71, 84, 87, 105, 108–10, 113, 117–19, 121, 206n (see also limited number of friends)
nurse 141, 159, 167
oath/swear 22, 125, 126n, 164, 174, 178–79, 190
— oath of friendship 164, 179
objectivity 36
official documents 189, 201
older-younger friendships 74, 96, 99–100, 108, 137n
one body, friends as 177, 179
one soul, friends are of 177n
oneness of mind/thought/purpose/spirit/feelings 21–23, 26, 47, 59, 65–66, 68, 84–85, 101, 129, 158, 210, 220, 232, 234, 238, 250, 252
opponents/rivals of Paul 228–31, 260
order 128
orphans 139
pairs of friends 145, 148, 151, 155, 157, 166, 168n, 174 (see also

canon of traditional pairs of friends)
parasite/parasitic 23–24, 159
parents/parental 51, 88, 150–51, 159, 203, 219
— parent-child friendship/relationship 45–46, 50–51, 55–56, 89n, 107, 159, 220
parody 5, 164–65, 168n
partner/partnership 101, 107, 158, 160, 179, 203, 210, 220
passions/emotions/feelings 15–21, 26n, 46–47, 49, 55, 59, 62, 71, 85, 96, 116, 140, 142, 151, 160–62, 168, 173, 175, 220, 232–33
pastoral theology and friendship 10n
patricians 123, 127, 130, 132–35, 144
patriotism 127
patristic views of friendship 10n
patron 45, 66, 71n, 107–9, 123n, 198, 230, 246, 247n (see also client)
— patronage 9n, 234, 246n, 247n
— patronal friendship 257n, 259
peace 128, 134, 136, 139, 174, 212
pederasty 137n
Peripatetics 3, 35, 45–57, 79
perjury 24, 173, 213
persistence/preservation of friendship 18, 48, 87, 89–90, 94, 100n, 102, 125, 137n, 138, 149n, 166n, 260 (see also friendship maintenance)
persuasion/persuade 20n, 108, 129, 132, 135, 143n, 144, 147, 150, 152, 154

petition 184
Pharisees 24n, 253n, 254–55
philanthropy 61n, 96, 129n, 133, 205, 247n
philosophers/philosophical schools
— communal setting of philosophical schools 229
— philosophers as associates of powerful people 249n
— philosophical treatments of friendship 2–6, 35–122, 165, 166n, 204, 207–8, 210–11, 213, 215–16, 222, 227, 229, 231, 234
— see also Cynics, Epicureans, Peripatetics, Platonists, Pythagoreans, and Stoics
planting/pruning/cutting trees 205–6, 208, 212
Platonists/Academy 54, 79, 102, 227
— Middle Platonism 54, 65n, 204, 209, 211n, 219
— Neoplatonism 80, 101
pleasure/pleasant 37, 41–47, 50, 55, 61n, 62n, 63, 68, 83–84, 108, 114–15, 119–20, 137n, 190, 208n
plebeians 123, 127–28, 130–33, 135–36, 139, 142–44
poetry/poem/poet 9, 26n, 29–30, 81, 88
polis/city/state 14, 27, 31, 35–36, 40–41, 43, 50, 52–53, 57, 60n, 66n, 67, 69n, 86, 107n, 109, 124–30, 133, 135–38, 140, 141n, 144, 149n, 150, 154, 160, 182, 190–91, 197, 212, 216, 221, 240n, 241, 243, 245

Index of Subjects

political/civic friendship 4–5, 14n, 36, 40, 43–44, 48, 50, 52–54, 56–57, 59–60, 62n, 63n, 66, 67n, 69n, 70n, 72n, 73n, 85, 98, 107n, 109–10, 123–45, 158, 162, 212, 240n
politics/political life 3, 5, 34, 40, 59–60, 62n, 64, 66–76, 78, 84–85, 96, 97n, 100, 106, 144, 161, 169, 179, 243n, 244n
poor 46, 74n, 109, 123, 128–31, 133–35, 143–44, 154, 169, 173, 176n, 177, 182, 202, 239n, 244n, 246, 249, 252
possession 39–40
possessions/property/assets 16n, 74n, 84, 91–93, 100, 128n, 137–38, 175, 181–82, 190, 193–95, 202, 206, 215, 238, 240–43, 244n, 245n, 246, 247n, 248, 251–57
— assist friends in acquiring or increasing property 170, 245n
— common ownership of property 238, 241n, 243–44, 245n, 251
— common use of private property 243, 244n
— friends as one's most valuable possessions 175, 179
— private property 238, 240–45, 251, 256n
— sharing possessions 236, 238, 242–43, 246–48, 251, 255
poverty 128, 130–31, 169
power 49, 66–68, 128, 132, 134–36, 141, 144, 175
pragmatism 69

praise/encomium/applause/congratulations 105, 113, 116–17, 124n, 131, 134, 137, 165–66, 170, 196, 203, 215
prayer 140–41, 149n
prefect 188, 201
— friend of the prefect 188, 201
presence 62n, 63n, 75, 172, 194, 196
primitivism 241n, 242
prison/imprisoned 65n, 130, 171–73
— friends in prison 65n, 171–72
progress 87, 89, 111, 205, 221, 241n
proofs of friendship/affection 101, 147, 156
proportion (proportional friendship) 45–46
proselytes 210n, 217–18
prostitution as counterfeit friendship 206
protection 59, 73–74, 76, 130, 196
proven friends 178
providence 126, 172n
proxies, friends as 6, 189–90, 201
prudence 95
Pythagorean:
— *akousmata/symbola* 81–82, 90, 93, 95n
— letters 4, 77, 80, 85–86
— life 4, 77–78, 82, 92
— pseudepigrapha 77, 79–80, 81n, 96
— sayings (collections of) 4, 77, 80–81, 86–90
— term for good friends 77
— traditions 4, 78–80

— writings 4, 77–103
Pythagoreans/Neopythagoreans
  3–4, 38n, 47, 52n, 64, 65n, 77–
  103, 222n, 229
quarrel/altercation 127
quietism 226
rape 170
rarity of true friends/friendship
  9n, 30, 63, 65, 156
reason/rational 55, 60–61, 71n, 84,
  98–99, 101, 125, 141–43
reciprocity/reciprocal 6, 18, 20n,
  25, 38–39, 52, 54, 59, 62n, 63,
  66–68, 71–73, 108n, 147, 167,
  169, 178, 227–28, 230, 232, 234–
  35, 237, 239–40, 246, 247n, 248,
  254, 257
  — reciprocity ethic 239–40,
  246–48
recommendation 230, 234 (see
  also letter of recommendation)
reconciliation/reconcile/restoration
  of friendship 4, 25–26, 32, 62n,
  84–85, 90n, 98, 125, 128–30, 132,
  136, 141–42, 144
refuge/shelter/safety 9n, 65n, 66n,
  129, 135, 140
regard 63n
religion/religious/piety 68, 87–88,
  95, 98–99, 136, 138, 142, 181,
  189, 196–97, 201, 218–19
repentance/repentant 113, 141,
  143–44, 153
reputation 65, 71, 214
requests 72, 92, 110, 134, 193–94,
  233n
resemblance 42, 43n

responses to a friend's misconduct
  32–33, 85, 89–90, 100, 125, 138,
  142, 215n (see also dissolving
  friendships and tolerance)
retaliation 32
reverence in friendship 96
revolt/revolution 124, 126
rhetoric/rhetorical/oratory 72, 86,
  107n, 161, 164, 166, 168, 187,
  201, 212, 227, 230–31
rich/wealthy 23, 71n, 109, 123,
  130n, 131, 144, 169, 182 (see also
  wealth)
riot 133
ritualized friendship 27n, 183,
  247n, 248n
robbery 171, 178, 244n (see also
  bandits)
Roman citizens as friends 197
romances, Greek (see novel)
ruler-advisor relationship 107, 110,
  158, 188–89, 201
rules/injunctions for friendship
  99–100
sacrifice 139, 165, 236
salvation/save 53, 128, 149, 151–
  52, 155, 168, 172
satire/satirist 5, 120n
Scheintod (apparent death) 149n,
  150
second (another) self, friend as a
  38, 48, 64n, 75, 77, 90, 94, 120,
  177n, 209–10, 227n, 252n
secrets
  — divulging a friend's 207
  — revealing secrets to a friend
  259

security 59–60, 61n, 69n, 76, 128, 147, 171
sedition 123, 127–28, 130, 142
selection/choosing of friends 59, 66, 87–88, 90, 93, 101–2, 174, 216n
self-accusation 171n
self-commendation 230
self-denial 89
self-interest 61n, 64, 68n, 69n, 73, 76, 89, 129n, 206
self-love (friendship toward the self) 37–38, 41, 50, 55–57, 61n, 64n
self-sacrifice 41, 234, 258–59, 261
self-sufficiency 37, 61n, 62n, 172, 235–36, 260
senate 69n, 70n, 109, 128–30, 132–33, 135–36, 140
sentimental/sentimentality 163–64, 169, 173, 179
servant 182, 259
service 70–71, 74, 132, 135, 142, 153–54, 169n, 193–94, 202
sexual symmetry 161
sharing 35, 38, 40, 43, 46, 54, 57, 65n, 71n, 77, 87, 91–95, 97, 102, 124n, 130, 134–35, 139, 142, 156, 160–61, 167, 171, 193, 215, 218, 222, 232, 235–36, 238, 246–47, 251, 255
— sharing of life 38, 40, 61n, 62n, 64, 68, 75, 227
— sharing of sorrow/pain/misfortune/dangers/burdens vii, 38, 63, 87, 91, 122, 149, 151, 155–56, 167, 171, 175, 227n, 229, 232
sincerity/sincere 67n, 72, 132, 187, 201

sister 107n, 126–27, 138, 141, 143, 155, 157, 178, 198, 258, 260
slaves/slavery/enslaved 71, 119, 128–30, 133, 140, 149n, 150–51, 155–56, 158–59, 161–62, 171, 178, 182, 198, 202, 219
— friendships of/with slaves 159, 162
social boundaries 246, 248n, 251–52, 255–56
social clubs/associations/sodalities 67, 70–71
soldier/mercenary/army 23, 123, 127–28, 130, 134, 149n, 154, 158, 164, 192, 212
— fellow soldier/warrior 26, 158
solidarity 60, 61n
son 137, 139–44, 190, 192–93
speech/speeches 125, 130–32, 140, 150, 152, 166, 172, 175n, 177–78
squire 20
status 6, 60, 87, 162, 170n, 180, 182, 190, 197–98, 202, 228, 230, 237, 239–40, 245–46, 248, 250–57, 259–60
Stoicism/Stoics 3, 6, 9, 47–53, 55, 57, 60, 61n, 62n, 63n, 65n, 68, 79, 86, 129n, 203–5, 206n, 208–9, 211, 212n, 213–16, 217n, 219–22, 227
— Middle Stoicism 209, 219–21, 244
student/pupil 65n, 224, 236
subjectivity 36
submission 126–27
suffering for a friend (see dying for a friend)

suffering(s)   85, 125, 133, 135, 137, 140, 153, 169, 233
suicide   141, 144, 150, 153, 155–56, 171, 178
suitors   25n, 176
supplication   252n
support   9n, 70n, 71n, 72–73, 74n, 139, 149, 158, 167–69, 195, 214, 230–31, 236, 246n
sympathy   18, 65n, 232
symposium/banquet   23, 126, 163
table and salt as signs of friendship   211
taxonomy (types/kinds/forms) of friendship   3, 37, 41–45, 49–50, 54, 57, 60n, 61n, 83–84, 97–98, 203–4, 207–8, 235
— two kinds   60n, 61n
— three kinds   37, 41, 43, 45, 49–50, 83, 208n
— four kinds   49
— five kinds   98
— six kinds   49
teacher   65n, 89n, 230, 236
temperance   98–99
temple/shrine   151, 157, 171, 192
testing/judging   24n, 30, 46, 62, 87, 92–94, 132, 175
Therapeutae   215
threaten friends   195, 202
tolerance   32, 46, 89–90
tranquility   110n, 111, 208n
transcendence   35, 56
transmission of Aristotelian texts   35n, 36n
treaties/diplomatic relations   21n, 86, 109, 124–25, 136, 141, 176
trial   7n, 125, 142, 149n, 150, 152–53, 158, 173
tribune   69n, 130, 132–34, 195
true friendship   33, 37, 46, 52, 54, 62–63, 75, 90, 100, 108, 156, 174, 211, 227–28
trust/faith   19n, 24, 29, 147, 158, 160, 194
trustworthy   19n, 23, 28, 30–31, 43
truth   62, 65, 129, 150, 178
uncle   127
unequal partners/friends/associates   45, 107–10, 121–22, 167n, 169, 185, 198, 207, 246–47, 250 (see also inequity)
unfriendliness   28
unanimity of spirit/views (see oneness)
unity/united   6, 102n, 132, 134, 239, 250, 260
universalism and universal friendship/ friendliness   6, 47, 52–53, 55–57, 85, 96–97, 102, 203, 220–22, 245n
untrustworthy/unreliable   30, 33, 228
utility/utilitarian   3, 21, 37, 42–47, 61n, 63–64, 66, 68, 73, 83–84, 108–9, 118–19, 145, 159–60, 162, 166, 181, 208n, 209, 235 (see also advantage)
utopia   238, 240–44, 257
vengeance/revenge   128, 135, 140, 142, 153–54
violence   131–32
virtue/virtuous   31, 35, 37, 39–41, 43, 45, 47, 53–55, 57, 61n, 62n, 63, 64n, 65–66, 69n, 71n, 77, 83,

86, 88–89, 93, 95, 99, 101–2, 108, 119, 128n, 136, 142, 160, 165–66, 170, 177, 196, 208n, 232, 234, 241n

vocabulary/terminology/language of friendship   5–6, 13, 20, 21n, 31n, 49, 60, 123n, 157–58, 168n, 181, 183, 187, 189, 200, 205, 210–11, 226, 231–32, 234, 247n, 261–62

war/battle(field)   21n, 25–26, 27n, 28, 76, 123–27, 129–32, 134–38, 154, 159, 174, 176, 178, 212

wealth/mammon/money/prosperity   68, 87, 91, 114, 128, 150, 160, 166–67, 168n, 169, 172–73, 176, 182, 194, 196, 206, 215, 244, 248n, 253n, 254–55
— friends as (better than) wealth   176, 256

widow/widower   141, 159

wife   127n, 134, 137–40, 149–50, 152, 154–55, 167, 169–70, 174, 178, 194 (see also husband and women)

willing/willingness/readiness/voluntary   76n, 89, 130, 150, 155–56, 171n, 176, 178, 234, 242, 245n, 250, 258

wills   6, 173, 189, 192–93, 199–202, 222n

wisdom/wisely   23, 46–48, 61n, 87, 95, 99, 124n

wise (the)/sages   47, 61n, 62n, 63n, 66, 75, 99n, 112, 140, 217, 218n

women   121, 137–43, 153–54, 159, 161, 167, 170, 174, 180, 182, 184, 186, 189–91, 193, 198, 202, 256 (see also wife)
— female-female friendships   5, 159, 162, 198
— female-male friendships   5–6, 137n, 198
— wife-husband as friends   5, 45, 85, 137n, 145, 160–62
— women and friendship   5–6, 159, 162, 186, 191, 198

worship   88, 166, 192, 218

Index of Greek and Latin Terms

ἀγαπάω 138, 248n, 258
ἀγάπη 38, 199, 231, 234
ἀγαπητός 140
ἀκοινώνητος 130
ἄλλος ἐγώ 77
ἀντιφιλέω 205n
ἀντιφίλησις 38
ἅπαντα (πάντα) κοινά 238, 250, 257
ἀρετή 39, 41, 108, 119, 218n
ἁρμονία 99n
αὐτάρκεια 61n
ἄφιλος 137n
γνώριμος 91, 107n, 199
εἰκὼν ψυχῆς 75n
εἰς ἕνα 177
εἷς ἄνθρωπος 177
ἐξαίρετος 148–50, 157
ἐπιτήδειος 107n, 183
ἔρως 38–39, 126, 151, 210n
ἐρωτική 49
ἑταιρία 210, 213
ἑταιρικός 49, 84, 107–8, 147–48, 157
ἑταῖρος 19, 28, 107n, 183, 207n, 210
ἕτερος αὐτός 38
εὐεργεσία 134, 140, 255
εὐεργέτης 256
εὐεργετική 49
εὐθυμία 110–11
εὔνοια 92, 96, 106n, 113–14, 119, 155, 158, 168n, 208–9, 211, 219, 221
εὔνους 113–14, 209n
ζεύγεα φιλίας 121
ἡδονή 43, 114, 119

ἡδύς 108, 114–15, 119
ἠθοποιία 151, 161
θεοφιλής 217
ἰατρός = φιλία 120
ἰσότης 77, 93, 208n, 250n
καταφιλέω 208
κοινὰ τὰ τῶν φίλων 64, 77, 92, 120, 168, 215–16, 229, 235, 243n, 244–46
κοινότης 84n, 98
κοινόω 134
κοινωνέω 149, 165n, 232
κοινωνία 96, 98, 128, 160, 165n, 210, 220, 232, 233n, 234–36, 245n, 250
κοινωνικός 51, 52n
κοινωνός 158
κολακεία 11, 109, 120, 207
κόλαξ 105, 113–15, 118–19, 121
λάθε βιώσας 66n
μία ψυχή 177n, 238, 250, 251n, 252, 257
νόμισμα = φίλος 121
νόμισμα παράσημον = κόλαξ 121
νόμισμα φιλίας 119
νόσημα = κολακεία 120
ξεινοδόκος 24n
ξενία 20, 247n, 248n
ξενική 49
ξένος (ξεῖνος) 17, 20n, 248n
οἰκειότης 217, 219–20
οἰκείωσις 50–52, 55, 56n, 57, 61n
οἶκος 14n, 43
ὁμιλία 96
ὁμοδοξία 65n
ὁμοιοπάθεια 115

Index of Greek and Latin Terms

ὅμοιος 107n, 115–16
ὁμοιότης 115, 117
ὁμονοέω 158
ὁμόνοια 65n, 99n, 131, 210, 220
ὁμοφροσύνη 22, 220
ὁμόφρων 22
ὄρεξις 121
παλαιός 148n, 156
παραμυθέομαι 151–54, 156
παρηγορέω 156n
παρρησία 11, 113, 116–17, 119, 121, 207
παρρησιάζομαι 116
παρρησιαστής 116
πασιφίλη 191
πιστεύω 154, 160
πίστις 62n, 155, 158
πιστός 19n, 148, 155
πολυφιλία 105, 108, 113, 121
πολύφιλος 109
προσκύνημα 189, 191–92, 201
συγγένεια 218–19
συγγενής 207, 210n, 217
συγγενική 49
συγκινδυνεύω 151
συζάω 40, 62n
συμφοιτητής 152
συμφωνία 210
σύν-compounds 156, 233n
συναποθνῄσκω 152–53, 156
συνήθεια 49, 108, 113, 117–18, 210
συνήθης 91, 107n, 117–18, 210n
συστρατιώτης 158
σχῆμα φίλου 153
φιλαδελφία 105–7, 226–27
φιλάλληλος 51, 52n
φιλανθρωπία 61n, 96, 129n, 133, 205

φιλάνθρωπος 10n, 55, 129, 132, 139
φιλαυτία 61n
φιλέω 18n, 20n, 22, 44, 126, 138–39, 158–59, 198, 205n, 208, 210, 257
φίλημα 20n, 208
φίλησις 47, 55
φιλητός 42
φιλία 11, 13–15, 35, 36n, 47, 50–52, 55, 61n, 83n, 84, 93–95, 98n, 99n, 101n, 106–7, 109n, 110, 112n, 114–15, 117–20, 129n, 147–48, 150, 157, 160, 162, 163n, 181, 183, 185, 189, 199, 203–13, 217–20, 225–27, 233–34, 248n, 250n, 257, 259
φιλικός 94
φίλιος 140
φιλοξενία 20
φίλος 15–21, 28, 31n, 36n, 37n, 64, 77, 92, 105, 107n, 109n, 110, 113–14, 116–21, 125, 132, 135–36, 137n, 141, 148–53, 155–60, 165n, 168n, 174, 181, 183–89, 193, 198–99, 204–5, 209n, 210, 211n, 217, 218n, 219n, 225–26, 229, 231, 233, 236–37, 257–59, 261
φιλοστοργία 105, 193
φιλόστοργος 141
φιλότης 20n, 26, 77, 132
φιλοφρονέομαι 134, 160
φιλοφρόνησις 74n, 75n
φιλοφρόνως 177n
χάρις 49, 68n, 114, 118–19, 129, 134, 138–40, 177n, 222n
χρεία 49, 108–9, 118–19

χρήσιμον 43
ὠφελέω 105
ὠφέλιμος 119

alter ego 75
amicitia 62n, 69n, 70n, 72n, 74n, 109
amicus 60n, 108n, 109
amor 61
beneficentia 68
benevolentia 60, 62, 68, 74n
caritas 60–61, 68
clientela 70n, 246n
collegium 71
consensio 66
constantia 62
diligo 61
familiaris 60n, 69n, 71n
familiaritas 60
fides 62, 68
honestum 63n
humanitas 53, 71n, 76n
moneo 116
parousia 75
probitas 62n
respublica 62n, 69n, 76n
societas 68, 69n
sportula 108n
utilis 63n
utilitas 66, 209
veritas 62

Index of Ancient Authors and Texts

The abbreviations used for the citation of primary texts follow, in general, the guidelines of the Society of Biblical Literature as published in the *Journal of Biblical Literature* 107 (1988) 579–96. Where no abbreviation has been recommended by the SBL, preference in the citation of ancient authors and texts is often given to the abbreviations employed by N. G. L. Hammond and H. H. Scullard (eds.) in *The Oxford Classical Dictionary* (2d ed.; Oxford: Clarendon, 1970). Other abbreviations are either self-evident or are derived from one or more of the following works: P. G. W. Glare (ed.), *Oxford Latin Dictionary* (Oxford: Clarendon, 1982); G. W. H. Lampe (ed.), *A Patristic Greek Lexicon* (Oxford: Clarendon, 1961); C. T. Lewis and C. Short, *A New Latin Dictionary* (New York: American, 1907); H. G. Liddell and R. Scott, *A Greek-English Lexicon* (rev. H. S. Jones and R. McKenzie; 9th ed.; Oxford: Clarendon, 1940); A. Souter, *A Glossary of Later Latin to 600 A.D.* (Oxford: Clarendon, 1949); and *The Studia Philonica Annual* 5 (1993) 250–56.

1. Hebrew Bible (Old Testament) 287
2. Apocrypha and Pseudepigrapha 289
3. Josephus and Philo 290
4. New Testament 294
5. Non-Canonical Christian Literature 297
6. Other Ancient Authors and Texts 297

NOTE: n = footnote(s). If the same page of this volume contains a reference in both the text and the footnotes to the same passage or author, only the reference in the text is indicated in the following index. Pseudonymous works are listed, in general, under the supposed author.

1. Hebrew Bible (Old Testament)

Exodus [Exod]
20:7 213
32:27 218n
33:11 204n, 215

Leviticus [Lev]
4:27 252

5:1 213n
19:3 219
19:23–25 206

Numbers [Num]
15:27 252
31:28 252

Deuteronomy [Deut] 212, 251
  4:29 251
  6:5 251
  10:12 251
  11:13 251
  11:18 251
  13:3 251
  13:7 204n, 209n, 252n
  15:4 251
  20:10–13 212
  20:19 212
  24:16 213n
  26:16 251
  30:2 251
  30:6 251
  30:10 251

Judges [Judg]
  5:30 204n
  14:20 204n
  15:2 204n
  15:6 204n

Jeremiah [Jer]
  9:4 204n
  20:4 204n
  20:6 204n
  20:10 204n
  37:14 204n

Micah [Mic]
  7:5 204n

Psalms [Ps]
  139:17 (138:17 LXX) 204n

Proverbs [Prov] 203
  3:29 204n
  5:19 203n
  6:1 204n
  6:3 204n
  7:18 203n
  10:12 203n
  12:26 204n
  14:20 204n
  15:17 203n
  16:7 (15:28a LXX) 204n
  16:28 204n
  16:29 204n
  17:9 203n, 204n
  17:17 204n
  17:18 204n
  18:1 204n
  19:4 204n
  19:7 203n
  22:24 204n
  25:1 204n
  25:8 204n
  25:10 204n
  25:10a (LXX) 203n
  25:17 204n
  25:18 204n
  26:19 204n
  27:5 203n
  27:6 204n
  27:10 204n
  27:14 204n
  29:5 204n

Job
  2:11 204n
  6:27 204n
  19:13 204n
  19:21 204n
  32:1 204n
  32:3 204n
  35:4 204n
  36:33 204n
  42:7 204n
  42:10 204n

Index of Ancient Authors and Texts

Esther [Esth]
1:3   204n
1:13   204n
2:18   204n
3:1   204n
5:10   204n
5:14   204n
6:9   204n
6:13   204n
9:22   204n

Daniel [Dan]
2:13 (Θ)   204n
2:17 (Θ)   204n
2:18 (Θ)   204n
3:24 (3:91 LXX)   204n
3:27 (3:94 LXX)   204n
5:23   204n
6:14   204n

1 Chronicles [1 Chr]
12:39   252
27:33   204n

2. Apocrypha and Pseudepigrapha

Epistle of Aristeas [Ep. Arist.]
125   207n
225   204n
228   204n
231   204n

1 Maccabees [1 Macc]   204n
8:1   203n
8:11   203n
8:17   203n
10:20   203n
10:23   203n
10:26   203n
10:54   203n
12:1   203n
12:3   203n
12:8   203n
12:10   203n
12:16   203n
14:18   203n
14:22   203n
15:17   203n

2 Maccabees [2 Macc]
4:11   203n
6:20   129n

6:22   203n

4 Maccabees [4 Macc]   127n, 204n
2:9–14   204n
2:11–13   143n
8:5   204n
12:5   204n
13:19–14:1   204n
13:23–14:1   143n
14:13   143n
14:13–15:23   204n
14:20   143n
15:4–17:10   143n
16:24   143n
18:6–19   143n

Pseudo-Phocylides   204n
91   207n
91–94   204n
195–97   204n
219   204n

Sirach [Sir]   204n, 229
6:5–17   204n, 216n, 229
6:7   229
6:9   229

6:13   229
6:17   203n
9:8   203n
11:29–12:18   204n, 216n
22:19–26   204n
22:20   203n
25:1   203n

27:18   203n
37:1–6   204n

Wisdom of Solomon [Wis]   229
7:14   203n
8:18   203n

3. Josephus and Philo

Josephus
Contra Apionem [CA]
   2.207   207n

Philo   3, 6, 203–23, 229
Abr.
   65   210n, 217n
   153   209n, 210n
   194   203n, 209n, 210n
   235   215n
   273   218n
Agr.
   25   218n
   88   211n, 213n
   155   210n, 217n
   159   211n
   164   206n
   168   218n
Cher.
   20   210n, 219n
Conf.
   48   206n, 207n, 209n
   106   216n
Congr.
   79   211n
   91   211n
   166   210n
Contempl.
   2–9   215n
   13   210n, 217n

   13–17   215n
   14   217n
   40–89   215n
   41   210n, 211n, 217n
   44   211n
   90   217n
Decal.
   41   220n
   89–90   213n
   132–134   220n
Det.
   15   210n
   33   209n
   37   210n, 211n, 213n
   67–68   222n
   165   211n, 213n, 219n
   166   210n
Deus
   27   210n
   55   210n
   79   217n
   98   210n
   167   211n
Ebr.
   58   218n
   66   219n
   69   211n, 219n
   94   218n
   159   210n

Index of Ancient Authors and Texts

165   211n
176   211n, 219n
Flacc.
  18   209n, 211n
  19   206n
  32   210n
  43   207n
  60   217n
  62   211n, 212n
  64   217n
  72   217n
Fug.
  3   210n
  6   207n, 209n
  29   215n
  40   209n
  58   210n, 217n
  89   219n
Gig.
  33   217n, 218n
  35   218n
  43   210n, 213n
  61   216n
  66   210n, 213n
Her. 207
  19–21   207n
  21   207, 217n, 218n
  42   208n, 210n
  44   208n, 210n
  48   210n
  51   208n
  83   209n
  186   218n
  203   210n, 213n
  243   211n, 218n
  246   210n
  313   222n

Hypoth.
  8.7.8   207n
  8.11.4–13   215n
  8.11.18   215n
Ios.
  74   207n, 209n
  79   209n, 210n
  210   211n
Leg.
  2.10   206n
  2.85   217n
  3.1   210n, 211n, 218n
  3.20   218n
  3.71   211n, 217n, 218n
  3.85   222n
  3.152   218n
  3.182   206, 209n, 210n, 219n
  3.204   218n
  3.205   217n, 219n
Legat.
  40   211n
  268   210n
  327–328   210n
Migr.
  44–45   218n
  45   218n
  59   216n
  111–12   206n
  112   210n
  115–117   207n
  116   209n, 210n
Mos. 217
  1.31   219n
  1.39   217n
  1.45   210n
  1.147–62   215n
  1.155–57   218n
  1.156–57   216n

1.157   216n
1.280   211n
1.303   217n
1.307   210n, 217n
1.310   211n
1.322   217n
2.42   217n, 219n
2.171   217n, 218n
2.273   217n, 219n

Mut.
40   215n
51–53   222n
52   222n
53   222n
57–60   222n
263   222n

Opif.
3   216n
8–9   211n
77   219n, 220n
142   216n
143   216n

Plant.
25   218n
90   209n, 217n
94   206n
95   206n
104–5   206n
104–6   206n, 210n
105   206n
106   208n, 209n

Post.
25   210n
91   210n, 218n
157   210n
172   210n, 217n

Praem.
17   217n

92   220n
118   211n
127   210n
134   219n
154   210n, 217n

Prob.
9   217n
35   217n
42   210n, 218n
44   210n, 218n
74–75   215n
79   218n, 219n, 220n
85–87   215n
88–91   215n

QE
2.34   222n
2.106   222n

QG
2.10   222n
2.60   220n, 222n
3.40   222n
3.42   222n

Sacr.
20   219n
36   210n
57   222n
129   219n
130   218n

Sobr.
55–57   218n

Somn.
1.110   213n
1.111   210n, 218n
1.191   207n
1.193   218n
1.193–94 218n
1.193–95 218n
1.193–96 218n

Index of Ancient Authors and Texts

1.193–200   218n
1.232   218n
2.104   210n
2.108   209n
2.219   218n
2.223–25   222n
2.237   222n
2.297   218n
Spec.   212
  1.51–52   217n
  1.52   209n, 217n, 218n, 219n
  1.68   210n, 217n
  1.69–70   217n
  1.70   210n
  1.97   213n, 219n
  1.247   217n
  1.250   209n, 219n
  1.313   211n, 219n
  1.316   211n
  1.316–17   209n
  1.317   209n, 218n 219n
  1.340   211n, 219n
  2.16   222n
  2.19   207n, 217n
  2.26   213n
  2.45   216n
  2.119   210n
  2.132   210n, 213n
  2.239–40   209n
  2.240   219n
  3.11   219n
  3.85   217n
  3.90   217n
  3.126   219n
  3.155   209n, 210n, 213n, 217n, 218n
  4.14   220n
  4.70   209n, 211n, 219n
  4.88   216n
  4.141   217n
  4.161   210n
  4.219–23   212n
  4.226–29   212n
Virt.   205, 212
  35   210n, 218n
  46   211n
  51–174   205n
  55   210n
  96   219n
  103   209n
  109   212n
  110–15   212n
  119   221n
  125   211n, 219n
  149–54   212n
  152   212n
  173   213n, 217n
  179   217n, 218n, 219
  195   211n, 219n
  218   219n

4. New Testament

Matthew [Matt]
5   248n
5:17   134n
5:19   134n
5:21–26   90n
11:19   225n
12:34   97n
12:46–50   218n
16:19   134n
18:21–22   89n
21:31   169n
21:40   169n
22:34–40   24n
23:33   97n

Mark
1:18   253n
1:20   253n
2:14   253n
3:31–35   218n
5:38–40   169n
10:8   177n
10:28   253n
10:29–30   167n
12:28–34   24n

Luke   6, 216, 225, 236–57, 261
1:3   237n
1:51–52   134n
5:11   253
5:28   253n
6:34–35a   248
6:35a   248n
7:6   225n, 236n, 237
7:34   225n, 236n
8:3   256
8:19–21   218n
10:27   53n
10:29   216n
11:4   130n
11:5   225n, 236n
11:5–8   237
11:6   225n, 236n
11:8   225n, 236n
12:4   225n, 236n, 237
13:32   97n
14:10   225n, 236n, 237
14:12   225n, 236n
14:12–14   237, 249
14:26   127n
15:6   225n, 236n, 237
15:9   225n, 236n, 237
15:29   225n, 236n
16:9   225n, 236n, 237
16:14   254
16:14–15   253n, 254
16:15   255
18:28   253
18:29   253n
19:28   253n
20:34–35   127n
21:16   225n, 236n, 237
22:25–26   256
23:12   225n, 236n, 237

John   6, 11n, 225, 257–59, 261
3:29   225n, 257
5:20   257
7:7   257
10:11   168n, 258
10:15   258
10:17–18   257
11:3   257
11:11   225n, 257
11:36   257

15:13   168n, 225n, 231, 258
15:14   225n
15:14–15   257
15:15   225n, 259
15:19   257
15:23   257
16:27   257
17:14   257
19:12   225n, 257
19:25–27   169n
20:2   257
20:30–31   172n
21:15   257
21:16   257
21:17   257
21:25   172n

Acts   6, 11n, 236–57, 261
1:1   237n
1:14   250
1:15   250
1:18   251
1:25   250
2   239–40, 242n, 250
2:1   250
2:44   238, 241n, 250
2:44–45   241
2:44–47   237
2:46   250
2:47   250
3:1–10   255
4   239–40, 242n, 248n, 250, 252
4:9   255
4:24   250
4:32   177n, 238, 241, 251n
4:32b   238
4:32–37   237
4:34   251
5:2   251
5:4   255
5:12   250
5:13–14   97n
10:24   225n, 236n, 237
11:29   256
12:12   256
13:1   256
16:15   256
16:19–40   171n
16:40   256
17:12   256
19:31   225n, 236n, 237
20:29   97n
20:33–35   256
20:35   249
27:3   129n, 225n, 236n
28:2   129n

Romans [Rom]   6, 226, 231–33
5:6–8   231
12:1   231–32
12:1–2   233n
12:1–15:33   231
12:3   129n
12:9   232
12:10   232
12:13   232
12:15   232
12:16   232
13:8–10   232
14:1–15:13   232
15:14   232
15:14–33   231
15:15   232
15:23–24   231
15:24   231
15:26   232
15:27   232
15:30   233n

16:1–16   233n
16:3–16   233
16:17   233n

1 Corinthians [1 Cor]   6, 226, 230–31, 260
9:1–23   230
12:26–27   177n

2 Corinthians [2 Cor]   6, 226, 230–31, 260
1:13–24   230
6:10   172n
10–12   230

Galatians [Gal]   6, 226–30
1:6–10   228
4:12   227
4:12–20   227–29
4:13–14   227
4:14–15   175
4:15–16   229n
4:16   228
4:17   228
4:18   228
4:19   228
6:1   88n
6:2   229
6:2a   171n
6:6   229, 236

Ephesians [Eph]
4:15–16   177n

Philippians [Phil]   6, 11n, 226, 233–36, 260
1:5   233n
1:6   233n
1:21–26   233n
1:27   233n, 234
1:30   233n

2:1   233n
2:2   233n, 234
2:6   233n
2:6–8   134n
2:6–11   234
2:17   233n
2:18   233n
2:20   233n
2:25   233n
2:30   234
3:2   97n
3:10   233n
3:17   233n
3:21   233n
4   11n, 234n
4:3   33n, 233n
4:10–11   234
4:10–20   11n, 234
4:11   11n, 234n
4:11–12   172n
4:11–13   235
4:12–20   234
4:13   236
4:14   233n, 235
4:14–16   235
4:14–17   236
4:14–20   235
4:15   233n, 234–35
4:17   235
4:17–18   235
4:17–19   235
4:18   235–36
4:19   236

1 Thessalonians [1 Thess]   6, 226–27
2:17   226
3:6–10   226
4:9–10   226

Index of Ancient Authors and Texts 297

2 Timothy [2 Tim]
   2:25 88n

Titus [Tit]
   1:12 97n

Hebrews [Heb] 11n

James [Jas] 10n
   2:23 225n

4:4 225n

1 John 6, 11n
   2:10 126n
   3:16 225n, 258

3 John
   15 257

5. Non-Canonical Christian Literature

Augustine
  De civitate Dei
  [*De civ. D.*]
    19.3 220n

Clement of Alexandria
  Stromata [*Strom.*]
    2 204n
    2.19.101.1 83

Didache [*Did.*]
   1.3–5 90n

Gospel of Thomas [*Gos. Thom.*]
   95 248n

Hippolytus
  Refutatio omnium
  haeresium [*Ref.*]
  (ed. Marcovich)
    6.27.5 90n

Synesius
  Epistulae [*Ep.*]
    100.17 90n

6. Other Ancient Authors and Texts

Achilles Tatius [Ach. Tat.] 146n, 149n, 156n
  Leucippe and Clitophon 146
    2.4.2 158n
    2.27.2 156n, 158n
    2.33.1 158n
    2.33.2 149n
    3.9–4.5 170n
    3.18.5 149n
    3.21.6 158n
    3.22.1 157n, 168n
    4.10.1 156n
    5.8.1 149n, 156n
    5.14.2 156n
    5.23 167n

    7.6.1 156n
    7.6.6 156n
    7.7.4 158n
    7.9.4 158n
    7.10.1 156n, 158n
    7.14.4 156n, 157n

Aeschines [Aeschin.]
  Or.
    19.248 27n

Aeschylus [Aesch.] 121
  Ag.
    537 32n
  Cho. 121

Albinus 54n
(See Alcinous)

Alcinous 3, 54
Didaskalikos
33.1   209n
33.1–2 (187.13–17)   54n
33.3   204n

Alexander of Aphrodisias [Alex. Aph.]   50
De Anima Mantissa, Supplementum Aristotelicum
2.1.151.7–13   50n

Alexander Polyhistor   82, 90n, 92–93

The Alexander Romance
3.6   173n

Ammonius
De adfinium vocabulorum differentia
208   211n

Andronicus of Rhodes   35, 51, 57, 209
De passionibus
6   209n

Anonymus Diodori   82, 91–92

Antiochus of Ascalon   51, 220

Antonius Diogenes   90n, 93
The Marvels beyond Thule   166n

Aphthonius
Progymn.
11   161n

Apollodorus
Epit.
6.28   157n

Apollonius of Tyana   4, 79, 82, 86, 96, 97n, 183
Epistulae [Ep.]   80–81, 86
1   81, 86
47   81, 86
52   81, 86

Apuleius
De Platone et eius dogmate
13   209n
13–14   204n

Archytas of Tarentum   78

Aristotle [Arist.]   3, 5, 13–15, 26–27, 33–57, 61n, 64n, 80, 83–84, 87–88, 90n, 92–93, 118n, 159–60, 162, 165, 183, 204, 207–11, 213, 243n, 245, 247n
Eth. Eudem. [E.E.]   35–36, 41–42, 54
7   35, 204n
7.1–2 (1234b29–1237a36)   37n
7.2.8 (1236a)   205n
7.2 (1236a15–32)   54n
7.2 (1236a15–35)   37n, 42n
7.2.16 (1236b)   205n
7.2.45–48 (1237b–1238a)   216n
7.2.46 (1238a2)   211n
7.4.7 (1239a)   207n
7.6.6 (1240b)   238n
7.7   62n
7.7.1–3 (1241a1–15)   209n
7.7.3–8 (1241a16–34)   210n
7.7–12 (1241a33–1246a25)   45n
7.10 (1242b31–32)   44n
7.12   62n
7.12.13 (1245a)   210n

Index of Ancient Authors and Texts

7.12 (1245b3–5)   156n
Eth. Nic. [*E.N.*]   35–36, 41–42, 47, 51–52, 54–55, 112, 147
1   36n
1.6 (1098a16–20)   39n
2   36n
2.3 (1104b9)   55n
3   36n
4.1 (1120a23–24)   41n
4.3.24–25 (1124b)   247n
5.3.7–17 (1130a–1131b)   240n
5.5.6 (1133a)   240n
5.6.4 (1134a)   240n
5.10 (1137b11–1138a3)   44n
7   36n
8   35, 36n, 38, 50, 53, 83, 167n
8–9   204n
8.1   64n
8.1 (1155a16–19)   40n
8.1 (1155a16–22)   50n, 55n
8.1 (1155a22–23)   52n
8.1 (1155a22–26)   44n
8.1 (1155a22–28)   40n
8.1 (1155a26–28)   44n
8.2–9.5   62n
8.2.3–4 (1155b–1156a)   209n
8.2 (1155b17–21)   42n
8.2 (1155b17–27)   50n
8.2 (1155b17–1156a5)   39n
8.2–3 (1155b17–1156b32)   37n
8.2 (1155b27–1156a5)   52n
8.2 (1155b32)   113
8.2.4 (1156a)   205n
8.3 (1156a9–10)   44n
8.3 (1156a10–12)   43n
8.3 (1156a19–20)   43n
8.3–4 (1156a35–1157a2)   42n
8.3.8 (1156b)   211n, 216n

8.3 (1156b6)   43n
8.3 (1156b7–32)   37n
8.3 (1156b11–12)   43n
8.3 (1156b25)   156n
8.4 (1157a14–15)   160n
8.4.3 (1157a)   227n
8.4 (1157a25–32)   54n
8.4 (1157a25–33)   42n
8.4 (1157b3)   37n
8.5 (1157b23)   54n
8.5 (1157b28–29)   47n, 55n
8.5.5 (1158a)   240n
8.6.2–3 (1158a)   216n
8.6 (1158a7–10)   52n
8.6.2 (1158a10)   31n
8.6 (1158a10–18)   52n
8.6 (1158b1)   54n
8.6 (1158b1–11)   43n
8.6–7 (1158b1–1159a12)   90
8.6 (1158b5–8)   42n
8.7 (1158b29–35)   87
8.7 (1158b35–1159a5)   87
8.7.5–6 (1159a)   217n
8.7 (1159a5)   86
8.8.1 (1159a)   207n
8.8.4 (1159a-b)   210n
8.8.5 (1159b)   213n, 240n
8.9.1 (1159b)   240n
8.9 (1159b27–28)   158n
8.10 (1160b22–1161a9)   53n
8.10 (1160a35–1160b22)   53n
8.11 (1161a15–29)   40n
8.11 (1161a25)   84
8.11.5 (1161a)   240n
8.11.6 (1161a)   259n
8.11–12 (1161b11–1161b13)   54n
8.12 (1161b12–13)   84

8.12 (1161b35)   84
8.12 (1162a7–9)   47n
8.12 (1162a15–33)   53n
8.12–14 (1162a34–1163b28)   45n
8.13.1 (1162b)   240n
8.13 (1162b21–23)   44n
8.13 (1162b21–1163a8)   44n
8.14 (1163b24)   54n
9   35, 38, 50
9.3.3–5   89n, 167n
9.4   64n
9.4.1 (1166a)   205n
9.4 (1166a1–33)   38n
9.4.5 (1166a)   210n
9.4 (1166a31)   90n
9.4 (1166a31–32)   38n
9.5 (1166b30ff)   113
9.5.1–4 (1167a)   209n
9.5.3 (1167a)   209n
9.6.1–4 (1167a-b)   210n
9.8 (1168a28–1168b10)   50n
9.8 (1168b)   64n, 216n
9.8.2 (1168b)   238, 240n
9.8 (1168b8)   158n
9.8 (1169a18–29)   39n
9.8 (1169a18–1169b2)   41n, 168n
9.9   62n
9.9 (1169b3–7)   38n
9.9 (1169b6–7)   38n
9.9 (1169b8–13)   39n
9.9 (1169b18–19)   40n
9.9 (1169b28–30)   39n
9.9 (1169b30–1170a4)   41n
9.9 (1170a4–11)   43n
9.9.10 (1170b)   210n
9.9 (1170b10–14)   43n
9.10   61n
9.10.1–6 (1170b20–1171a20)   52n, 216n
9.11 (1171b3)   156n
9.12 (1171b33)   158n
10   36n
Magn. Mor. [*MM*]   35, 36n
2.11 (1209a8–9)   54n
2.11 (1209b11–15)   54n
2.11 (1210a7–9)   54n
2.15   90n
2.15.5 (1213a)   210n
Περὶ φιλίας   35n
Pol.   35, 52, 243n
1.1 (1152a24–31)   53n
1.1 (1253a3)   52n
2.1.2 (1261a)   243n
2.1.5 (1261a)   240n
2.1.8–10 (1261b–1262a)   241n
2.1 (1262b7–9)   44n
2.1.15–2.6 (1262b–1263b)   241n
2.2.1 (1262b)   243n
2.2.4–5 (1263a)   244n
2.2.5 (1263a)   244n
4.2 (1289a26–1289b26)   53n
Rhet. [*Rh.*]   35, 47
1.5 (1361b37)   37n
2.1 (1378a18–19)   47n
2.4.1–2 (1380b–1381a)   205n
2.4.1–29 (1380b34–1381b37)   118n
2.4 (1380b37)   37n
2.4 (1381a2)   39n, 52n
2.13   85n
2.13.4 (1389b)   213n
2.21   85n
2.21.13–14 (1395a)   213n

Index of Ancient Authors and Texts

Fragmenta (ed. Rose)
  195   90n

Aristoxenus   91n, 92–93, 97, 99, 101
  Fragmenta (ed. Wehrli)
  31   94n, 97n, 100n

Arius Didymus [Ar. Did.]   3, 36n, 49–53, 55–57
  Epitome (*ap.* Stobaeus, *Ecl.*)   49n
  2.7.52.10   36n
  2.7.73–74 (51)   210n
  2.7.106 (11k)   210n
  2.7.108 (11m)   210n, 217n
  2.7.109.18   52n
  2.7.116.19–152.25   49n
  2.7.118.11–119.4   50n
  2.7.119.22–120.20   56n
  2.7.119.22–121.21   50n, 55n
  2.7.120.8–20   51n
  2.7.120.14   51n
  2.7.120.15–17   52n
  2.7.120.17–20   52n
  2.7.120.20–121.3   53n
  2.7.121.3–8   53n
  2.7.121.4–5   56n
  2.7.137.13–142.13   51n
  2.7.140.8   51n
  2.7.140.12ff   51n
  2.7.143.1–16   49n
  2.7.143.5–8   49n
  2.7.143.8–9   50n
  2.7.143.11   50n
  2.7.143.11–16   50n
  2.7.147.26–152.25   53
  2.7.148.5–8   53n
  2.7.148.16–19   53n
  2.7.151.3–5   53n

Aspasius [Asp.]   3, 35, 36n, 50n, 54–57
  In Ethica Nicomachea [*In Eth. Nic.*], *CAG*   35, 36n
  19.44.12–19   55n
  19.159.26–160.1   56n
  19.159.26–160.7   55n
  19.160.1–2   56n
  19.163.27–164.11   54n
  19.172.8–12   55n

Athenaeus [Ath.]   112n
  Deipnosophistes [*Deipn.*]
  6.236D-E   23
  6.248E   175n
  6.249A   175n
  12.546   63n
  13.561C   210n

Atticus   36n
  Frg.
  2.9   36n

Aulus Gellius
  (see Gellius, Aulus)

Avianus
  Fabulae
  22   175n

Babrius (ed. Perry, *Babrius and Phaedrus*, App.)
  no. 284   176n
  no. 580   175n

Boethus of Sidon   50

Callicratidas   4, 80, 84
  On Household Happiness [*De dom. felic.*] (ed. Thesleff)   84
  103.28–104.3   84
  104.8   84
  104.19–24   84

Calligone 176n

Callimachus 91

Catullus 9
  73 33n

Chariton 3, 5, 145–62, 172
  Callirhoe 5, 145–62, 171n
    1.4.1 159
    1.5 172n
    1.5.2 148, 150, 155
    1.5.2–6.1 150
    1.6.1 150
    1.6.2 150
    1.6.4 157
    1.7–3.2 150
    1.12.6 158–59
    1.12.10 160
    1.13.2 160
    1.13.7–11 161
    1.14.3 160
    1.14.4 160
    1.14.6 160
    2.2.3 157
    2.4.1 158
    2.5.1 157
    2.6.3 158
    2.6.5 159
    2.7.5 159
    2.10.2 159
    2.10.3 159
    2.11.6 159
    3.1.7 157
    3.4.14 150
    3.4.16 151
    3.4.16–18 150
    3.5.7 151, 156
    3.6.2–8 151
    3.6.8 156
    3.7.3 151, 156
    4.2 167n, 173
    4.2.1–2 151
    4.2.2 148
    4.2.11 158
    4.2.14 152, 156, 157
    4.3.1 148
    4.3.4 148
    4.3.5 152, 156
    4.3.6 158
    4.4.1 152, 156
    4.4.7 148, 152
    4.6.1 158
    4.6.5 158
    5.1.1 148
    5.1.4–7 161
    5.2.4 148, 152
    5.2.6 152, 156
    5.4.7 152, 158
    5.4.12–13 158
    5.6.2 158
    5.7.7 158
    5.8.6–7 158
    5.8.9 159
    5.10.6–10 153
    5.10.10 148
    6.2.8 148
    6.2.8–11 153
    6.8.5 158
    6.9.5–7 159
    7.1.2 148, 153
    7.1.2–6 153
    7.1.7 156–57
    7.1.7–8 154
    7.1.10–11 154
    7.2.3 148
    7.3.2 158
    7.5.10 158

Index of Ancient Authors and Texts 303

7.6.5   161
8.1   171n
8.1.6   156
8.1.6–9   154
8.1.12   154
8.1.13   154
8.2.10   158
8.2.13   158
8.3.8   159
8.4.3   158
8.4.4–6   161
8.4.8   159
8.6.9   154
8.7.8   155–56
8.8.4   158
8.8.7   155–56
8.8.10   158
8.8.12   148, 155

Chrysippus   205n, 215n

Cicero [Cic.]   3, 45n, 46n, 47–48, 59–76, 123, 129n, 144, 165, 183, 207, 209, 211, 213n, 214, 244–45, 255
Amic. [= *Lael.*]   3, 14n, 47–48, 59–60, 69, 214
  1.3   68
  4.15   66, 68, 166n, 174n, 240n
  5.18–19   66
  5.19   61n, 68n, 203
  5.19–20   60, 74n, 209n
  6.20   47n, 65–66, 68, 240n
  6.20–22   48n
  6.22   62, 66, 68, 75n, 209n, 259
  7.23   62, 66, 75n, 227n
  8.26   61n, 207n, 210n
  8.26–9.32   60
  8.27   61, 62n, 220n

9.30   66, 172n
9.30–31   68n
9.31   66
9.31–32   66
9.32   62n, 63
9.33–10.35   73n
10.34   64
10.34–13.44   214n
11.36   48n, 135n
11.37   65
11.38   66
12.40   48n, 214n
12.42   48n, 140n, 142n
13.44   48n, 167n, 207n, 214n
13.46   127n
13.46–15.54   63
13.47–48   47n
14.49   62
14.50   62
14.51   66, 89
15.52   62
15.53   68n, 137n
15.55   68, 175n
16.56–17.61   64
16.59   213n
17.61   48n, 65, 214n
17.62–63   65
17.62–64   62–63
17.63–64   66
17.64   64–65, 69n, 137n
18.65   62, 68
18.65–66   62
19.67   211n
19.69–70   64
20.71   133n
20.71–73   64
20.74   68, 166n
21.76   214n

21.77   64
21.78   33
21.80   48n, 68, 75n
22.82   214n
22.83–84   64
22.84   62n, 65
23.86   62n
24.88–25.91   88n
24.88–26.100   23, 207n
24.89–90   62
24.89–26.100   65
25.92   156n
26.100   65
27.100   61, 66, 210n
27.100–1   61
27.104   65

Att.
1.9   75n
1.18.6   69n
1.19.7   63n
1.20.2   69n
1.20.2–3   63n
2.1.6–7   63n
2.3.3   69n
3.15.4   75n
4.1.7   75n
4.7.1   75n
4.15.10   69n
4.19.2   69n
7.15.1   74n
8.14.1   75n
9.10.1   75n
11.5.4   73n
12.34.2   74n
12.39.2   75n
12.53   75n
14.13B.4   73n

Brut.
1.15.2   75n

Cato major [= Sen.]
9.28–29   74n

Comm. petitionis
(see Quintus)

De or.
1.198   75n

Fam.   60n
1.1.3   69n
1.8.1–4   69n
1.9.11   69n
1.9.12   69n
1.9.17–18   69n
1.9.19   73n
1.9.20   69n
2.4.1   74n
2.9.2   75n
2.15.4   75n
3.1.2   71n
3.1.3   60n
3.10.9   60n
3.11.2   75n
4.12.2   60n
5.2.3   68n
5.3.5   75n
5.7   60
5.13.4   75n
5.14.3   75n
5.17.3   75n
5.18.1   75n
5.21.5   75n
6.4.4   74n
6.5.4   75n
6.6.1   74n
6.6.12–13   74n
6.10.4   74n
6.10.4–6   74n
7.1.6   74n

Index of Ancient Authors and Texts

7.5.1   75n
9.14.6   75n
11.15.2   75n
12.26.1   74n
13   76n
13.1.1   75n
13.4.1   67
13.70–71   76
14.7.1   67
15.4   75n
15.4.16   68
15.5.2   67
15.16   75n
16.16.2   75n

Fin.
1.20.65   166n
1.20.67   61n
2.9.28–10.30   214n
2.14.45   220n
2.24.78   210n
2.24.78–26.85a   209n
2.26.82   68
3.6.20   61n
3.19.62–63   220n
3.21.70   209n
5.23.65   220n
5.23.65–66   61n

In Verr.
2.3.181   70n

Inv.
2.166   68n

Lael. (see *Amic.*)

Leg.
1.34   220n
1.49   209n

Mur.
70–71   71n

Off. [*De off.*]   47

1.7.20   68
1.11.34–35   213n
1.13.41   71n
1.15.47   67
1.16.51   56n, 68, 244
1.16.51–52   244
1.16.52   56n
1.17.55–56   47n
1.17.56   68, 75n, 90n, 210n
1.17.58   61n, 74n
1.42.150–51   253n
1.44.158   61n
2   63n
2.2.5   211n
2.15.54   244n
2.15.55–16.56   245n
3   61n
3.10.45   91n
3.17.69   74n

Part. or.
78   68
88   68

Phil.
1.10.   73n
1.14   73n
5.19   73n
12.14   73n

Planc.
5   68
80   68n
81   67–68

Pro S. Roscio Amerino
111   68n

QF
1.1.20   68n
1.1.45   74n, 75n
1.2.10   68n
2.2.2   69n

2.9.2   69n
2.12.5   69n
Rep.
  1.43   71n
  1.69   71n
  2.16.59 71n
Sen. (see *Cato major*)
Tusc. disp. [*Tusc.*]
  5.1–4 75n
  5.22   91n

CIJ
  1452   191n
  1453   191n
  1456   191n
  1460   191n
  1464   191n
  1466   191n
  1468   191n
  1470   191n
  1471   191n
  1473   191n
  1474   191n
  1475   191n
  1483   191n
  1488   191n
  1490   191
  1493   191n
  1494   191n
  1495   191n
  1497   191n
  1498   191n
  1500   191n
  1501   191n
  1502   191n
  1504   191n
  1512   199
  1513   191n
  1514   191n
  1518   191n
  1519   191n
  1521   191n
  1523   191n
  1526   191n
  1528   191n

Cleanthes 205n

Clitarchus 81n, 86
  Sayings/Sentences of Clitarchus
    [*Sent.*]   4, 81, 86–87
    88   87
    90   87
    91   87
    92   87
    141 87

Commentariolum petitionis (see under Quintus)

Corpus paroemiographorum Graecorum (ed. Leutsch and Schneidewin)
  2.359   85n
  2.760   90n

Ps.-Crates
  Ep.
    7   172n

Demetrius of Scepsis 24

Ps.-Demetrius 185
  Typoi Epist. 183n
    1   185n

Democritus 81, 247n
  Fragmenta (Diels-Kranz, *Vorsokr.*)
    47   89n

Index of Ancient Authors and Texts

Demosthenes
  Orationes
    Or. 18 (*De corona*)
      109 27n
    Or. 23 (*Ag. Arist.*)
      122 213n

Dio Chrysostom [Dio Chrys.]
  Orat. [*Or.*]
    4.42 158n
    17.9–10 240n
    44.2 256n

Diodorus Siculus (Diodorus of Sicily) [Diod. Sic.] 82, 85, 91–92, 94, 138n
  10.3–11 91
  10.3.5 91
  10.4.1 91
  10.4.2 91
  10.4.3 94n
  10.4.3–6 91
  10.8.1 92
  10.8.2–3 92
  12.20.3 85, 93n

Diogenes Laertius [Diog. Laert. = D. L.] 82, 96
  Vitae philosophorum
    1.87 213n
    6.63 216n
    6.69 65n
    7.32–33 217n
    7.115 209n
    7.116 209n
    7.120 51n
    7.124 61n, 210n, 217n
    7.174 205n
    8 80, 92–93
    8.1–50 92
    8.10 64, 77n, 90n, 92, 208n, 216n, 240n
    8.16 93
    8.17 90n
    8.23 92, 213n
    8.33 90n, 93
    8.35 90n, 93
    10.120 61n, 63n

Dionysius of Halicarnassus [Dion. Hal.] 3–4, 123–44
  Ant. Rom. [*AR*] 4, 123–44
    2.8–11 123n
    2.11 132n
    3 123–27, 143
    3.3.1 124
    3.3.5 124
    3.5.2 124
    3.6.3 124
    3.7.1 125
    3.7.3 125
    3.8.4–5 125
    3.9.2 125
    3.9.4 125
    3.9.7 125
    3.10–11 125
    3.11.9 137
    3.13.4 126
    3.15.2 126
    3.16.2 126
    3.16.3 126
    3.17.5 126
    3.18–20 126
    3.21.3 126
    3.21.6 97n, 126
    6 123, 127–31, 144
    6.22–92 127
    6.22.1 127
    6.23.1 127

6.23.3 130n	6.83.3 129–30
6.24.3 127	6.83.4 130
6.26 130	6.86.1 129–30
6.26.1 127	6.92.3–93.3 132
6.26.2–3 128	6.92–8.62 131
6.28.1 127	6.94.2 131
6.35.2 128	7 123, 131–35, 144
6.36.1 97n, 128	7.4.4 132
6.40.3 128	7.8.1 130n
6.41.1 128	7.15 132
6.41.2 128	7.18.1 132
6.43.1 128	7.20.4 132
6.45.2–3 129	7.21.1 132
6.47.4 128	7.21.3 132
6.49.2 128	7.22.1 132
6.51.1 128	7.23.4 132
6.54.1 128	7.27.1–2 132
6.54.2 129	7.27.3 132
6.55.3 129	7.30.1 132
6.56.3 129	7.32.3 132
6.56.5 129	7.33.1 132
6.58.3 129–30	7.34.1 129n
6.59.1 129	7.34.2–5 133
6.59.3 129	7.35.3 133
6.60.1 129	7.44.1 133
6.60.3 129	7.44.2 133
6.63.3 129	7.44.3–4 133
6.66.1 129	7.45.4 133
6.69.2 129	7.46.6 133, 135
6.71.2 128	7.47.2 133
6.73.1 129	7.53.3 133
6.78.1 129–30	7.53.6 133
6.78.4 129–30	7.54.3–4 133
6.80.2 130	7.54.5 134
6.80.4 130	7.55.2 134
6.81.3 130n	7.58.3 128n
6.82.1–3 130	7.59.2 134
6.83.2 130	7.59.3–6 128n

7.59.8 134	8.39.3 138
7.60.1–2 134	8.39.4–5 139
7.62.2 134	8.40.3 139
7.62.3 134	8.40.4 138n
7.63.1 133	8.41.2 139
7.63.3 134	8.41.4 139
7.64.6 134	8.41.6 134
7.65.1 130, 134	8.42.1–2 139, 142
7.65.5 134	8.44.2 126
7.66.3 131, 135	8.44.4 139
7.66.5 131, 135	8.45.2 140
7.67.3 134	8.47.3 138
7.70–73 134n	8.47.4 140
8 123, 135–44	8.48–53 140
8.1.2 135	8.48.1 140
8.1.4 129n	8.48.4 140
8.1.5–6 135	8.49.2 140
8.2.38–40 138n	8.49.6 140
8.2.45–46 138n	8.50 141
8.6.2–3 128n	8.50.3 138, 143
8.7.1 135	8.50.4 141n, 143
8.7.3 136	8.51.3 141
8.9.3 136	8.51.5 141n
8.10.1 136	8.52.2 141
8.15.2 136	8.53.1–3 141
8.22.4 136	8.53.4 141, 143
8.23.2 136	8.54.1 141
8.25.2 136	8.54.2 141
8.25.3 136	8.56.1 141
8.28.1 137	8.57 142
8.28.4 137	8.59.1–2 142
8.29.1–2 137	8.60 142
8.32.3 137	8.61.1 142
8.32.5 138, 141n	8.61.2–3 143
8.33.3 136	8.61.3 142
8.34.1 138, 141n	8.62.3 131
8.34.1–3 138, 142	14.5.5–6 218n
8.35.4 138	

Ennius   56n, 244n

Epictetus [Epict.]   9, 81
   Diss.
      2.4.8–11   241n
      2.7.3   168n, 231n
      2.22   9n
      2.22.37   156n
      3.13.5   52n
      3.22.62–66   9n
      3.24   62n
      4.5.10   52n
   Ench.
      32.3   156n

Epicurus [Epicur.]   8, 61n, 63n, 65n, 208, 214, 249n
   Epistulae [Ep.] Letter to Pythocles
      62n
   Ratae sententiae [RS] (Principal Doctrines)
      18   63n
      26   63n
      27–28   61n
      29   63n

Eratosthenes   218n

Eudemus   45, 54

Euripides [Eur.]   7, 121n
   El.   121
      1249   157n
   Or.   121n
      1658   157n

Eustathius
   In Iliadem [In Il.]
      4.54.22   90n

Fragmente der Vorsokratiker (ed. Diels-Kranz)
   1.389–91 [39]   83n
   1.462–66 [58C]   82n
   1.471–73 [58D7]   97n
   1.477–78 [58D9]   97n
   1.478–80 [58E]   78n
   2.156 [66.47]   89n

Gellius, Aulus [Gell.]   46n, 48, 49n, 214
   Noctes Atticae [NA]
      1.3.8–14   46n
      1.3.10–11   48n
      1.3.10–13   214n
      1.3.10–18   48n
      1.3.10–29   48n
      1.3.19–20   48n
      1.3.21–29   46n
      1.3.23   214n

The Golden Verses (ed. Thom)   4, 81, 87–90
   1–4   88
   5–8   88
   6   89
   8a   90
   8b   90

Heliodorus [Hel.]   167n
   Ethiopian Story   146
      1.9   167n

Hermippus   35n

Hesiod [Hes.]   3, 13, 15, 30–32
   Op.
      174–201   30
      184   30n
      707–14   32

Index of Ancient Authors and Texts

Hippodamus 4, 80, 83–84
  On Happiness (ed. Thesleff) 83
    97.14–15 83

Homer [Hom.] 3, 13–29, 31, 156n, 179
  Iliad [*Il.*] 15, 25–26, 28
    1.1 25
    2.379–80 26
    3.73 21n
    3.256 21n
    3.323 21n
    3.354 24n
    3.453–54 26n
    4 21
    4.360–61 22
    5.695 19n
    6 21n
    6.14 21n
    6.14–15 21n
    6.119–236 21n
    7.301–02 23n
    9.120 26n
    9.204 19
    9.205 19
    9.528 18n
    9.630 19
    9.630–31 28
    9.641–42 19
    10.522 19n
    11.616 19
    13.249 20
    13.487 22
    13.653 19n
    15.650 19n
    15.710 22
    16 25
    16.219 22
    16.280–82 26
    16.491 19n
    17.267 22
    17.411 20
    17.557 19n
    17.576–77 23
    17.577 23
    17.578 24
    17.589–90 23
    17.642 19
    17.655 20
    18.80 19
    18.80–82 20n
    18.98 20n
    18.114 19
    18.233 19
    18.235 19n
    18.460 19n
    19.305 19
    19.315 20
    21.106 18n
    22 22
    22.262–65 22
    22.263 22n
    22.390 19
    23.77 19
    23.178 19
    23.556 19n
    23.563 19n
    23.695 19n
    24.123 19
    24.591 19
    24.775 15n
  Odyssey [*Ody.*] 15, 25n
    1.313 15n
    2.333 18n
    3.103 22
    3.126–29 23
    3.130–50 23

3.199   22
3.211   22
3.313   22
3.375   22
4.722   18n
6.121   20n
6.180–85   22
7.301–02   26n
8   24
8.21   21n
8.209–11   24
8.576   20n
8.585–86   19n
13.202   20n
15.22   18n
15.68–74   25
15.195–98   22

Horace [Hor.]   9
Epistulae [Ep.]
    1.18.44–45   88n

Hyginus
Fabulae [Fab.]
    257   91n

Iamblichus
Babyloniaca
    3   176n

Iamblichus of Chalcis [Iambl.]   80, 82–83, 87, 91n, 93n, 96n
De vita Pythagorica [VP]   83, 95–102
    32   95
    37–44   96
    40   96
    45–46   99n
    60–62   98n
    69   83n, 93, 97
    69–70   97
    70   99
    86   90n, 95n
    101   88n, 89n, 99–100
    101–2   89n, 97
    102   100
    107–8   98n
    134–56   95
    157–66   95
    162   90n, 95n
    167–68   99n
    167–69   238n
    167–86   95
    168   98n, 238n
    185   100n
    187–213   95
    189–94   94, 95n
    214–28   95
    229   83n, 93, 97, 222n
    229–30   97, 99, 222n
    229–40   95
    230   77, 89n, 99
    230–31   88n, 89n
    230–32   97
    231   88n, 100
    232   89n, 100
    233   100
    233–36   97n
    234–36   91n, 94n, 101
    234–39   101
    237–38   101
    239   101
    240   101
    259   96
In Nicomachi arithmeticam [In Nicom. arith.]
    35.6   90n

Index of Ancient Authors and Texts

Prot.
  108.2   90n
  122.15–21   90n
  123.12   52n

Isocrates [Isoc.]   218
  Orationes
  Or. 1 (*To Demonicus*)
    22   207n
    24   207n
  Or. 4 (*Panegyricus*)
    50   218n
  Or. 7 (*Areopagiticus*)
    35   244n
    83   244n
    84   244n

Julius Victor   184
  Art of Rhetoric
    27   184n

Juvenal [Juv.]   9, 105, 108n, 120n
  Sat.   120n
    1.95–126   108n, 109n
    5.12–23   249n
    5.167–73   249n
    10.12–18   109n
    10.43–46   108n

Libanius [Lib.]   107n
  Progymn.
    3   156n

Ps.-Libanius
  Epist. Char.   183n

The Life of Secundus
  11   9n

Livy
  1.22–26   124
  2.21–25   127
  2.33–35   131
  2.36–40   135n

Longus   146n
  Daphnis and Chloe   146

Lucian   3, 5, 163–80
  De Syria Dea   165n
  Merc. Cond.
    19–20   238n
  Navig.   163n
  Peregr.   173n
  Philops.   163n
    13   168n
  Tox.   5, 147–48, 155, 163–80, 206, 227n
    6   149
    7   156n, 158n
    8   166n
    9   166
    10   148n, 156n, 157n, 166n
    10–11   164
    12–18   127n, 148, 166, 206n
    15   167n
    18   156n, 167n, 171n
    19   168n
    19–21   168, 174n
    20   158n, 168n
    21   168
    22–23   169, 176n
    22–24   179
    23   169
    24–26   169
    26   170n
    27–34   148, 170
    28   158n
    30   171n
    32   158n, 171n, 209n
    34   175n

35   166n, 172n, 174n
36   174n, 231n
37   174, 206n, 209n, 217n
38   166n
38–41   174
41   175n
42   175n
44–55   169n, 176
46   177
53   177, 179n
56   178
58   156n
58–60   157n
60   156n, 157n
61   178
62–63   164
63   166n
Ver. Hist.   163n
1.6   168n
1.25   175n
2.4   168n

Lucretius [Lucr.]   8
De rerum natura

**Marcus Aurelius
[Mar. Ant.]**
Med.
7.13.55   129n

Martial   9n

Maximus of Tyre [Max. Tyr.]   207
Orationes [Or.]
14   23, 65n
14.18   207n

Menander   7n, 229
Dysk.
233–392   157n
748–83   157n

Nicomachus of Gerasa   79, 82, 94, 97n

Numenius of Apamea   79

Olympiodorus [Olymp.]
In Platonis Alcibiadem [In Plat. Alcib.]
31.18   90n

P. Amh.   186n
II.131   194n
II.154   189

Panaetius   8, 48n, 49n, 56n, 63n, 213

P. Ant.   186n
I.44   194

P. Cair.
47992   176n

P. Col.   186n

Petronius [Petron.]
Sat.   168n
1.1   175n
144.10   168n

P. Fay.   186n
131   194

P. Freib.   186n

P. Giss.   186n

P. Harris   186n

P. Heid.   186n

P. Herc.
(See Philodemus)

P. Hib. 186n

Philodemus 23n, 116n, 207
  De adulatione [*Adul.*] (*On Flattery*) 207n
    [PHerc. 222, 223, 1082, 1089, 1457, 1675]
  De libertate dicendi 23, 207 [*Lib.*] [PHerc. 1471] (*On Frank Criticism*)

Philostratus [Philostr.] 196n
  Vita Apollonii [*VA*] 81

Phocylides [Phoc.]
  2A 33n

Plato [Pl.] 3, 7, 38–40, 43, 57n, 208, 216, 240–42, 245n
  Ap.
    31B-C 65n
  Critias
    110C 238n
    110D 241n
  Crito
    45A-B 65n
  Gorg. [*Grg.*]
    420C 65n
    507E-F 99n
  Leg.
    678B 241n
    716C 54
    888A 88n
  Ly. 7n, 205, 208n
    207c 216n
    208e 227n
    211e2–3 39n
    211e7 39n
    212a5 39n
    212a-b 210n
    214d–216e 216n
    223b 205n
  Phdr. 7n
    233C 89n
  Resp.
    3.413C–417B 241n
    3.416D–417B 241n
    5.462C 238n
    5.462E–464B 241n
    8.543A-C 241n
  Soph.
    233D 65n
  Symp. 7n, 39
    179b 168n, 231n
    192e 177n
    199e6–201a7 39n
    200d2 39n
    204a1–2 39n
    208d 168n, 231n
  Tim.
    18B 241n

P. Leid.Inst. 186n
  31 193, 194n

Pliny 9n, 183

P. Lond. 186n
  II.356 194
  II.2448 195n

Plotinus 57n, 101n, 196n

Plutarch [Plut.] 3–4, 23n, 45, 105–22, 127n, 137n, 165, 207, 211, 217–18, 240n, 245
  Moralia [*Mor.*] 106, 111, 114, 116, 122
  De liber. ed.
    12E 90n

Quomodo adulator ab amico internoscatur ["Flatterer"]
  4, 11n, 23, 65n, 105, 110, 113n
  48E–59A 207
  48E–74E 207n
  49C 109
  49C-D 120
  49D-E 121
  49F 114, 118–19
  51A-B 114
  51B 115, 118
  51C 240n
  51C-D 119
  52A 116–17
  53B 113
  53C 113
  53F–54B 207n
  54D-E 114
  54F 119
  55A 115, 120
  55D 119
  55E–60B 113
  55E–62B 116
  56A 113
  59A–74E 207
  61B 121
  65A 120
  65B 121
  65E–74E 116
  70E 116
  73C-D 117
De cap. ex in. ut. 105
De amicorum mult. ["Friends"] 4, 31n, 105, 108, 110, 113n, 122
  93A–97B 217n
  93C 121
  93D 117
  93E 107n, 120–21, 156n, 157n, 166n
  93F 119, 158n, 209n
  94A 211n
  94A-B 109
  94B 89, 108
  95B 113
  95C 156n
  96A 90n
  96D-F 240n
  96F 156n, 158n, 238n
  96F–97A 115
Coniug. praec. 105, 106n
  140D 245n
  143A 238n
Reg. et imp. ap. 111
  173D 249n
  181–82 249n
Ap. Lac. 111
In. Lac. 111
Lac. ap. 111
Mul. virt. 164n
Quaest. Rom.
  266A 245n
De Alex. fort.
  329C-D 218n
  329D 218n
De coh. ira
  457D 110n
De tranq. anim. 111
  464F 110n
De frat. amor. 89n, 105, 106n
  478B 209n
  478E 220n
  479C-D 106, 220n
  481C 209n
  482B 209n, 211n
  487A 107

Index of Ancient Authors and Texts

490E   120n
De amor. prol.   105, 106n
De invid. et odio   106, 118n
  538E   118
De se ips. c. i. laud.   105
Quaest. conv.
  644C-D   245n
  743E   245n
Amat.   137n
  750D   137n
  751B   137n
  751C-D   137n
  752C   137n
  756E   137n
  757C-E   137n
  758C   137n
  766D–771C   137n
  767E   137n, 245n
  768E   137n
  769A   137n
  769C-D   137n
  770A-B   137n
Max. c. princ. phil.
  778C   249n
Praec. ger. reip.   106
Vit. X orat.
  842D   116
De Stoic. repugn.
  1039D   205n, 215n
Non poss. suav. viv.
  sec. Epic.
  1102F   120n, 245n

Adv. Colotem
  1127D   214n
Fragmenta
  159–71 (*Epistle on Friendship*)
  106

Vitae parallelae   106, 111, 114, 116, 122
  Alc.   105n
  Alex.
    64   173n
  Cor.   138n
De vita Homeri [*Vit. Hom.*] (ed. Bernadakis)
  151   90n

P. Mert.   186n
  I.12   186, 201
  I.24   193, 194n
  I.28   193n

P. Mich.   186n

P. Michael.   186n

Polybius [Polyb.]
  1.14.3–5   124n

Porphyry   80, 82, 91n, 93–94
  De vita Pythagorae [*VP*]   93–95
    13   93
    23–25   98n
    33   38n, 90n, 94
    59–61   91n, 94

P. Oslo   186n

P. Oxy.   186n
  I.32   195, 197
  I.110   191n
  I.111   191n
  I.112   191n
  I.115   194
  III.472   191n
  III.490   193, 199
  III.523   191n
  III.524   191n
  III.530   194n

IV.706   188
IV.724   190
IV.742   194
IV.745   195
IV.747   191n
VI.907   193
VI.926   191n
VI.933   194
VII.1062   195n
VIII.1109   190
VIII.1155   193n
VIII.1158   194, 195n
IX.1214   191n
XII.1427   190n
XII.1477   190, 191n
XII.1483   195
XII.1484   191n
XII.1485   191n
XII.1486   191n
XII.1487   191n
XIV.1635   188n
XIV.1657   194, 198
XIV.1676   193n
XVI.1841   189n
XVI.1843   189
XVI.1845   189
XVI.1863   189
XVI.1872   199n
XXII.2348   192
XXXI.2603   187, 195, 199, 201
XXXIV.2726   194, 195n
XXXIV.2732   195n, 199n
XXXVI.2754   188
XXXVIII.2855   190
XXXVIII.2861   195n
XXXVIII.2869   190n
XLI.2975   195n
XLI.2976   191

XLI.2983   195n
XLI.2996   195n
XLII.3022   188
XLII.3069   196
LI.3643   195
LI.3644   195

P. Petrie   186n

P. Princ.   186n

Proclus   183n

P. Ryl.   186n
  II.153   192

PSI
  981   176n

P. Strassb.   186n

P. Tebt.   186n
  I.33   170n
  II.314   196
  II.412   193n
  II.413   198
  II.418   194

Ptolemy   35n, 36n

P. Wash. Univ.   186n

Pythagoras   3–4, 77–78, 80–82, 91–94, 96–98, 99n, 208n, 210n, 216, 222n
  Orat. (ed. Thesleff)
    1.178–80   96

Pythgorean Golden Verses (see *The Golden Verses*)

Pythagorean Letters [*Pyth. Ep.*]   85–86
  Ep. 6 (Theano to Nicostrate)   4, 81, 85
  6.5   85

Index of Ancient Authors and Texts 319

Pythagorean Memoirs 82, 93

Pythagorean Sayings 4, 81, 86–87
  33 87
  34 87
  76 87
  97 87

Quintus 3, 59, 66n
  Commentariolum petitionis 3, 59, 66, 69–73
    3 70–72
    4 72
    5 70
    16 70, 72–73
    17 71
    18 70
    19 71
    20 72
    25–26 73
    29 71
    31 71
    31–32 73
    32 71
    33 72
    36–38 71

Royal Correspondence in the Hellenistic Period (ed. Welles)
  1 67n
  14 67n
  15.10–12 67n
  22.15–17 67n
  23 67n
  45 67n
  65–67 67n

Sacred Discourse 92n, 96

Sayings of Clitarchus (see Clitarchus)

Sayings of Sextus (see Sextus)

SB 186
  I.4456 192
  I.5629 198
  III.6041 192
  III.6230 191n
  V.7883 191
  V.8089 193n
  V.8230 188n
  V.8664 192
  V.8874 188n
  V.8892 188n
  VI.9017, no. 20 198
  X.10463 199n
  X.10500 192
  X.10664 188n
  XII.10803 193n
  XII.10841 199n
  XII.11016 193n
  XII.11127 193n

Scholia in Iliadem [Schol. *Il.*]
  18.82 90n

Secundus 9
  (see also *The Life of Secundus*)

Seneca [Sen.] 8, 79, 183, 233, 245, 247n
  Moral Epistles 112
  Ep.
    3 8n
    6.2 157n
    9 8n, 62n
    9.10 167n, 168n, 231n
    9.14–15 238n
    33.7 111
    35 8n, 64n
    48 8n
    55 62n
    63 8n, 62n

81   245n
81.17   249n
89.5   211n
90   238n
90.2–6   240n
90.38   241n
94   8n
95.48   68n
103   8n
109   8n
Moral Essays   112
Ben.
  4.17.2   219n
  4.20.3   68n
  6.34   61n
  7.4.2   245n
  7.4.7   245n
  7.12   65n
  7.12.3–5   245n
De moribus
  frg. 13   116

Sentences of Clitarchus (see Clitarchus)

Sentences of Sextus
  (see Sextus)

Sextus   81n, 86
  Sayings/Sentences of Sextus [*Sent.*]
    4, 81, 86–87
  86b   87
  105   87
  293   89n

Sextus Empiricus [**Sext. Emp.**]
  Math. [*M*]
  9.13   211n
  9.75   211n

Simplicius [**Simplic.**]   46, 47n
  In Aristotelis Categorias [*In Ar. Cat.*],
    CAG
  8.235.3–13   46n

Sophocles [**Soph.**]   141n
  Aj.
    679–83   213n
  Ant.   141n
    10   36n
    11   36n
    73   36n
    99   36n
    847   36n
    898–99   36n
  El.   121

Statius   9n

Stobaeus [**Stob.**] (ed. Wachsmuth
  and Hense)   80, 97n, 207
  Ecl.   49
    2.7 (see Arius Didymus)
    3.13 (3:453–68)   207n
    3.14 (3:468–76)   207n
    3.41 (3:757–59)   207n

Stoicorum Veterum Fragmenta [*SVF*]
  (ed. von Arnim)
  1.54 (§222)   217n
  1.61 (§263)   210n
  1.107 (§481)   205n
  2.15 (§36)   211n
  2.112 (§311)   211n
  3.12 (§43)   209n
  3.25 (§106)   62n
  3.26–27 (§112)   62n, 204n,
    210n
  3.105 (§431)   209n
  3.105 (§432)   209n

Index of Ancient Authors and Texts

3.160–61 (§630)   210n, 217n
3.161 (§631)   210n, 217n
3.166 (§661)   210n
3.172.14–173.3 (§686)   52n
3.181.32–37 (§723)   48n, 61n, 204n
3.182 (§724)   205n, 215n
3.183.22–25 (§731)   51n

Strabo [Strab.]
  1.4.9   218n

Tacitus   9n

Teles   172n

Terence [Ter.]   247n

Theano (see *Pythagorean Letters*)

Theognis = Theognidea   3, 13, 15, 29–32, 34n
  61–68   29
  63–65   29
  69–72   29
  73–74   29
  75–76   29
  77–78   30
  79–82   30
  83–86   30
  87–90   29
  91–92   29
  93–96   29
  97–100   30
  101–04   29
  105–12   29
  113–14   29
  115–16   30
  117–18   30
  119–28   30
  209–10   30
  213–18   29
  221–26   30
  237–54   30
  253–54   29
  271–78   29
  283–86   29
  299–300   30
  301–02   29
  305–08   29
  309–12   29
  313–14   29
  323–24   29
  325–28   33
  332a-b   30
  333–34   29
  399–400   29
  415–18   30
  447–52   30
  511–22   30
  529–30   30
  571–72   30
  575–76   29
  599–602   29
  641–42   30
  643–44   30
  645–46   30
  697–98   30
  811–13   29
  851–52   29
  857–60   30
  861–62   29
  869–72   30
  929–30   30
  963–66   29
  963–70   30
  967–70   29
  979–82   29
  1016   30
  1071–74   29

1079–80   30
1082c–f   29
1083–84   29
1087–90   30, 32
1097–1100   29
1101–02   29
1104a–06   30
1151–52   29
1164a–d   30
1164e–h   30
1219–20   30
1238a–b   29
1238a–40   29
1239–40   29
1241–42   29
1243–44   29
1245–46   29
1263–66   29
1278a–b   29
1283–94   29
1311–18   29–30
1361–62   29
1363–64   30
1377–80   29

Theophrastus   3, 35, 45–46, 48, 49n, 51, 57, 120n, 207, 213–14
  Fragmenta (ed. Fortenbaugh, Huby, Sharples, and Gutas)
    2.264 (frg. 438)   46n
    2.352 (frg. 532)   45n
    2.352 (frg. 533)   45n
    2.353–73 (frgs. 532–46)   214n
    2.354 (frg. 534)   46n
    2.356 (frg. 534)   214n
    2.358 (frg. 534)   214n
    2.360 (frg. 535)   46n
    2.360 (frg. 536)   46n
    2.360 (frg. 537)   46n
    2.362 (frg. 538A)   46n
    2.362 (frg. 538B)   46n
    2.362 (frg. 538C)   46n
    2.362 (frg. 538D)   46n
    2.364 (frg. 538E)   46n
    2.364 (frg. 538F)   46n
    2.364 (frg. 540)   46n
    2.366 (frg. 541)   46n
    2.366 (frg. 542)   46n
    2.368 (frg. 543)   46n
    2.373 (frgs. 547–48)   207n

Thucydides [Thuc.]   7, 249n
  2.40.4–5   7n
  2.97.4   249n

Timaeus of Tauromenium   90n, 92, 96

Valerius Maximus
  4.7   166n

Vita Aesopi
  109   88n

Xenarchus   50

Xenophon [Xen.]   7, 36n, 229
  Cyr.
    8.2.1–22   249n
    8.2.7   249n
    8.2.14   249n
    8.7.13   7n
  Hell.
    2.3.15   7n
    2.3.43   7n
    4.1.34–35   27n
  Mem.
    1.2.7   65n
    1.2.8   7n
    1.2.14   65n

1.2.52–55   7n
2.2.2   36n
2.4.1–2.6.39   7n
2.4.6   65n
2.6.23   65n
2.9–10   89
3.7.9   36n
3.11.4   65n
4.2.40   65n

Xenophon of Ephesus [Xen. Eph.]
   146n, 149n
Ephesian Tale   146
   2.14.2   149n
   3.3.6   149n
   3.6.4   158n

4.4.1   172n
5.7   169n
5.8   167n
5.9.9   149n
5.9.13   149n
5.15.3–4   149n

Zaleucus   4, 80, 84–85, 93n, 96
   Preambles to the Laws [*Prooem.*] (ed. Thesleff)   84–85
   226.18–21   85
   226.21–22   85
   227.29–228.1   85
   228.10–12   85

Zeno of Citium   210n, 217n

INDEX OF MODERN SCHOLARS

Adkins, A. W. H.   13, 15n, 16n, 21n
Albrecht, M. von   95n, 98n, 99n, 101, 102n, 103n
Alföldy, G.   246n, 252n
Alfonsi, L.   9n
Allen, W., Jr.   8n
Anderson, G.   149n, 163n, 165, 176n, 178n
Annas, J.   7n
Antonaccio, C. M.   27n
Argyle, M.   2n
Armstrong, A. H.   36n
Arnim, H. F. A. von   7n, 49n, 52n, 204n
Atkinson, K. C.   188n
Aune, D. E.   vii, 9n
Babbitt, F. C.   107n, 116, 122n
Badhwar, N. K.   2n
Balch, D. L.   4, 53, 79n, 80n, 82n, 84, 93n, 97n, 103n, 123, 127n, 130n, 134n, 170n, 204n, 233n, 246n
Baldry, H. C.   220n, 240n, 245n
Balsdon, J. P. V. D.   69n
Bammel, E.   10n
Barton, C. A.   178n
Bell, R. R.   2n
Benveniste, É.   16n, 17n, 18n, 20n
Berkowitz, L.   87n
Bernard, A.   186n
Bernard, E.   186n
Berry, K. L.   11n, 234n
Bethge, E.   2n
Betz, H. D.   88n, 166n, 171n, 175n, 227–29
Billerbeck, M.   9n

Birnbaum, E.   221n, 222n
Blake, W. E.   148n
Bloom, A.   2n
Blum, L. A.   2n
Blundell, M. W.   9n, 22n, 141n
Boas, G.   241n
Boehm, F.   82n
Bohnenblust, G.   14n, 112n, 147n, 156n, 157n, 158n, 227n, 240n, 256
Bollack, J.   8n
Bolotin, D.   7n
Bompaire, J.   164n
Bonhoeffer, D.   2n
Bonhöffer, A.   9n
Borgen, P.   221n
Bowersock, G.   166n
Bowie, E. L.   145n, 146n
Bowman, A. K.   194n, 197n
Bowra, C. M.   30n, 31n
Braun, H.   242n
Brawley, R. L.   124n
Brescia, C.   8n
Breytenbach, C.   125n, 141n
Brinckmann, W.   8n
Bringmann, K.   47n, 48n, 49n, 60n
Brown, P. G. McC.   8n
Brown, R. E.   258n, 259n
Brunt, P. A.   9n, 62n, 69, 135n
Buechner, K.   9n, 60n
Bultmann, R.   248n, 258n
Burkert, W.   79n, 82n, 84n, 91n, 94n, 95n, 96n, 97n
Cameron, A.   137n
Carpenter, E.   14n
Carrière, J.   29n, 34n

324

Index of Modern Scholars

Cary, E.   123n
Caster, M.   178n
Cerfaux. L.   237n, 238n, 250n
Cesa, M.   138n
Chadwick, H.   81n, 86n
Chantraine, P.   15n, 17n
Charlesworth, J. C.   221n
Cobb-Stevens, V.   29n
Cobet, C. G.   94n
Conzelmann, H.   237n, 243n, 249n
Cooper, J. M.   41n, 44n, 208n
Craik, E. M.   16n
Cranfield, C. E. B.   231n
Croix, G. E. M. de Ste.   127n
Culham, P.   146n
Culpepper, R. A.   258n
Curtius, E.   16n
Danker, F. W.   256n
David, J. L.   126n
Degenhardt, H. J.   239n, 242n, 247n, 249n, 251n, 253n
Deissmann, A.   231n
De Lacy, P.   118n
Delatte, A.   77n, 82n, 90n, 92
Della Casa, A.   79n
Del Re, R.   79n
Del Verme, M.   242n, 251n
Den Boer, W.   245n, 246n
Denton, J.   138n
Derrida, J.   2n
Derron, P.   204n
Deubner, L.   95n
De Witt, N. W.   8n
Diano, C.   8n
Dibelius, M.   258n
Diels, H.   78n, 82n, 83n, 89n, 97n
Dihle, A.   10n, 89
Dillon, J.   82n, 95n, 222n

Dirlmeier, F.   14n, 99n
Dobbeler, A. von   258n
Donlan, W.   28–29, 30n, 31
Donner, H.   10n
Dorey, T. A.   67n, 69n, 72n, 73n, 74n
Dörrie, H.   78n
Drinkwater, J.   247n
Duck, S.   2n
Dugas, L.   14n, 61n, 62n, 64n, 65n, 66n, 67n
Dupont, J.   237n, 238n, 239n, 242n, 243n, 250n, 251n, 252n, 256n
Ebner, M.   234–36, 259–69
Eckert, K.   9n
Edgar, G. C.   170n
Edmunds, L.   146n
Edwards, M. W.   20n
Edwards, R. A.   81n, 86n, 248n
Edwards, R. R.   10n
Egenter, R.   10n
Egger, B.   147n
Eglinger, R.   14n
Einarson, B.   118n
Eisenstein, E. L.   110n
Eliot, G.   59
Elter, A.   81n
Engberg-Pedersen, T.   9n, 11n, 23n, 57n
Enright, D. J.   2n
Ernest, J. D.   17n
Esler, P.   246, 253n
Evans, K. G.   5, 181, 184n
Exler, F. X. J.   184
Faerber, H.   60n
Fagles, R.   21n, 26n
Faltner, M.   60n
Farrington, B.   8n

Ferguson, E.   10n, 127n, 170n, 204n, 233n
Ferguson, J.   14n, 16n, 17n
Festugière, A.-J.   8n, 82n
Figueira, T. J.   28n, 29n
Finley, M. I.   20n, 253n
Fiore, B.   3, 45n, 59, 129n, 231–32
Fiske, A. M.   10n, 199n
Fitzgerald, J. T.   vii, 9n, 10n, 11, 13, 20n, 23n, 24n, 33n, 233n, 234n
Fitzmyer, J. A.   242n, 248n, 249n, 254n
Flanagan, O.   2n
Foakes Jackson, F. J.   238n, 242n
Ford, J. M.   217n
Fortenbaugh, W. W.   42n, 43n, 45n, 46, 47n, 48n, 49n, 55n
Fowler, H. N.   89n
Fraisse, J.-C.   14n, 38n, 44n, 45n, 47n, 48n, 49n, 56n, 61n, 62n, 63n, 96n, 99n, 101n
Fränkel, H.   16n, 18n, 22n
Fredrickson, D. E.   11n
Frey, J.-B.   186n
Friedländer, L.   108n, 110n
Friedman, M.   2n
Frischer, B.   8n
Frisk, H.   15n
Fritz, K. von   78n, 82n
Gabba, E.   123n, 131n
Gadamer, H.-G.   7n
Gantar, K.   9n
Garnsey, P.   247n
Gärtner, H.   146n
Giannantoni, M.   8n
Gigante, M.   8n
Gigon, O.   7n
Glad, C. E.   11n, 23n

Gleichen-Russwurm, A. V.   14n
Glidden, D.   7n
Goergemanns, H.   49n, 51n, 52
Goold, G. P.   148n
Goold, J.   252n
Gorce, D.   20n
Gottschalk, H. B.   35n, 36n, 50n, 51n, 55n
Grenfell, B. P.   191n
Grundmann, W.   257n
Guillemin, A.-M.   75n
Gurdin, J. B.   2n
Hadot, I.   74n, 75n
Haenchen, E.   238n, 242n, 249n
Hägg, T.   145n
Hainsworth, J. B.   15n, 28n
Hallett, J. P.   140n
Halperin, D. M.   19n
Hamp, E. P.   16n
Hands, A. R.   140n, 244n, 247n
Harder, R.   60n
Harmon, A. M.   163n, 173n, 176n, 177n
Harnack, A. von   258n
Harrison, S. J.   145n, 146n
Hauck, F.   10n, 257n
Havener, I.   248n
Hawthorne, G. F.   67n
Hellegouarc'h, J.   68n
Helmbold, W. C.   112n, 114n
Helms, J.   148n
Henderson, M.   2n
Hengel, M.   238n, 241n
Herman, G.   11n, 27n, 183n, 247n
Hershbell, J.   82n, 95n, 222n
Heubeck, A.   15n, 16n
Hicks, R. D.   93
Hiltbrunner, O.   10n, 20n, 129n

Index of Modern Scholars

Hock, R. F.   5, 145, 167n, 172n
Hölk, C.   82n
Holland, G. S.   2n
Holmberg, B.   252n
Hooker, J.   16n, 17n, 18n
Hudson-Williams, T.   29n
Hunt, A. S.   170n, 191n
Hunt, H. A. K.   61n, 63n
Hunter, R. L.   9n, 146n
Hutter, H.   4n, 7n, 8n, 9n, 14n, 240n
Hyatte, R.   10n
Jaquette, J. L.   233n
Jaubert, A.   222n
Jervell, J.   258n
Johnson, L. T.   10n, 233n, 237n, 241n, 243n, 250n, 251n, 253, 256
Jones, C. P.   164, 165n, 173, 178n
Judge, E. A.   257n, 259
Kahn, C. H.   49n
Kaiser, O.   7n
Kakridis, H. J.   17n, 19n, 20n
Karris, R. J.   239, 249n, 253n, 254–56
Keck, L.   242n
Kenny, A.   35n
Kilpatrick, R. S.   9n
Kirk, G. S.   18n, 20n, 28n
Kittay, E. F.   2n
Klassen, W.   11n
Klauck, H.-J.   127n, 204n, 227n, 229, 231n, 237n, 242n, 258n, 259–60, 261n
Klein, E.   14n
Klein, U.   95n
Kloppenborg, J. S.   248n
Klostermann, E.   254n
Knoche, U.   8n, 75n

Knox, B.   21n
Konstan, D.   7n, 8n, 10n, 11n, 13, 14n, 20n, 23n, 33n, 34n, 127n, 137n, 146n, 157n, 161
Koskenniemi, H.   75n, 184n, 185
Kosman, A.   7n
Kretschmar, P.   16n
Kuntzmann, R.   212n
Kupfer, J.   2n
LaFleur, R.A.   9n
Lake, K.   238n, 242n
Landfester, M.   15n, 16n, 17n
Lattimore, R.   21n, 26n
Leach, E. W.   48n
Légasse, S.   212n
Lesses, G.   9n
Levy, H. L.   25n
Lewis, N.   190n
Leyerle, B.   223n
Liviabella Furiani, P.   147n
Lloyd-Jones, H.   28n
Long, A. A.   50n
Lossmann, F.   68n, 75n, 76n
Louw, J. P.   97n
Lovejoy, A. O.   241n
Lualdi, M.   7n
MacLeod, M. D.   163n, 177n
MacMullen, R.   252n
Maguinness, W. S.   9n
Malherbe, A. J.   1–2, 11n, 88n, 89n, 127n, 170n, 183n, 184n, 185n, 187n, 204n, 226, 227n, 233n, 234n, 258n, 259
Manzanedo, M. F.   8n
Marshall, P.   126n, 225, 228–30, 234, 237, 247n, 257n, 259n, 260
Martin, C.   33n
Marty, M. E.   2n

Martyn, J. L.   242n, 259n
Maurach, G.   8n, 75n
Mauss, M.   247n
McGuire, B. P.   10n, 199n
Mealand, D. L.   238n, 241n, 242n, 253n
Meeks, W. A.   127n, 130n, 170n, 204n, 233n, 252n, 258n
Meilaender, G.   2n
Meister, K.   9n
Meyers, D. T.   2n
Michel, O.   231n
Mielenbrink, E.   10n
Millett, P.   247n
Mitchell, A. C.   6, 11n, 45n, 175n, 225
Mitchell, L. G.   14n
Mitchell, T. N.   63n, 68n, 70n, 71n
Mitsis, P.   8n, 208n
Moessner, D. P.   249n
Moles, J. L.   9n
Momigliano, A.   10n
Mondolfo, R.   79n
Moraux, P.   36n, 49n, 50n, 54n, 55n
Morgan, J. R.   165n
Mott, S. C.   67n, 68n
Motto, A. L.   8n
Moxnes, H.   246n, 247n
Moxon, I. S.   131n
Muellner, L. C.   26n
Murray, A. T.   21n, 22n
Nagy, G.   28n, 29n
Nauck, A.   94n
Neumark, H.   217n
Neyrey, J. H.   184n, 246n
Nida, E. A.   97n
Noè, E.   131n

Nugent, S. G.   2n
Nussbaum, M. C.   7n, 36n, 160, 161n
Nygren, A.   38
Oates, J. F.   185n, 197n
O'Connor, D. K.   2n, 8n, 208n
Oden, R.   165n
Oldfather, C. H.   85, 91
Olivieri, A.   207n
O'Meara, D. J.   80n, 83n
O'Neil, E. N.   4, 45n, 105, 112n, 114n, 162n, 166n, 211n
Osborne, C.   7n
Osiek, C.   127n
Otto, A.   10n
Pakaluk, M.   2n
Parsons, P. J.   196n
Paton, W. R.   124n
Pearson, L.   28n, 126n
Pedrick, V.   252n
Pembroke, S. G.   50n, 51, 52n
Penella, R. J.   81n, 86n
Perry, B. E.   148, 156–57, 164, 175n, 176n
Pervo, R. I.   5, 163, 171n, 206n
Peterson, E.   10n
Pizzolato, L. F.   9n, 10n, 14n, 30n
Places, E. des   91n, 93n, 94n
Plepelits, K.   146n
Plümacher, E.   238n, 239n, 241n
Pohlenz, M.   7n
Polag, A.   248n
Porter, R.   2n
Powell, J.   176n
Powell, J. G. F.   214n
Prandi, L.   138n
Preisigke, F.   183
Price, A. W.   7n, 208n

Index of Modern Scholars

Puthenkandathil, E. 17n
Raaflaub, K. A. 127n
Rader, R. 10n
Raffaelli, L. M. 138n
Rapske, B. 171n
Rasco, R. 250n
Rattenbury, R. 176n
Rawlinson, D. 2n
Reardon, B. P. 145n, 146n, 148, 149n, 155, 176n
Regenbogen, O. 51n
Renehan, R. 20n
Rensberger, D. 259n
Reumann, J. 11n, 234n
Rhodes, P. J. 14n
Richardson, N. 18n
Rieu, D. C. H. 19n, 25n
Rieu, E. V. 19n
Rist, J. M. 8n, 206n, 208n, 214
Robinson, D. B. 7n, 16n, 18, 21n, 205n
Rohde, E. 82n, 97n, 145n, 163n
Rönsch, H. 10n
Rorty, A. O. 2n, 208n
Rosén, H. B. 16n, 17n
Rostovtzeff, M. 176n
Rouner, L. S. 2n
Rouse, W. H. D. 21n, 22n
Ruiz-Montero, C. 146n, 147n, 158n
Runia, D. T. 211n
Rupprecht, K. 10n
Russell, D. A. 105n, 138n
Rusten, J. S. 7n
Sacks, K. S. 138n
Saller, R. P. 9n, 247n
Sandbach, F. H. 106
Sanders, E. P. 222n
Sandnes, K. O. 10n
Scarcella, A. M. 147n
Schlosser, J. 212n
Schmeling, G. 145n
Schmidt-Berger, U. 7n
Schnackenburg, R. 258n
Schneider, G. 249n
Schottlaender, R. 8n
Schroeder, F. M. 3, 35, 36n, 57n, 208n, 223n
Schultze, C. E. 131
Schulz, S. 248n
Scullard, H. H. 67n, 69n, 70n, 72n
Seager, R. 9n
Seccombe, D. P. 238n, 241n, 250n, 251n, 255n
Segovia, F. 10n, 258n
Sevenster, J. N. 221n, 233, 259n
Shelton, J. C. 191n
Sinos, D. S. 19n
Spector, S. 10n
Spicq, C. 16n, 17n, 33n
Squitier, K. A. 87n
Städele, A. 81n, 86n
Stählin, G. 15n, 16n, 112n, 121, 156n, 165n, 177n, 204n, 225n, 236n, 237n, 257n, 261n
Stambaugh, J. E. 246n
Stanton, G. R. 7n
Steffen, W. 30n
Steinberger, J. 60n, 61n, 62n, 64n, 66n
Steinmetz, F.-A. 8n, 49n
Stephens, S. A. 176n
Sterling, G. E. 6, 203, 215n, 225n
Stern-Gillet, S. 8n, 57n
Stock, St. G. 14n
Stocker, M. 2n
Stoneman, R. 165n

Stowers, S. K.   2n, 233n
Strecker, G.   258n
Swain, S.   165, 176n
Tannehill, R.   248n, 253n, 255n
Tatum, J.   147n
Taylor, A. E.   7n
Theissen, G.   98n
Thesleff, H.   79, 80n, 81n, 83n, 84n, 85n, 92n, 96n
Thom, J. C.   4, 77, 78n, 81n, 82n, 88n, 102n, 222n
Thomas, L.   2n
Thomaselli, S.   2n
Thraede, K.   74n, 75n, 183n, 200n
Trenkner, S.   163n, 166n, 168n, 171n, 178n
Treu, K.   10n, 16n, 77n, 112n, 137n
Tuilier, A.   8n
Tyler, J.   7n
Ulf, C.   19n
van der Horst, P. W.   204n, 207n
Versenyi, L.   7n
Veyne, P.   137n, 247n, 255n
Vidal, M.   10n
Vlastos, G.   7n, 37–40, 208n
Vogel, C. J. de   96n, 97n, 98n, 99, 100n, 101n
Wadell, P. J.   2n, 199n
Waerden, B. L. van der   78n, 79n, 82n, 88n
Waithe, M. E.   86n
Wallace-Hadrill, A.   9n, 247n
Wedderburn, A. J.   233n
Wehr, H.   20n
Wehrli,   97n
Weinreich, O.   163n
Welles, C. B.   67n
Wender, D.   32n
Werkmeister, W. H.   7n
West, M. L.   19n, 24n, 30n, 32n
West, S.   15n
Wettstein, J. J.   237n
White, C.   10n, 147n, 156n
White, J. L.   186n
White, L. M.   24n, 130n, 170n, 233n, 234, 246n, 260
White, N. P.   51n
White, P.   9n
Whittaker, J.   54n
Wilckens, U.   231n
Wild, R. A.   81n, 86n
Williams, M. F.   9n
Williams, W. G.   76n
Willis, W. H.   146n
Winkler, J. J.   176n
Winston, D.   205n, 217n, 220n
Winter, S. C.   11n
Wolter, M.   231n
Wood, N.   61n, 66n, 69n, 70n, 71n, 73n, 74n, 240n, 245n
Woolf, G.   247n
Yarbrough, O. L.   24n, 130n
Yuen, S. Y.   9n
Zeller, D.   231n
Zeller, E.   78n, 79n
Ziebis, W.   7n
Zimmermann, F.   176n
Zucker, F.   8n

www.ingramcontent.com/pod-product-compliance
Lightning Source LLC
Chambersburg PA
CBHW031705230426
43668CB00006B/109